Muslim Civilization
in India

BY S. M. Ikram

EDITED BY Ainslie T. Embree

Columbia University Press
New York and London

S. M. Ikram is a member of the Pakistan Civil Service and has on several occasions been a Visiting Professor of International Affairs at Columbia University. He has written a number of books in Urdu and English on the history of Islam in India and is the co-editor of *The Cultural Heritage of Pakistan*. Ainslie T. Embree is Assistant Professor of History at Columbia University. He is author of *Charles Grant and British Rule in India* and co-editor of *Approaches to Asian Civilization* and *A Guide to Oriental Classics*.

Copyright © 1964 Columbia University Press

First printing 1964
Second printing 1965

Library of Congress Catalog Card Number: 64-14656
Printed in the United States of America

Preface

AN APOLOGY is hardly needed for bringing out this small volume on the political and cultural history of Muslim India and Pakistan. In the past the study of Muslim civilization has been largely confined to the Arab countries, or at best extended to Iran or the Ottoman Turkey, but the need for studying the background of modern countries like Pakistan and Indonesia is too obvious to be ignored. Muslims in the Indo-Pak subcontinent number more than 100 millions, and the sections of the community dispersed in surrounding regions like East Africa, Burma, Ceylon are not without importance. Apart from numbers, the story of this civilization is full of great achievements. For several centuries Islam dominated the subcontinent which now includes India and Pakistan, and rulers like Akbar, Shah Jahan, and Aurangzeb, in addition to their achievements in the political and administrative field, left a rich cultural heritage. Above all, the history of Muslim rule in India is the story of Islam in a predominantly non-Muslim environment. This led to conflicts, tensions, and assimilations which make the record of particular interest to students of culture and politics.

In addition to the political narrative which furnishes the essential background, the book gives an account of the cultural developments, the changes in political philosophy and institutions, the rise of Indo-Muslim law, and above all, those religious and intellectual movements which in the long run proved more powerful than the mighty rulers. The general features of the cultural, administrative, social, and economic history have been outlined in separate chapters, but the developments in these fields which were closely associated with any particular period or regime have been summarized along with the political narrative of that period.

An attempt has also been made to give a fuller background of events relating to the areas, like Muslim Bengal, that have gained in importance with the birth of Pakistan, but that did not receive

adequate attention in older historical works. This narrative naturally involves going over the past, but the ground has been covered, so to say, "facing forward." The interest in the happenings of the past is partly because of their contribution to the making of the present. This has led to devotion of greater space to the political and cultural developments in the eighteenth century than is customary. It was a period of transition and confusion, but modern Muslim India and Pakistan are more closely rooted in the eighteenth century than in the days of the grand Mughals, and the present cannot be understood without a satisfactory study of the period which saw the rise of Urdu and the systematization of the local Islamic tradition by Shah Waliullah.

A word must be said about the transliteration of the many words used from Arabic, Persian, and Indian languages. The spelling generally adopted is that of the *Cambridge History of India,* but the diacritical marks have not been used. It was felt that these sometimes distract rather than help the reader who is not familiar with Indo-Muslim names and terminology. Some spellings that have been widely accepted in writings on Indian history have been retained, even though they may not be strictly correct transliterations. This is especially true of place names. Furthermore, translators have used such a variety of spellings that consistency is difficult to maintain when quotations are given. It should also be remembered that the Urdu version of words is sometimes different from the Persian original, and it is the Urdu spelling which is common in modern India and Pakistan.

The present volume is an abridgment of the author's fuller *History of Muslim Civilization in India and Pakistan (712–1858),* published in Lahore in 1962. In compressing an account of such a long period in some 300 pages, much has necessarily had to be sacrificed— including the long introduction on historiography of Muslim India —but the aim has been to ensure that nothing basic or essential is omitted in the abridgment. The success that has been achieved in this attempt is due to the thought and labor bestowed on the task by Professor Ainslie T. Embree of Columbia University. He took my abridged version as the basis, thoroughly revised it, rearranged

certain chapters, and even recast some portions, to make the material more intelligible to the Western reader and to improve the presentation. My grateful thanks are due to him. I also acknowledge with thanks a grant made by the Rockefeller Foundation to Columbia University, which facilitated the completion of the earlier book.

S. M. IKRAM

Lahore, Pakistan
March, 1964

Contents

Part One: The Early Invasions and the Delhi Sultanate, 712-1526

Chronology		2
I	The Impact of the Arabs	3
II	The Heritage of Ghazni and Bukhara	22
III	The Establishment of the Delhi Sultanate	37
IV	Consolidation of Muslim Rule in the North	55
V	Expansion in the South: The Khaljis and the Tughluqs	61
VI	The Disintegration of the Sultanate	76
VII	The Administrative System of the Sultanate	86
VIII	Society and Culture under the Sultanate	107
IX	The Interaction of Islam and Hinduism	123

Part Two: The Mughal Period, 1526-1858

Chronology		134
X	The Establishment of the Mughal Empire	135
XI	The Age of Akbar	143
XII	Religion at Akbar's Court	156
XIII	The Orthodox Reaction	166
XIV	The Age of Splendor	175
XV	Aurangzeb	189
XVI	Mughal Administration	209
XVII	Economic and Social Developments under the Mughals	223
XVIII	The Mughals and the Arts	238
XIX	A Century of Political Decline: 1707-1803	254
XX	The Beginning of a New Era: 1803-1857	277
XXI	Conclusion	295

Glossary and Suggested Readings

Glossary   299

Suggested Readings   308

Index   311

Maps

  India at the End of the Ninth Century   13

  India in 1236   47

  The Empire of Muhammad bin Tughluq in 1335   71

  Regional Kingdoms at the End of the Fifteenth Century   81

  The Mughal Empire at the Death of Akbar in 1605   147

  The Mughal Empire in 1700   203

  India in 1780   271

Part One

The Early Invasions and the
Delhi Sultanate
712-1526

Chronology and Dynasties, 712-1526

First Phase

c.570–632   Life of the Prophet Muhammad.

711–713   Conquest of Sind and Multan by Muhammad ibn Qasim.

998–1030   Reign of Mahmud of Ghazni. Raids on India.

1020   Lahore becomes part of Ghaznavid empire.

1151   Rise of Ghuri empire.

1186   Capture of Lahore by Muhammad Ghuri.

1192   Defeat of Prithvi Raj by Muhammad Ghuri at Tarain.

The Sultanate

1206–1210   Aibak, first sultan of Delhi and founder of the Slave dynasty, 1206–1290.

1211–1236   Reign of Iltutmish.

1266–1287   Reign of Balban.

1290–1320   The Khalji dynasty.

1296–1316   Expansion to South India under Ala-ud-din.

1320–1413   The Tughluq dynasty.

1325–1351   Reign of Muhammad Tughluq.

1351–1388   Reign of Firuz Shah.

c.1300–1500   Establishment of regional kingdoms.

1414–1451   The Sayyid dynasty.

1451–1526   The Lodi dynasty.

I. The Impact of the Arabs

ISLAM, the youngest of the three great Semitic religions, dates from the early years of the seventh century.[1] Its founder, the Prophet Muhammad, was born in 570 A.D. in Mecca, an important center on the caravan route along the western coast of Arabia. At the age of forty he saw visions and received revelations which, as embodied in the Quran, constitute the message and teachings of Islam. The tremendous vision of the majesty and power of God which came to Muhammad found expression in the central creed: "There is no God but God and Muhammad is his prophet." This uncompromising declaration of faith in the unity of God was a challenge to the polytheism that flourished in Arabia, especially in Mecca where the main temple, the Kaaba, housed more than three hundred idols. While the proclamation of God's oneness was originally the main feature of Islam, other characteristics gradually developed, particularly an emphasis on the brotherhood of all believers and the equality of all men before God, irrespective of class, color, or race. Specific injunctions, such as the prohibition of the use of intoxicants, also became an essential feature of the Islamic way of life, helping to weld the believers in Islam into a cohesive, self-conscious social group. These beliefs and practices finally found vivid form in the "Five Pillars of Islam," an easily remembered summary of ritual and doctrine. These are: 1) profession of faith in the unity of God and the prophetic mission of Muhammad; 2) the observance of the five daily prayers; 3) the giving of alms; 4) fasting during the month of Ramadan; and 5) the making of a pilgrimage to Mecca. Each of these was open to interpretation and elaboration, but they provided, in their simplicity and inclusiveness, a framework that proved capable of binding people of the most diverse races and of levels of cultural achievement into a brotherhood that built, with astonishing rapidity, a civilization that stretched from the Iberian peninsula to the islands of the Eastern Seas.

[1] "Islam" is used for the religion, "Muslim" for a member of the religious community.

Despite the special features it had from its birth and the others it acquired in the course of its history, Islam essentially claims to be a continuation of the earlier religions of western Asia, particularly Judaism and Christianity. According to the Quran, prophets were sent to all nations and social groups to show them the right path. Four of them, Adam, Abraham, Moses, and Jesus, find a frequent mention in the Quran. The ritual code of Islam is, indeed, largely based on that of Judaism as practiced in Arabia in Muhammad's time. There are, for example, ceremonial prayers, with Friday taking the place of the Saturday Sabbath; a month of fasting (Ramadan); festivals including the celebration of Old Testament events such as the sacrifice of Isaac (Ismail, in the Islamic version). There is the Judaic conception of "unclean meats," including the prohibition of pork. The references to Christianity and Christians in the Quran are friendly; Jesus is referred to as the spirit of God and many miracles are ascribed to him. But Islam firmly rejected belief in the Trinity as a reversion to polytheism.

Muhammad received a very poor response in his own birthplace. He and the few followers he was able to gather were persecuted, and in 622 he had to flee from Mecca to Medina. This migration, known as the Hijra, proved highly propitious, for, from this time, Islam rapidly gained adherents. In Medina the Prophet was not only the founder of a new religion but he was also the head of a city-state. Gradually Islam began spreading outside Medina, and before the Prophet died in 632, almost the entire peninsula of Arabia had adopted Islam.

Muhammad left no male heir. On his death claims were made on behalf of his son-in-law and cousin Ali, but senior members of the community elected as their leader or caliph, the Prophet's companion, Abu Bakr, who was one of the earliest converts to Islam. He successfully dealt with the local rebellions, and sent troops against the Byzantine and the Persian empires, with whom disputes had arisen during the last days of the Prophet. The two great empires had weakened themselves by centuries of mutual warfare, and the ill-equipped Arab armies were victorious. Abu Bakr died after only two years in office, and was succeeded by Umar (r. 634–644), under whose leader-

ship the Islamic community was transformed into a vast empire. Syria and Egypt in the west and Persia in the east were conquered, and an administrative basis was devised for the organization of Islamic territory. The sanctions for this governmental structure were the precepts of the Quran and the example of the Prophet, but Umar's administration reflects his own robust common sense and his knowledge of the experience of other rulers. After the conquest of Iran, for example, he invited a group of Iranian officials to Medina to explain its government under former rulers. His system of maintaining a bureau of official registers was derived from Iranian practice, as was the idea of *jizya,* the poll tax levied on non-Muslims. After ten years, Umar was succeeded by Usman (r. 644–656), who was followed by Ali (r. 656–661), the last of the four "Righteous Caliphs."

Owing to his relationship with the Prophet as well as to personal bravery, nobility of character, and intellectual and literary gifts, Caliph Ali occupies a special place in the history of Islam, but he was unable to control the tribal and personal quarrels of the Arabs. After his death, Muawiyah (r. 661–680), the first of the Umayyad caliphs, seized power and transferred the seat of caliphate from Medina to Damascus. In 680 occurred the tragedy of Karbala when Imam Husain, son of Ali and grandson of the Prophet, fell a martyr. Three years later the succession passed from Muawiyah's grandson to another branch of the Umayyad dynasty, which continued in power until 750. During this period the Muslim armies overran Asia Minor, conquered the north coast of Africa, occupied Spain (711), and were halted only in the heart of France at Tours (732). In the east the Muslim empire was extended to Central Asia, and, as we shall see, it was during this period that a part of the Indian subcontinent was annexed. In the course of these conquests, the Arabs became subject to older civilizations. Damascus was located in the heart of Syria, where Greek and Syrian culture had flowered for ages, and the Umayyad capital displayed a cultural and social life quite different from that of puritanical Medina. As heirs to the Byzantine civilization, the Umayyads developed the postal service, introduced a new coinage, established a state archive in Damascus, and introduced other changes in the organization of government.

Religious schisms in Islam began early and often paralleled political divisions. The two principal sects are Shia and Sunni. The former, more correctly known as Shian-i-Ali (the partisans of Ali), hold that Ali should have succeeded the Prophet. The Sunnis, who make up the vast majority of the Muslim world, accept the order in which the succession of the "Righteous Caliphs" actually took place. The Shias were subdivided into two branches—the Ismailis, who played a more important role in the early history of Islam than they do today, and the main Shia group, whose creed is the state religion of Iran.

The Arab Conquest of Sind

It was against this background of rapid expansion that the first contacts between Islam and India took place. Since time immemorial spices and other articles from India and southeast Asia had been in great demand in Egypt and southern Europe, with the transit trade largely in the hands of Arabs, who brought merchandise from the Indian ports to Yemen in southern Arabia. The goods were then sent by land to the Syrian ports to be shipped again to Egypt and Europe. The rise of Islam did not, therefore, give rise to the connection with India, but it added a new dimension. Trade continued after the Arabs had embraced Islam, and the first major conflict between the Indian subcontinent and Muslim Arabia arose out of developments connected with Arab sailors plying their trade about the Indian Ocean. They sailed as far as Ceylon, and when some of them died on that island, the local ruler thought it expedient to send their widows and children to Arabia, with gifts and letters of goodwill for Hajjaj (661–714), the powerful viceroy of the eastern provinces of the Umayyad empire. Unfavorable winds drove the vessels carrying the gifts and the survivors close to the shores of Debul (an inland port near modern Karachi). Here pirates attacked them, plundered the gifts, and took the Muslim women and children as captives. Hajjaj, on learning of this, protested to Dahar, the ruler of Sind, and demanded the release of the prisoners and restoration of the booty, but he received only an evasive reply. The enraged Hajjaj, famous in Arab history as

much for his severity as for his administrative ability, persuaded Caliph Walid, to authorize punitive measures against Dahar.

Two expeditions sent against Dahar ended in failure, but for the third, Hajjaj sent a hand-picked body of soldiers under the command of his son-in-law, Muhammad ibn Qasim. The Arab general, with six thousand horsemen, a camel corps of equal strength, and a baggage train of three thousand camels, marched against Debul by way of Shiraz and through Makran. He received reinforcements on the way and in the autumn of 711 appeared before Debul. Hajjaj, who had made very thorough preparations, sent the siege artillery by sea, including a huge balista, affectionately called *al'arus,* "the bride," which was worked by five hundred men. Protected by strong stone fortifications the Debul garrison offered stiff resistance, but ultimately the fort was captured and the Muslim flag was hoisted for the first time on the soil of the Indian subcontinent.

Making light of the fall of Debul as a mere commercial town, Dahar made plans to give battle before the strong fortress of Brahmanabad. A decisive encounter did not take place for several months, however, owing to the difficulties confronting the Arabs. Apart from the greater forces assembled by Dahar, an epidemic of scurvy broke out among the Arab troops, and their horses also suffered from sickness. Hajjaj sent reinforcements, but perhaps even more valuable was the assistance he rendered in dealing with the scurvy. His manner of transporting a large supply of vinegar in concentrated form illustrates the resourcefulness of the early Arabs. Cotton was soaked in thick concentrated vinegar and dried. This operation was repeated until the cotton could hold no more liquid; then the cotton was sent to Sind, where the vinegar was extracted by soaking the cotton in water. This supply of vinegar brought the scurvy under control, and in the extreme heat of June, 712, the Arabs crossed the river and faced Dahar's army. The battle was fought with great vigor on both sides, but the superior Arab generalship and the skill of the Arab archers gave them the victory. Dahar lost his life on the battlefield, and with his death the Hindu army lost heart and fled from the field. Muhammad captured Brahmanabad, married Rani Ladi, Dahar's widow, thus becoming the master of Lower Sind.

The Arab general spent some time in organizing the administration of the conquered area, then he started for Aror (near modern Sukkur), Dahar's capital, now held by one of his sons. After a brief siege the town surrendered and soon Muhammad proceeded to complete the conquest of Upper Sind. He moved towards Punjab. Multan, the leading city, was well fortified, but a deserter brought information about a stream which supplied water to the city, and by diverting it the Arabs were able to force the garrison to surrender in 713. Muhammad was now master of the whole of Sind and part of the Punjab. After the occupation of Multan, he advanced to the borders of the kingdom of Kashmir. Threatened by this move, the raja of Kashmir sent an envoy to the Chinese emperor asking for help. He received no aid but events at home stopped further Arab advance. Hajjaj, Muhammad ibn Qasim's father-in-law and the viceroy of the eastern provinces, died in 714, and in the following year the Caliph Walid, who had been his supporter, also died. The new caliph was Sulaiman, a bitter enemy of Hajjaj's family. The policy of extremism, partisanship, and violence which Hajjaj had followed now brought its nemesis. Death saved him from the new caliph's wrath, but his family had to pay the penalty. Sulaiman appointed a new governor, recalled Muhammad ibn Qasim, and handed him to an officer who had the young conqueror of Sind tortured to death in an Iraqi prison.

The comparative ease with which the Arabs defeated the Indian forces and occupied a large territory calls for explanation. It was due partly to the quality of their troops, the ability of the military commander, and the superiority of the Arab military technique. But the conciliatory policy which Muhammad ibn Qasim adopted towards all those who submitted to the Arabs also facilitated his task, and the Arab conquest was noteworthy more for voluntary surrenders than for bloody battles. At Nirun, for example, the Buddhist priests welcomed the general, and at Sehwan the populace revolted against the Hindu governor and submitted to Muhammad ibn Qasim. Popular dissatisfaction with the former rulers, or at least indifference to their fate, seems in fact to have contributed substantially to Arab success. A large proportion of the population of Sind and Multan was Buddhist, but Chach, a Brahmin minister of the Buddhist king, had

usurped the throne in 622, and his dynasty was not popular with large sections of the people. Even the chiefs and officials were quick to offer allegiance to the Arabs. As R. C. Majumdar has remarked: "To the inexplicable want of strategy on the part of Dahar and the treachery of the Buddhists of the south, we must add the base betrayal of the chief officials and grandees of Sind to account for its ignominious end. All important chiefs and officials seem to have deserted his cause. This is partly accounted for by the superstitious idea prevailing among the people that according to the Hindu Sastras the country was destined to fall into the hands of the Muhammadans, and it was, therefore, useless to fight. But the attitude of chiefs was perhaps due also to personal feelings against the son of the usurper who had driven out the old royal family." [2]

Dahar's hold over southern Sind, largely Buddhist, was also very feeble, as this area had come under his rule only a short time before the Arab invasion. Chach (r. 622–666) had tried to buttress his position by a policy of ruthless suppression of the dissident groups. He inflicted great humiliation on the Jats, who were forbidden to carry swords or wear fine garments or to ride on horseback with saddles, and they were commanded to walk about with their heads and feet bare, accompanied by dogs.[3] Muslims who were fighting his son won the sympathies of the oppressed classes, and perhaps the most important cause of the Arab success was the support of the Jats and the Meds. At an early stage they started enlisting under Muhammad ibn Qasim's banner, "which independent of its moral effect in dividing national sympathies, and relaxing the unanimity of defense against foreign aggression, must have been of incalculable benefit to him, in his disproportionate excess of cavalry, which could be of little service in a country intersected by rivers, swamps, and canals." [4]

Muhammad ibn Qasim was only seventeen when he was appointed to a hazardous military command in a distant and little-known territory. Apparently he was selected because of his kinship with the all-

[2] R. C. Majumdar, "The Arab Invasion of India," *Journal of Indian History,* Vol. X (1931), supplement.

[3] H. M. Elliot and John Dowson, *The History of India as Told by Its Own Historians* (London, 1867–1877), I, 151.

[4] Elliot and Dowson, I, 435.

powerful Hajjaj, but he had already been a successful governor of Shiraz and his efficiency in carrying out his assignment in Sind fully justified the choice. His great achievement was, of course, as a military commander and the way in which he and his troops overwhelmed bigger forces. He combined great courage and resourcefulness with moderation and statesmanship of a high order. He had a warm personality, ready to enjoy the humor of new and odd situations and to exchange jokes with his companions. With all this he was a disciplined soldier, as is evident from the manner in which he carried out Hajjaj's directions and later quietly, without demur, submitted to the orders of the new caliph in his last supreme act of self-renunciation. In emphasizing this side of Muhammad ibn Qasim's character it should be remembered that he was the leader of a punitive expedition. At Debul, where he had to blot out the memories of the defeat and massacre of the Arab forces sent earlier against Dahar, and later at Multan, where he was stubbornly resisted, he was harsh and ruthless, but such occasions were exceptional. Normally he was humane and considerate, and though no subordinate of Hajjaj could afford to show any weakness, Muhammad achieved his object more by negotiation and grant of liberal terms than by warfare. He made systematic efforts to seek out the officers of the old regime, showered honors and favors on them, and made them his collaborators in the task of administration.

Foremost among these were Sisakar, Raja Dahar's minister, and Kaksa, the raja's nephew. Sisakar won his way into Muhammad ibn Qasim's favor by restoring the widows and children of the Arabian sailors, whose capture by pirates had originally brought down Hajjaj's wrath on Dahar. Sisakar was made principal adviser in affairs relating to Lower Sind. Kaksa's position was even more important. "The minister Kaksa," according to an early historian, "was a learned man and a philosopher of Hind. When he came to transact business, Muhammad ibn Qasim used to make him sit before the throne and then consult him, and Kaksa took precedence in the army before all the nobles and commanders. He collected the revenue of the country and the treasury was placed under his seal. He assisted Muhammad ibn Qasim in all his undertakings, and was addressed by the title of

mubarak mushir (prosperous counsellor)." [5] The generosity shown by Muhammad to the leading Indian administrators was rewarded by their loyal cooperation.

Arab Administration

The Arab administration in Sind followed the general pattern adopted by the Arab conquerors in other countries. The normal rule was to employ local talent and make minimum changes in local practices. Caliph Umar, acknowledged as the chief creator of the Arab system of administration, had laid down the working principle that Arabs should not acquire landed property in conquered territories. Under his system the conquering general of a new territory became its governor, but "most of the subordinate officers were allowed to retain their posts." Available evidence about Sind shows that these injunctions were observed. The Arabs established themselves in large towns, which were also military cantonments, and provided the military garrisons, but civil administration was left largely in the hands of the local chiefs, only a few of whom had accepted Islam.

The administrative arrangements which Muhammad ibn Qasim made with the non-Muslims after his victory over Dahar are often referred to as "the Brahmanabad settlement." The basic principle was to treat the Hindus as "the people of the book," and to confer on them the status of the zimmis (the protected). In some respects the arrangements were even more liberal than those granted to "the people of the book" by the later schools of Islamic law. For example, according to later opinion the zimmis could not repair their places of worship, although existing ones were allowed to stand. The question of repairing a damaged temple came up before Muhammad, who referred the matter to Hajjaj. The latter, having consulted the ulama of Damascus, not only granted the permission asked for, but declared that so long as non-Muslims paid their dues to the state they were free to live in whatever manner they liked. "It appears," Hajjaj wrote, "that the chief inhabitants of Brahmanabad had petitioned to be allowed to repair the temple of Budh and pursue their religion. As they have

---

[5] Elliot and Dowson, I, 203.

made submission, and have agreed to pay taxes to the Khalifa, nothing more can properly be required from them. They have been taken under our protection, and we cannot in any way stretch out our hands upon their lives or property. Permission is given them to worship their gods. Nobody must be forbidden and prevented from following his own religion. They may live in their houses in whatever manner they like." [6] According to one early Muslim historian, the Arab conqueror countenanced even the privileged position of the Brahmans, not only in religious matters, but also in the administrative sphere. "Muhammad ibn Qasim maintained their dignity and passed orders confirming their pre-eminence. They were protected against opposition and violence." Even the 3 percent share of government revenue, which they had received during the ascendancy of the Brahman rulers of Sind, was conceded to them. In his arrangements for the collection of taxes Muhammad ibn Qasim also made an attempt to provide some safeguards against oppression by appointing "people from among the villagers and the chief citizens to collect the fixed taxes from the cities and the villages so that there might be the feeling of strength and protection." [7]

When the Abbasids overthrew the Umayyads in 750 they sent their own officers to Sind. The Abbasid governor, Hisham, who came to Sind in 757, carried out successful raids against Gujarat and Kashmir, but no permanent additions to Arab dominion were made. Later, through preoccupations at home, Arab control over Sind weakened, with the process of disintegration being accelerated by tribal conflicts among local Arabs. One governor went so far as to revolt against Caliph al-Mamum. The rebellion was put down but Musa (son of Yahya the Barmakid, the famous wazir of Harun-al-Rashid), who was placed in charge of the affairs of Sind, nominated as his successor on his death in 836 his son Amran. The caliph recognized the appointment, but the beginning of the hereditary succession to governorship meant a weakening of the hold of Baghdad. An energetic ruler, Amran dealt firmly with the disturbances of the Jats and the Meds, but internecine quarrels among the Arabs flared up and he lost his life

[6] Elliot and Dowson, I, 185–86.
[7] Elliot and Dowson, I, 183–87.

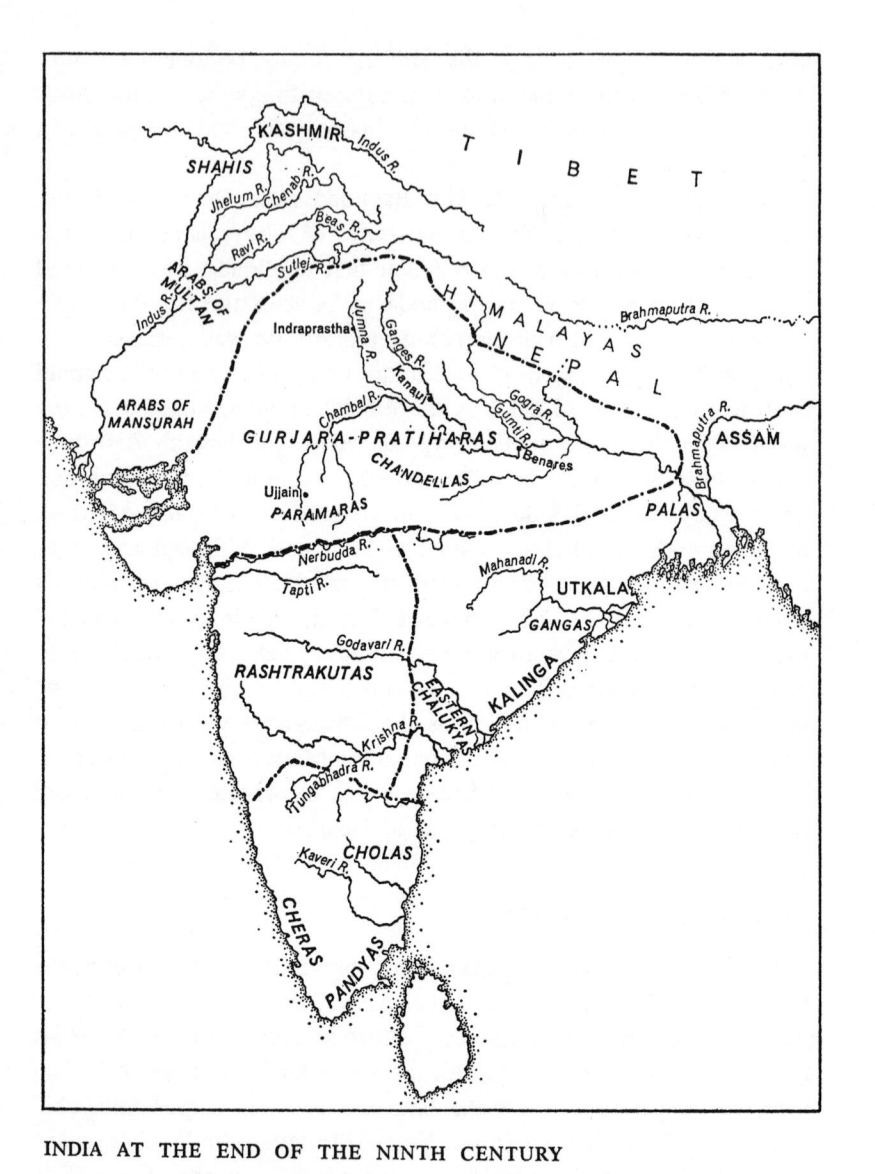

INDIA AT THE END OF THE NINTH CENTURY

From: *An Historical Atlas of the Indian Peninsula* (Oxford University Press, Bombay, 1961).

after a brief reign. In 854 the Hibbari family became hereditary
rulers of Sind, with Mansura as their capital. In course of time, Multan became independent and the Hindus reestablished themselves in
Rohri.

The severance of contacts with Baghdad made Sind and Multan
a happy hunting ground for the emissaries of the rivals of the Abbasids, the Ismaili rulers of Cairo. Their first missionary came to Sind
in 883 and started secret propaganda in favor of the Ismaili caliph.
After the ground had been prepared, military aid was obtained from
Cairo, and through a *coup d'état* Multan was captured in 977. Ismaili
doctrines were now adopted as the official religion, and the *khutba*
was read in the name of the Egyptian ruler. The Ismailis destroyed
the old historic temple of Multan, which Muhammad ibn Qasim had
left in charge of the Hindus, and built a mosque on its site. Mansura
remained with the Hibbari family, at least until 985, but at a later
date this also became a small Ismaili stronghold. The Ismailis suffered
a setback with the rise of Mahmud of Ghazni, who in 1005 compelled
the ruler of Multan to recant his Ismaili beliefs and some twenty
years later conquered Mansura on his return from Somnath. The
Ismaili creed regained strength as the Ghaznavids weakened, but in
1175 Sultan Muhammad Ghuri captured Multan and appointed an
orthodox Sunni as governor. The area was incorporated in the Sunni
sultanate first of Ghazni, and later of Delhi.

Intellectual Achievements

During the Umayyad and the early Abbasid period, when the Arabs
were at the height of their political power, they were also active in
the intellectual field, making every effort to acquire knowledge from
all sources. Sind became the link through which the fruits of Indian
learning were transmitted to the Arabs, and by them made available
to the rest of the civilized world. Indo-Arab intellectual collaboration
was at its height during two distinct periods. During the reign (753–
774) of Mansur, embassies from Sind to Baghdad included scholars
who brought important books with them.[8] The second fruitful period

[8] E. C. Sachau, *Alberuni's India* (London, 1914), I, xxxi.

was the reign (780–808) of Harun-al-Rashid when the Barmakid family, which provided wazirs to the Abbasid caliphs for half a century, was at the zenith of its power. Arab bibliographers especially mention Harun's wazir, Yahya the Barmakid, Yahya's son Musa, and grandson Amran (both of whom governed Sind for some time) for their interest in India and Indian sciences. Besides sending scholars to India to study medicine and pharmacology, they brought Hindu scholars to Baghdad, made them chief physicians of their hospitals, and commissioned them to translate, into Arabic, Sanskrit books on such subjects as medicine, pharmacology, toxicology, philosophy, and astrology.

The earliest recorded Indo-Arab intellectual contact came in 771, when a Hindu astronomer and mathematician reached Baghdad, bringing with him a Sanskrit work (*Brahma Siddhanta* by Brahmagupta) which he translated into Arabic with the help of an Arab mathematician. Titles of three other works on astronomy translated from Sanskrit have been preserved by Arab bibliographers, but *Siddhanta,* which came to be known in Arabic as "Sindhind," had the greatest influence on the development of Arab astronomy. In mathematics the most important contribution of the subcontinent to Arabic learning was the introduction of what are known in the West as "Arabic numerals," but which Arabs themselves call "Indian numerals" (*al-ruqum-al-Hindiyyah*).

Indian medicine received even greater attention; the titles of at least fifteen works in Sanskrit which were translated into Arabic have been preserved, including books by Sushruta and Caraka, the foremost authorities in Hindu medicine. One of the translated books was on veterinary science, and another dealt with snakes and their poisons. None of these translations are now known to exist, except a rendering of a book on poisons, which was originally translated into Persian for Khalid-al-Barmaki, the Abbasid wazir, and later was translated into Arabic. Indian doctors enjoyed great prestige at Baghdad, and although their names, like the titles of their works, have been mutilated beyond recognition in Arab bibliographies, their number was very great. One of these men, Manka, was specially sent for when Harun-al-Rashid fell ill and could not be cured by Baghdad doctors.

Manka's treatment was successful and not only was he richly rewarded by the grateful caliph but he was entrusted with the translation of medical books from Sanskrit. Another Indian physician was
called in when a cousin of the caliph suffered a paralytic stroke and
was given up for lost by the Greek court physician. Many Indian
medicines, some of them in their original names such as *atrifal,* which
is the Hindi *tri-phal* (a combination of three fruits), found their way
into Arab pharmacopoeia.

Astrology and palmistry also received considerable attention at
Baghdad, and titles of a large number of books, translated from
Sanskrit on these subjects have been preserved. Other books which
were translated were on logic, alchemy, magic, ethics, statecraft, and
the art of war, but literary works gained the greatest popularity. Some
of the stories of the *Arabian Nights' Entertainments* are attributed to
Indian origin, and Arabic translations of the *Panchtantra,* popularly
known as the story of Kalila and Dimna, have become famous in
various Arabic and Persian versions. The games of chess and *chausar*
were also brought from India and transmitted by Arabs to other parts
of the world.

Sind also made a contribution in spheres other than science and
learning. While the debt of the Sufis, the Islamic mystics, to Indian
religion in general is not certain, the links of Sind with Islamic Sufism
are fairly definite. The great early Sufi, Bayazid of Bistam, had a
Sindhi as his spiritual teacher. "I learned," he said, "the science of
annihilation (ilm-i-fana) and unity (Tauhid) from Abu Ali (of Sind)
and Abu Ali learned the lessons of Islamic unity from me." [9] The
close association of Sind with Sufism is maintained to this day, and
one of the most marked features of Sind is the dominant place which
Sufism occupies in her literary and religious life.

Our knowledge of India's impact on Arab cultural life is based
on contemporary Arab sources, but it is far from complete. No title
of any Sanskrit book on music translated at Baghdad is available, but
it is known that the music of the subcontinent influenced Arab music.
That it was appreciated in the Abbasid capital is indicated by the

[9] Jami, *Nafahat al-uns* (Bombay, 1872), p. 60.

famous Arab author Jahiz (fl. 869), who wrote in his account of the people of the Indo-Pakistan subcontinent that "Their music is pleasing. One of their musical instruments is known as Kankalah, which is played with a string stretched on a pumpkin." This would seem to be a reference to an Indian instrument, the kingar, which is made with two gourds. Another indication of widespread knowledge of Indian music is a reference by an Arabic author from Andalusia to an Indian book on tunes and melodies.[10] It has even been suggested that many of the technical terms for Arab music were borrowed from Persia and India and that Indian music itself has incorporated certain Perso-Arab airs, such as *Yeman* and *Hijj* from Hijaz and *Zanuglah,* corrupted into *Jangla.*[11]

No connected history of Sind and Multan after the recall of Muhammad ibn Qasim is available but works of Arab travelers and geographers enable us to fill the gap. In particular Masudi, who visited what is now West Pakistan in 915–916, has left a brilliant account of the conditions in the Indus valley, from Waihind in the north to Debul in the south. Ibn Haukul, another traveler, visited the area some years later. Both agree that the principal Arab colonies were at Mansura, Multan, Debul, and Nirun, all of which had large Friday mosques. Non-Muslims formed the bulk of the population, and were in a preponderant majority at Debul and Alor. The relations between the Arabs and the non-Muslims were good. Unlike the historians of the sultanate period the Arab travelers refer to the non-Muslims as zimmis and not as kafirs (infidels). Soon after the conquest of Sind and Multan, the killing of cows was banned in the area. The reason may have been a simple desire to preserve the cattle wealth, but regard for Hindu sentiments may also have been partly responsible for this step. Some Hindu chiefs showed a sympathetic interest in Islam, for in 886 a Hindu raja commissioned an Arab linguist from Mansura to translate the Quran into the local language.[12] Another indication of the integration of the population into the gen-

[10] S. S. Nadwi, *Arab wa Hind ke ta'alluqat* (Allahabad, 1950), pp. 127, 157–58.
[11] S. A. Halim in *Journal of the Asiatic Society of Pakistan,* vol. I (1956).
[12] A. Z. Nadvi, *Tarikh-i-Sind* (Karachi, 1947), p. 196.

eral life of the ruling class was the use of Sindhi troops in Arab armies. Contemporary records mention their presence in areas as distant as the frontiers of the Byzantine empire.[13]

Arab rulers adopted local practices to a much greater extent than the Ghaznavids did later at Lahore, or the Turks and the Afghans at Delhi. According to Masudi, the ruler of Mansura had eighty war elephants and occasionally rode in a chariot drawn by elephants. The Arabs of Mansura generally dressed like the people of Iraq, but the dress of the ruler was similar to that of the Hindu rajas, and, like them, he wore earrings and kept his hair long.

After Muhammad ibn Qasim there were no large-scale Arab immigrations and Arab influence gradually diminished, but Sind and Multan remained in contact with the Arab countries, particularly Iraq and Egypt. At the time of Masudi's visit Arabic and Sindhi were spoken in Sind but Iranian influences were also strong, particularly after the rise of the Dailamites, when the use of Persian became more prevalent, especially in Multan.

Arab rule produced men of note in Sind and Multan, some of whom achieved fame and distinction in Damascus and Baghdad. One of them, Abu Maashar Sindhi (fl. 787), an authority on the life of the Prophet, was so eminent that when he died in Baghdad the reigning caliph led the prayers at his funeral. A number of other scholars and poets connected with Sind are also mentioned in Arabic anthologies. Some of them were from the immigrant families but many were of Sindhi origin and included descendants of captives taken as slaves during the Arab conquest or the later wars. The most notable Arabic poet of Sindhi origin was Abul Ata Sindhi, who was taken to Syria as a captive during his childhood, and earned his manumission with a *qasida* or ode. In spite of his command of literary Arabic, his pronunciation of Arabic words bore such traces of his origin that he had to engage a *ravi* to recite his verses. He wrote forceful *qasidas* in praise of the Umayyad rulers and poignant elegies on their downfall.

Life in the Arab dominion of Sind and Multan was simple, but agriculture and commerce were highly developed. Masudi mentions a large number of hamlets in the principalities of Multan and Mansura,

---

[13] Elliot and Dowson, I, 465.

and apparently the whole country was well cultivated. There was active commerce between Sind and other parts of the Muslim world, with caravans going to Khurasan, most commonly by the route of Kabul and Bamian. There were also communications with Zabulistan and Sijistan through Ghazni and Qandahar. Sindhi Hindus, who were excellent accountants and traders, had a major share in this commerce, and Alor is mentioned as a great commercial center. The prosperity of the area may be judged by the fact that Sind and Multan contributed eleven and a half million dirhams to Abbasid revenue, while the total revenue from the Kabul area in cash and cattle was less than two and a quarter million dirhams.[14]

Results of Arab Rule

Time, man, and natural calamities have dealt harshly with the traces of Arab rule in Sind. In 893 Debul was visited by a terrible earthquake which practically destroyed the whole city; the number of deaths was estimated at 150,000. A similar calamity affected Brahmanabad at a later date, but more permanent causes of damage were the floods and the changes in the course of the Indus. The cumulative result is that not one of the Arab cities has survived, and their very sites are uncertain.

It is not surprising, therefore, that historians attach little importance to Arab rule in Sind; yet though the visible traces of Arab ascendancy have been obliterated its invisible effects are many and far-reaching. Most of them, of course, relate to the former province of Sind. The script adopted for the Sindhi language is Arabic, not the Perso-Arabic script used for other Muslim languages of the subcontinent, and it contains a large proportion of Arabic words, mutilated or intact. Several leading Sindhi families are of Arab origin, and many more, although indigenous, have changed their genealogical tables to claim Arab ancestry. Until recently the social pattern in Sind was largely tribal, the place of the Arab shaikh being taken by the Sindhi wadera (the word itself is a literal translation of the Arabic counterpart). Such Arab virtues as hospitality have always distin-

[14] Elliot and Dowson, I, 471–72.

guished Sind, and the standard of Arabic scholarship has also remained high. Even the landscape, before the recent construction of
two barrages in Upper and Lower Sind, contained much to remind
one of Arabia—the desert, the pastoral scene, many large groves of
date-palm trees, and the strings of camels.

In two important spheres the impact of the Arabs—as we have
already seen—was felt far beyond Sind and Multan. In the political
field, the arrangements made by Muhammad ibn Qasim with the non-
Muslims provided the basis for later Muslim policy in the subcontinent. By the time Muslim rule was established at Lahore and Delhi,
Islamic law had been codified and contained stringent provisions regarding idol-worshipers. The fact that those provisions were not followed and the Hindus were treated as "people of the book" was
largely due to the fact that they had been given this status by Muhammad ibn Qasim and that for centuries this liberal practice had
been built up in Sind and Multan.

The second important consequence of the Arab conquest of Sind
—the cultural and intellectual contacts—came to an end when Baghdad lost political control over the area. Arabic literature henceforth
looked elsewhere than to India for inspiration, and Sanskrit works
were no longer translated by Hindu scholars in Baghdad.

Although Arab conquest had been confined to the southern part of
what is now West Pakistan, peaceful contacts were far more extensive. Arab sailors and traders plied their trade along the coast and
soon after the rise of Islam we find colonies of Muslim Arabs at a
number of major ports such as Cambay, Chaul, and Honawar. Muslims had reached Ceylon even earlier, and the Arab invasion of Sind
was, as we have seen, a measure of reprisal for the plunder and imprisonment of Muslim widows and orphans returning from Ceylon.
Hajjaj, who organized the expedition to Sind, was also indirectly responsible for the establishment of a large colony of Muslim Arabs in
the South. When he became the viceroy of Iraq, many political
enemies fled his jurisdiction, seeking refuge on the southern coast of
the subcontinent. They form the nucleus of the important Nawayat
community found on the Konkan coast of Bombay and in Tinnevelly

district of Madras. Others settled along the Bay of Bengal, where the presence of Muslims is traceable back to the eighth century.

The largest Arab coastal settlements, however, were in Malabar, where Muslims now form a substantial part of the population. One result of the Arab settlement was the conversion of a local ruler to Islam, an event which undoubtedly helped the position of the Muslim community. Another influence of the arrival of Muslims may possibly be seen in the great religious movements in South India in the ninth century. It has been suggested, although without very clear proof, that the religious ferment of the period may have owed something to Muslim ideas.

These Muslim colonies on the coast are of interest also as they provided the base from which missionaries, traders, and sailors went to the Far East and spread Islam in Malaya and Indonesia. The movement to the East was not only a result of the Arab share in the spice trade of Southeast Asia but also a continuation of traditional Indian relations with the countries further east. Southeast Asia has since ancient times been greatly influenced by Indian religion, literature, and art, and with the spread of Islam to the key points of contact, Muslim influence replaced that of Brahmanism and Buddhism. Bali remains Hindu to this day, but Malaya, Java, and Sumatra are predominantly Muslim and owe their present religious and literary tradition largely to the influences emanating from the Muslim colonies on the coastline of the subcontinent. Emigrants who brought about this transformation in Southeast Asia included Arab and Persian sailors and traders, but the role of Muslims from Gujarat, Malabar, Coromandal, and Bengal was not less important.

II. The Heritage of Ghazni and Bukhara

THE ARAB conquest of Sind and southwestern Punjab was completed by 714, and during the following three centuries there was no further extension of Muslim dominion. The second phase of Muslim expansion, beginning with the establishment of a Turkish Muslim dynasty in Ghazni, followed the traditional northwestern routes for the invasion of India.

In 642 the Arabs had defeated the Sassanid ruler Yezdegerd and become masters of Iran. After this, operating from Fars by way of Kirman, they set about conquering the eastern provinces of the Iranian empire. Under Qutaiba ibn Muslim they conquered Transoxiana as far as Khwarizm and Samarqand (711–712), and within a century of the death of the founder of Islam the Arabs were masters of Khurasan, Balkh, and Mawara-un Nahr (Transoxiana). It was the Arab occupation of Transoxiana that paved the way for the Muslim conquest of India, for it established a link between the Turkish homeland and Islam. From this time the Turks were to play an important role in the Muslim world, and were the main force behind the conquest of the subcontinent.

Invasions from Ghazni

The first inroad into the heart of the area which is now Afghanistan was made by Yaqub ibn Lais, the Saffarid, who captured Kabul in 870 and founded Ghazni at about the same time. Kabul was, however, lost by his successor to Hindu rulers known as the Hindu Shahis, whose capital was at Waihind (Ohind), near modern Peshawar, and whose rule extended to Kabul in the west and the Bias River in the east.

In the meantime the Samanids (874–999) had established them-

selves at Bukhara and gradually brought the greater part of the territory to the east of Baghdad under their sway. Persian in origin,
they favored the Persian language. Rudaki, the Chaucer of Persian
poetry, flourished at the Samanid court, and Persian replaced Arabic
as the official language.

Under the Samanids Turkish slaves gained political and military
importance. One of these, Alptigin, rebelled against his Samanid
masters and established himself at Ghazni in 962. In 977, Subuktigin,
a Turkish slave upon whom Alptigin had bestowed the hand of his
daughter, ascended the throne of Ghazni and proceeded to expand
his kingdom by annexing adjacent areas in Khurasan, Seistan, and
Lamghan. Alarmed at the rising power of the new Turkish principality, Jaipal, Shahi raja of Waihind, took the offensive and advanced toward Subuktigin's capital. The two armies met between
Lamghan (modern Jalalabad) and Ghazni. Jaipal was defeated, and
was forced to agree to pay a large indemnity to the Turkish ruler. He
defaulted and tried to avenge his loss, but he was again decisively
defeated, and Subuktigin followed up his success by forcing Jaipal to
cede the territory between Lamghan and Peshawar.

Later Muslim historians often represent Subuktigin as a champion
of the faith, whose "chief occupation was the propagation of Islam
with fire and sword among the idolators of India," but, in fact, he
never crossed the Indus, and the only two expeditions in which he
took the initiative "were undertaken rather as measures of reprisal
and for the purpose of securing his dominion than with any intention
of propagating his faith." [1] Subuktigin, however, paved the way for
the more active efforts of his son Mahmud by occupying the key
city of Peshawar and building roads leading to the Indian frontiers
along which his son marched during his numerous expeditions.

Even more important was the development of Ghazni as a base of
operations against India. It reached its zenith in the succeeding reign
when it became a center of political power, organized administration, and literary culture, second in importance only to Baghdad in
Muslim Asia. Even under Subuktigin it surpassed Bukhara in im-

[1] Sir Wolseley Haig in *The Cambridge History of India* (Cambridge, 1928),
III, 12.

portance, and began to attract a large number of Turks who were to form the spearhead of the attack against the Indian subcontinent.

Subuktigin died in 997, and after a brief struggle his son, known to history as Mahmud of Ghazni, succeeded him. Brilliant and ambitious, Mahmud at once turned his attention to India. He had taken part in all of his father's campaigns against Jaipal, and knew the weakness of the Indian armies as well as the riches of the kings and temples. The series of invasions he launched against the subcontinent were to carry his armies farther than any previous Muslim ruler had penetrated. His first important battle was fought near Peshawar on November 28, 1001, and ended with the defeat and capture of his father's old opponent, Raja Jaipal. Jaipal obtained his release by paying ransom, but his repeated defeats had lost him the confidence of his people, and he named his son Anandpal as his successor. Following the Rajput custom, he immolated himself on the flames of a funeral pyre.

Three years later Mahmud made another expedition to India to punish the raja of Bhatiya (the modern Bhera), a principality that had been friendly to Subuktigin but had failed to provide help against Jaipal. The raja was defeated, but on his return Mahmud found himself in a difficult position. He lost most of his baggage in crossing the rivers of western Punjab, and was attacked by Abul Fath Daud, the Ismaili ruler of Multan. In 1005 Mahmud returned to punish Daud, but his passage was obstructed by Anandpal. Daud shut himself up in the fort at Multan and obtained pardon on payment of ransom and the promise to abjure Ismaili doctrines. Anandpal was defeated, and Mahmud appointed Sukhpal (a grandson of Jaipal who had accepted Islam and was now known as Nawasa Shah), as governor of Waihind and returned to Ghazni.

This first attempt to establish a center of Muslim authority east of the Indus through a scion of the old ruling family did not succeed. Nawasa Shah apostasized, started expelling Muslim officers, and proposed to rule either as an independent king or as the vassal of his uncle Anandpal. Mahmud returned to deal with the situation in 1008 and found Anandpal fully prepared. He had obtained help

from the Hindu rajas of Ujjain, Gwalior, Kalinjar, Kanauj, Delhi, and Ajmer. It appears that by now Hindu India was alive to its peril. Not only did the rulers from northern and central India send their contingents, but, according to Firishta, even the masses were highly enthusiastic, and the Hindu women sold their ornaments and sent their savings to help the army. The battle was fought at a place between Peshawar and Waihind. Mahmud took special precautions, for his army was breaking down under the charge of the warlike Khokhars when a fortunate accident decided the day in his favor. Anandpal's elephant took fright and fled with his royal rider. The Rajput army, believing the raja's flight to be intentional, broke up and dispersed, hotly pursued by the Muslims, thus converting what looked like a Hindu victory into a defeat.

The defeat of the great Hindu confederacy was a turning point in Mahmud's career. So far his campaigns had been confined to the neighborhood of the Indus. The breakup of the Hindu army emboldened him, and now he marched against the more distant Nagarkot (Kangra), where there was no resistance. Nagarkot contained an ancient temple which, like other Hindu temples of the period, was a great repository of wealth donated by rich votaries. Mahmud returned laden with booty, and for the rest of his life the ancient Hindu religious centers with their treasure hoards accumulated over centuries were to exercise a powerful fascination over him. His future expeditions went even farther afield. Tarain (1010), Thanesar (1014), the distant Kanauj (1018), and Kalinjar (1022) were scenes of Mahmud's exploits, in which he was uniformly successful. He did not try to establish his rule at any of these places, but he left a governor at Lahore in 1020, which now became incorporated into the Ghaznavid empire.

The most dramatic of Mahmud's campaigns was against Somnath, the wealthy religious center on the shores of the Indian Ocean. The dash to this distant goal, through an unknown and unfriendly area, across the deserts of Rajputana and marshes of Cutch, was a remarkable feat of courage, planning, resourcefulness, and tenacity of purpose. In spite of the hardships which Mahmud and his army had

to suffer on the return journey, the expedition was completely successful in its object. Mahmud returned laden with riches of an extent until then unheard of in Ghazni.

Mahmud set out on the expedition to Somnath in October, 1024, and did not return to his capital until the spring of 1026. Except for a brief punitive expedition in the autumn of the same year against the Jats of Sind who had harassed him during his return from Somnath, Mahmud did not return to India. Henceforth affairs in Central Asia occupied him until his death in 1030.

A brave and resourceful general during thirty years of ceaseless warfare, Mahmud never suffered defeat. He was a cultured monarch, and by his munificence attracted great poets and scholars to his court, making Ghazni the rival of Baghdad in the splendor of edifices and the number of men of culture and learning. He lacked the constructive genius of Muhmad Ghuri, and in spite of having overrun a great part of northern India, established Muslim dominion only up to Lahore, but he made the work of the later conquerors easier.

India at the Time of the Invasions: Al-Biruni's Account

For our knowledge of India in this period we are indebted to one of the most remarkable of Islamic writers, Abu Raihan al-Biruni. His stay in what is now West Pakistan could not have been long, but his accounts of Indian customs and manners, as well as his observations on the Islamic conquest, are among the most penetrating that we have. He was born in about 973 in Khwarizm (modern Khiva) and soon distinguished himself in astronomy, mathematics, logic, and history. Some time before 1017 Mahmud was able to persuade him to come to Ghazni, but evidence of close contact between the sultan and al-Biruni is lacking. He was evidently in greater favor with the next ruler, Masud, to whom he dedicated his work, *Qanun-i-Masudi.* His other works include the *Chronology of Ancient Nations,* an introduction to astrology, a treatise on materia medica, astronomical tables, a summary of Ptolemy's *Almagest,* and several translations from Greek and Sanskrit. He must have written some books in

Sanskrit as at one place he writes of "being occupied in composing for the Hindus a translation of the books of Euclid and of the *Almagest,* and dictating to them a treatise on the construction of the astrolabe, being simply guided herein by the desire of spreading science." [2] However the work which is of special interest is his famous *Kitab-ul-Hind,* a masterly survey of the religion, sciences, and social customs of the Hindus, which was completed shortly after Mahmud's death. As a study of an alien civilization his book represents the peak of Muslim scholarship and remains unsurpassed as a masterpiece of erudite learning, penetrating observation, and unbiased appraisal of Hindu culture. In the preface to his book al-Biruni discussed the principles which should guide a scholar in treating of societies and religious systems other than his own. He criticized the tendency to misrepresent other societies or to depend on "second-hand information which one has copied from the others, a farrago of materials never sifted by the sieve of critical examination." The principle which he adopted was to adhere to the accounts of the Hindus as given in their own authentic works. Of his own work he said: "This book is not a polemical one. I shall not produce the arguments of our antagonists in order to refute such of them as I believe to be in the wrong. My book is nothing but a simple historic record of facts. I shall place before the reader the theories of the Hindus exactly as they are, and I shall mention in connection with them similar theories of the Greeks in order to show the relationship existing between them." [3]

Al-Biruni considered the Hindus to be excellent philosophers, good mathematicians, and sound astrologers. He fully appreciated their mental achievements, and when he came across anything noble in their sciences or practical life he did not fail to praise it. Writing about the great tanks, or reservoirs, at holy places he remarked, "In this they have attained a very high degree of art, so that our people when they see them wonder at them and are unable to describe them, much less to construct anything like them." [4]

[2] E. C. Sachau, *Alberuni's India* (London, 1914), I, 137.
[3] Sachau, I, 6–7.
[4] Sachau, II, 144.

But while al-Biruni had a sympathetic understanding of the profound achievements of Hindu society, there were Indian attitudes and customs that seemed to him to indicate fundamental weaknesses. The chief of this is summed up in his often-quoted analysis of the tone and temper of contemporary Hindu society: "We can only say that folly is an illness for which there is no medicine, and the Hindus believe that there is no country but theirs, no nation like theirs, no kings like theirs, no religion like theirs, no science like theirs. They are haughty, foolishly vain, self-conceited, and stolid. They are by nature niggardly in communicating that which they know, and they take the greatest possible care to withhold it from men of another caste among their own people, still much more, of course, from any foreigner." [5]

There can be little doubt that these attitudes help to explain the successes of Mahmud and later invaders. An open, dynamic society, which had adopted ideas and techniques from many quarters, had an enormous advantage when it faced a culture that had ceased to be receptive to alien influences.

Mahmud's Successors

After Mahmud's death in 1030, his son Masud, succeeded in establishing his claim to the throne. Masud soon turned his attention to India and replaced the governor of Lahore with Ahmad Niyaltigin, his father's treasurer. The instructions issued to the officers at Lahore at the time of Ahmad's administrative reorganization are interesting. "They were not to undertake, without special permission, expeditions beyond the limits of the Punjab, but were to accompany Ahmad on any expedition which he might undertake; they were not to drink, play polo, or mix in social intercourse with the Hindu officers at Lahore; and they were to refrain from wounding the susceptibilities of these officers and their troops by inopportune displays of religious bigotry." [6]

[5] Sachau, I, 22–23.
[6] *Cambridge History of India*, III, 29.

Ahmad Niyaltigin soon got into difficulties, however, with Abul Hasan, who had been sent by Masud to collect the revenue and inquire into the affairs of the earlier administration. It seems that when Ahmad returned in 1034 from a very successful raid against Benares he had failed to remit the spoils of victory to Ghazni. This gave Hasan the opportunity to send reports to Masud that Ahmad, utilizing the plunder of Benares to raise a powerful army, was on the point of revolt. Masud decided upon punitive action against the governor, and the command of this responsible and hazardous expedition was entrusted to Tilak, one of his Hindu generals. "When Tilak arrived at Lahore, he took several Musulmans prisoners, who were the friends of Ahmad, and ordered their right hands to be cut off; . . . the men who were with Ahmad were so terrified at this punishment and display of power, that they sued for mercy and deserted him." [7] Tilak pursued Ahmad with a large body of men, chiefly Hindu, and after the erstwhile governor was killed in an encounter, his head was taken to Ghazni.

Masud came to India in 1037 and, in fulfillment of a vow taken during an illness, attacked and captured the fortress of Hansi, hitherto considered impregnable by the Hindus. During his absence the Saljuq Turks invaded the western and northern territories of the Ghaznavid empire and occupied Nishapur. Masud returned to deal with them, but his Hindu contingent failed conspicuously against the Saljuqs, and Masud fled toward Lahore. When the royal party reached Marigal pass between Rawalpindi and Attock, Turkish and Hindu guards mutinied, and the sultan's brother was placed on the throne. However Masud's son, Maudud, defeated his uncle and in 1042 became sultan.

During Maudud's reign, Mahipal, the raja of Delhi, made a determined attempt to oust the Ghaznavids from the Punjab. He recaptured Hansi, Thanesar, and Kangra and besieged Lahore, but was unable to take the town. In 1048 Maudud appointed two of his sons to the government of Lahore and Peshawar, and sent Bu Ali Hasan, the kotwal of Ghazni, to deal with the Hindu resurgence. These

[7] H. M. Elliot and John Dowson, *The History of India as Told by Its Own Historians* (London, 1867–1877), II, 132.

measures were successful, but Maudud died shortly thereafter in December, 1049.

The next important ruler was Sultan Ibrahim, whose long and peaceful reign of forty years (1059–1099) constitutes the golden period of Ghaznavid Punjab. Ibrahim had ensured the stability of his northern and western frontiers by entering into a treaty with the Saljuqs and his son Masud II married the daughter of Sultan Malik Shah. Secure at home, Ibrahim could pay full attention to India, and in 1079 he crossed the southern border of the Punjab, capturing Ajodhan, now known as Pakpatan. His military commander at Lahore, the brilliant Abul Najm Zarir Shaybani, was constantly on the offensive, and carried out successful raids against Benares, Thanesar, and Kanauj. The main achievement of Ibrahim's reign, however, was Lahore's rise as a great cultural center under the viceroyalty of Shirzad, his grandson. Ibrahim was succeeded by his son Masud III, who ruled peacefully for sixteen years (1099–1115). Shirzad succeeded him, but he was deposed in the following year, and then after a brief rule by Arsalan, Bahram came to the throne, which he held for thirty-four troubled years (1118–1152).

The trouble came mainly from the chiefs of Ghur, a hilly area between Herat and Kabul that had been conquered by the Ghaznavids in the time of Mahmud, but that had remained virtually independent. Out of the quarrels was to come the destruction of the Ghazni dynasty and its replacement by one based on Ghur. During Bahram's reign Qutb-ud-din Muhammad, a Ghuri chief, took the title of malik-ul-jabal (the king of the mountains). Bahram gave him his daughter in marriage, but later, suspecting treachery, had his son-in-law poisoned. To avenge his death, his brother Saif-ud-din collected a large body of men at Firuz Kuh, the capital of Ghur, and set out for Ghazni. He defeated Bahram and forced him to flee to India, but in 1149 Bahram returned suddenly to Ghazni, surprised Saif-ud-din, and reoccupied his capital. Saif-ud-din, who had surrendered on the promise that his life would be spared, was put to death under abhorrent circumstances. This aroused the ire of another brother, Ala-ud-din Husain, known to history as Jahan Saz (the world-burner), who took a terrible vengeance. Capturing Ghazni in 1151, he reduced its splendid

buildings to ashes and desecrated the graves of its kings. The same process of destruction was repeated in the provinces.

Bahram reoccupied what remained of Ghazni when Ala-ud-din Husain was defeated and temporarily imprisoned by the Saljuq Turks. This relief was only temporary, however, for after Bahram's death in 1152 his successor was driven out of Ghazni by the Ghuzz tribe of Turkmans. All that was left to the Ghaznavids was their Indian province of Lahore, where they maintained their rule after the loss of Ghazni.

Meanwhile the power of the Ghuri chieftains revived, and in 1173 two nephews of Ala-ud-din Husain succeeded in taking the city from the Turkmans. The older of the two, Ghiyas-ud-din, became sultan of the Ghuri kingdom, which he governed from Firuz Kuh, in the area now known as Hazarajat. The younger brother, Muiz-ud-din Muhammad, was stationed at Ghazni as the deputy of the sultan, and from here he undertook the conquest of the subcontinent. His first move was against Lahore, where the last of the Ghaznavids, Khusrau Malik, was finally defeated in 1186, and the area was added to the Ghuri kingdom. The subsequent career of Muiz-ud-din, or, as he is known in Indian history, Muhammad Ghuri, will be traced in the following chapter, but since his triumphs mark the end of one period of Muslim-Hindu contact and begin another, it will be convenient at this point to summarize the general results of the impact of Islam after the time Mahmud of Ghazni made his first raids at the beginning of the eleventh century.

Results of the Ghaznavid Invasions

The example set by Mahmud of Ghazni of raiding India and sacking its wealth, particularly that stored in the great temples, was repeated by his successors whenever the opportunity arose. The effect of this on the country can easily be imagined, and al-Biruni's description of the result of Mahmud's raids can scarcely be doubted. "Mahmud," he wrote, "utterly ruined the prosperity of the country, and performed wonderful exploits by which the Hindus became like atoms of dust scattered in all directions, and like a tale of old in the

al-Biruni report of the raids

mouth of the people. Their scattered remains cherish, of course, the most inveterate aversion towards all Muslims. This is the reason, too, why Hindu sciences have retired far away from those parts of the country conquered by us, and have fled to places which our hand cannot yet reach, to Kashmir, Benares, and other places." [8]

Over against this dark picture, however, must be set evidence that suggests that even during the Ghaznavid period there were peaceful contacts between Hindus and Muslims. The caravan routes between Kurasan and India were reopened, for example, as soon as military operations were over. Furthermore, according to Ibn-ul-Athir, there had been Muslims in the Benares area "since the days of Mahmud bin Subuktigin who continued faithful to the law of Islam, and constant in prayer and good works." [9] There is a persistent local tradition in certain old centers in the heart of Uttar Pradesh that Muslim families had settled there long before the conquest of the area by Muhammad Ghuri. In the city of Benares there are Muslim *mohallas,* which, it is said, are anterior in date to the conquest of Benares by the Muslims, and similar traditions are current about Maner in Bihar.[10]

The only area of which anything like a recorded history for the Hindu period is available is Kashmir, and from there we get information regarding the peaceful presence of the Muslims among the Hindus. "Muslim traders and soldiers of fortune began to enter Kashmir from an early date. Kalhana records that Lalitaditya's son and successor Vajraditya sold many men to the *mlecchas,* and introduced practices which befitted the *mlecchas.*" Later Harsa (d. 1101) employed Turkish soldiers and, under Muslim influence, adopted elaborate fashions in dress and ornaments. During the brief reign (1120–1121) of Bhikshachara, Muslim soldiers were again employed. From the accounts of Marco Polo, it appears that by the end of the thirteenth century there was a colony of Muslims in Kashmir, for he says that the people of the valley do not kill animals, but that if they want to eat meat, "they get the Saracens who dwell among them, to play the butcher." These "Saracens" must have been

[8] Sachau, I, 22.
[9] H. M. Elliot and John Dowson, *A History of India as Told by Its Own Historians* (London, 1867–1877), II, 251.
[10] H. R. Nevill, ed., *Benares: A Gazetteer.* Vol. XXIV of *District Gazetteer of the United Provinces of Agra and Oudh* (Lucknow, 1922).

either emigrants from Turkistan or Hindus converted to Islam by the pietist missionaries from India and Central Asia.[11]

The position of Hindu generals, soldiers, and scholars at the Ghaznavid court is also significant. Even Mahmud, the iconoclast, had a contingent of Hindu officers and soldiers. He richly rewarded at least one Sanskrit poet and had Hindu pandits at his court. He also issued coins with Sanskrit inscriptions. The Hindu position seems to have improved greatly in the days of his successor, Masud. Only fifty days after the death of Mahmud, his son despatched Sewand Rai, a Hindu chief, with a large body of Hindu cavalry in pursuit of the nobles who had espoused the cause of his brother. Sewand Rai died in the ensuing battle, but his selection for this important assignment indicates his position of trust and eminence. Five years later, Tilak, another Hindu general, acquired a dominant position. The son of a barber, he became a confidant of Khwaja Ahmed Hasan Maimandi, the influential wazir of Sultan Mahmud. The khwaja made Tilak his secretary and interpreter, and in 1033, when news was received from Lahore of the rebellion of Ahmad Niyaltigin, it was Tilak who was sent to deal with the situation. The extreme measures taken by the Hindu general against the Muslim partisans of Ahmad show his confidence and sense of security.

The importance of the Hindus in Masud's army may be judged by the fact that at the battle of Kirman they formed half of the cavalry, there being two thousand Hindus, one thousand Turks, and one thousand Kurds and Arabs. They fared very badly in this battle, and later six of their officers committed suicide in accordance with Rajput practice. The Hindu contingent was later equally ineffective at Merv. These repeated disasters must have led to the reduction of the Hindu element in the Ghazni army, but contemporary evidence suggests that the Hindu position under the Ghaznavids was very much better than it was to be in the early days of the Delhi Sultanate.

The Cultural Legacy

Of more lasting importance than the vicissitudes of the house of Mahmud is the cultural heritage of Ghazni, particularly in relation

[11] Mohibul Hasan, *Kashmir under the Sultans* (Calcutta, 1959), pp. 234–35.

to that part of the Ghaznavid empire which now constitutes West Pakistan. The court chroniclers of Ghazni have not paid the subject much attention, but there are ample indications in contemporary literature that the Muslim government at Lahore was well organized and vigorous and that the city had become a great cultural center. Usually a distinguished royal prince was appointed the naib (viceroy or deputy) of the Punjab, and maintained an elaborate court. The long and peaceful reigns of Ibrahim and his successor Masud III, provided the opportunity for the cultural growth of Lahore. The city owed much to Abu Nasr Farsi, the distinguished secretary of Shirzad who was viceroy for many years. He established a *khanqah* (hospice) at Lahore which attracted scholars from far and near. "In large numbers seekers after knowledge from all parts of India, and the territories of Kashgar, Transoxiana, Iraq, Bukhara, Samarqand, Khurasan, Ghazni, Herat, etc., benefited by the same. Consequently a new settlement grew up in the neighborhood of Lahore." [12]

The first Persian poet of the area mentioned in literary histories was Masud Razi (d.1077). Razi recited a poem in Masud's court in which he appealed to the sultan to deal with the growing menace of the Saljuqs. "The ants have become snakes," he said, and "may become dragons, if neglected." The sultan, resenting this overt reference to his weakness, exiled the poet to the Punjab.[13] Next year he relented and put Razi in charge of affairs at Jhelum, but did not permit his return to Ghazni. With the exception of a few verses his work has perished, but the *diwan* of his distinguished son, Abul Farj Runi, who spent most of his time at Lahore, has survived and has been published in Iran.

The most notable poet of the period, however, was Masud Sa'ad Salman, whose father held a high office under the viceroy. Masud was born in Lahore about 1048. A great favorite of Prince Saif-ud-daula Mahmud, the viceroy of Hindustan, he composed many *qasidas* eulogizing the victories of his patron. When the prince fell out of favor with the sultan the poet lost his *jagir,* and was later imprisoned

---

[12] Quoted in M. A. Ghani, *Pre-Mughal Persian in Hindustan* (Allahabad, 1941), p. 194.
[13] M. H. K. Sherani, *Panjab men Urdu* (Lahore, 195?), pp. 32–33.

for ten years because of his suspected share in Saif-ud-daula's treasonable proceedings. Released shortly before Sultan Ibrahim's death in 1099, he was given responsible posts, including the governorship of Jullundur. When his patron Abu Nasr Farsi incurred royal displeasure, Masud was again imprisoned. He was released in about 1107, became the royal librarian, and after arranging his voluminous *diwan,* died in 1121 or 1122. Masud wrote in Persian, Arabic, and old Hindi, but no specimen of his verses in the last two languages is extant. His Persian works have led an Iranian critic to include him among the ten greatest poets of the Persian language.[14] His most moving poems were composed in captivity and express a nostalgic longing for Lahore. In one he wrote:

> Thou knowest that I lie in grievous bonds, O Lord!
> Thou knowest that I am weak and feeble, O Lord!
> My spirit goes out in longing for Lahore, O Lord!
> O Lord, how I crave for it, O Lord!

And in another he remembers how,

The Id festal time is come, and I am far from the face of that charming
    sweetheart;
How can I live without the sight of that houri of Paradise?
Who shall say to me, "O friend, a happy Id to thee!"
When my sweetheart is at Lahore and I in Nishapur?
Why do I long for the city of Lahore and my beloved?
Well, was there a man who did not miss his sweetheart and his native
    land?

Among the prose writers of this period the most famous was the saint Ali Hujwiri, popularly known as Data Ganj Bakhsh of Lahore, who died in 1071. He wrote both in prose and verse, but his *diwan* was lost during his lifetime, and the few verses that are quoted in his prose works are not of a high order. His fame as an author rests on *Kashf-al-Mahjub* (The Unveiling of the Hidden), the oldest extant work on Sufism in Persian.[15] The value of *Kashf-al-Mahjub* lies not only in the authentic information which it gives about the earlier and contemporary mystic orders, but also in the fact that it is a systematic

[4] Ghani, pp. 200–2.
[15] *Kashf al-Mahjub,* trans. by R. A. Nicholson (London, 1911).

exposition of mysticism. It has long been regarded as a standard text-book by Sufis.

The Central Asian Heritage

Arab rule in the Sind had brought Islam to India, and had set a pattern for dealing with the conquered peoples as well as facilitating fruitful contact between Hindu and Islamic civilizations; the Ghaznavid occupation of Lahore had even more far-reaching cultural results. Persian, which was adopted as the court language and was the vehicle of literary and cultural expression during the Ghaznavid period, continued to hold this position throughout Muslim rule. The branch of Persian which remained current in Muslim India was the eastern branch in vogue in Afghanistan and Central Asia and not the pure Persian of Isfahan and Shiraz.

Partly because the linguistic affinity, and partly because the waves of the immigrants who established Muslim culture in India came through Ghazni and Bukhara, the entire cultural pattern of Muslim India was dominated by the Central Asian tradition. This continued until the days of the Mughals who, although themselves Turks from Central Asia, established closer contacts with Iran and Arabia. Even then, out of several strands which provided the warp and woof of Muslim civilization in India, the most dominant was the influence of Central Asia. After the establishment of Muslim Delhi, the administrative system was modeled on that of Ghazni. Muslim political institutions, military and administrative organization, ethics, and jurisprudence, in fact the entire pattern of Muslim life, bears the imprint of Ghazni and Bukhara. It was the *Hidaya* of a Central Asian lawyer which became the standard legal textbook in Muslim India. The same tradition gained preeminence in other spheres. This tradition became firmly entrenched when a large number of Muslim scholars, writers, and darvishes from Central Asia took refuge in Muslim India to escape Mongol atrocities.

III. The Establishment of the Delhi Sultanate

AFTER the death of Mahmud in 1030 there were occasional incursions into Hindu territory from Ghazni and the Ghaznavid base at Lahore, but no major territorial change took place and Hindu India enjoyed a respite from foreign invasion for a century and a half. This did not lead, however, to national consolidation, and a number of principalities grew up in different parts of the subcontinent. In the north, the most important were the kingdoms of Delhi and Ajmer, Kanauj, Bundhelkhand, Gujarat, Malwa, and Bengal. Occasionally they would come together for some common purpose, but normally there was no cooperation among them, even in the face of the danger that threatened them from the northwest. Perhaps the relative freedom from Muslim raids during the first part of the twelfth century made them forget their perilous position, but, for whatever reason, their disunity made it possible for a determined leader to deal with them one after the other.

Muhammad Ghuri's Conquests

It was this situation that was exploited to the full by Muhammad Ghuri, who had been placed in charge of Ghazni by his brother, the sultan of Ghur, in 1173. For the next thirty years Ghazni was the base from which Muhammad mounted his attacks on India; unlike the raids of the previous Muslim rulers of the mountain areas, these were aimed not at acquiring plunder and glory but at the political control of northern India. From this time on, the story of Islam in India is one of expansion and the building up of a great empire that would be based not on Ghazni or Ghur but on Lahore and Delhi.

To attain his object, Muhammad first had to bring the Muslim kingdoms on the frontier under his control. Soon after the conquest of Ghazni he accomplished this by occupying Multan and Uch in

1175. At that time the most frequented route from Ghazni into India was not the well-known Khyber pass, or the Bolan pass in the south, but the Gomal, which leads to the district of Dera Ismail Khan in what is now West Pakistan. Muhammad Ghuri followed this route, and for some years left Peshawar and Lahore undisturbed. After occupying Upper Sind he turned in 1178 to Anhilwara or Patan, the capital of Gujarat, possibly with the hope that its riches would provide an economic basis for his military schemes. He was defeated, however, and had to change his strategy. Turning to the Khyber and the Punjab, he took Peshawar in 1179, Sialkot in 1185, and Lahore in 1186. In the winter of 1190–91 he conquered the Hindu fort of Bhatinda and placed it in charge of a governor. He was returning to Ghazni when he received information that Prithvi Raj of Ajmer and Delhi was on his way to Bhatinda and that immediate help was needed. Part of the sultan's army had already dispersed, but in view of the danger to which Bhatinda was exposed, Muhammad Ghuri returned and met the forces of Prithvi Raj at Tarain (modern Taraori), near Karnal. The Rajputs attacked with such vigor that both wings of the Muslim army were driven from the field. Its center stood firm under Muhammad Ghuri and, in a determined charge on the Hindu center, he attacked Govind Rai, the raja's brother and the commander-in-chief of the Indian army. Muhammad Ghuri struck Govind Rai with a lance, shattering his teeth, but the Hindu general drove his javelin through his opponent's arm. The sultan, faint from pain and loss of blood, was about to fall from his horse when a young Khalji with great presence of mind sprang upon his horse, steadied him, and carried him back to the place where the Muslim army had halted. Here a litter was hastily prepared, and the army returned to Ghazni in comparative order.

This was the first major defeat suffered by Muslims in northern India, and on his return to the capital Muhammad Ghuri meted out exemplary punishment to the army chiefs who had fled from the battlefield. As a severe penance for himself, he did not wear fine clothes or engage in any festivities for a year, but concentrated all his energies on preparations for a return to India.

The two armies met again in 1192 on the battlefield of Tarain. The

Indian army far exceeded Muhammad Ghuri's forces in number, but his brilliant generalship and superior tactics gave him a decisive victory. The Indian commander-in-chief fell on the battlefield, Prithvi Raj was captured in the course of flight, and the Indian army was completely routed. This victory made Muhammad Ghuri master of Delhi and Ajmer. He left Qutb-ud-Din Aibak to consolidate the new conquests at Kuhram (in East Punjab), but in conformity with Muhammad ibn Qasim's policy of appointing local governors, a son of Prithvi Raj, was made governor of Ajmer. Prithvi Raj himself was taken to Ajmer, where, after some delay, he was found guilty of treason and executed. A few of his coins with the Sanskrit superscription "Hammira" (Amir) on the obverse have been found, suggesting that he had initially accepted Muslim suzerainty.

Muhammad Ghuri, who had returned to Ghazni after the battle of Tarain, was back again two years later to deal with the powerful raja of Kanauj. The ensuing battle was severely contested, but the Muslims were victorious and added a great kingdom to their dominion. Meanwhile, early in 1193, Aibak had occupied Delhi, the future seat of Muslim power in India. Hazabr-ud-din Hasan Adib, an adventurous officer, had conquered Badaun in the heart of the Gangetic plain even before Muhammad Ghuri had taken Bhatinda, and Malik Hisam-ud-din Aghul Bak, another leader of the vanguard of Islam, had established himself in Oudh.

These brilliant victories, indicative of the spirit and resourcefulness of early Muslim officers, were soon eclipsed by the exploits of Ikhtiyar-ud-din Muhammad, the son of Bakhtiyar Khalji, who had been assigned certain villages in Oudh. From his advance base between the Ganges and the Son he raided Bihar and Tirhut. His successes attracted so many adventurers that he was able to invade and conquer southern parts of Bihar, probably in 1199. Later he presented himself to Aibak, who gave him his recent conquests as a fief.

This encouraged Ikhtiyar-ud-din to extend the Muslim dominion to the most eastern parts of the subcontinent. In 1201 he left Bihar with a large body of horse and marched so rapidly against Nadiya, the capital of Bengal, that when he arrived at the city only eighteen of his companions had been able to keep pace with him. Nadiya was

partly deserted at this time, and the Muslim commander and his eighteen companions were able to pass through the city gates un- challenged as horse dealers from the north. Reaching the raja's palace on the banks of the Ganges, they cut down the guards, but Raja Lakshmansena escaped through a postern gate by boat. The valiant eighteen held their own until the rest of the army arrived; then took complete control of the capital, laying the foundation of Muslim rule in the northwestern part of Bengal. The raja fled to Vikrampur (near modern Dacca), where his family continued to rule for three genera- tions.

After his victory over the raja of Kanauj Muhammad Ghuri was preoccupied with the affairs of Central Asia, as he had succeeded his brother as sultan in 1202. He suffered a defeat in 1205 at the hands of the Qara Khitai Turks, and rumors spread that he had been killed. This led the Khokhars and some other tribes in the Salt Range of the Punjab to rebel under the leadership of a renegade raja. They de- feated the deputy governor of Multan, plundered Lahore, and, by stopping communication between that city and Ghazni, prevented the remittance of revenue from the Punjab. The situation became so serious that it required the sultan's personal attention and in October, 1205, he left Ghazni for India. Only after the arrival of Aibak with fresh reinforcements was the rebellion completely crushed. Muham- mad permitted his troops to return to their homes to prepare for his planned operations in Central Asia, and he himself was returning to Ghazni with a small contingent when on March 15, 1206, he was assassinated near Damiyak, probably by an Ismaili fanatic.

The death of Ghuri within fourteen years of the victory at Tarain was a great blow to the rising Muslim power in India, but his task had been nearly accomplished. Nearly all of northern India was under Muslim rule, and in Aibak, Iltutmish, Nasir-ud-din Qabacha, and Muhammad bin Bakhtiyar Khalji, he left a group of capable officers who could complete his task. Many of them, including Aibak and Iltutmish, who later became rulers of India, were slaves, a reminder of the important place well-trained and loyal slaves had in the early Muslim dynasties. Brought from all over Central Asia, often members of ruling families that had been defeated, they provided generals and

governors who were often more trustworthy than sons or other relatives.

Causes of Muslim Success

The sweeping victories won by Muhammad Ghuri and his generals at the end of the twelfth century tend to give the impression that the conquest of North India was an easy and uninterrupted process. That this was not the case is shown by the reverses suffered by Ghuri himself as well as by the strong counteroffensives mounted by individual Hindu rulers. The most important factor in the success of the Muslims at this time was probably the quality of the rank and file and of their commanders. Not only were Muslim commanders able to wipe out the effects of various setbacks, but they showed superior generalship against heavy odds in victories such as that at Tarain. They were able also to exploit their limited resources to the fullest possible advantage by adopting the most suitable tactics, such as the feigned withdrawal of Ghuri at Tarain and the shock of a sudden surprise at Nadiya by Muhammad bin Bakhtiyar. Another factor which materially contributed to Muslim success was superior horsemanship, and in fact the victories of Muslims over much larger Hindu armies may be considered the victory of the horse over the slow-moving elephant.

Other factors also contributed to Muslim success. They were always on the offensive and had the advantage of greater initiative and selectivity. Fighting hundreds of miles away from their homes, they had to fight desperately as they had no easy means of escape. Religious ardor must also have acted as a spur to their fighting qualities. The soldiers were not confined to one class, as was generally the case with Indian armies, but contained picked and zealous soldiers from all classes and even different ethnic groups, such as the Turks, Tajiks, Khaljis, and Afghans.

While these factors were responsible for the speedy conquest of northern India, the consolidation of Muslim rule owed not a little to another event which was a tragedy for the Muslim countries of central and western Asia. This was the Mongol invasion, which drove

large numbers of refugees, amongst whom were princes, chiefs, soldiers, scholars, and saints, to Muslim India. Thus a vast reservoir of manpower became available to the new government at Delhi, and these people, having suffered so much, did not spare themselves in making India a "Citadel of Islam."

Organization of the Delhi Government

After Muhammad Ghuri's assassination in 1206 the control of his Indian possessions passed to his slave Qutb-ud-din Aibak, while the rest of his empire became the scene of a struggle between various claimants for power. This meant, in effect, that henceforth the Indian provinces of the Ghuri dynasty were independent; Aibak may thus be reckoned the first independent Muslim ruler of northern India, the founder of the Delhi Sultanate. He had been bought as a young man by the qazi of Nishapur who, recognizing his ability, gave him a good education. After the qazi's death he was sold to Muhammad Ghuri, under whom he served as a commander, and when Ghuri returned to Ghazni as sultan, Aibak remained as viceroy of his Indian province. In the inevitable confusion that followed the sultan's death, Aibak had himself crowned at Lahore, and although he acknowledged the supremacy of the new ruler at Ghuri, he himself was given the title of sultan, and was virtually independent. A source of perplexity for later jurists in connection with this assumption of power was that Aibak's formal manumission from slavery did not take place until 1208; yet under Islamic law an unmanumitted slave could not be a ruler. In any case, his own successors for the next ninety years were originally either slaves or descendants of slaves.

Aibak's main work had been accomplished as the deputy of Sultan Muhammad Ghuri. After his accession to the throne he made no new conquests but consolidated the Muslim dominion by following a policy of conciliation and open-handed generosity which earned him the title of *lakhbakhsh,* or "the giver of lakhs." Aside from this, he commenced building two magnificent mosques at Delhi and Ajmer. He was evidently a patron of letters, for two historians, Hasan Nizami and Fakhr-i-Mudabbir, dedicated their works to him. His career was cut short by early death in 1211 as the result of a polo accident.

Aibak's son succeeded him, but the Delhi nobles soon replaced him by Shams-ud-din Iltutmish, Aibak's son-in-law. The new ruler was faced with a very difficult task, for not only was Muslim rule in India far from consolidated, but powerful military leaders in Bengal, Punjab, and Multan challenged his authority. Yildiz, the ruler of Ghazni, laid claim as Muhammad Ghuri's successor to suzerainty over all the latter's Indian conquests. The Hindu chiefs had by now recovered from the stunning effects of Muslim victories and were winning back many of the strongholds originally conquered by the Muslims. Kalinjar had been recovered as early as 1206, and in course of time Jalor, Ranthambhor, Gwalior, and even Badaun, where Iltutmish held his last post before accession to the throne, were lost to the Muslims. In Oudh and the Doab the situation was even worse, and Minhaj-us-Siraj speaks of a Hindu chief named Bartu "beneath whose sword above a hundred and twenty thousand Musalmans had attained martyrdom." [1]

Iltutmish, trained in the traditions of Ghuri and Aibak, moved slowly against his host of enemies. He first consolidated his authority in the areas of Delhi, Badaun, Oudh, and Benares, and then dealt with his Muslim opponents one by one. In 1216 he defeated and captured Yildiz who, after his expulsion from Ghazni by the Khwarizm-shahis, had occupied Lahore. In 1225 he turned his attention to Bengal and forced the local ruler to abandon his royal title, acknowledge the authority of Delhi, and pay regular tribute. After this he dealt with Nasir-ud-din Qabacha, the powerful and popular ruler of Sind and western Punjab. On February 9, 1228, he arrived at Uch, Qabacha's capital, and opened siege. Uch surrendered on May 4, and a few days later Qabacha, who had moved to the island fortress of Bhakkar (situated between modern Sukkur and Rohri), found a watery grave in the Indus.

Mongol Invasions

An important development of Iltutmish's reign which had indirect but far-reaching consequences for the new empire was the rise of the

[1] Minhaj-us-Siraj, *Tabaqat-i-Nasiri*, trans. by H. G. Raverty (Calcutta, 1881), I, 628–29.

Mongols under Chingiz and Hulagu, and their "dance of death" in central and western Asia. The Mongol invasion, the greatest blow which the Muslim world ever suffered, is the dividing point of Islamic history. The modern evaluation of the Mongol advance as a catastrophe for Islam was shared by contemporaries, one of whom, the historian Ibn-ul-Athir, called it, "the death blow of Islam and the Muslims." Beginning in 1219 with Chingiz Khan's invasion of Transoxiana, it brought destruction to large cultivated areas, ruin to libraries and *madrasas,* and endless slaughter to men, women, and children. It culminated in the sack of Baghdad, and the end of the Abbasid caliphate at the hands of Hulagu Khan in 1258. A quotation from E. G. Browne summarizes the extent of the catastrophe: "In its suddenness, its devastating destruction, its appalling ferocity, its passionless and purposeless cruelty, its irresistible though short-lived violence, this outburst of savage nomads hitherto hardly known by name even to their neighbors, resembles rather some brute cataclysm of the blind forces of nature than a phenomenon of human history. The details of massacre, outrage, spoliation, and destruction wrought by these hateful hordes of barbarians who, in the space of a few years, swept the world from Japan to Germany would . . . be incredible were they not confirmed from so many different quarters." [2] That India was spared the full force of invasion can be attributed in large part to the vigilance and resourcefulness of the Delhi sultans.

Iltutmish's government first felt the impact of the gigantic military movement when Jalal-ud-din, the ruler of Khwarizm, whose father had attracted the wrath of Chingiz Khan, crossed the border with 10,000 men and sought aid from Iltutmish. Realizing the peril of getting embroiled in a dispute with the Mongol chief, Iltutmish gave skillfully evasive replies, and thus averted the danger of the India subcontinent being involved in the first onrush of the Mongol invasion. But the Mongols continued to move toward the subcontinent, and in 1241, during the chaos following Iltutmish's death, they destroyed Lahore. They remained entrenched on the frontier for several years, and for nearly half a century the principal preoccupation of the Delhi government was the defense of the subcontinent from the

[2] E. G. Browne, *A Literary History of Persia* (Cambridge, 1928), II, 427.

fate suffered by central and western Asia. Thanks to Balban's efficient measures and Ala-ud-din Khalji's military prowess this danger was averted, but the indirect consequences of the Mongol eruption and their activities beyond the border were not trifling. The danger in the north was partly responsible for Balban's ruthless policy of internal consolidation and centralization (about which more will be said later). The Mongol atrocities in Muslim countries and the threat to their newly won empire also steeled Muslim hearts in the subcontinent and inspired them to great efforts. And, again, the great influx of refugees from the Muslim countries of Central Asia, Khurasan, Iran, Iraq, and modern Afghanistan into the newly conquered territories provided the human resources needed for the consolidation of Muslim rule and the firm planting of Islamic religion in the subcontinent. These developments continued throughout the greater part of the thirteenth century, but they began during Iltutmish's reign, and a large number of distinguished refugees came to his court.[3]

Administration

Iltutmish rivals Balban for the distinction of being the greatest of the Slave Kings. Although it was Balban's transformation of the royal position that became firmly ingrained in the fabric of Muslim government, Iltutmish's work was historically of great importance. Aibak had done little but maintain the position he had acquired from Ghuri; it was Iltutmish who consolidated the Indian possessions into an independent kingdom. Not only had he to deal with powerful Muslim rivals and the Hindu counter-offensive, but he also had to build up the fabric of a new administration and organize different departments of the central government at Delhi. A skillful organizer, he dealt with the problems of administration in the same manner that he handled threats to the security and the integrity of the realm. In this his task was greatly facilitated by the model of government organization that had been established at Ghazni and the copious literature that had appeared on statecraft and the art of government in

[3] H. M. Elliot and John Dowson, *A History of India as Told by Her Own Historians* (London, 1867–1877), III, 98–99.

Muslim countries. By now some of the classics of Muslim political theory, such as the Arabic *Ahkam-us-Sultania,* the Persian *Qabus Namah* (1082), and the *Siasat Nama* (1092) had already been written, in addition to similar works that have perished. The historian Ziya-ud-din Barani (1285–1357) quotes Balban as speaking of two works on statecraft—*Adab-us-Salatin* and *Maasir-us-Salatin*— which were brought from Baghdad in Iltutmish's reign.[4] He also seems to have received assistance from scholars versed in the principles of Muslim political theory and governmental organization, and *Adab-ul-Muluk,* the first Indo-Muslim classic on the art of government and warfare was written for him. With this background, he was able to lay the basis of a well-coordinated structure of government.

Aside from the influence of the Ghaznavid system of government and the principles of statecraft learned from the texts on politics, the pattern of the new government established at Delhi was determined by Iltutmish's own temperament and the realities of the Indian situation. Much of the territorial expansion of Muslim India had been the work of individual nobles and resourceful adventurers. These men and others who had risen to prominence in the service of Muhammad Ghuri or Iltutmish by this time possessed large tracts of land. Since their privileges were not curtailed, a loosely knit, decentralized form of administration came into existence. Iltutmish made no attempt to weaken the position of his nobles, and indeed felt himself one of them. He used to declare that God Almighty had raised him above his peers who were a thousand times better than he. Barani quotes him as saying: "When they stand before me in the *durbar* I feel abashed at their grandeur and greatness, and desire that I should descend from the throne and kiss their hands and feet."[5]

It was also typical of Iltutmish that he did not adopt a hostile policy towards the Sufis but valued and respected them as a source of spiritual and moral strength. The high education which he gave to his daughter Raziyya, and his preference of her as his successor to the throne, suggests that he was free from the prejudices of his Turkish

---

[4] Ziya-ud-din Barani, *Tarikh-i-Firuz Shahi,* ed. by S. A. Khan (Calcutta, 1862), pp. 144–45.
[5] Barani, p. 137.

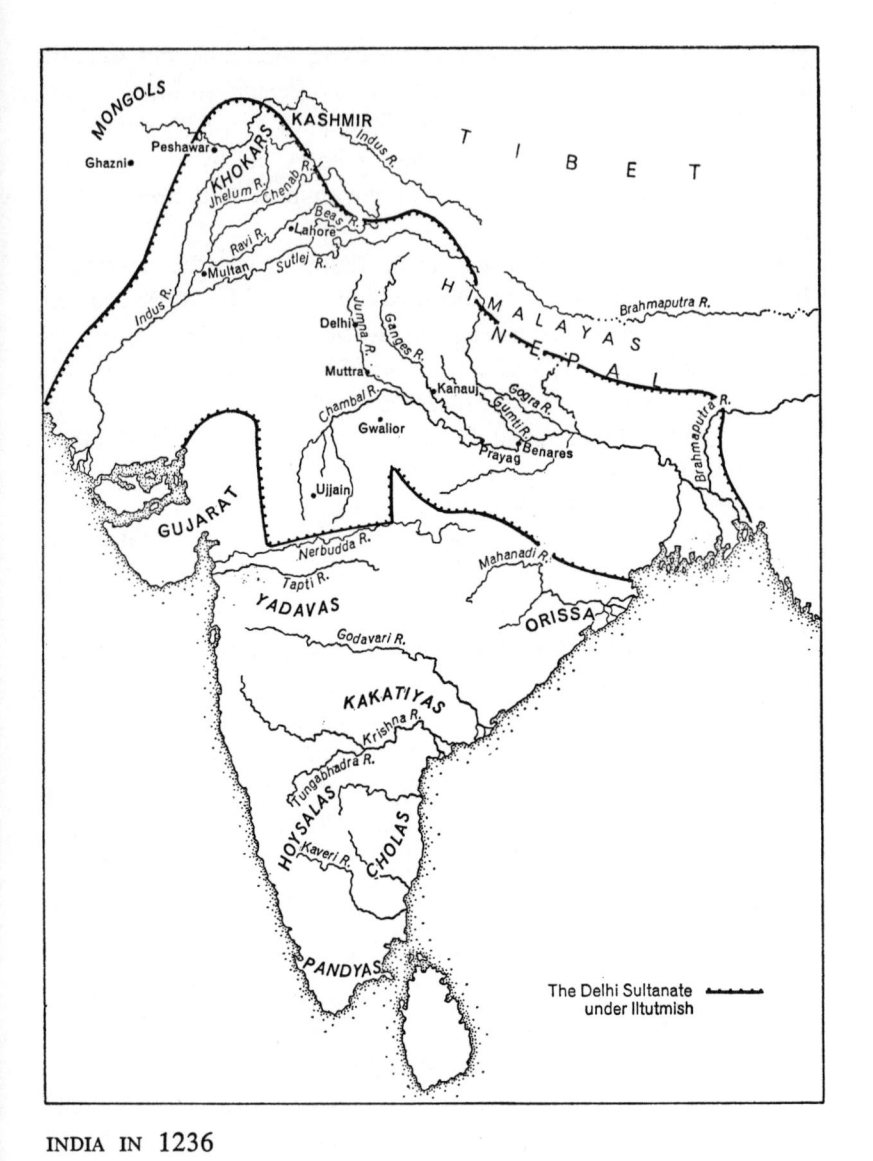

The Delhi Sultanate ⊷
under Iltutmish

INDIA IN 1236

From: *An Historical Atlas of the Indian Peninsula* (Oxford University Press, Bombay, 1961).

nobles. He tried to maintain a balance between the Turks, who were the all-powerful generals and governors, and the Persian-speaking Tajiks, who provided the scribes who dominated the imperial secretariat. After his death the balance was seriously upset, but by then the basic task of organizing the new Muslim government had been accomplished.

One of the crucial problems facing Iltutmish was the position of Hindus in a Muslim state. By this time Muslim law had been codified, and the freedom of action enjoyed by Muhammad ibn Qasim five centuries earlier in Sind was denied him. Three out of four schools of Islamic law favored the extermination of all idolators, but the practice, initiated by Muhammad ibn Qasim and maintained by the Ghaznavids, of treating idolatrous Hindus at least as privileged zimmis proved more powerful. When the ulama urged Iltutmish to give effect to the opinion of the majority of the founders of Islamic schools of law, he convened a conference and called upon his wazir, Nizam-ul Mulk Junaidi, to explain the position. The wazir argued that since India had only recently been conquered, and since the Muslims were fewer in number than the Hindus, it would not be wise to attempt a course of action that might lead to disturbances. This argument was accepted, and the status quo was maintained. The possibility of imposing the viewpoint of the majority Islamic law was never again raised in the form urged by the ulama. The course adopted was in consonance with fourth school of law (Hanafi), which has been accepted by the vast majority of Indian Muslims.[6]

Iltutmish took other steps to strengthen the fabric of the new government. To give it a legal basis in the eyes of the orthodox, he is said to have sought confirmation of his royal title from the Abbasid caliph of Baghdad. On February 19, 1229, the caliph's envoy arrived with a robe of honor and delivered to Iltutmish a patent which conveyed recognition of his title as the sultan of India. The caliph's recognition was largely a formality, and this seems to be one of the two occasions when a ruler of Delhi troubled himself about obtaining foreign recognition, but in the initial stages of Muslim rule this step was useful. It confirmed the sovereignty of Delhi against the claims of

[6] S. A. Rashid in *Medieval Indian Quarterly*, Vol. I, No. 3 and 4, pp. 104–5.

Ghazni, giving it a legal basis in the eyes of the orthodox, and it also silenced those local rivals who challenged the sultan's authority.

After this investiture, Iltutmish attended to the coinage, an important symbol of sovereignty. The name of the caliph was inscribed on the coins issued from the royal mint, and the sultan was described as "Helper of the Commander of the Faithful." So far the Muslim rulers had issued small bullion coins of the native form inscribed in Devanagari, the Indian script, or in Arabic characters, and bearing symbols familiar to the Hindu population such as the Bull of Shiva and the Chauhan horseman. Iltutmish now introduced purely Arabic coinage, discarding Hindu symbols, and adopted as a standard coin the silver tanka, the ancestor of the modern rupee.

Delhi was founded in the tenth century, but before the Muslim occupation it was not a large city, ranking below Ajmer in the Chauhan kingdom. Since it could not meet the requirements of the large population attracted by the seat of the new government, Iltutmish had to provide it with proper amenities and adorn it as the imperial capital. He built or completed the Qutb Minar, greatly extended the Quwwat-ul-Islam Mosque, giving it a distinctly Islamic look, and constructed a large water reservoir (Hauz-i-Shamsi) to meet the needs of Delhi citizens. The educational needs of the people were also looked after, for the Madrasa-i-Nasiri, of which the historian Minhaj-us-Siraj was the head at one time, was built in his reign.[7]

While Iltutmish's outlook and political philosophy were reflected in the salient features of his administration, he was fortunate in receiving competent assistance and guidance from some able and farsighted people. Principal amongst these co-workers was his wazir, Nizam-ul-Mulk Kamal-ud-din Muhammad Junaidi, a man of culture, a distinguished patron of learning, and a statesman of strong views. The historian Aufi dedicated his famous *Jawami-al-Hikayat* to him, and in a number of verses and poems interspersed in the book he praised Junaidi's wisdom, statesmanship, skill in warfare, and generosity. The contemporary poet Reza also wrote many poems extolling these qualities of Junaidi and has mentioned as well his callig-

---

[7] U. N. Day, *The Administrative System of the Delhi Sultanate* (Allahabad, 1959), p. 160.

raphy and excellent literary style. Isami also praises him in his history, *Futuh-us-Salatin,* mentioning that it was Junaidi who had purchased Balban as a present for Iltutmish. Junaidi's strength of character may be seen from the fact that when Iltutmish's worthless son, Rukh-ud-din Firuz, began to squander public money after his father's death, the wazir risked his office and refused to support him. He also refused to take the oath of allegiance to Raziyya, who had ascended the throne without consultation with the provincial chiefs and the wazir. The most fruitful part of Junaidi's career was under Iltutmish, when he was in charge of the entire government, including civil and military departments, and even religious functions which were later entrusted to the sadr-i-jahan. Barani's account of the conference which was convened to determine the treatment of the Hindus shows that in such major political issues Junaidi's opinion counted for much. He advocated a humane line of action, and though he based his viewpoint on the grounds of expediency, he achieved the practical end he had in view. The prominent role which he played in dealing with this difficult and crucial question would suggest that he had an equally important part in the formulation of other decisions and actions of Iltutmish's government.

The Problem of Succession

The problem of a successor troubled Iltutmish during his last days. His eldest son had died, and his other sons were worthless; his own choice was his able daughter Raziyya, but he knew the Turkish nobles were opposed to the idea of a woman ruler. He tried various solutions to deal with the situation. When he set out for Gwalior in 1231, he left Raziyya in charge of the capital, and was so satisfied with her handling of government affairs during his long absence that on his return he considered issuing a proclamation appointing her his heir. Her name was included along with that of the sultan in a series of coins, but for one reason or another Iltutmish did not take the final step of naming her his successor. He entrusted the vice-royalty of Lahore to his eldest surviving son, Rukh-ud-din Firuz, to see how he fared. Before he could decide the question of succession,

Iltutmish fell seriously ill and the matter was still unsettled when he died. Firuz ascended the throne with the support of army leaders, but he started squandering public funds and misusing power in such a way that the provincial governors revolted. Firuz left the capital to deal with the rebels when one of the most gruesome tragedies of early Muslim rule took place.

Firuz's misbehavior and the high-handedness of his mother Shah Turkan had offended so many people that even the Wazir Nizam-ul-Mulk Junaidi left the sultan to join his opponents. This brought to a head the bitter antagonism that existed between two court factions, the Tajiks and the Turks. The Tajiks were Persian-speaking Turks who had migrated from Turkish homelands. Their contribution to the building of the early Muslim state at Delhi was very substantial, and not only did they monopolize the higher posts in the Delhi secretariat, but also they dominated the literary and intellectual life. The wazir himself was a Tajik. So was Minhaj-us-Siraj, the historian and the future chief justice. Along with other notables they were openly hostile to Firuz. This so enraged the sultan's Turkish supporters that they massacred all the Tajik notables who were present in the royal camp. The list of casualties preserved by Minhaj-us-Siraj reads like a roll-call of the Delhi court.[8] Practically all the leading literary figures of Iltutmish's reign were extinguished on one dark day. The tragedy damaged irreparably the influence of the Tajiks and also impoverished the intellectual life of the new state.

While Rukn-ud-din Firuz's supporters were destroying the flower of the imperial secretariat, his sister Raziyya made a bold bid for the throne. Clad in red, she appeared before the people gathered for Friday prayers in the principal mosque at Delhi and appealed to them in the name of Iltutmish to give her a chance to prove her worth. This dramatic gesture evoked great response, and the people of Delhi, who so far had not taken the oath of allegiance to Firuz, accepted her claim. On his return, Firuz was imprisoned and subsequently put to death, but Rizayya's accession, which had been effected without consent of the provincial governors or even of the wazir, was doomed from the beginning. For the powerful nobles considered her accession

[8] Minhaj-us-Siraj, I, 635.

was unprecedented; her discarding of the veil and her severity swung public opinion against her. She tried to create dissension among her opponents, but the elevation of an Abyssinian to the major post of amir-i-akhur (commander of the cavalry) gave serious offense to the Turkish nobles and they rose in rebellion against her. Her followers murdered the Abyssinian and imprisoned her while she was camping at Bhatinda to deal with the rebels. Her efforts to weather the storm by marrying Altuniya, the rebel governor of Bhatinda, failed to save her. Her brother Bahram, who had been proclaimed sultan of Delhi during her absence, entrusted young Balban, their father's slave, with the task of dealing with Raziyya and her husband's troops, and Balban carried out the mission with the competence which was, in course of time, to carry him to the throne of Delhi. Raziyya and Altuniya were defeated, deserted by their troops, and murdered by the Hindus in the course of their lonely flight (October 14, 1240).

Raziyya's brief reign also saw a bid for power by the Ismailis, a heretical sect which once had sought to assassinate Iltutmish. On Friday, March 5, 1237, nearly a thousand of them, incited by the harangues of a fanatical preacher, Nur Turk, entered the great mosque of Delhi from two directions and attacked the congregation. Many fell under their swords, but the Turkish nobles assembled their troops who, aided by the congregation, overpowered and slaughtered the insurgents.

The Struggle between the Nobles and the Sultan

Raziyya's end highlighted a development which, though visible even in the success of nobles in sponsoring the claims of Iltutmish against those of Qutb-ud-din, Aibak's son, had become more marked since the death of Iltutmish. This was the question of the right and power of the nobility to determine the choice of the sultan and place limitations on his power and sphere of activity. After Raziyya was defeated and imprisoned, her half-brother Muizz-ud-din Bahram was proclaimed sultan, but "on the stipulation of Deputyship being conferred on Malik Ikhtiyar-ud-din Aetkin," who "by virtue of his Deputyship . . . took the affairs of the kingdom into his own hands,

and, in conjunction with the wazir [Muhazzab-ud-din] . . . and Mu-hammad Iwaz, the mustaufi [the auditor-general] assumed control over the disposal of state affairs." [9] There is an analogy in this action to that taken in the same century by King John's barons in England, but the arrangement at Delhi broke down at once.

The basic responsibility for the failure was that of the deputy who, as the nominee of the nobles, started assuming royal prerogatives and took steps which alarmed the new monarch. He married the sultan's sister, assumed the triple *naubat,* the drums which were a symbol of sovereignty, and stationed an elephant at the entrance of his residence. These developments annoyed the youthful monarch, and he secretly encouraged violent measures to deal with the situation. Within three months of his assumption of office, the deputy was assassinated in the royal presence at a gathering arranged to hear a sermon. The wazir was also attacked by the assassins but managed to escape.

This was not the end of the struggle between the nobles and the sultan. Badrud-din-Sunqar, the amir-i-hajib (lord chamberlain) as-sumed the direction of state affairs, but he suffered from the sultan's hostility and lack of cooperation from the wazir. He called a meeting of the principal nobles, including the highest financial and judicial officials of the realm. They discussed recent events among themselves and sent the mushrif-i-mumalik (accountant-general) to invite the wazir to join them. The wazir promised to come, but instead conveyed the news of what was happening to the sultan. Bahram immediately mounted his horse and reached the place where the meeting was being held. He took Sunqar with him, but so strong was the power of the nobles that no real punishment was inflicted on the leader of the con-spiracy. He was sent to Badaun, which was given to him as a fief. Qazi Jalal-ud-din was relieved of the office of the chief qazi (which was a few weeks later conferred on Minhaj-us-Siraj), and some of the other collaborators left the capital, fearing unpleasant developments.

The wazir now became all-powerful, but the attack had shown Bahram's real sentiments toward him. He soon joined hands with the nobles to depose Bahram, who was dethroned on May 10, 1242. The principal senior noble, Izz-ud-din Kishlu Khan, now made a bid for the

[9] Minhaj-us-Siraj, I, 649–50.

throne, but his associates repudiated him, choosing instead Iltutmish's grandson, Ala-ud-din Masud. Qutb-ud-din Husain of Ghur was named deputy, but the real power remained with the wazir. The Turkish amirs, the soldier-administrators of the realm, did not like the concentration of power in the hands of someone selected from the "writer" class, so they joined forces and had him assassinated. The submissive Najm-ud-din Abu Bakr now became wazir, and Balban, Iltutmish's slave, was appointed to the key post of Amir-i-Hajib. Ala-ud-din Masud continued to rule for more than four years with tolerable success, but later when he tried to curb the power of the nobles he alienated the most powerful of them. He was deposed on June 10, 1246, and the nobles, among whom Balban played a dominant role, enthroned Iltutmish's youngest son, Nasir-ud-din Mahmud.

IV. Consolidation of Muslim Rule
in the North

THE SULTANATE of Delhi suffered grievously in the ten years following the death of Iltutmish. The Mongols who had been hovering on
the frontier grew bolder and in 1241 sacked Lahore. They harried
Multan, Sind, and central Punjab, and were in virtual control of this
area for a number of years. In the east, Bengal and Bihar became independent. To the south of Delhi, the Hindus began to reassert themselves, and the Muslims lost many important strongholds which had
been captured in the days of Aibak and Iltutmish. Gwalior and
Ranthambhor were abandoned during Raziyya's reign. Now, even
in areas nearer to the capital such as Katehar (modern Rohilkhand)
and the Doab, Hindu resistance was intensified.

Not less important than these material losses were the fissures and
weaknesses displayed by the administrative structure built up by
Iltutmish. The lines on which he had organized the new government
required for their success a man of great ability, wisdom, and resourcefulness, but as he had feared, there was nobody equal to the
task in his family. In the scramble for power which followed his death,
Tajiks were pitted against Turks, the nobility was at loggerheads with
the king, and the conflicting ambitions of the individual nobles prevented any united action.

Balban's Administration

With the accession of Nasir-ud-din in 1246 this period of acute
conflict ended, but it was not due to the ruler's abilities. The real
power was in the hands of Balban, who had been largely instrumental
in bringing him to the throne. Although Balban did not actually become sultan until 1265, the whole period from 1246 to 1287—including the years of Nasir's rule and his own—may well be designated

the "Balban Era." A member of a noble family of the Ilbari Turks, Ghiyas-ud-din Balban had been captured during the turmoil that followed the Mongol invasions of Central Asia and sold as a slave in Baghdad. He was taken to Delhi in 1232, where he was purchased by Iltutmish to serve as a personal attendant. He became chief huntsman, commander of the cavalry, and, after Iltutmish's death, lord chamberlain.

Balban's ascendancy over the sultan was challenged, most notably in 1253 when Imad-ud-din Raihan made an attempt to oust him. This particular episode is of special interest, as Raihan was an Indian convert to Islam, and seems to have rallied the non-Turkish element in the court to his support. Balban was saved by the Turkish governors of the provinces, who rallied to his side. Balban maintained his position in the sultan's government until 1265, when, on Nasir-ud-din's death, he added the formal title of sultan to the power he had held for twenty years.

Balban's work, both before and after he became sultan, involved not only the defense of the country against foreign aggression and internal dangers but also a reorganization of the administration with the aim of increasing its effectiveness. Iltutmish had organized the administration in the newly conquered territories as a decentralized system in which the fiefholders enjoyed wide power and high nobles were treated almost as peers of the king. A pious Muslim, disdaining show, he had not sought to assert royal superiority over the nobility. The disturbed conditions which followed his death, marked by a struggle between king and nobility, showed the dangers inherent in this attitude. His successor, Nasir-ud-din Mahmud had lived an unassuming life, leaving real power with the deputy. Balban's attitude, however, was completely different. Influenced by the Iranian theory of kingship, and noting the anarchy which prevailed after the death of Iltutmish, he proceeded to raise the royal status far above that of the nobles. He used to say that next to prophethood, the highest office was that of kingship, and that the ruler who did not maintain the dignity of his office failed to perform his functions properly, and his subjects, resorting to insubordination, would fall prey to crime.

As soon as he ascended the throne, Balban provided a material

basis for the heightened royal status by strengthening the army. Aibak and Iltutmish had relied largely on the contingents of the fiefholders, and the ariz, or war office, had been a subordinate branch of the central secretariat under the overall control of the wazir. Balban re-organized the war office, raised the status of ariz-i-mamalik, his chief of staff, and dealt directly with him. He increased the army's size, placed the troops under hand-picked commanders, and raised their emoluments. He kept it in fighting trim by taking it on long, arduous expeditions and large-scale hunting parties. The result was an instru-ment adequate for combatting external and internal enemies and for making the position of the king immeasurably stronger than that of the nobles and fiefholders.

Balban took other steps to enhance the royal status. Great impor-tance was attached to the observance of an impressive and elaborate court etiquette. When the royal cavalcade moved, hundreds of im-posing heralds, dressed in brilliant uniforms, preceded it; it was such a magnificent show that according to the historian Barani, people came from great distances to witness the procession. At the royal court, there was such an atmosphere of awe and majesty that ambas-sadors presenting their credentials and rajas coming to pay tribute became nervous and occasionally stumbled on the steps. Very metic-ulous about the royal dignity, Balban imposed a rigorous discipline on himself. No valet ever saw him without a cap or socks or shoes, and throughout his long period of kingship he never laughed aloud before others, nor had anyone the courage to laugh aloud in his presence.[1]

A major problem with which Balban was faced was the all-powerful military oligarchy which had dominated the politics of the sultanate since the death of Iltutmish. This aristocratic corps, commonly known as the Chihilgan or "the Forty," had at one time played a constructive role, but in the days of Iltutmish's weak successors it had become a major threat to the state. Originally Balban had been one of the Forty, but now he set about breaking their power by all possible means, including the use of poison and the assassin's dagger.

[1] H. M. Elliot and John Dowson, *A History of India as Told by Its Own Historians* (London, 1867–1877), III, 100.

As a natural consequence of this policy the provincial governors lost much of their power and privilege. The instructions which Balban gave to his son Bughra Khan, while entrusting to him the government of Bengal, laid down the relationship which was to exist between the central government at Delhi and the governors of the provinces.[2] Even more effective were the practical steps he took to control the provincial chiefs. In all provinces he appointed barids (intelligence officers) to report on the local dignitaries. On the basis of these reports Balban meted out exemplary punishments to the provincial governors for any misbehavior. This was one aspect of Balban's attempt to transform Iltutmish's decentralized organization, with the nobles possessing great powers, into a highly centralized government under the control of an autocratic king. Henceforth, subject to occasional variations, this was to be the normal pattern of Muslim government in India.

Although he insisted on the rights of kingship, Balban acknowledged the duty of a ruler to provide peace and tranquility within his dominion. This the early Muslim rulers had not always been able to ensure. The Jats, the Mewatis, and the Khokhars were a constant menace to the peaceful subjects of the sultanate. The Muslim rulers had broken the power of the organized Hindu armies, but warlike, restless tribes had taken to robbery. Every year there was some major disturbance of the peace, and even the city of Delhi was not immune to plundering operations. Thieves infesting the jungles around Delhi robbed travelers under the very walls of the city. The gates on the south side of the city had to be shut immediately following afternoon prayers, and it was dangerous to leave the city at night.

Balban spent the first year of his reign in enforcing law and order in the city and its suburbs. The jungle was cleared, the Mewati robbers who had made it a base for their operations were destroyed, a fort was built to guard the city's southwestern approaches, and police posts were established around Delhi. Balban dealt equally firmly with the people of the Doab, who had closed the road between Bengal and the capital. He spent nearly a year in the districts of Patyali, Bhojpur, and Kampil, extirpating the highway robbers, building forts at suit-

[2] Elliot and Dowson, III, 111.

able centers, garrisoning them with Afghan soldiers who received lands in the area for their maintenance, and granting large areas to powerful nobles so that they could bring the land under cultivation and clear the jungles. The methods he used against the local population were undoubtedly ruthless, but they secured the roads between Delhi and Bengal for nearly a century. Similar measures were taken against the Rajputs in the trans-Gangetic tract in the charge of the governors of Budaun and Amroha. Balban ordered a terrifying slaughter of the insurgents, had their houses and hiding places burned, cleared the country of forests, built roads, and introduced orderly civil government.

Although Balban built up a powerful army, he made no attempt to extend his dominion or to recover areas such as Malwa, once controlled by the Muslims. When these measures were suggested to him he replied that he had even higher ambitions, but could not expose Delhi to the fate of Baghdad. A stern realist, he abandoned the expansionist policy of his predecessors and concentrated on the consolidation of Muslim power in India. What he did instead with his army was to use it to overawe his nobles, and, in the last two decades of his reign, to defend his frontiers against the Mongols.

Hulagu Khan who, with his sack of Baghdad in 1258 had wiped out the great center of Abbasid culture, was still alive, and the Mongols now constituted a standing threat to the subcontinent. As a preliminary measure of defense in 1270, Balban restored the fortifications of Lahore, which had been virtually deserted since its sack by the Mongols in 1241. While this facilitated the defense of the northwest, other vigorous military measures were needed to deal with the Mongol menace, and Balban erected a chain of fortifications in the northwest. The command of this strategic area Balban entrusted initially to Sher Khan Sunqar, his most distinguished general, and on Sunqar's death to Prince Muhammad Khan, Balban's favorite son and heir-apparent. Prince Muhammad Khan was killed in 1285 in a battle with the Mongols, but the arrangements that had been made for the defense of the northwestern frontier kept Hulagu Khan in check.

Although Balban had succeeded for forty years in maintaining his control over most of North India, he was not able to ensure a peace-

ful succession. After the death of Prince Muhammad Khan, he named as his heir Bughra Khan, the governor of Bengal, but Bughra refused to remain in Delhi. On his deathbed, Balban selected a son of Prince Muhammad Khan, but his nobles disregarded his will and placed on the throne Kaiqubad, the worthless, pleasure-loving son of Bughra Khan. Unable to control the fierce rivalries of the factions that were struggling to gain power, Kaiqubad soon ceased to play an effective role in the government. The group that emerged triumphant out of the breakdown of the sultan's authority was the Khalji family, one of the Turkish clans that had been settled so long in Afghanistan before entering India that their Turkish origin was almost forgotten. The Khalji chief, Makik Jalal-ud-din Firuz, as head of the army department, had one of the most important offices in the realm. He used this position to have himself proclaimed sultan in 1290, after a Khalji noble had murdered Kaiqubad.

With Kaiqubad's death the Slave dynasty of the Ilbari Turks came to an end. It had established the political dominance of Islam throughout North India, and had laid the foundations for an administrative structure that was more than a military occupation. The violence that marked the last years of the dynasty continued under the Khaljis, but beyond the intrigues of the palace factions the position of the Muslim rulers was consolidated, and a great new movement became possible —the conquest of South India.

V. Expansion in the South: The Khaljis and the Tughluqs

ON THE surface, the seizure of the throne by Jalal-ud-din Firuz in 1290 was the act of a strong and ruthless individual; in reality, it was the achievement of power by one large clan, the Khaljis. Their triumph illustrates one of the basic ingredients in the history of Islamic India: the role in the continual power struggles of different groups within the ranks of the Turkish invaders. Ethnically the Khaljis were Turks, but because of their earlier migration from the Turkish homelands they constituted a group quite distinct from those who had come into the Ghazni and Ghuri areas at a later time. Although they had played a conspicuous role in the success of the Turkish armies in India, they had always been looked down upon by the Ilbari Turks, the dominant group during the Slave dynasty. This tension between the Khaljis and other Turks, kept in check by Balban, came to the surface in the succeeding reign, and ended in the displacement of the Ilbari Turks.

Khalji success against the aristocratic Turks had far-reaching sociopolitical results. Muslim government ceased to be a close preserve of the Turkish aristocracy and not only the Khaljis but other groups such as the indigenous Muslims began to share power. For the first time, the historians refer to the "Hindustanis," the local Muslims, and soon converts such as Malik Kafur were occupying the highest position in the state. The efforts of the Muslim missionaries and Sufis had begun to bear fruit and a sizable number of Muslim converts was available for the service of the state. The rule of the Khaljis did not last more than thirty years, but the social revolution which their success engendered, and the large increase in manpower which resulted from it, enabled the Delhi government to take a major step forward and conquer the vast areas south of the Vindhyas.

When Jalal-ud-din came to the throne he followed a policy of exceptional mildness and forbearance. This reconciled the general popu-

lation to him, but the Khalji nobles were shocked at the sultan's behavior. They attributed it to senility—he was more than seventy when he came to the throne—and openly started plotting against him. The plot which succeeded was that of his nephew and son-in-law, Ala-ud-din. This ambitious young man had been appointed governor of Kara (near modern Allahabad), and there, surrounded by other discontented officers, he organized an army to make a bid for the throne of Delhi. To support his army he plundered neighboring unconquered Hindu territories.

First Conquests

Ala-ud-din started by invading Malwa and capturing the town of Bhilsa, a wealthy commercial center. He decided next on a bolder step. At Bhilsa he had heard of the wealth of the great southern kingdom of Devagiri. Without obtaining the permission of his uncle, and making arrangements at Kara for supplying Delhi with such periodical news about his movement as would allay suspicion, he set out in 1296, at the head of 8,000 horse. So far, no Muslim ruler had crossed the Vindhyas, and Devagiri was separated from Kara by a two-month march through unknown regions. The success of this extraordinary raid against a powerful kingdom is explained partly by good luck and partly by Ala-ud-din's ability and courage. He returned to Kara with a huge booty—17,250 pounds of gold, 200 pounds of pearls, 58 pounds of other gems, 28,250 pounds of silver, and 1,000 pieces of silk. Some of Jalal-ud-din's nobles, particularly the loyal and vigilant Ahmad Chap, were critical of Ala-ud-din's moves, but his brother, who was at the court, lulled the sultan's suspicions. He was able even to persuade Jalal-ud-din to go to Kara to meet Ala-ud-din, who, he said, was too penitent to come to Delhi after having undertaken a major military operation without royal authority. The sultan, according to a contemporary historian, was blinded by greed, and, welcoming the suggestion, he proceeded to Kara, where he was assassinated. Ala-ud-din Khalji ascended the throne, and, with a judicious distribution of riches brought from Devagiri, he was able to win over the public of Delhi.

Ala-ud-din's twenty-year reign may be divided into three phases. During the first period (1296–1303) he defeated the Mongols, re-conquered the Hindu kingdom of Gujarat, and reduced Ranthambhor (1301), Chitor (August, 1303), and other Hindu strongholds in Rajasthan. In the second period (1303–1307) his attention was given largely to securing and consolidating his power. He continued, how-ever, to extend his territory. In 1305 he sent Ain-ul-Mulk Multani to Central India, where he subdued Malwa and conquered the forts of Ujjain, Chanderi, and Mandawar. Malwa was annexed, and Ain-ul-Mulk appointed its governor. In the final period, he was engaged in the conquest in the South.

The Mongols had continued to threaten India, and in 1290 they raided as far as Delhi. They returned in 1303 with an army of 120,000, besieged Delhi, and forced Ala-ud-din to retire to the fortress of Siri. Their reason for withdrawing after two months is not clear; and while Barani attributed it to the power of the prayers of a local saint, Ala-ud-din realized that more effective steps were necessary to deal with the Mongol menace. He proceeded to reorganize the defenses in the western Punjab, where the fortifications established by Balban had fallen into disrepair, and placed the frontier province of Dipalpur under Ghiyas-ud-din Tughluq, the ablest soldier of the realm. He also raised a powerful standing army independent of the contingents of the fiefholders, and made it adequate for all offensive and defensive pur-poses. This meant that Ala-ud-din's officers could take the offensive against the Mongols, and they raided their territory as far as Kabul and Ghazni. After 1306, partly because of these measures, partly be-cause of the death of the Mongol ruler of Transoxiana, India ceased to be troubled by the Mongols.

During the third period (1307–1313), Ala-ud-din completed the conquest of South India. The ground had been prepared for this by his conquests in Central India, and in 1307 his general, Malik Kafur, de-feated Raja Ramchandra of Devagiri, who had withheld the tribute he had promised to pay after Ala-ud-din's first raid. The raja was brought to Delhi, and, reaffirming his submission, he received the title of Rai Rayan. Two years later Malik Kafur led another expedition to the south and conquered Warangal. Among the booty was a great dia-

mond, identified by some with the famous Koh-i-Nur. In this campaign the raja of Devagiri gave the Muslims considerable help, including a force of Marathas. Next year Malik Kafur set out on a year-long expedition which, through the defeat of the rajas of Madura and Dvarasa Mudra, extended the Muslim dominion to the southern seacoast. During this expedition, the Muslim officers built a mosque, either at Rameshwaram on the island of Pamban, or on the mainland opposite.

Ala-ud-din did not bring the newly conquered territories in the south under his direct administration. Devagiri was an exception. When the raja of Devagiri died in 1311 and his successor refused to accept the suzerainty of Delhi, it was annexed as part of the sultanate of Delhi. Other conquered territories such as Warangal, Madura, and Dvarasa Mudra continued under local rajas who paid an annual tribute.

Ala-ud-din Khalji was a soldier, undisciplined by formal education. When fortune smiled on all his early projects, his fancy soared high and he began to think of conquests in other fields. He played with the idea of establishing a new religion, and at times expressed a desire to sally forth from Delhi, and, like Alexander, to embark on a career of world conquest. He even issued coins referring to himself as Alexander the Second. Luckily his nobles were not afraid of giving him sound advice, and he had the good sense to listen to them. He had four principal counsellors, but it was the old Ala-ul-Mulk, the kotwal of Delhi, who dissuaded the king from attempting to carry out his plans. Ala-ul-Mulk's interview is vividly described, perhaps with a touch of imagination, by his nephew, the historian Barani.[1] Ala-ul-Mulk told the sultan that the introduction of a religion was a matter for the prophets and not for kings, and pointed out that the Mongols, in spite of their great power, had not been able to replace the Islamic religion. As for foreign conquests, the sultan could not undertake them until he had completely conquered and established his rule in the whole of India, and even then he could leave his realm only if he had a sagacious and dependable deputy like Alexander's Aristotle to look after the kingdom during his absence. Ala-ud-din had an uncertain temper, but he recognized the wisdom of the old

---

[1] H. M. Elliot and John Dowson, *A History of India as Told by Its Own Historians* (London, 1867–1877), III, 169–71.

counsellor. He never talked again about religious innovations, and he dropped his plans for world conquest.

During the early years of his reign, two rebellions—one at Delhi and another in Oudh—and an attempted assassination forced Ala-ud-din to consider precautions against attempts to overthrow his rule. According to his advisers the rebellions had four main causes: 1) an inefficient system of intelligence which prevented the sultan from knowing what was happening; 2) the widespread use of wine, which loosened tongues, encouraged intimacies, and bred plots and treason; 3) the strengthening of the position of the nobles by intermarriage; and 4) the possession· of wealth by certain sections of the people, which, relieving them of the necessity of work, left them leisure for mischievous thoughts.[2] Ala-ud-din dealt systematically with all these causes. He set up an efficient system of intelligence and taught himself to read the illegible handwriting known as *shikasta,* in order to be able to decipher the reports of his informers. He prohibited the use of intoxicating liquor and set an example by causing his wine vessels to be broken and having the wine poured out. He regulated marriages among the nobles and revised the taxation system so as to reduce the surpluses of the prosperous classes. This latter measure hit both the Muslim and Hindu privileged classes. It included the Muslim holders of *inam* lands (rent-free grants) and *waqf* (pious endowments), and those Hindu chiefs who had been allowed to retain their lands in return for the payment of tribute. Apparently many of them had used their positions to build up centers of intrigue against the ruler.

Among the most interesting of Ala-ud-din's actions were the famous price-control measures. Modern historians, following Barani, have generally held that these were introduced in order to keep the cost of the new army at a low level.[3] Other contemporary or near-contemporary writers such as Afif, Ibn Battuta, Isami, and Hazrat Nasir-ud-din Chiragh-i-Delhi indicate that Ala-ud-din controlled prices of the necessities of life so that the general public might benefit.[4] Barani's explanation appears odd, since a ruthless ruler like Ala-ud-

[2] Elliot and Dowson, III, 178.   [3] Elliot and Dowson, III, 191–97.
[4] Shams-i-Siraj-i-Afif, *Tarikh-i-Firuzshahi,* ed. by Maulvi Wilayat Husain, (Calcutta, 1890); A. M. Husain, *The Shahnama of Medieval India of Isami* (Agra, 1938), p. 293; Mahdi Husain, *The Rehla of Ibn Battuta* (Baroda, 1953).

din could easily have provided for the upkeep of his army by other means, such as additional taxation. In order to deal with a limited problem it was hardly necessary for him to introduce a detailed and complicated system involving elaborate administrative measures over wide areas. All contemporary authorities except Barani indicate that Ala-ud-din, in spite of his obvious defects, had firm ideas of the responsibilities of kingship. Their interpretation is that he felt that the most effective way to benefit the public and achieve lasting renown was to place reasonable price controls on the necessities of daily life. Those who have seen the difficulty of enforcing a rigid price control in India and Pakistan in modern times know that this could not be achieved by royal edict, and one cannot read Barani's account of various regulations and administrative steps taken by Ala-ud-din without admiring his administrative ability and the competence of his officers. To enforce his orders regulating prices he introduced the following: the system of obtaining land revenue in the form of food grains; the buildup of vast stores from which corn could be issued at the time of need; control of transport; a simple method of rationing when necessary; and the buildup of an elaborate organization to carry out the whole system. Ala-ud-din made a success of this scheme, which continued in operation throughout his reign. It is no wonder that after his death the poor forgot his cruelty and remembered his rule with gratitude; they even visited his grave as if it were the tomb of a holy man.[5]

It is only recently that scholars, piecing together bits of information from different sources, have begun to realize the extent of Ala-ud-din's administrative achievements. K. R. Qanungo, for example, credits him with organizing the army on a new model. He accomplished this, according to Qanungo, by arming it directly through the *Ariz-i-Mamalik,* paying in cash from the state treasury, choosing the officers himself, and stamping out corruption in the supplying of horses by requiring that they be branded.[6]

Ala-ud-din kept in touch with the army when it was on the move through an elaborate system of *dak-chauki,* or postal relay. When he

[5] S. M. Ikram, *Ab-i-Kausar* (Lahore, 1958), pp. 163–68.
[6] K. R. Qanungo, *Sher Shah* (Calcutta, 1921), p. 361.

sent an army on an expedition he established posts on the road at which relays of horses were stationed, and at every half or quarter *kos* runners were appointed. "Every day or every two or three days," according to Qanungo, "news used to come to Sultan reporting the progress of the army, and intelligence of the health of the sovereign was carried to the army. False news was thus prevented from being circulated in the city or the army. The securing of accurate intelligence from the court on one side and the army on the other was a great public benefit." While this system was not original with Ala-ud-din—the Abbasids had used it—the efficiency with which it was set up indicates Ala-ud-din's thoroughness in matters of administration.

More important for Ala-ud-din's subjects were his arrangements for proper assessment of land revenue—a continuing concern of Indian governments. He introduced the method of assessment of revenue on the basis of land measurement, as this appeared to him more satisfactory from the point of view of the state than merely exacting as much as seemed feasible from the peasants. While the system was not extended very far and did not take sufficient root to survive the death of Ala-ud-din, it shows that the most important feature of Sher Shah's revenue system was originally introduced by the Khalji ruler.

A full assessment of cultural aspects of his rule is yet to be made, but the scattered indications on the subject are enough to show that it was a very important period in the cultural life of medieval India, comparable almost to that of Akbar during the Mughal period. Indeed it may be said that if consolidation of Muslim rule was the work of Balban, Muslim India attained cultural maturity in the days of Ala-ud-din Khalji. The wealth that poured into Delhi after the conquests in South India made possible the maintenance of a large army, and enabled the ruler and other beneficiaries to undertake cultural activities on a lavish scale. Ala-ud-din did not live long enough to realize all his architectural dreams, but he has left many splendid monuments. Developments in the realm of music were even more significant. After the conquest of the Hindu states in the south, musicians moved north to seek the patronage of Muslim kings and nobles. Luckily Delhi had men such as Amir Khusrau who availed them-

selves of the situation, and a new era in Indo-Muslim music was opened.

Developments in literature were equally remarkable. Amir Khusrau (c.1254–1324), one of the greatest of Indo-Islamic poets, lived during the reign of seven monarchs, but the royal court with which he was associated longest was that of Ala-ud-din. The Khalji king's outlook was too practical to permit him to appreciate literature, but the poet must have benefited by the general prosperity of the period. As a poet, musician, historian, biographer, courtier, and mystic, he assisted in the evolution of a new pattern of culture, humanistic, artistically rich, and in harmony with the environment.

Unlike earlier poets, Amir Khusrau was not an immigrant, but was born in India of an Indian mother. Living in an era which saw the large-scale expansion of Muslim rule in the south and its consolidation in the north, including the defeat of the Mongols, his works breathe a spirit of exultation, self-confidence and local pride. His liberal Sufi outlook and probable Indian origin on the maternal side enabled him to admire and imbibe the praiseworthy elements of the old Indian tradition. He studied Indian music and introduced changes and innovations which made it acceptable to the new Muslim society. He wrote long poems on local themes. His poetry is full of pride in his native land, its history, its people, its flowers, its *pan* and its mango; he also held that Persian as spoken, and written in India was purer than the language used in Khurasan, Sistan, and Azerbaijan. A poem written in the last year of Ala-ud-din's reign gives vivid expression to this spirit:

Happy be Hindustan, with its splendor of religion,
Where Islamic law enjoys perfect honor and dignity;
In learning Delhi now rivals Bukhara;
Islam has been made manifest by the rulers.
From Ghazni to the very shore of the ocean
You see Islam in its glory.
Muslims here belong to the Hanafi creed,
But sincerely respect all four schools [of law].
They have no enmity with the Shafites, and no fondness for the Zaidis.
With heart and soul they are devoted to the path of *jamm'at* and the
    sunnah.

It is a wonderful land, producing Muslims and favoring religion,
Where the very fish of the stream are Sunnis.

While this outburst of intellectual creativity was at its height, control of the kingdom began to slip from the aging Ala-ud-din's hands. The excesses of a luxurious court had left him an invalid. Instead of the group of counsellors which had helped him in his days of triumph, he was dominated by Malik Kafur, a eunuch who had been one of his most successful generals. After Ala-ud-din's death in January, 1316, Kafur blinded the heir to the throne, intending to seize power for himself, but he was murdered by another son of Ala-ud-din, who became sultan under the name of Mubarak Shah.

Mubarak Shah's brief reign was the beginning of a grim but curious episode in the history of the Delhi Sultanate. His favorite was Khusrau Khan, a convert from a low Hindu caste who, after four years of dominating his master, had him murdered. Khusrau Khan ascended the throne, put to death all members of Ala-ud-din's family, and tried to make his rule secure by various devices including a liberal distribution of gifts, on the line adopted by Ala-ud-din when he had usurped the throne. His treatment of his patron and his family, however, had alienated public opinion. Furthermore, the behavior of Khusrau's companions, many of whom were Hindus, convinced leading Muslims that there was a possibility of the revival of Hindu supremacy or at least displacement of Islam from the position it occupied. It is conceivable that if the insurgents had had a suitable leader capable of winning the respect of Hindu chiefs and the public, they might have reestablished Hindu power. But Khusrau's low-caste companions behaved with incredible stupidity, destroying mosques and copies of the Quran. Important Muslims outside of Delhi, led by Ghazi Malik, who had been one of Ala-ud-din's frontier generals, gathered an army and attacked the sultan. Khusrau's forces were totally defeated, and since he had murdered all the members of Ala-ud-din's family, the nobles made Ghazi Malik the new sultan. As Ghiyas-ud-din Tughluq Shah, he became the first ruler of the Tughluq dynasty, which maintained itself for nearly a hundred years.

The Consolidation of Muslim Rule

According to generally accepted accounts, Ghiyas-ud-din Tughluq, who became sultan of Delhi in September, 1320, was the son of a Turkish slave of Balban and a Jat woman. With a distinguished record as a defender of the sultanate against the Mongols, he faced first the task of restoring the authority of the Delhi government, which had been weakened during the disorders that followed Ala-ud-din's death. In the south, the tributary raja of Warangal had declared his independence; Ghiyas-ud-din met the challenge by annexing his kingdom. The governor of Bengal had also revolted, and while suppressing this rebellion Ghiyas-ud-din expanded his boundaries by the conquest of Tirhut (the ancient Mithila), which had remained outside Muslim rule. This was his last campaign, however, for he was killed in 1325 in the collapse of a victory pavilion erected to celebrate his triumphal return from Bengal.

The son who succeeded him was Muhammad Tughluq (r. 1325–1351), whose character was a puzzle both to contemporary and later historians. Highly gifted and accomplished, and possessing great purity of character, he endeavored throughout his reign to create a just and orderly society. Instead, he soon gained a reputation for barbarous cruelty, and his rule brought misery to his people and greatly weakened the power of the Delhi Sultanate.

Admittedly this was due partly to natural calamities, for his reign coincided with a long period of drought which in intensity and extent was one of the worst the subcontinent has ever known. From 1335 to 1342 there was widespread famine, and although the king tried to deal with the situation by opening poor houses and distributing free grain, the problem was beyond his resources. But his misfortunes were not all due to natural and unavoidable causes. A man of ideas, he continually conceived new schemes, and if they were not well received, he lost patience and resorted to ferocious cruelty to enforce them. The most famous incident of this kind occurred in 1327. He had decided, in view of repeated rebellions in the south, that it was necessary to shift the capital to a more central place. He selected

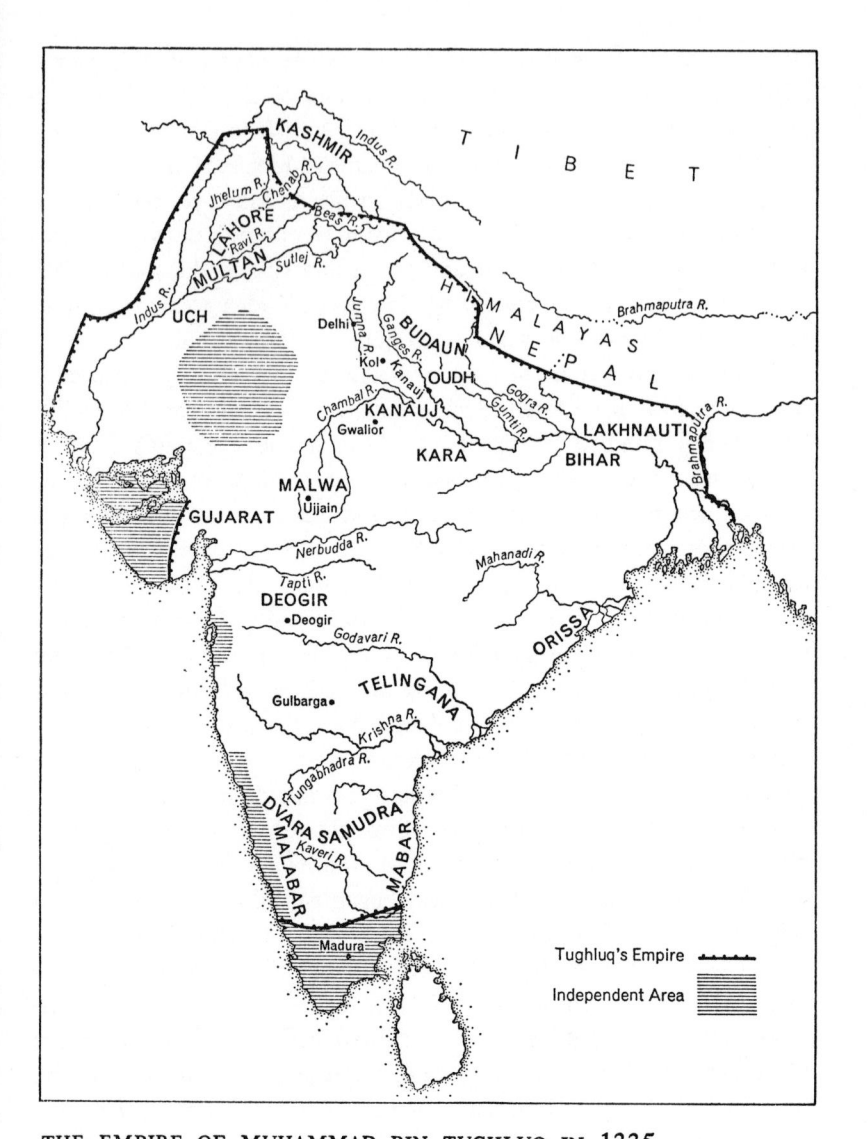

THE EMPIRE OF MUHAMMAD BIN TUGHLUQ IN 1335

From: *An Historical Atlas of the Indian Peninsula* (Oxford University Press, Bombay, 1961).

Devagiri, which he named Daulatabad, as the new seat of government, and he forced the Muslim inhabitants of Delhi to migrate to the new capital. Many perished on the long march to Daulatabad, and eventually the sultan allowed them to return to Delhi. On the face of it, the operation seems to have been an act of folly, yet there is no doubt that the migration of a large Muslim population drawn from all sections of society helped to stabilize Muslim rule in the south. Like many of his schemes, it failed, not because his idea was wrong, but because his organization was not adequate to carry it out.

Another controversial measure was the sultan's issue of token currency. The prolonged famine, the expensive wars, and royal liberality had severely strained the exchequer. Muhammad Tughluq's solution was to issue brass and copper tokens in place of silver coins. Again, the idea was probably sound enough, and one that has been adopted everywhere in the modern world. However the measure was too unfamiliar and too complex for fourteenth-century India. The result was severe dislocation of the economy. Counterfeiting became common and as Barani says, "every Hindu's house became a mint." The king had the good sense to acknowledge his failure, and the token currency was withdrawn from circulation after three or four years. Its introduction and failure neither enhanced public confidence in the sultan nor restored economic prosperity to the country.

There were widespread rebellions throughout Muhammad Tughluq's reign, and the vast empire which Ala-ud-din Khalji and Ghiyas-ud-din Tughluq had governed with success began to fall apart. Early in his reign he had to deal with the revolt of Baha-ud-din Gurshashp, a cousin who was given shelter by the Hindu rajas of the south. Muhammad Tughluq sent a powerful force against the defiant rajas, annexed Kampili, sacked Dvarasa Mudra, and forced its ruler to surrender Gurshashp and to reiterate his submission to the government of Delhi. The cousin's fate was indicative of the sultan's treatment of rebels. He was flayed alive, his flesh was cooked with rice and was sent to his wife and children, while his skin, stuffed with straw, was exhibited in the principal cities of the kingdom. But even such ferocious punishments did not prevent rebellion; perhaps they drove men to rebel out of desperation and fear.

In 1335 Ma'bar, in the extreme south, became independent, fol-

lowed three years later by Bengal. The Hindu rajas in the south organized a confederacy, and in 1336 Vijayanagar became the nucleus of a powerful Hindu state. A year later, when the Muslim chiefs in the Deccan set up the independent Bahmani kingdom, the entire area south of the Vindhyas was lost to Delhi. In the same year Gujarat and Kathiawar revolted, but the sultan was able to quell the rebellions in these two areas. Next it was Sind, and in 1351 he was marching towards Thatta to put down the revolt when he fell ill and died. As Badauni says, "The king was freed from his people and they from their king."

While the breakup of the Delhi Sultanate began in the reign of Muhammad Tughluq, the disasters which overtook him during the last years of his reign need not be the only basis for assessing his character and abilities. Until extreme irritation at the failure of his plans had warped his judgment, driving him to revolting cruelties, he had tried, as a man of ideas, to steer his course according to certain intelligent plans and considerations. His policy toward the Hindus, for example, was conciliatory, and he had tried to introduce social reforms, such as the abolition of *sati*. He appointed a Hindu as governor of Sind, and employed others in high positions. The Jain chroniclers remember with gratitude the respect with which he received their theologians. When northern India was afflicted by the seven-year famine, he built a new town on the Ganges near the worst affected area, giving it the Hindu name of Svargdvara, the "Gate of Heaven."

Muhammad Tughluq's greatest achievement was in the south. Previous rulers, particularly Ala-ud-din Khalji, had established suzerainty over the Hindu princes of the south, but in general had left them in possession of their territories as long as they paid tribute. Muhammad Tughluq, however, set out to end Hindu rule in the south. Warangal and Madura had already been incorporated in the Tughluq dominions and now Kampili and a large part of the Hoysala dominions shared the same fate. Not all of these conquests were maintained, for even during Muhammad's lifetime a powerful Hindu reaction led to the foundation of Vijayanagar, but much remained. Above all, the creation of Daulatabad out of the old fortress city of Devagiri gave the Muslims a great stronghold.

Mention must be made also of the attempt by Muhammad Tughluq

to establish links with other Muslim countries. Among the many distinguished visitors who came to Delhi at this time perhaps the most famous was Ibn Battuta (c.1304–1378), the Moorish traveler who was appointed chief judge in the capital. He has left an interesting account of the capital as well as of places in Sind, Multan, and the Punjab which he visited on the way to Delhi. He was sent on a diplomatic mission to China, and although he did not return to India, his *Book of Travels* is a useful source for the history of Indo-Islamic society.

Muhammad Tughluq's successor was his cousin, Firuz Tughluq, who reigned from 1351 to 1388. While the commencement of the Tughluq rule had seen a new emphasis on orthodoxy, Firuz's reign saw an even greater attempt to govern India in conformity with Islamic law. Until Aurangzeb, in fact, no other ruler made such a serious endeavor to champion orthodoxy as a guide for the state. The study of Islamic law was encouraged, and Firuz attempted to enforce the law not only among orthodox Muslims, but also among sects such as the Ismaili Shias and the non-Muslims. For the first time *jizya* was levied upon the Brahmans, who had hitherto remained exempt from the tax. On appeal, the king reduced the amount to be levied from 10 tankas to 50 jitals, but maintained the tax as a legal formality.

In this support of orthodoxy Firuz was probably swayed by personal religious beliefs, even though he was not, in his private life, a strict follower of the Islamic code. Probably he was conscious also that one reason for Muhammad Tughluq's failures was lack of support from the powerful religious leaders, and therefore he was anxious to win them to his side.

The measures by which Firuz helped to gain a reputation for orthodoxy were of a formal nature; the developments which shed luster on his reign were the steps taken in the furtherance of public welfare. In many ways he was the ablest of the Muslim rulers of Delhi previous to Akbar, and contemporary historians describe at length the steps he took to assist agriculture, promote employment, and secure the happiness and prosperity of the people. He initiated extensive irrigation schemes, digging five canals to distribute the water of the Sutlej and Jhelum over a large area. One of these continues to be used up to the

present day. Also he set up an employment bureau where young men who were without work in the city of Delhi gave their qualifications, and occupations were found for them.

The greatest monuments of Firuz's rule, however, are the buildings and the towns founded by him. He is credited with the erection of 200 towns, 40 mosques, 30 colleges, 30 reservoirs, 50 dams, 100 hospitals, 100 public baths, and 150 bridges. He built a magnificent new capital near Delhi, and the two important towns of Jaunpur and Hissar were founded by him. He set up a regular Department of Public Works, which erected new buildings and took steps to restore the structures of former kings. He removed two gigantic monolithic pillars of the emperor Ashoka, one from a village in the Ambala District and the other from Meerut, and had them set up near Delhi. He also showed his interest in India's past by having translations made of a number of Sanskrit books which he found during his conquest of Kangra in 1361.

But Firuz did little to prevent the disintegration of the sultanate which had already set in during the last years of the reign of his predecessor. The process was speeded by his death, for a civil war broke out between his son and grandson. The Hindu chiefs threw off their allegiance and governors of provinces became independent. The weakness of the kingdom invited foreign invasion and in 1398 Timur, the Barlas Turkish chief who ruled at Samarqand, invaded India. He had no intention of staying in India, but came, as had the invaders of four centuries before, to take back slaves and booty. After terrible destruction, including the sacking of Delhi, he returned home, but he had helped to destroy the Delhi Sultanate. Possibly it could not have survived long in any case, but certainly Timur's raid effectively prevented the Tughluqs from regaining their control.

The familiar story of dynastic decay thus repeated itself. In the decade following Firuz's death, six sultans briefly occupied the throne. The last of the Tughluq line, Mahmud, fled from Delhi during Timur's invasion. Although he returned after his departure, managing to stay on the throne until 1413, he was not able to ensure the succession to a member of the house.

VI. The Disintegration of the Sultanate

IN THE century that intervened between the death of the last of the Tughluq kings in 1413 and the emergence of a new Turkish power, the Mughals, in the early years of the sixteenth century, two main processes can be seen at work in Muslim India. One is the disintegration of the power of the Delhi Sultanate; the other, and complementary to it, is the rise of independent regional Muslim kingdoms. The centralizing authority of the Delhi sultan that had been asserted with varying success since the time of Muhammad Ghuri (d.1206) ceased to be a paramount factor in Indian political life, and its place was taken by kingdoms, many of which were centers of great artistic achievement, and some of which were better organized and more powerful than Delhi.

This did not mean, however, that the Delhi Sultanate passed away; on the contrary, as a symbol of prestige and a source of wealth it remained the great prize for which factions struggled and fought. The group that succeeded to the sultanate on the death of Mahmud Tughluq are known as the Sayyids, although there is little evidence, as their name would suggest, that they were descendants of the Prophet. The first of them, Khizr Khan, considered himself to be the viceroy of Timur's son, which in itself was an indication of the change that had come over the sultanate. Three more members of the family continued to maintain some show of authority until the last of the line, Alam Shah, retired from the turmoil of Delhi to the relative peace of the provincial city of Badaun in 1448. It was against this background of confusion that the wazir and nobles turned to Buhlul Lodi, the able governor of Sirhind, and invited him to come to Delhi. Buhlul responded with alacrity and in 1451, without any opposition from Alam Shah, he occupied the throne, becoming the first Afghan ruler in India.

The First Afghan Kings

Buhlul Lodi was a member of an Afghan family that had been re-warded by the Sayyid sultans with control of the Sirhind district in the Punjab in return for service as defenders of the northwestern frontier. From this base Buhlul Lodi had gained control over eastern and central Punjab, and by the time the invitation came from Delhi he was virtually independent of the sultanate. After he had succeeded to the throne he sought to strengthen his position by bringing in Afghans from the northwestern highlands, attracting them by grants of lands and estates. Energetic and ambitious, he overlooked no op-portunity of extending his dominion, and throughout the nearly forty years of his reign he concentrated his power on attempts to overcome the chiefs, both Hindu and Muslim, who had established independent kingdoms during the previous reigns and now opposed the new cen-tralizing force emanating from Delhi. That part of this resistance met by the Lodi kings was related to groups with attachments to the dis-placed Sayyid sultans is suggested by the attitude of the ruler of Jaunpur, an important kingdom in the central Gangetic plain. The ruler, Husain Sharqi, had married Jalila, a daughter of the last Sayyid sultan of Delhi, and she persuaded her husband to invade Delhi. This led to the defeat of the Jaunpur ruler and the annexation of his terri-tory.

Buhlul's policy was continued by his son Sikandar (r. 1489–1517), and while he did not succeed in regaining the full territory that the Delhi sultans had once controlled, at least he made the chiefs within the narrower boundaries recognize his power. He spent four years (1499–1503) in thoroughly organizing the administration of the trans-Gangetic province of Sambhal, and soon after he transferred his capital from Delhi to Sikandara, a suburb of Agra, to be nearer the areas which required his attention. This was, incidentally, the begin-ning of the future importance of Agra, which hitherto had been a dependency of the more important fortress of Biana.

A patron of learning who himself wrote poetry, Sikandar attracted many scholars to his court, including the well-known poet and mystic

Jamali (d.1535). One of the most interesting works of the period, which was sponsored by his wazir, Miyan Bhuva, was a voluminous book on medicine entitled *Ma'dan-ul-Shifa* or *Tib-i-Sikanadari,* in which theories and prescriptions of Indian medicine were consolidated. A work on music, *Lahjat-i-Sikandar Shahi,* of which the only existing copy is in the Tagore Library of the University of Lucknow, was another important contribution.[1]

Muslim historians, including Nizam-ud-din Bakshi, the author of *Tabaqat-i-Akbari,* have accused Sikandar of religious bigotry, but it was during his reign that Hindus began to adjust to the new conditions, and a great many of them started to learn Persian. Muslim interest in Indian medicine and music in the highest circles has already been mentioned. In spite of Sikandar's reputation for bigotry it seems fair to surmise that in the cultural sphere his period was one of active mutual interest "among Hindus and Muslims for each other's learning, thus conducing to a reapproachment." Sikandar died in 1517 and was succeeded by his son, Ibrahim Lodi. Soon disputes between the sultan and his Afghan nobles which simmered throughout the Lodi period became acute, and Daulat Khan Lodi, the governor of the Punjab and the king's uncle, invited Babur, the ruler of Kabul, to invade India. After early incursions confined to the northwest and the Punjab, Babur met Ibrahim in the first battle of Panipat on April 21, 1526, and, by defeating him and capturing Delhi and Agra, laid the foundation for the Mughal rule.

The Rise of Regional Kingdoms

One aspect of the history of Islamic civilization in India in the fifteenth century, the collapse of the Delhi Sultanate, led to anarchy and turmoil, but the second important feature, the rise of independent kingdoms, prevented the disintegration of central authority from becoming an unqualified disaster. It can be argued, indeed, that splitting the realm into regional kingdoms resulted in Muslim penetration of areas hitherto unconquered, such as Kathiawar and eastern Bengal.

[1] R. C. Majumdar, ed., *The Delhi Sultanate*. Vol. V of *Culture and History of the Indian People* (Bombay, 1960), p. 146.

The administration of smaller and more compact territories was certainly more effective, and it is doubtful if the loosely controlled and vaguely demarcated *iqtas* of the sultanate could have developed into the well-organized *subas* of the Mughal period without the rise and consolidation of regional kingdoms. Because of these kingdoms, closer administrative control over areas where old Hindu chiefs had exercised a great degree of autonomy became a reality for the first time.

The rise of the regional kingdoms also helped the spread of Islam and Muslim culture. During the days of the sultanate, Delhi was the one major center of Islamic culture and religion; now Ahmadabad, Jaunpur, Gulbarga, Sonargaon, Gaur, Pandua, and other provincial capitals became active centers of Muslim religious and cultural activity. Delhi had a large number of influential immigrants, and the cultural traditions of the capital reflected mainly the Central Asian pattern. At the capitals of the regional kingdoms, Muslims and immigrants were not in a majority, and the cultural activity in these areas mirrored the indigenous tradition to a much greater extent. It was in these regional kingdoms, therefore, that Muslim impact led to the rise of vernaculars and paved the way for the religious synthesis advocated by some leaders of the *bhakti* movement. Music was more actively patronized in such regional centers as Kashmir, Jaunpur, Malwa, and Gujarat than at the capital of the sultanate. Another important difference between the capital and the regional kingdoms which affected culture was the fact that the rulers of the regional kingdoms were not preoccupied with the threat of Mongol invasions and other similar problems of the central government. They were able to devote greater attention to cultural pursuits at their courts than was possible in Delhi. The elaborate literary and cultural activity which was carried on in Kashmir under Zain-ul-Abidin's direct patronage, for example, finds no parallel in the annals of the sultanate.

These cultural activities of the regional kingdoms paved the way, moreover, for the broader basis of Mughal culture. The Mughal cultural pattern was derived primarily from Herat, Samarqand, Tabriz, and Isfahan; yet it included many features which were absent during the sultanate. A possible explanation is that these had gained prominence in the regional kingdoms. Examples of this process are the at-

tention paid to the development of vernacular, the official patronage of music, and the greater scope offered to Hindu thought and art forms. The extraordinarily rapid rise of Urdu during the eighteenth century was made possible by the slow maturing of the Deccani in the courts of Bijapur and Golkunda, and many other features of the regional cultural traditions were absorbed in the pattern of the Mughal culture.

Among the areas which became independent during the weakness of the sultanate, Bengal was probably the most important. Although Muhammad bin Bakhtiyar Khalji had made the first Muslim conquest about 1202, his hold extended over only a small portion of northern Bengal. After conquering Nadiya, the old Hindu capital, he withdrew northward and confined himself to the areas near Bihar. His successors gradually extended the Muslim dominion in the east, but their efforts were fitful and often accompanied by defiance of Delhi's authority. We hear about Sonargaon (near modern Dacca) for the first time in 1280 when Balban, in pursuit of Tughril, the rebellious deputy in Bengal, compelled the Hindu raja of Sonargaon to undertake a search for the rebel. Tughril's revolt forced Balban to face the problem of chronic rebellion in Bengal, and he tackled it with his usual thoroughness. After dealing with the rebels he stayed on to reorganize the administration, appointed his son Bughra Khan as the viceroy of the territory, and left a team of carefully selected officers to assist the prince.

The measures taken by Balban in Bengal proved fruitful. The consequences of posting a team of highly educated and cultured officials from Delhi were soon evident, and the Islamization of the territory was begun. Although Bughra Khan lost his chance of succeeding Balban at Delhi because of his preference for Bengal, this enabled Balban's family to continue their sway in the eastern territory long after its rule had ended at Delhi. The reigns of Bughra Khan's successors from 1286 to 1328 constituted a period of active expansion. Southern and eastern Bengal came under their control, and important centers were established at Satgaon (Hugli district) and Sonargaon. One of these rulers, Shams-ud-din Firuz (r. 1301–1322) extended Muslim dominion across the Brahmaputra into the Sylhet district of

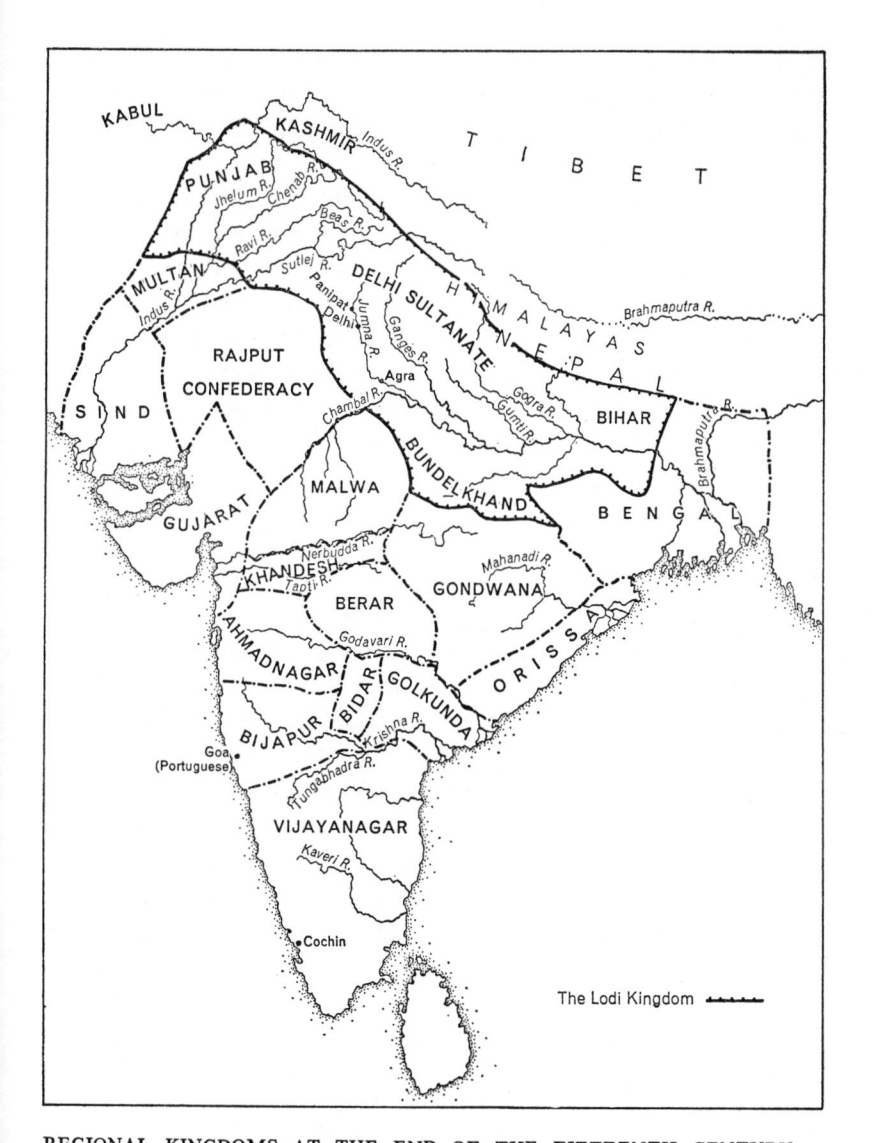

REGIONAL KINGDOMS AT THE END OF THE FIFTEENTH CENTURY

From: *An Historical Atlas of the Indian Peninsula* (Oxford University Press, Bombay, 1961).

Assam. These efforts were facilitated by the arrival of a large number of Turkish officers and soldiers who had been displaced by the Khaljis at Delhi. In addition, the volunteers for *jihad,* or holy war, locally known as ghazis, and other spirited volunteers actively assisted in Muslim expansion. The conquest of Sylhet in 1303, for example, is attributed by both Muslim and Hindu accounts to the support which the Muslim troops received from a contemporary soldier-saint, Shah Jalal, who lies buried at Sylhet. Many other warrior-saints, such as Zafar Khan Ghazi of Tribheni near Hugli and Shah Ismail Ghazi in Rangpur district, are mentioned in contemporary accounts.

Although Ghiyas-ud-din Tughluq reasserted the authority of Delhi over Bengal in 1234, the troubles which broke out in the reign of his son Muhammad Tughluq resulted in the independence of the area once more. The two expeditions of the next ruler, Firuz Tughluq, could not reverse this process, and Bengal remained independent until its conquest by Akbar in 1576.

Independent Bengal was ruled by a succession of dynasties, of which two are noteworthy. The rulers of the Ilyas Shahi dynasty, who were on the throne of Bengal from 1338 to 1415, and again from 1437 to 1487, secured the independence of the province, dealt with the two expeditions of Firuz Tughluq, revived Bengal's contacts with the outside world, and won notable victories against neighboring non-Muslim rulers of Tirhut, Nepal, and Orissa. Among them, Ghiyas-ud-din Azam Shah (r. 1393–1410) tried to attract the great Persian poet Hafiz to his court, sent large sums of money to holy places in Hijaz, and exchanged envoys with the contemporary Chinese emperor. His small, beautiful tomb at Sonargaon is the oldest Muslim monument in East Pakistan. Soon after his death, Ganesh, a Hindu zamindar of Dinajpur, seized power, and the local Muslims sought aid from the Muslim ruler of the neighboring kingdom of Jaunpur. When the Sharqui king threatened to intervene, Ganesh vacated the throne in favor of his son, who accepted Islam. He ruled from 1415 to 1431. Six years later his successor was assassinated, possibly as a result of rivalry between the Hindu and Muslim nobles, and the Ilyas Shahi dynasty was restored to power.

Much briefer, but somewhat better documented, was the tenure of the Hussain Shahi dynasty (1493–1539). It produced two able rulers —Ala-ud-din Husain Shah (r. 1493–1519) and his son Nusrat Shah (r. 1519–1532). They were competent rulers, liberal in outlook, and great patrons of cultural activities. They recovered lost territories, and left magnificent buildings at Gaur and Pandua. Their patronage of letters was not confined to Persian, the court language; they gave encouragement to the rising Bengali literature, and many Sanskrit works were translated into Bengali at their court. The confusion following the assassination of Nusrat Shah in 1532 enabled the Afghan, Sher Khan Suri, to intervene, and he conquered the province in 1539. It remained in Afghan hands until 1576, when Akbar annexed it to the Mughal empire.

Another important independent kingdom was the Bahmani sultanate in the Deccan which lasted from 1347 to 1527. For a little less than a century and a half (1347–1482) it prospered until it extended from the western to the eastern coasts of South India. Ultimately it broke into five principalities—the Adil Shahis of Bijapur (1490–1686), the Nizam Shahis of Ahmadnagar (1480–1633), the Imad Shahis of Berar (1410–1568), the Barid Shahis of Bidar (1580–1609), and the Qutb Shahis of Golkunda (1512–1687).

The rulers of these Deccan kingdoms attracted scholars, poets, and statesmen from Persia and Iraq, but local talent was employed to a much larger extent than was the case at Delhi. At one time the principal ministers at Bijapur were Hindu, and the Maratha chief, Shahji of Ahmadnagar, the father of Shivaji, occupied a distinguished position in the army. In linguistic matters also there was closer collaboration between the Hindus and the Muslims. Marathi was the language used for village records, and the rulers helped the development of the Deccani variety of Hindustani. They themselves composed verses in that language and encouraged others, and it was no accident that although Hindustani appeared in northern India in the very beginning of the Muslim rule, it was the Deccani idiom that first attained literary status.

Other important regional kingdoms which rose were Gujarat (1403–

1572), Jaunpur (1393–1479), Malwa (1400–1561), Khandesh (1382–1601), and Multan (1444–1524). Sind was also independent at this time, as indeed it had been for centuries. During the two centuries of their independent rule the kings of Gujarat built many magnificent buildings and founded new cities, including Ahmadabad. Their encouragement of arts and crafts laid the foundation of many of the industries for which Gujarat became famous during the Mughal period. Jaunpur, in the central Gangetic plain, became a great cultural center after Timur's destruction of Delhi. The rulers provided asylum for the leading scholars from the capital, and by bestowing rich endowments on scholarly families laid the foundation for that intellectual preeminence of the region which has been maintained until recent times. The last king of Jaunpur, Sultan Husain Sharqi, was an ineffective ruler, but, because of his patronage, he occupies an important place in the history of Indian music.

Kashmir was also an independent Muslim kingdom, having remained outside the kingdom of Delhi until its conquest by Akbar in 1586. Muslim rule had been established there in the first half of the fourteenth century. Its most noteworthy ruler was Zain-ul-Abidin, who ruled from 1420 to 1470. He abolished *jizya* and freely patronized Hindu learning. At his court several works were translated from Sanskrit into Persian and Persian and Arabic works were translated into Kashmiri.

The breakup of the Delhi Sultanate led not only to the establishment of a number of Muslim kingdoms, but in certain areas the Hindu chiefs also reasserted themselves. In addition to the minor chieftains who became independent, a powerful state was established at Mewar in Rajputana. Rana Sanga, who came to the throne in 1509, was successful in battle against the Muslim kings of Gujarat and Malwa as well as the Lodi ruler of Delhi. By 1526 he had become the most powerful ruler of northern India, and when Babur was establishing Mughal rule, his most important victory was not that against the Lodi ruler at Panipat but against Rana Sanga and his Afghan confederates at Kanwah in 1527. Sanga was poisoned shortly after his defeat, and Mewar's importance declined.

In the south an even more important Hindu kingdom was estab-

lished in 1336 at Vijayanagar. This lasted until 1564, when the Muslim rulers of the Deccan united and administered a complete defeat to the Vijayanagar army at Talikota.

Mention must be made also of another power that made its appearance at this time. On May 27, 1498, the Portuguese admiral Vasco da Gama, guided by the Arab pilot Ahmad ibn Majid whom he had pressed into service on reaching the East African coast, appeared before Calicut. A new chapter had opened not only in the history of India but of the entire East. Soon the Portuguese established themselves as the masters of the Indian Ocean. They did not establish a regional kingdom but instead occupied and fortified the key points of Daman, Diu, and Goa. They controlled Indian coastal waters until their mastery was challenged first by the Dutch and then by the British.

VII. The Administrative System
of the Sultanate

Good summary statement

A RAPID survey of the three-hundred-year history of the Delhi Sultanate is likely to leave the reader with two impressions. One is of a political structure in which violence, based on a powerful fighting force, was the only support of a ruler's government; the other is that anything like a coherent political philosophy was completely lacking. What is becoming increasingly plain, however, as the period is studied in more depth, is that the sultanate under its abler rulers had a quite sophisticated administrative structure. In addition, the Turkish sultans were heirs to a tradition in which political theory had been considerably evolved, and there were many scholars in Islamic India who had given thought to both the general principles underlying government and the techniques of public administration. We know of the works of some of these writers only from casual references in other books, but a number which have survived suggest the background of thought against which the sultanate's actual administrative structure developed.

Political Theory

The earliest work of importance for the history of political thought of Muslim India was probably intended to be a blueprint for the first Muslim government at Delhi. It was written by a contemporary of Iltutmish, Fakhr-i-Mudabbir, who had spent a considerable part of his life at Lahore where he met Sultan Muhammad Ghuri and Sultan Qutb-ud-din Aibak, to whom one of his works, a book on genealogies, was presented in 1206. The historical introduction to this work has been translated into English,[1] but his more important work, variously styled *Adab-ul-Muluk wa Kifayat al Mamluk* (Rules for the Kings

[1] E. Dennison Ross, "The Genealogies of Fakhr-ud-Din," in T. W. Arnold and R. A. Nicholson, eds., *A Volume of Oriental Studies* (Cambridge, 1922), pp. 392–413.

and the Welfare of the Subjects) or *Adab-ul-Harab wal-Shujaat* (Rules of Warfare and Bravery) has not yet been published in its entirety. It was undoubtedly intended to be a guide for rulers and administrators. The first part of this book deals with the privileges and responsibilities of kings, with separate chapters giving the qualifications and functions of different officers of state. The rest of the book is a manual dealing systematically and in some detail with the art of war. The work was presented to Iltutmish and, as the contemporary histories show, the government organization set up by him corresponded very closely to the structure visualized by Fakhr-i-Mudabbir.

Another early work, of which only an incomplete copy has survived, belongs to a different category. This is *Fatawa-i-Jahandari* (Rulings on Government) by Ziya-ud-din Barani (1285–1357), the greatest of fourteenth-century historians of Muslim India. A political phantasy consisting mainly of a number of discourses purporting to have been addressed by Sultan Mahmud of Ghazni to his successor, it was written after Barani had retired from the royal court in disgrace. It reflects Barani's bitterness against recent trends, his extremism, and his acute class-consciousness. He is bitter not only against the Hindus but also against the Muslim lower classes who, he believed, should not be "taught reading and writing, for plenty of disorders arise owing to the skill of the low-born in knowledge . . . For on account of their skill, they became governors, revenue collectors, auditors, officers and rulers." If the teachers disregard this edict, and it is discovered that "they have imparted knowledge or taught letters or writing to the low-born, inevitably the punishment for disobedience will be meted out to them." [2] *Fatawa-i-Jahandari* represents an individual's views and made no impression on the course of Indo-Muslim history or political thought. Indeed, it is not referred to by any later writer or historian, and is not included in the fairly full list of Barani's works given by his contemporary, Amir Khurd. The importance of the book is partly personal, as an insight into the mind of Barani, and partly topical, as it gives his views in the context of the political and social situation then prevailing. In spirit and sentiments, *Fatawa-i-Jahandari*

---

[2] Ziya-ud-din Barani, *Fatawa-i-Jahandari*, trans. by Afsar Khan in *The Political Theory of the Delhi Sultanate* (Allahabad, n.d.), p. 49.

is in complete contrast with Fakhr-i-Mudabbir's book, which is throughout inspired by practical idealism, moderation and good sense.

Barani dealt at length with political philosophies of early Muslim rulers, statesmen, and religious leaders in his great historical work, *Tarikh-i-Firuz Shahi*. The long discourses on political affairs and statecraft contained in his book are dramatizations and expansions by an eloquent historian who is also a creative artist. Among the most interesting of these discourses are Nur-ud-din Mubarik Ghaznavi's advice to Iltutmish on the responsibilities of a Muslim "Defender of the Faith" (Din Panah); Balban's views on kingship, and his long lecture to his son, Bughra Khan, the governor of Bengal, on the relationship between the central and the provincial governments; Ahmad Chap's advice to Jalal-ud-din Khalji; Kotwal Ala-ul-Mulk's discourses at Ala-ud-din's consultative assemblies; and Qazi Mughis' views on major political and legal problems of the day. They are presumably colored by his own predilictions, and should not be treated as verbally authentic, but the views attributed to different rulers and dignitaries are so distinct and so much in character that they may be taken to represent generally the individual views of the persons to whom they are attributed.

To turn from theory to practice, the first comment that should be made on the Islamic state in India is that it was not a theocracy, as sometimes has been suggested. Aside from the question of the relevance of the concept of a theocracy to a society that does not recognize a priesthood, by the time the Delhi Sultanate was established the religious function of the caliph had ceased to be of much significance for the outlying Islamic world. It is true that a few of the Delhi rulers obtained formal recognition of their titles from the caliph, but this pious legal fiction did not alter the reality. The temporal authority of the caliph at Baghdad dwindled to a mere shadow even within his own territories, and the actual reality of the Indian links with the caliphate may be judged by the fact that occasionally a caliph would have been dead for years before Delhi became aware of the event. The patents obtained by the rulers meant so little that at one time a caliph sent patents simultaneously to both rulers of Delhi and Bengal.

In any case the policy adopted by the early sultans under the stress

of circumstances with which they were confronted could scarcely permit the growth of theocracy. Iltutmish, recognizing the essentially secular nature of the sultanate saw that under the conditions prevailing in India, it was not possible for him to be a "Defender of the Faith" except in limited spheres. Balban went even further. In spite of his courtesy to the leading ulama and his personal observance of religious practices, in matters of administration, he was guided by the needs of the state, not Islamic law. Ala-ud-din Khalji followed the same policy. "When he became sultan," Barani records, "he came to the conclusion that polity and government are one thing, and the rules and decrees of Islamic law are another. Royal commands belong to the sultan, Islamic legal decrees rest upon the judgment of the qazis and muftis." [3] It was under the Tughluqs, particularly under Firuz, that Muslim jurists gained some recognition, but by then the pattern of Muslim rule in India had become firmly established.

The early ulama, realizing the complexity of the Indian situation and the need for strengthening the Muslim government, accepted Iltutmish's policy. Their lack of power may be judged by the fact that Raziyya ascended the throne of Delhi although Muslim legal opinion is firmly opposed to female rulers; it was left to a much later scholar, Shaikh Abdul Haq Muhaddis (1551–1642), in the more legalistic days of the Mughals, to criticize the selection of Raziyya and express surprise at the action of the contemporary jurists and Shaikhs in confirming it. There was an equally glaring departure from the correct legal position in Qutb-ud-din Aibak's acceptance as sultan before his manumission. In general, then, the position was that so long as a sultan undertook to safeguard the honor and the observances of Islam, did nothing in open defiance of the principles of *shariat,* appointed qazis and made arrangements for religious education and observance of religious practices, the ulama did not interfere in the affairs of the state.

The use of the title "sultan" in itself indicates the transition from the quasi-theocratic caliphate to a secular institution. Although the process was implicit in the establishment and administration of the

---

[3] H. M. Elliot and John Dowson, *The History of India as Told by Its Own Historians* (London, 1867–1877), III, 183.

Umayyad caliphate, it was strengthened by the Persian belief in the divine right of kings. This idea, which had become dominant in Baghdad under the later Abbasids, was even more marked at Ghazni. At Delhi, in the early days of the Turkish rule, there was some opposition to it in orthodox Muslim circles, and Iltutmish was almost apologetic about his kingly role.[4] The position completely changed with Balban, who was an advocate of Persian ideas, modeled his court after the Persian style, assumed the title of zillulah, and introduced Persian etiquette, court ceremonial, and festivities. With him Persian ideas of monarchy became dominant. The process was facilitated by the fact that the Hindus regarded a king as a representative of divine powers.

These theories gave medieval rulers powers which occasionally were used arbitrarily, but a number of checks remained on the absolute exercise of authority by the sultan. For one thing, the Islamic theory curtails the law-making power of a ruler, and although there was nothing to stop an autocratic ruler from becoming a law unto himself, he could do so only in defiance of the system which gave him power. Even the autocratic Ala-ud-din Khalji admitted that administration of justice was the concern of the Muslim jurists.

Equally important was the opinion of the nobility. The sultans consulted their chief nobles and the routine affairs of the state were left to them. Minhaj refers to a dignitary, Amir-i-Majlis, whose duty was to arrange meetings of the sultan's closest associates. Important questions were discussed freely, and some favorite royal schemes (such as Ala-ud-din's proposal to establish a new religion) were ruled out. Together with the influence of public opinion and the natural desire of the sultan to maintain his position, the nobles in this way exercised a check on the theoretical absolutism enjoyed by him.

According to Muslim theory, held particularly by the Sunnis who formed the bulk of Muslim population in India, election was the accepted method for selecting the ruler. This was rarely observed anywhere, and both Turko-Iranian and Hindu conceptions of sovereignty were opposed to it, but a form of limited election or acceptance was generally followed at Delhi. The oath of allegiance taken by the gov-

[4] See p. 46.

ernors of the provinces, the principal nobles of the capital, and the chief theologians was taken as a symbol of the indirect consent of the mass of the people.

Structure of Government

Fakhr-i-Mudabbir lists the principal dignitaries of the state as follows: wazir, wakil-i-dar, amir-i-dad, amir-i-hajib, mushrif, mustaufi, and sahib-i-barid. The wakil-i-dar (not to be confused with the wakil-i-sultanat of the Sayyid dynasty and the wakil-i-mutliq of the Mughals) was the controller of the household. The amir-i-dad (literally lord of justice) was the most important judicial dignitary. The amir-i-hajib is often designated as the chief chamberlain, but this does not fairly describe the functions and duties of this officer. He was the master of ceremonies at the court; no one could enter the royal presence without being introduced by one of his assistants, and all petitions were presented to the sultan through him. The post, therefore, was one of great prestige and was reserved for trusted nobles. One holder of this post, Balban, was the most powerful noble of his day. The mushrif was the accounts officer responsible for income, and the mustaufi for expenditure. The sahib-i-barid was in charge of communications and intelligence.

The chief minister of the sultan was called the wazir. Fakhr-i-Mudabbir considered the wazir a "partaker in sovereignty" and recommended that in his own technical domain he must be left free by the monarch. He describes the normal functions of the wazir in the following passage: "The kings know well how to lead expeditions, conquer countries, give rewards, and shine in the assembly or battlefield; but it is the domain of the wazir to make a country prosperous, to accumulate treasures, to appoint officials, to ask for accounts, to arrange for the stock-taking of the commodities in the *karkhanas,* and the census of horses, camels, mules, and other animals, to assemble and pay the troops and artisans, to keep the people satisfied, to look after the men of piety and fame and to give them stipends, to take care of the widows and the orphans, to provide for the learned, to administer the affairs of the people, and to organize the business of

the state." [5] This was the position in early days, when the wazir was in charge of the entire government, both the civil and the military departments and the functions which were later entrusted to Sadr-i-Jahan, but this arrangement underwent drastic changes in the light of practical experience. In view of the importance of the office, and to illustrate the administrative experiments that were carried on under the sultanate, it will be useful to sketch the history of the wizarat.

Although few details are known about administrative arrangements during the brief rule of Qutb-ud-din Aibak, presumably the practice of combining civil and military offices (which was introduced by the Ghaznavids at Lahore, and was continued under the Ghuris) remained in operation. This was also the position under Iltutmish. His first wazir, Nizam-ul-Mulk Junaidi, was in charge of all sections of the government, and in addition to his civil duties, was occasionally entrusted with military commands. During the troubled reign of Raziyya and her successors, Khwaja Muhazzab-ud-din used his influence with the weak rulers and his own capacity for intrigue to consolidate his position by taking all power out of the hands of the nobles. An attempt was made to curb the wazir's powers by the creation of the post of naib (deputy of the realm), but this was unsuccessful and the wazir continued to be all-powerful. Muhazzab's opponents, therefore, joined forces and had him assassinated.

His death marks the close of a period in the history of the wizarat. The provincial governors and other administrative officers would not permit an individual selected for his ability in office to obtain so much power. His successors were selected for their docility. Balban, even before he became deputy, was more powerful than the wazir, and when he became sultan, he took away the military functions of the wizarat. The rawat-i-arz (the muster-master, who was originally in charge of the finances and records of military personnel) was made independent of the wazir.

Some fifty years later, Ghiyas-ud-din Tughluq made an even more interesting experiment. He created a board of three ex-wazirs, with the senior having the high title of malik-ul-wuzara (chief minister).

[5] Quoted in I. H. Qureshi, *The Administration of the Sultanate of Delhi* (Karachi, 1958), pp. 78–80.

Ghiyas consulted them in all important matters, but the routine work of the wizarat was carried on by Malik Shadi, his son-in-law.

With the general policy of the Tughluqs to approximate standard Muslim practice in all matters and with Muhammad Tughluq's preference for Arab and Persian ways, we notice a reversion to the earlier character of the wizarat. Khwaja Jahan, though essentially a civil servant, was occasionally entrusted with military duties. This change is more marked under Firuz, whose wazir fulfilled the Arab notion of an all-powerful wazir. Khan Jahan, a Hindu from Telingana who had accepted Islam at the hands of Hazrat Nizam-ud-din Auliya, exercised both civil and military powers. His position may be judged by Firuz's frequent remark that Khan Jahan was virtually the sultan of Delhi. After his death in 1372, his son became wazir and followed his father's ideas for a long period, but this led to jealousy, and in 1387 he was killed in a quarrel with a noble. This also marked the end of Firuz Tughluq's power and the decline of the dynasty. Khwaja Jahan Sarvar-ul-Mulk, the wazir (1390–1394) of Muhammad Shah, exercised authority both in civil and military spheres, but realizing that the sultanate was tottering, he had one of the military leaders made wakil-i-sultanat, and he himself left for the eastern provinces, where he carved out a kingdom for himself in Jaunpur.

With the accession to power of the Lodi dynasty, the wizarat lost some of its importance, for Buhlul Lodi, with his tribal conception of kingship did not establish an organized wizarat. Sikandar Lodi, however, saw the impossibility of applying this tribal conception to a huge territory and had a regular diwan and a wizarat. His wazir, however, seems to have confined himself to civil work.

The developments that took place under the Mughals will be described later, but essentially their wizarat was based on Balban's model, with the holder of the office confined to civil duties. This meant that the wazir in the Indian Islamic state had less power than that assigned to him by Muslim political theorists, but the system worked fairly well. Indian tradition and the needs of the Islamic rulers favored strong monarchs. It is probably true that the people, insofar as they had a preference, preferred an absolute monarch to an absolute wazir.

Revenue

The financial arrangements of the sultanate were in accordance with the normal Islamic theory and practice as inherited from the Ghaznavid predecessors, but they were modified in the light of local needs and usages. Land revenue was, as in Hindu India, the mainstay of the government. Sultan Qutb-ud-din Aibak, the first Muslim ruler, fixed the state demand (*kharaj*) at one-fifth of the gross produce. In land revenue, as in other spheres, Balban laid down the administrative pattern for the sultanate. According to W. H. Moreland, one of the most careful students of Indian economic history, Balban "had grasped the main principles of rural economy in an Indian peasant-state, at a period when the environment afforded little scope for individual advance; he aimed at a peaceful and contented peasantry, raising ample produce and paying a reasonable revenue; and he saw that it was the king's duty to direct the administration with this object in view." [6] Under Ala-ud-din Khalji, because of the need to build up a large army, the state demand was raised to one-half of the produce, the uppermost limit allowed by Muslim law. In the following reign the heavy demands were lowered. The scale of demand in the reign of the first Tughluq king has been a matter of dispute. According to R. R. Tripathi, Ghiyas-ud-din Tughluq fixed the demand at 10 percent of the produce; according to Moreland, the relevant reference in the contemporary history refers to the limit of increase being 10 percent. I. H. Qureshi, on the other hand, holds that except for a few areas the general charge on land was a fifth of the produce, which was maintained from the earliest days of the sultanate until the end of Firuz Shah's reign. Under the Mughal rulers who followed Timur's precedent in charging a third of the produce as land revenue, the scale was raised and Sher Shah, who had seen the increase in the state demand under Babur and Humayun, followed their example.[7]

[6] W. H. Moreland, *The Agrarian System of Moslem India* (Cambridge, 1929), pp. 30–31.

[7] R. P. Tripathi, *Some Aspects of Muslim Administration* (Allahabad, 1936), pp. 338–40; Moreland, p. 41; and Qureshi, pp. 111–14.

Apart from the land revenue there were a number of local imposts imposed on various occasions. Orthodox Muslims considered them illegal and the two monarchs who made an attempt to run the state in accordance with Islamic law, Firuz Tughluq and Aurangzeb, abolished these taxes. These imposts were of ancient origin, however, and most sultans permitted them. And when the rulers abolished them, they were realized by corrupt officials or even by panchayats. A tax which gained importance during Firuz's reign was the charge levied for use of canal water. Firuz was not the first to dig canals, but he was the first monarch to ask Muslim jurists whether an irrigation tax was lawful. The jurists' reply was in the affirmative, and so a 10 percent addition was made to the land revenue in cases where canal water was used for irrigation.

During the early period, when the subcontinent was being conquered and new areas were being occupied, the *ghanimah* (the spoils of war) provided an important source of state income. According to Islamic law, all booty should be collected and a fifth set apart for the state, the rest being distributed among the soldiers. Later the practice was reversed and four-fifths of the booty was appropriated by the state treasury. Firuz's ulama considered it illegal, and Firuz ordered the restoration of the old rate as fixed by the law.

The taxes which had a special religious significance in an Islamic state—*zakat* and *jizya*—have been the subject of much controversy, both as regards their nature and their actual imposition during Muslim rule in India. *Zakat* was imposed only on Muslims; it is not, strictly speaking, a tax in the normal sense, since its payment was an act of piety. Contemporary historians do not record that *zakat* was levied by the sultans of Delhi, and their silence has been taken to mean that the procedure, common to all Islamic states, was followed. There were, at any rate, arrangements for the receipt of *zakat*, paid voluntarily by Muslims as a religious duty, and Fiqh-i-Firuz Shahi mentions a separate treasury for *zakat*. Toward the end of the sultanate, Sikandar Lodi abolished the *zakat* on grain and it was not renewed by any subsequent sultan.

The question of *jizya* is even more complex, not only because of the lack of clarity in the contemporary records but also because of

the strong emotional reaction that has been aroused in discussion concerning it. Under Islamic law, *jizya* was a tax levied on non-Muslims. This action can be interpreted as an equitable arrangement, since only Muslims had to pay *zakat;* and, in addition, they alone were liable to military service. From this point of view it was, in the words of a modern historian, a poll tax levied on non-Muslims "in return for which they received protection of life and property, and exemption for military service." [8] In the Quran *jizya* is used in the same sense as *kharaj,* meaning simply a tax, and the fact that early Muslim writers in India preserve this usage without attaching any technical significance to the term suggests that it was not levied during the first conquests. However it was later levied as a poll tax. As such it was borrowed from Persia, where it was called *gezit*. The failure of the historians to indicate when *jizya* was paid cannot be taken as an indication, as has been sometimes suggested, that some rulers, notably Ala-ud-din, did not levy *jizya* because they refused to accord the Hindus the status of zimmis, or protected peoples.[9] The reason *jizya* is not more definitely mentioned in the records is probably that for the sake of convenience in rural areas, where the population was overwhelmingly Hindu, *jizya* and *kharaj,* the land tax, were realized as a consolidated tax. In the early days of the sultanate the rulers had not built up an elaborate organization, and tax farming—through Hindu middlemen—was the normal means of recovery. It appears unlikely that apart from a comprehensive demand made on a village or a territory, separate or specific realization of *jizya* was feasible. Where *jizya* was recovered it was charged in three categories. The wealthy paid four dinars per head per annum, the middle groups two dinars, and the poor, one dinar.[10] Women, children, and those on a bare subsistence level were excused.

Nothing better illustrates the practical approach of the early Muslim rulers to administrative problems than the cautious evolution of their coinage system. Muhammad Ghuri has usually been pictured as an ardent Muslim, zealous in the destruction of Hindu idols and the estab-

[8] Sir Thomas Arnold in *Cambridge Medieval History* (Cambridge, 1936), IV, 287.
[9] Reuben Levy, *The Social Structure of Islam* (Cambridge, 1957), p. 406.
[10] Qureshi, p. 97.

lishment of Islamic religion. Yet of the three of his coins which are extant, two are mere imitations of earlier Hindu coins, with even the figure of the goddess Lakshmi reproduced, the only distinguishing element being the sovereign's name inscribed in Indian characters. The third coin, though based on the dinar of the Muslim countries, bears a Devanagri legend and the figure of a horseman, much in the tradition of the Hindu coins. This evidence suggests that Muslim rulers, faced with the problem of establishing a new currency among a people unacquainted with the Muslim coinage system, much less with Arabic, disturbed existing usages and practices as little as possible. Not until sixty years after the conquest of Delhi did Balban finally complete the process, begun by Iltutmish, of replacing the Hindu device of the bull and horseman with the sovereign's name in Devanagari characters.

In the early days of the sultanate, the jital, an adaptation of the old dehliwala current before Muslim rule, was the token coin in use. Iltutmish introduced the silver tankah (which was replaced by the rupiah of Sher Shah and Akbar), but even this innovation, in addition to its indigenous name, was linked to an Indian weight standard. Once the monetary system was established, the rulers introduced changes and improvements in the designs and legends of their coins and made them approximate to the normal Muslim coinage in legend and appearance. Apart from Muhammad Tughluq's unsuccessful effort to introduce token currency of mixed metals, the coins were made of pure metal and the state took precautions to maintain their purity and weight.

The Army

An effective army was a vital feature of the administrative structure of the Islamic state in India; it is significant that Fakhr-i-Mudabbir's book on government was largely a war manual. Good generalship, disciplined troops, and sound knowledge of warfare techniques had been responsible for the conquest of India, and the ablest of the sultans were aware that continuance of power depended upon these same factors.

The steps taken by Balban to keep his troops in good trim and by Ala-ud-din Khalji to raise and maintain a large standing army, have been described by Barani. The cavalry was the backbone of the army, but the sultans did not confine their organization to the traditional pattern. They soon began to employ elephants on an extensive scale, and Balban considered a single war elephant to be as effective in battle as five hundred horsemen. The foot-soldiers (payaks) were mainly Hindus of the lower classes. The military grades were organized on a decimal basis: a sar-i-khail had ten horsemen under him; a sipah salar commanded ten sar-i-khails; an amir ten sipah salars; a malik ten amirs; and a khan ten maliks.[11]

The use of naphtha and Greek fire was known from early times. Incendiary arrows and javelins as well as pots of combustibles were hurled against the enemy. The Delhi army used grenades, fireworks, and rockets against Timur, but although there are references to a crude form of cannon, and in the provincial kingdoms of Gujarat and the Deccan this weapon was properly developed, the sultanate of Delhi had not made much progress in the use of artillery. It was the neglect of this weapon which turned the scales against the Delhi forces in the battle of Panipat in 1526.

For maintaining the army, the important functionary within the central government was the ariz. Although Fakhr-i-Mudabbir, writing at the beginning of the sultanate, does not emphasize the office of ariz, possibly because it was directly under the wazir, by the time of Balban the position was independent of the wizarat. With the expansion of the empire and the growth of the military side of the government, the importance of the ariz increased. Not only did he function sometimes as the general of the forces, but he also acted as the chief recruiting officer and fixed the salary of each recruit. The commissariat was under him, and his office, diwan-i-arz, disbursed salaries to the troops. Even the poet Amir Khusrau and the other court officials who held a military rank received salaries from this office. Thus already under the sultanate we can see the beginnings of the Mughal system of placing all public servants on the army pay-list and giving them mansabs. The ariz-i-mumalik was not the commander-in-chief,

[11] Qureshi, p. 153.

or even the senior general—the sultan named the generals for different campaigns—but it is not difficult to see in contemporary accounts the power and the importance of the head of the diwan-i-arz. Jalal-ud-din Khalji held this post before he ascended the throne, and the part played by Shaikh Farid, who held the corresponding position of mir bakhshi under Akbar, in securing the accession of Jahangir is well known.

Justice

The administration of justice received attention quite early in the sultanate, and here as elsewhere traditional Islamic practice was modified to suit the peculiar problems of India. Four types of courts were normally recognized in Islamic society: the diwan-i-mazalim, the court of complaints, presided over by the ruler or his representative; the qazi's court, which administered the Holy Law of Islam; the courts of the muhtasib, or censor, which dealt with public morals and offenses against religious ordinances; and the shurta, or police courts. In India the third type of court gained in power and prestige under the Tughluqs, and later under Aurangzeb.

The first important judicial dignitary of the sultanate at Delhi to whom a reference is found in contemporary records was the amir-i-dad, or chief magistrate. He was a layman, and the office was usually reserved for a leading noble with special aptitude for judicial work. Fakhr-i-Mudabbir suggested that only a member of the royal family, or a nobleman known for piety and learning, should be appointed to this post. A large salary was to be paid to him, as he might have to try complaints against governors and high commanders. In the absence of the sultan, who functioned as supreme judge throughout Muslim rule, the amir-i-dad presided over the court of complaints, but his office had many other functions. He controlled the police, was responsible for public works, including the maintenance of the city walls, kept copies of documents registered with the qazi, and forbade covenants which transgressed the law.[12] If he felt that there had been a miscarriage of justice he could either draw the attention of the qazi

[12] Qureshi, p. 162.

to the fact or delay the execution of the decision until the matter was reconsidered by a fuller or a higher court; he also ordered the arrest of criminals, dealt with breaches of law, and tried cases, where necessary with the assistance of a qazi who functioned as a legal adviser.

While the system of dispensation of justice by the sultan or his representative continued, administration of justice by the qazis grew in importance and became a prominent feature of the Tughluq rule. The main concern of the qazi was civil disputes among Muslims, although later his jurisdiction was widened to include the supervision and management of the property of orphans and lunatics. Appointed by the central government, he was completely independent of the provincial governors. The office of the qazi-i-mumalik, or chief judge, was normally held by the head of the ecclesiastical department, who was generally known as the sadr-i-jahan. It is not certain whether he heard appeals against the judgments of the qazis. He was also the sultan's legal adviser in matters relating to shariat, the holy law of Islam. With the monarch retaining the powers of appointment of the chief qazi, though the enlightened opinion and books on Muslim statecraft emphasize the importance of appointing only honest, pious, and well-qualified qazis in the realm, the sultan had the final say in the framing of the judicial structure. Public opinion was critical of the appointment of chief qazis for considerations other than those of merit, and most of the kings took steps to uphold the prestige of the judiciary. The manner in which on one occasion Muhammad Tughluq appeared like an ordinary plaintiff in the court of a qazi and saluted him may be nothing more than a theatrical gesture, but such episodes built up the prestige of the courts and enabled the general public and the legal profession to realize what was expected of the judges. Although under a despotic monarchy there were obvious limitations to the role which an individual could play, the jurists generally acted with courage and independence. When Jalal-ud-din Khalji wanted Sayyid Maula, who was accused of high treason, to vindicate himself by walking through fire, the jurists vetoed the idea by contending that fire did not distinguish between the innocent and the guilty. The sultan bowed to their decision, though he later connived at Sayyid's murder. Similarly, in spite of Ala-ud-din Khalji's reputation for ruthlessness,

Qazi Mughis-ud-din did not fail to criticize his actions, and in spite of this condemnation, he rewarded the qazi. The sanctity attached to the office of qazi, as an expert in Islamic law, and the pressure of public opinion, encouraged an honest and independent judiciary, the need for which was universally recognized.

An important development during the sultanate was the crystallization of the Indo-Muslim legal tradition. The first important figure in the legal history of the Delhi Sultanate was Sayyid Nur-ud-din Mubarik, originally of Ghazni (d.1234). He was held in high regard by Sultan Muhammad Ghuri, and he maintained his position even though he was extremely critical of court etiquette and the mode of living adopted by Muslim rulers. He wanted Iltutmish to deal firmly with non-Muslims, and he condemned not only all heresy but also the study of philosophy. Barani often puts some of his own ideas in the discourses which he attributes to important personalities, but the puritanical, ascetic approach which he attributes to Nur-ud-Din Mubarik appears typical of the early days of Muslim India, when simplicity and piety found favor with the jurists and the ruling monarch.

A different type of personality, and one whose policy left a great mark on the history of Islamic law in India, was Qazi Minhaj-us-Siraj, the most important historian of the Slave dynasty. A native of Ghazni, he came to the subcontinent during the reign of Iltutmish and received many important assignments. In the days of Iltutmish's successors, including Nasir-ud-din Mahmud, he held the important office of the chief qazi of the realm. It is said that the *sama* (ecstatic dances performed by groups similar to the "whirling dervishes") to which most orthodox lawyers objected, became prevalent in Delhi when Minhaj was qazi. A contemporary of Minhaj thought that he was not fit to be a qazi, but should have been the principal Sufi shaikh. These statements give a clue to his policies, for as he himself has recorded, he was so unpopular with other ecclesiastics that once they even attempted to have him assassinated.[13]

In the light of these observations it is reasonable to infer that Minhaj was not rigid in the application of Islamic law, and that his

[13] Elliot and Dowson, II, 342.

long tenure as chief qazi contributed toward the evolution of a suitable *modus operandi* for the new Muslim government. His views on Islamic law in fact appear to have been in agreement with those of Balban. Although personally punctilious in his religious observations, and careful about showing formal courtesy to religious leaders, Balban attached no importance to the views of ulama in political and administrative matters. He used to say that these things had to be decided in accordance with political considerations and not the views of jurists. According to Barani, "he would order whatever he considered to be in the interest of the realm, whether it was or was not sanctioned by Islamic law." Balban's practice and Minhaj's theory united to provide the flexibility needed by Islamic law if it were to operate in the peculiar conditions created by the existence of a tiny Muslim ruling class and a vast Hindu populace. The tradition of strong common sense and a realistic approach to problems built up by Minhaj was maintained by his daughter's son, Sadr-ud-din Arif, who was a deputy to the chief qazi for a long time, and whom Ala-ud-din Khalji promoted early in his reign. According to Barani he was not distinguished for scholarship, but he was a strong executive officer who understood the temperament of the people, so that "in spite of the freed slaves who overran Delhi, it was not possible for anyone to resort to swindling, deception, or trickery before his court." [14]

The man who most directly influenced the course of Indo-Muslim legal history was not a high official, as was Minhaj, but a scholar who introduced the systematic study of Islamic law into India. This was Maulana Burhan-ud-din, who brought with him to India from Balkh the *Hidaya,* the great legal textbook. This remained the basis of Muslim law for centuries, and was finally translated into English by officials of the East India Company. So great was Burhan-ud-din's reputation as a teacher that Balban, accompanied by his entire royal retinue, visited him after Friday prayers. Despite his orthodoxy, he was not particularly rigid in his application of Islamic law. On the crucial question of *sama,* the ecstatic dances, which remained the major legal controversy of the day and generally provided the divid-

[14] Ziya-ud-din Barani, *Tarikh-i-Firuz Shahi,* edited by S. A. Khan (Calcutta, 1862), p. 351.

ing line between the mystics and the ecclesiasts, his practice was not different from that of the more tolerant Minhaj. "I have not committed any major sin in life," he said, "except hearing of *sama,* which I have heard and want to hear again, if I have an opportunity." [15] The popularity of *Hidaya* and other textbooks from Central Asia ensured that in legal affairs, as in much else, Muslim India followed the traditions of Central Asia. These books, which were brought to India mainly by refugees during Balban's reign, were in Arabic. With the efforts made by Firuz Tughluq to run the government according to Islamic law, it became necessary to have summaries and abstracts of Islamic law in Persian, the court language of Muslim India. We accordingly see a large number of manuals prepared in his reign, usually based on the compilations of the lawyers of Central Asia. In addition more substantial efforts for compilation of books on Islamic law in Persian and Arabic were made. The earliest of such compilations prepared in India was in the time of Balban and was dedicated to him. Others were prepared during the Tughluq period but the most comprehensive digest compiled in Muslim India prior to the compilation of *Fatawa-i-Alamgiri* in Aurangzeb's reign was the *Fatawa-i-Tatar Khania,* named after the pious nobleman, Tatar Khan, who sponsored the compilation. Prepared by a committee of ulama it consisted of thirty volumes. It attracted attention ouside the subcontinent, and a summary was prepared by Shaikh Ibrahim, the imam of the mosque of the Ottoman sultan, Muhammad the Conqueror, in Istanbul.

Provincial Administration

Although contemporary historians give meager details about the provincial governments, it seems a fair inference that the provincial administrative structure did not crystallize until the days of Sher Shah and Akbar. It is possible that this development was facilitated by the establishment of regional kingdoms in the original *iqtas* (regions) of the Delhi Sultanate. From the earliest period governors were appointed for large *iqtas* which later became provinces, but their respon-

[15] Hasan Sijzi, *Fawaid-ul-Fawad* (Lucknow, 1885), p. 239.

sibilities were mainly the maintenance of peace, establishment and extension of the authority of the government, and recovery of tribute from the Hindu chiefs and others. The observance of state laws and the maintenance of order depended on the ability and the interest of the individual governor, and in some areas their authority must have been confined to main centers of administration and places easily accessible. The provincial boundaries were shifting and vague, and it was a long time before the territorial units took a stable form. Even the powers of all the governors were not identical. Governors in charge of bigger or more important areas or with special personal claims exercised wider powers than ordinary muqtis and were referred to as walis.

Before Balban's time, the governors were often semi-independent military chiefs of the territories conquered by them or by their ancestors, but even then many functions remained outside their domain. They were not given authority in religious and judicial affairs, nor were the local intelligence officers under their control. The governor's main concern was military control and revenue collection. With Balban the wizarat became more organized at the center and the provincial diwans were posted from Delhi, and a close check was exercised by the central government over the recovery and transmission of revenue. The provincial sahib-i-diwan was appointed by the sultan on the recommendation of the wazir, and submitted detailed statements of provincial accounts to the capital. On the basis of these statements the wazir's department settled the accounts with the muqtis. Even in the military sphere the powers of the provincial governors came to be regulated by the presence of the provincial ariz who was under the chief ariz at Delhi.

Balban had asserted the authority of the central government over the provincial chiefs, and Ala-ud-din Khalji tried to introduce system and uniformity in the administration of the Doab (the fertile area between the Ganges and the Jamna), the most dependable source of state revenue. Ghiyas-ud-din Tughluq, who had a long experience of provincial administration in the Punjab, tried to improve the administration, but details of his provincial administration have not been recorded. Under his son, Muhammad Tughluq, we get details of the hierarchy of provincial officials, and this possibly follows a pattern

introduced earlier. The empire consisted of twenty-four provinces divided into a number of *shiqs,* or rural districts. The next smallest unit after the *shiq* was the *pargana,* or group of villages. In a *pargana* and in the villages the old Hindu organization continued. The head of each *pargana* was a chaudhari, while a muqaddam or a mukhiya was the head man of the village. The most important feature of Muslim administration in India was the acceptance of the local autonomy enjoyed by rural areas. This policy had been followed by Muhammad ibn Qasim in the earliest days of Muslim rule in the Sind and was maintained by the sultans of Delhi. Qutb-ud-din Aibak, who originally handed back Ajmer to a son of Prithvi Raj, first adopted the policy of appointing Hindu officers for the administration of the country. "The Hindu chief played such an important role in the rural life of the period that to many he was the government, whereas the sultan was almost a mythical figure." [16]

The position of the nobility and the officers was so dominant in the early period that Minhaj, the historian of the period, devotes more space to an account of the principal officers of the realm than to the sultans. The existence of this bureaucracy made possible a large degree of stability in administration, and even in the periods of decline the succession of dynasties at Delhi was not usually reflected in changes of government at the local level.

Emphasis on administrative stability during the sultanate should not be taken as an indication that the period was peaceful or that normal judicial processes were always respected by either the sultans or their officials. Maintenance of control in a conquered area requires force, and, in addition, the ceaseless struggle for power that went on made violence commonplace. The smallest incident could be turned into a pretext for the drawing of the sword and the shedding of blood. Nor was violence confined to the cruel and heartless. Rulers such as Balban were not deficient in a sense of justice or in political ability, but these qualities did not deter him from severe punishments and free spilling of blood. At times a sense of justice and concern for the public welfare seemed to militate against human kindness. Once the deterrent theory of punishment was adopted and carried to extremes, all other human considerations gave way before it. In vain

[16] Qureshi, p. 211.

did the religious lawyers and intellectuals try to curb the extreme punishments inflicted by the sultans. Qazi Mughis argued before Ala-ud-din Khalji that his punishments were unauthorized and opposed to Islam, and the historian Barani told Muhammad bin Tughluq that human life could be taken only for eight specific crimes, but the autocratic sultans listened unmoved.

Not only was human life held in little esteem, but there were abhorrent cases of torture and mutilation. In this Muhammad bin Tughluq, who was a highly educated monarch and enjoyed the company of intellectuals and philosophers, was the worst offender. Some of the punishments meted out by him—for example to his cousin Gurshashp —are truly revolting. The Moorish traveler Ibn Battuta wrote of him: "Notwithstanding all his modesty, his sense of equality and justice, and his extraordinary liberality and kindness to the poor, he had immense daring to shed blood. His gate was hardly ever free from the corpse of a man who had been executed. And I used to see frequently a number of people killed at the gate of the royal palace and the corpses abandoned there. . . . The sultan used to punish all wrongs whether big or small and he would spare neither the men of learning and probity, nor those of high descent. Every day hundreds of people in chains with their hands fastened to the neck and their feet tightened were brought into the council hall. Those who were to be killed were killed and those who were to be tortured were tortured and those who were to be beaten were beaten. . . . May God save us calamity." [17]

It is true that these punishments were reserved for treason, and it is also true that conditions in the medieval ages in other parts of the world were not very much better, but the position in Muslim India in this respect seems to have worsened distinctly during the hundred years or so following the death of Iltutmish. Possibly the instances of brutality and cruelty during the sultanate in the thirteenth and fourteenth centuries reflect the impact of the Mongols; certainly the extremes of ruthless severity associated with Muhammad Tughluq or even with Balban and Ala-ud-din Khalji, did not exist in the days of Muhammad ibn Qasim, Aibak, and Iltutmish.

[17] Mahdi Husain, *The Rehla of Ibn Battuta* (Baroda, 1953), p. 85.

VIII. Society and Culture under the Sultanate

WHILE the historians of the Delhi Sultanate have left full accounts that make possible a reconstruction of military and political affairs, unfortunately no such records exist for social and economic history. Scattered comments in the histories, however, as well as such works as the *Travels* of Ibn Battuta, the narrative poems of Amir Khusrau, and the table talk of Hazrat Nizam-ud-din, illuminate the social life of the time.

Muslim society during the period was dominated by the Turkish rulers and nobles who sought to maintain their position not only against non-Muslims or the Muslims of indigenous origin, but also against other non-Turkish immigrants or over other Turks whose long separation from the Turkish homeland marked them off themselves. It can be argued that most of the sultans and nobles were ultimately Turkish in origin, even though they bear different designations, but the first hundred years of the Delhi Sultanate was clearly a period of Turkish supremacy: rule by groups that regarded themselves as Turks, and heirs of a definite cultural and historical tradition. During this time they produced not only three great rulers, Iltutmish, Ala-ud-din Khalji, and Balban, but also a great poet—Amir Khusrau.

One of the most interesting features of Islamic society during the sultanate is the long struggle of Indian Muslims—Hindu and Buddhist converts or their descendants—to assert themselves. They tried to gain power in the middle of the thirteenth century, but Balban and other Turkish nobles were too powerful for them. Their position gradually improved under the Khaljis, and under the Tughluqs a distinct change can be seen. Ghiyas-ud-din Tughluq had an Indian mother, Muhammed Tughluq appointed a Hindu as the governor of Upper Sind, and the dominant personality of the reign of Firuz Tughluq was Khan-i-Jahan, a Hindu convert from Telingana.

Although it took a long time for the Indo-Muslims to reach posi-

tions of power, local usages and customs influenced social life and behavior at an early period. The Indian *pan* (betel leaf) soon became popular among the Muslims; the use of spices for seasoning food became common; and standard Muslim dishes such as *pilau* were transformed. The newcomers also adopted Indian headgear; but, more significantly, religious ceremonies, especially those related to marriage and death, showed a definite Indian influence. The popularity of music, as well as its forms, reflected the local atmosphere.

The lives of Muslim upper classes, especially in Delhi, were modeled on those of their Turkish and Persian counterparts, with the sports of a society that valued the horse—polo, riding, racing—being the chief outdoor amusements; these were the prerogatives of the rich. All classes enjoyed chess and backgammon, although the more orthodox regarded them with disapproval. Most of the Muslims, at least during the earliest period of the sultanate, were city dwellers, many of them attached to the garrisons. For this reason there was a good deal of communal life among the ordinary people. There were, for example, bakeries instead of individual kitchens, and *hammans* (Turkish baths) in the larger towns.

As for the Hindus, their social life was relatively unchanged, although during military operations they suffered losses in property and life. Even when the harsh laws of war gave place to peace, the Hindus were burdened by certain handicaps. The loss of sovereignty itself was a major loss, especially in the case of the Brahmans and the Kshatriyas. The sultanate period was more difficult for them than any other period of Muslim rule. The liberal and conciliatory policy adopted by Muhammad ibn Qasim had given place to a new relationship, and the integration of the Hindu population into the political and administrative structure was not to come about until later. Muslim conquest of Sind and Multan and even of Lahore and Peshawar had not led to the same tensions and conflicts which followed their domination over the heart of Aryavarta. Even the indirect effect of the Mongol invasion of Muslim lands led to a stiffening of attitude, as the Muslim refugees, who had suffered so much at the hands of the pagan Mongols, were not disposed to be friendly towards the non-Muslims of India.

All these factors make the sultanate a period of tensions and conflicts. The theory of Turkish racial superiority which held sway during the rule of early Slave kings was not favorable to the employment of Hindus—or even indigenous Muslims—in high civil and military appointments, as was the case under the Arabs in Sind or even under the Ghaznavids. It would, however, be wrong to think that the Hindus were completely excluded from service. In rural areas the Hindu landed aristocracy still occupied a position of prestige and power, and the muqqadams, the chaudharis and the khuts had important roles in the administration. The land system was not altered, and the Hindu peasant must have led much the same kind of life as he did before the coming of the Muslims. Trade and commerce also remained in Hindu control, for to the Muslim invader from Central Asia, the complex Hindu banking system would be unfamiliar and unworkable. The Hindu merchant might be heavily assessed, or, during a war have his movable goods confiscated, but he was too much a part of the intricate commercial structure to be easily replaced. The money lender thrived under the new, as under the old, dispensation. We hear, for example, about the large incomes of the Muslim grandees and the splendor of their households, but Barani leaves us in no doubt that most, if not all, borrowed from the Hindu money lenders. "The maliks and the khans and the nobles of those days were constantly in debt, owing to their excessive generosity, expenditures, and beneficence. Except in their public halls no gold or silver could be found, and they had no savings on account of their excessive liberality. The wealth and riches of the Multani merchants and the shahs [money lenders] were from the interest realized from the old maliks and nobles of Delhi, who borrowed money from them to the maximum limit, and repaid their debts along with additional gifts from their [lands]. Whenever a malik or a khan held a banquet and invited notables, his agents would rush to the Multanis and shahs, sign documents, and borrow money with interest." [1] That the money lenders recovered their money along with interest (forbidden under Islamic law), is an

[1] Ziya-ud-din Barani, *Tarikh-i-Firuz Shahi,* edited by S. A. Khan (Calcutta, 1862), pp. 210. For a general discussion of social life, see K. M. Asraf, *Life and Condition of the People of Hindustan* (Delhi, 1959).

indication of how vital they were to the system. Even the powerful Ala-ud-din Khalji who, seeing the danger to his government from the power of the Hindu rural chiefs, made a determined attempt to curb their power and reduce their wealth, found it necessary to make Hindu traders the main instrument of his price control measures.[2]

Industry and Trade

Hindus occupied an important role in foreign, as in domestic trade, although foreign Muslim merchants, known as khurasani, also had a large share of it. The rulers of the coastal kingdoms in the Deccan accorded to foreign merchants certain extra-territorial rights and special concessions in consideration of the heavy taxes which they paid to the treasury. An organized class of brokers handled the business on the coast and inside the country. The imports consisted mainly of certain luxury items for the upper classes and a general supply of all kinds of horses and mules, in which India was deficient. Hindus had never attached any importance to cavalry, but seeing the success of the Muslim horsemen, they started to substitute horses for elephants. The exports included large quantities of food-grains and cloth. Among the agricultural products were wheat, millet, rice, pulses, oilseeds, scents, medicinal herbs, and sugar. Some of the countries around the Persian Gulf depended on the subcontinent for their entire food supply. Cotton cloth and other textiles were especially important items of export, particularly to Southeast Asia and East Africa, although some reached Europe. They were carried by the Arabs to the Red Sea and from there found their way to Damascus and Alexandria, from where they were distributed to the Mediterranean countries and beyond.

Many industries of considerable size and importance developed during this period, the most important of which were textiles, various items of metal work, sugar, indigo, and in certain localities, paper. The Indian textile industry is very old but the variety of cloth produced was originally limited. Taking advantage of the local talent, the

[2] I. H. Qureshi, *The Administration of the Sultanate of Delhi* (Karachi, 1958), p. 226.

Muslims introduced a number of fine varieties of textiles, most of which had Persian or Arabic origin. Bengal was the main center of this industry, but Gujarat rivaled it as a supplier of the export trade during the sultanate period.

Next in importance were a number of industries connected with metal work: the manufacture of swords, guns, and knives, as well as household needs such as trays and basins. Manufacture of sugar was also carried on on a fairly large scale and in Bengal enough was produced to leave a surplus for export after meeting the local demand. Paper-making was a minor industry of which little is known except that Delhi was the center of a considerable market.

These industries were mainly privately owned, but the government equipped and managed large-scale *karkhanas,* or factories, for supplying its requirements. The royal factories at Delhi sometimes employed as many as four thousand weavers for silk alone. The example of the sultan of Delhi was followed by the rulers of the regional kingdoms, and the contribution of the state to the development of the industry was not a minor one.

In certain aspects of social life, the Hindus had virtual autonomy during the sultanate. This was in accordance with the established axiom of Islamic law that while Muslims are governed by the *Shariat,* non-Muslim zimmis are subject to their own laws and social organization, but it was also a product of the Indian situation. The Muslim rulers from the days of the Arab occupation of Sind accepted the right of the village and caste panchavats to settle the affairs of their community. This meant that the Hindu villages remained small autonomous republics, as they had been since ancient times, and in commerce and industry the Hindu guilds were supreme. This position continued throughout the Muslim rule, but during the sultanate, when the provincial administration had not been properly organized, Hindu autonomy outside the principal towns was particularly effective.

It is often forgotten—and Muslim court chroniclers were not anxious to mention it—that a large number of independent or quasi-independent Hindu chiefs remained after the establishment of the sultanate. Some of them were rajas, or kings; others were only petty chieftains, controlling a few villages. Many of them belonged to old

families, but new principalities grew up even after the establishment of Muslim power at Delhi. Rajputs often found new kingdoms for themselves in remote, easily defended areas in Rajputana and the Himalayas. From such movements during the sultanate come also some of the large landed estates still held by Rajputs in Oudh and in Bihar. In these predominantly Hindu areas the old religion was fostered, and its cultural expressions kept alive even in the periods of greatest Islamic power.

Learning, Literature, and the Arts

After the sack of Baghdad in 1258 Delhi was perhaps the most important cultural center in the Muslim East. Heir to the traditions of Ghazni and Lahore, its importance increased when the Mongols destroyed the cultural centers of Central and Western Asia, and the poets, scholars and men of letters from these areas took refuge in Muslim India. Balban, who gave high offices of the state only to persons of good families, welcomed these distinguished refugees, and many illustrious families of Muslim India trace their origin to this period. This influx bore fruit in a large number of works, many of which are lost, but the contemporary historians attest to their worth. During the reign (1296–1316) of Ala-ud-din Khalji the general prosperity engendered by his conquests enabled the nobles, and not just the sultan, to become literary patrons. This probably explains why Barani could devote fourteen pages to an account of the scholars, poets, preachers, philosophers, physicians, astronomers, and historians who thronged Delhi in the days of Ala-ud-din Khalji. If the surviving poetry of Khusrau, the historical works of Barani, and the table talk of Hazrat Nizam-ud-din Auliya are any indication of the cultural vitality and richness of the age, one can well understand why Amir Khusrau and others felt that Delhi was the metropolis of the Muslim East.

Yet despite the cultural eminence of the capital, it cannot be claimed that the sultanate is a period marked by that solid scholarship and study of sciences which distinguished Baghdad and Cordova. The reason is obvious. Learned and gifted men had come to India, but

without their libraries. Those who were escaping with their lives could not be expected to carry heavy loads of books over long distances. We get a glimpse of this in the case of Fakhr-i-Mudabbir, who fled from Ghazni without even his family papers, and had to wait for an opportunity to go back to reclaim them. The result was that only those cultural activities gained prominence which, like poetry, *belles-lettres,* local history, architecture, and music, were not dependent on accumulated stores of knowledge.

Probably for the same reason—the lack of libraries—great educational institutions of the kind found in Baghdad and Cairo did not develop in India. There were, however, schools and colleges in Delhi and all the important provincial capitals.

In Muslim society, teaching and the promotion of educational enterprises are regarded as necessary marks of religious vocation, and the Muslim state is expected to facilitate this by providing teachers with ample means of subsistence. This was the procedure generally adopted during Muslim rule in India, and the official in charge of religious endowments, the sadr-i-jahan, arranged for the grant of tax-free lands to imams, qazis, and other religious groups who provided education, particularly in Islamic subjects. This education was usually on the elementary level, but the system also provided for the maintenance of scholars who had specialized in different branches of learning. We find even nobles and distinguished men of affairs teaching subjects in which they had become proficient. Hazrat Nizam-ud-din Auliya, for example, studied under Shams-ul-Mulk, who became the wazir of Balban. The children of nobles were taught at their own residences by private tutors, whose guidance was often available for other students also.

For advanced students *madrasas,* or colleges, were set up by pious and public-spirited rulers, and this activity received special attention during the early period. Two major *madrasas* called Muizziya and Nasiriya were established during the beginning of Muslim rule at Delhi. Details about these *madrasas* are lacking, but probably one of them was the college built by Iltutmish and repaired a century later by Firuz Tughluq. Similar steps to establish educational institutions were taken by Muslim rulers in the distant provinces, and we read

of Muhammad Bakhtiyar Khalji setting up *madrasas* at Devkot and other places in Bengal. Firuz Tughluq was unusual in that he looked after the institutions established by his predecessors; probably most of these establishments fell into decay when the original founders passed away, and the grants made for the *madrasas* were diverted to other purposes.

Historians give little information about the staff or the curriculum of *madrasas,* but some details are available for one founded by Firuz Tughluq near Hauz-i-Alai in Delhi. Barani has given a lengthy account of the beautiful building and gardens which provided a center around which people built their houses. Both Barani and Mutahar, a well-known poet, praise the comprehensive knowledge of Maulana Jala-ud-din Rumi, the head of the institution. The main subjects taught seem to have been religious—*tafsir* (interpretation of the Quran), *hadith* (tradition), and *fiqh* (jurisprudence).

The intellectual activity of the schools owed much to the refugee scholars from Central Asia, Persia, and Iraq who came to Delhi in the thirteenth century. After this influx had ceased and the Mongols had established their rule in the northwestern borderland, communication between Central Asia and northern India became difficult. It appears that in the Deccan, where contact was maintained with Iran by the sea route, intellectual activity during the later centuries encompassed a wider range than was the position in the north. In northern India, apart from religious subjects, literature, history, mysticism, and ethics were the principal subjects studied. In the Deccan, scientific subjects also received attention. The great Bahmani king, Firuz (1397–1422), for example, encouraged botany, geometry, and logic. He was interested also in astronomy, and in 1407 started work on an observatory near Daulatabad. The untimely death of Hakim Hashim Gilani, the astronomer who was to supervise the observatory, put an end to the project. When Sayyid Gisu Daraz, who has left a large number of books on mysticism and who was famous for his knowledge of religious subjects, reached the Deccan, Firuz went to meet him. The historian Firishta records that the sultan found the saint lacking in solid scholarship, and made no secret of his disappointment. The fact that Firuz was not alone in intellectual pursuits is evident from the

account of a prince who used to teach students mathematics (including Euclid), theology, and rhetoric.[3] Promotion of learning in the Deccan was largely the work of Persian statesmen and scholars whom the rulers had attracted from Iran, and an interesting monument to the age is the ruined college of the Bahmani minister, Mahmud Gawan, in Bidar. It was a magnificent building, as can be seen from its beautiful minarets and facade, but it was badly damaged during the wars of the Deccan kings with Aurangzeb.

The one scientific subject that received considerable attention in the schools was medicine. The earliest work on medicine, of which an imperfect manuscript copy has survived, was written about 1329 in the reign of Muhammad bin Tughluq. Its author Zia Muhammad, went to the Deccan under the orders of the sultan. His book, *Majmua-i-ziai,* based on Arabic and Indian sources, gives local counterparts for Arabian medicines as well as the prescriptions of Hindu physicians. Following this work, other writers combined Greek and Indian works. The history of Indo-Islamic medicine has not yet been carefully studied, but it is reasonably certain that in the books written in India during the sultanate one sees the blending of the three streams of Greek, Arabic, and Hindu medical knowledge. The most famous of these works is the *Tibh-i-Sikandari,* written by the court physician Mian Bhuwa about 1512. It draws freely on the classical Sanskrit writers, and it long remained a standard textbook for followers of the indigenous medical systems.

Of the purely literary works of the early period, very few have survived. This is especially true of poetry, for barring the works of major poets like Amir Khusrau and Hasan, only those poems have been preserved which, because of their topical nature were included in general histories. Examples are the poems of Sangreza on the arrival of Iltutmish's patent of sovereignty from the Abbasid caliphate and his verses on the accession of Iltutmish's son or Ruhani's poem on Iltutmish's conquest of Ranthambhor. While these poems have the usual limitations of occasional poetry, they indicate high poetic skill.

The early men of letters represented a trans-Indus tradition. Most

[3] N. N. Law, *Promotion of Learning in India during Muhammadan Rule* (London, 1916), p. 181, n. 1.

of them had received their education beyond the border, and although they had settled down in Islamic India, an indigenous literary tradition was slow in developing. The two most important representatives of the early tradition were Muhammad Aufi and Muhammad bin Mansur Qureshi, generally known as Fakhr-i-Mudabbir. Aufi (c.1172–1242), a native of Bukhara who lived in Lahore and Delhi, was the author of the earliest extant collection of biographies of Persian poets, *Lubab-ul-Albab*. He also completed the voluminous encyclopedia of anecdotes, *Jawami-al-Hikayat,* which, apart from its literary interest, is a mine of curious and interesting information relating to this and earlier periods. The major work of Fakhr-i-Mudabbir, who lived in Lahore at the beginning of the thirteenth century, was a study of statecraft; this has already been discussed in Chapter VII.

The first Persian poet of eminence who was born in India was Reza, or, as he was sometimes known, Sangreza. He was Iltutmish's secretary. The most distinguished writer of the early sultanate, however, was Amir Khusrau (c.1253–1325). His father, a junior Turkish officer under Iltutmish, had married a daughter of Rawat-i-Arz, Balban's famous minister. Khusrau showed literary promise at an early age, and, after spending some time at the provincial court of Oudh, became attached at first to Prince Bughra Khan, the governor of Samana and later of Bengal, and subsequently to Prince Muhammad, the heir-designate of Balban, who maintained a magnificent court at Multan. The prince lost his life in a skirmish with the Mongols in 1285, and the poet went to Delhi. Balban's successor, Kaiqubad, was Khusrau's first royal patron. In all, seven rulers were to be his patrons, but it is doubtful whether he was greatly concerned by the kaleidoscopic changes of royalty.

Apart from lyrics, Khusrau wrote poems relating to contemporary events. *Qiran-us-Saadain,* completed in 1289, gives an account of the historic meeting of Bughra Khan and Kaiqubad on the banks of the river Sarju, and contains an interesting description of the Delhi of those days. *Miftah-ul-Futuh* (1291) is a versified account of the exploits of Jalal-ud-din Firuz Khalji; in *Ashiqa* (1315) is an account of the romance of the Gujarati princess Deval Devi and Prince Khizr Khan, son of Ala-ud-din Khalji. The latter's conquests are the subject

matter of *Khazain-ul-Futuh* (1311), an ornate prose work, while *Nuh Sipihr,* completed in 1318, celebrates the reign of Qutb-ud-din Mubarik Shah. In this book Amir Khusrau challenged the poets of Iran and sang of his native land, its hoary past, its love of learning, its flowers, and its fair, intelligent people. *Tughlaq Nama* describes the successful expedition of Ghiyas-ud-din Tughluq against the usurper Khusrau Khan. Khusrau was also among the earliest writers of Hindi poetry, and though the origins of the Hindi poems attributed to him are doubtful, he referred to his Hindi verses in the introduction to one of his Persian *diwans*. He also played a major role in the development of Indian music, as noted below.

The work of Hassan (c.1252–1337), a friend of Khusrau, was praised by Jami, the great Persian poet, a rare distinction for an Indian writer. He wrote prose as well as verse, and his *Fawaid-ul-Fuad,* a record of the table-talk of his spiritual guide, Nizam-ud-din Auliya, is a literary classic. Equally interesting, though not so well known, was Ziya Nakhshabi (d.1350), who was a master of simple and eloquent prose. His *Tuti Namah* (The Book of the Parrot) was based on a Sanskrit original. It has been translated into Turkish, German, English, and many Indian languages. His other translations include the *Kok Shastra,* a Sanskrit text on erotics.

While there were many distinguished names in poetry, perhaps the most important literary contribution during the sultanate was in the field of history. Since classical Hindu culture produced almost no historical literature, the Muslim works are of special significance for Indian historiography. Written by contemporaries who had taken part in the events they describe, these histories are of enormous value for an understanding of the period. They are marred, however, by certain defects which their very excellence tends to conceal. One is that many of the chronicles were written specifically for certain rulers and nobles whom the historians glorified at the expense of rivals; another is the tendency to picture the conquerors as actuated by unselfish and religious motives. These peculiarities of method can generally be discounted, however, and the historians do not seem to have falsified historical facts even when they were writing panegyrics.

The number of historical works of the sultanate period which have

reached us is not large, but the works possess rich variety. The historians of the period, many of whom have already been mentioned, include Barani, Fakhr-i-Mudabbir, Hasan Nizami, Minhaj-us-Siraj, Aufi, Khusrau, Yahya, and Isami. Most of them occupied high official positions and wrote from personal knowledge. Barani is the most interesting, but he is not very particular about dates (normally the strong point of the Muslim historians), and this detracts from the value of his book, *Tarikh-i-Firuz Shahi*. But he wrote history as an artist, selecting and carefully arranging his material so that his book, instead of being a chronicle of events, emphasized the characteristics of various rulers and different reigns. He does not confine himself to the kings but gives details about the political philosophies of different monarchs and leading men of the times, the literary and the religious history, the prices in the market, and other matters of concern to the ordinary people. Even more interesting is the gallery of portraits which he has brought to life by a skillful analysis of personalities and by providing those significant small details which most Indian historians omit.

As already noted, the rise of regional kingdoms in the fifteenth century played an extremely important role in the dissemination of Islamic culture.[4] One significant feature of this disintegration of the central authority, with its dependence on Persian as the official language, was the rise of regional languages. Hindu kings had given their patronage to Sanskrit as the language of religion and the classics; Muslim rulers felt no such compulsion, and supported the common languages of the people. It was Muslim rulers, therefore, who were responsible for many of the first translations of the Sanskrit classics into the provincial languages. The Muslim rulers of Bengal engaged scholars to translate the *Ramayana* and the *Mahabharata* into Bengali. Maladhar Vasu translated the *Bhagavata Purana* into Bengali under the patronage of Sultan Husain Shah (r. 1493–1518), and Chuti Khan, governor of Chittagong, employed Srikara Nadi to translate parts of the *Asvamedha Parva* of the *Mahabharata* into Bengali. In Kashmir, Hindu literature and philosophy were studied enthusiastically at the court of Zain-ul-Abidin (1420–1470). *Rajatarangini,* one of

4 See p. 79.

the few histories written in Sanskrit, was translated into Persian, with a supplement to bring the account up to date. Other works on music and mathematics were composed by Hindu scholars at the Kashmir court. In the south the Muslim rulers of Golkunda and Bijapur employed Hindus as ministers, and maintained the state records in the Marathi language. Cultural histories of the various provincial governments are yet to be written, but a similar process was at work at all places.

Among the nonliterary arts, music, rather than painting or sculpture, underwent important developments during the period of the sultanate. As already noted, Indian music had made an impact on the Arab systems as early as the conquest of Sind, and the interchange between the two forms was even more fruitful when the rich heritage of Persia and Central Asia was added. The result was the creation in North India of a new type of music, quite different from traditional Indian music, which maintained its hold in South India.

Credit for this important work of synthesis is given to the poet Amir Khusrau, whose fame helped to give prestige to the new music, which had as its rival in the Delhi court the musical modes favored by the Turkish rulers. The interest of the Chishti Sufis in "Hindustani" music and its practical cultivation by them further ensured its popularity. The next stage was reached during the establishment of the independent Muslim kingdom at Jaunpur, not far from Benares and Kanauj, the old centers of Hindu arts. Here music received special attention, both at the royal court and in the Sufi monasteries. The two most important Indian Muslim musicians of the day were Sultan Husain Sharqi, the last king of Jaunpur, and the contemporary saint, Pir Bodhan of Barnawa. The saint's dwelling became a rendezvous for musicians from Delhi, the Deccan, and Jaunpur. The contribution of Sultan Husain to the development of Indian music was much more specific. He is regarded as the original founder of the *khiyal* (or romantic) school of music, which slowly matured and took its final shape in the days of the later Mughals, particularly under Muhammad Shah. Related to a Hindu devotional form that dealt with the love of Krishna for the milkmaids, the *khiyal* transformed the devotional theme to thinly veiled invocations of human love and romance.

Another regional kingdom where music was highly cultivated after the breakdown of the sultanate was Gwalior. Here the ruler, Raja Man Singh (r. 1486–1516), was a Hindu, but the chief musician at his court, Nayak Mahmud, was a Muslim. Under his leadership a band of musicians systematized Indian music in the light of the changes it had undergone since the advent of the Muslims. This resulted in the compilation of *Man Kautuhal,* which contains almost all the airs introduced by the Muslim musicians.[5]

Probably the greatest artistic achievement of the sultanate was neither literature nor music, but architecture. As with the musicians, the creativity of the Muslim architects was nourished by the mature styles of both the existing Islamic and Hindu traditions. The Muslims brought to India the experience gained in the great buildings of Cairo, Baghdad, Cordova, and Damascus, and they were able to draw upon the skill of Indian stonemasons. The result was a profusion of mosques, palaces, and tombs unmatched in any other Islamic country.

In the same year in which Delhi was occupied, the foundation of the mosque of Quwwat-ul-Islam was laid by Qutb-ud-din Aibak to commemorate the capture of Delhi and, as the name implies, to glorify the power of Islam. Aibak however spent most of his brief reign at Lahore, and adornment of the new Muslim capital was essentially the work of his successor, Iltutmish. He more than doubled the size of the Quwwat-ul-Islam mosque, built the Qutb Minar, one of the world's loveliest towers, erected the buildings for Nasiriya Madrasa, and, to meet the needs of the growing population of Delhi for water, excavated the great water reservoir, the Hauz-i-Shamsi. He also changed architectural methods. Previously material from Hindu buildings had been used for constructing mosques, but in 1230, when he extended the Quwwat-ul-Islam mosque, he used stone especially quarried for the purpose. This gave the addition a more Islamic appearance.

In architecture, as in other spheres of culture, the Indo-Islamic society was enriched by the dislocation in Central Asia and Persia caused by the Mongol invasion. Not only scholars but artisans as well came to Delhi as refugees, and they found a ready market for their

[5] S. A. Halim, *Journal of the Asiatic Society of Pakistan,* vol. I (1956).

skills in the expanding Muslim state. One important result was that the indigenous Indian artistic element ceased to be dominant in Delhi during this period. By the time of Ala-ud-din Khalji, Muslim traditions had become firmly established on Indian soil, with the result that methods of construction were revolutionized and ornament became an integral part of the scheme, rather than a quasi-independent accessory, as was the case in the earlier buildings. The Jama'at Khana mosque, constructed in the reign of Ala-ud-din, is the earliest surviving example in India of a mosque built wholly in accordance with Muslim ideas.

In the provincial capitals, however, the influence of the refugee artisans was slight, and the indigenous styles remained important. In Bengal the Muslim rulers decorated their buildings with carving which is obviously the work of Hindu craftsmen, and in Gujarat they adapted the local style to Muslim needs to create some of India's most beautiful buildings. Yet even where most was owed to native Indian skills and tradition, the peculiar Muslim architectural characteristics of spaciousness and graceful forms are present. Furthermore, the Muslims made full use of concrete and mortar, which were known but scarcely used before their arrival in India. "Thanks to the strength of their binding properties, it was possible for the Muslim rulers to span wide spaces with their arches, to roof immense areas with their domes, and in other ways to achieve effects of grandeur such as the Indians had never dreamt of." [6]

The Tughluqs in the fourteenth century introduced a new and austere phase in architecture. Muhammad Tughluq, who shifted his capital from Delhi to Daulatabad, had no interest in the old city. The many buildings erected in Delhi during the reign of his successor Firuz show a severe simplicity, possibly due as much to the need for economy as Firuz's own strict orthodoxy. Hindu influences were reduced to the minimum, and Tughluq buildings are lacking in elegance and refinement. Under the Lodis there reemerged a vigorous and catholic spirit of design, replete with creative energy and imagination.

[6] Sir John Marshall, *Cambridge History of India* (Cambridge, 1928), III, 573.

The explanation is probably that with the conversion of the Mongols to Islam and the reduction of chaos in Central Asia, inspiration from Persia was now available in architecture as in literature. The Lodis were soon replaced by the Mughals, under whom Persian influences became even more dominant.

IX. The Interaction of Islam and Hinduism

AN ASPECT of the cultural life of Islamic India that demands special consideration is the nature of the interaction of faith and practice that took place between Islam and Hinduism. There are, however, a variety of factors involved that make the study of this interaction exceedingly complex and prevent any very assured conclusions being attained. One is simply the lack of evidence, for the religious movements of medieval India have left few records. Then there is the uncertainty at times whether a pattern of behavior and belief in both religions has a common origin in one, or if it grew up independently in both cultures. The intricate question of the relation of Hindu and Islamic mystical movements is an example of this difficulty. Finally, since one is confronted not just with the problem of identifying Islamic influence on Hinduism but also Hindu influences on Islam, it is clear that the process of interaction may be complicated by a double movement. Original Hindu influences, for example, may have passed over into Islam; the movement or process that resulted from this may then in turn influence Hinduism, causing a rather different phenomenon. Mysticism again provides a possible illustration.

The most obvious result of the religious impact of Islam on Hinduism is, of course, the existence of a large Muslim population in India. The view that Islam propagated itself in India through the sword cannot be maintained; aside from other evidence, the very distribution of the Muslim population does not support it. If the spread of Islam had been due to the might of the Muslim kings, one would expect the largest proportion of Muslims in those areas which were the centers of Muslim political power. This, however, is not the case. The percentage of Muslims is low around Delhi, Lucknow, Ahmadabad, Ahmadnagar, and Bijapur, the principal seats of Muslim political power. Even in the case of Mysore, where Sultan Tipu is said to have forced conversion to Islam, the ineffectiveness of royal

proselytism may be measured by the fact that Muslims are scarcely 5 percent of the total population of the state. On the other hand, Islam was never a political power in Malabar, yet today Muslims form nearly 30 percent of its total population. In the two areas in which the concentration of Muslims is heaviest—modern East and West Pakistan—there is fairly clear evidence that conversion was the work of Sufis, mystics who migrated to India throughout the period of the sultanate. In the western area the process was facilitated in the thirteenth century by the thousands of Muslim theologians, saints, and missionaries who fled to India to escape the Mongol terror. The names and careers of some of these are well known. Thus Pir Shams Tabriz came to Multan; Khwaja Qutb-ud-din Bakhtiyar went to Delhi; and Syed Jalal settled in Uch, the great fortress south of Multan. The influence of such men, and of many others, can be traced through the families of their spiritual descendants.

In Bengal, the Muslim missionaries found the greatest response to their message among the outcastes and the depressed classes, of which there were large numbers in Bengal. To them, the creed of Islam, with its emphasis on equality, must have come as a liberating force. Then too, the acceptance of the religion of the conquerors would have been a powerful attraction, since it would undoubtedly carry with it possibilities of advancement they had never known before. Another factor in the large number of conversions is the somewhat peculiar religious history of Bengal. From the eighth to the twelfth century the Pala dynasty had supported Buddhism. Then in the twelfth century the Sena dynasty, which had its roots in South India, began to encourage Hindu orthodoxy. The result was probably a good deal of religious unrest and uncertainty, which made it possible for Islam to find an opening for its work of proselytization. When the Islamic missionaries arrived they found in several instances that the conquering armies had destroyed both the temples of revived Hinduism and the monasteries of the older Buddhism; in their place—often on the same sites—they built new shrines. Moreover, they very frequently transferred ancient Hindu and Buddhist stories of miracles to Muslim saints, fusing the old religion into the new on a level that could be accepted by the masses.

By the end of the fourteenth century Islam had permeated all parts of India, and the process was fully under way which led to the conversion of a large section of the Indian population to Islam, and resulted in far-reaching cultural and spiritual changes outside the Muslim society. The developments in the cultural sphere—development of regional languages, the rise of Hindustani, and the evolution of Indo-Muslim music and architecture—have been outlined in the preceding chapter; here an attempt will be made to examine those religious movements which seem to owe something to the interaction of Hinduism and Islam.

The process of interaction is undeniably obscure, and knowledge of many vital links is lacking, but what is certain is that the period was of great importance for the development of the religious and cultural traditions of modern India. The fifteenth century, it has been observed, "was marked by an extraordinary outburst of devotional poetry inspired by these religious movements, and this stands out as one of the great formative periods in the history of northern India, a period in which on the one hand the modern languages were firmly established as vehicles of literary expression, and on the other the faith of the people was permeated by new ideas." [1]

The religious schools and movements which arose in the fifteenth and sixteenth centuries are generally characterized as variants of *bhakti,* or devotional religion, and the influence of Islam has been seen as a determining factor. This understanding of the movements is, however, an oversimplification of a very complex phenomenon. It is important to remember, first of all, that many of the elements associated with the religious movements at the end of the sultanate had already been dominant in Hinduism itself for many centuries. This is especially true of those areas of South India where Muslim influence had not been strong. It is also quite possible that the Islamic mystics, the Sufis, had been directly or indirectly influenced by Hindu thought and institutions before the conquest of India. Hinduism in the fifteenth century, then, was receiving in an elaborated form what it had already given to Islam. But of even greater importance in examining

[1] W. H. Moreland and A. C. Chatterjee, *A Short History of India* (London, 1945), p. 193.

the religious movements of the fourteenth and fifteenth centuries is an awareness of two very different attitudes which Hindu religious leaders had toward Islam. One group accepted what was congenial to it in the new spiritual system; the other group adopted a few elements from the spiritual structure of the dominant race in order to strengthen Hinduism and make it better able to withstand Islam. Both reacted to Islam, but one was sympathetic while the other was hostile. The two trends are similar to the growth of the tolerant, cosmopolitan Brahmo Samaj and the militant Arya Samaj, when Hinduism was confronted with Christianity in the nineteenth century. Kabir, Guru Nanak, Dadu, and other founders of syncretic sects are included in the first group, while the movement in Bengal, associated with Chaitanya, mirrors the latter tendency.

One of the earliest of the religious leaders, and probably the most influential, was Kabir. His dates are uncertain, some scholars giving his birth date as 1398, and some as late as 1440, but it is generally agreed that he flourished in the middle of the fifteenth century. There has also been much controversy concerning his religious origins, but it is quite certain that he was born into a Muslim family. The names of Kabir and Kamal, his son, are both Islamic. According to the popular *Tazkirah-i-Auliya-i-Hind* (Lives of Muslim Saints), he was a disciple of the Muslim Sufi, Shaikh Taqi. A further indication of his Muslim origin is that his grave at Maghar has always been in the keeping of Muslims. But Kabir was above all a religious radical who denounced with equal zest the narrowness of Islamic and Hindu sectarianism. According to one tradition he was a disciple of Ramananda, the great mystic who is credited with the spread of *bhakti* doctrines in North India. That Ramananda himself was influenced by Islam is not certain, but his willingness to admit men of all castes, including Islam, as his disciples, suggests the possibility of this. The right conclusion seems to be that Kabir was a Muslim Sufi who, having come under Ramananda's influence, accepted some Hindu ideas and tried to reconcile Hinduism and Islam. However it was the Hindus, and particularly those of the lower classes, to whom his message appealed.

With many of his works not available for study, and serious doubts

existing about the genuineness of others, it is difficult to assess Kabir properly, but there is no difference of opinion about the general tenor of his writings. He often uses Hindu religious nomenclature, and is equally at home in Hindu and Muslim religious thought, but there is no doubt that one of the most salient features of his teachings is denunciation of polytheism, idolatry, and caste. But he is equally unsparing in his condemnation of Muslim formalism, and he made no distinction between what was sane and holy in the teachings of Hinduism and Islam. He was a true seeker after God, and did his best to break the barriers that separated Hindus from Muslims. What has appealed to the millions of his followers through the ages, however, is his passionate conviction that he had found the pathway to God, a pathway accessible to the lowest as well as the highest. That he has in the course of time become a saint of the Hindus rather than of the Muslims is a reflection of the temper of Hinduism, which finds it easier than Islam to bring new sects and doctrines within its spiritual hegemony.

The second great religious leader whose work shows undoubted Islamic influence is Guru Nanak (1469–1539). The Sikh religion, of which Nanak was the founder, is noted for its militant opposition to Islam, but this is largely a product of historical circumstances in the seventeenth century. Nanak's own aim was to unite both Hindu and Muslim through an appeal to what he considered the great central truths of both. He acknowledged Kabir as his spiritual teacher, and their teachings are very similar. His debt to Islam is shown in his rigorous insistence on the will and majesty of God, while the underlying structure of his thought, with its tendency to postulate a unity that comprehends all things, suggests his Hindu inheritance. Accompanied by two companions, one a Muslim and the other a Hindu, he wandered throughout North India and, according to some accounts, to Arabia, preaching his simple gospel. The followers he gained became, in the course of a century, a separate religious community, but the Sikh scriptures, of which Nanak's sayings provide the core, are a reminder of the attempt to bridge the gap between Hinduism and Islam.

Dadu (1544–1603) was the third of the religious leaders through

whose teachings Islamic ideas found wide currency among non-Muslims. While he does not belong chronologically in a survey of the early interaction of Hinduism and Islam, since he lived into the seventeenth century, his membership in a Kabir sect makes a brief consideration of his career useful. Furthermore, his biography shows the same process at work that is seen in the accounts of the life of Kabir. Dadu is stated by his later followers to have been the son of a Nagar Brahman, but recent researches have shown that he was born in a family of Muslim cotton-carders. This is borne out by his own works and the fact that all the members of his family have Muslim names: his father's name was Lodi, his mother's, Basiran; his sons were Garib and Miskin and his grandson, Faqir. His teacher was Shaikh Budhan, a Muslim saint of the Qadri order. The early Hindu followers of Dadu were not disturbed by the knowledge that he was a Muslim by birth, but later ones were. The legend of his Brahmanical origin made its first appearance in a commentary on the *Bhaktamala,* written as late as 1800. It is said that until recent times documents existed at the monasteries of the followers of Dadu which suggested that he had been a Muslim, but that these were destroyed by the keepers who were unwilling to admit that his origins were not Hindu.[2]

The metamorphosis which the life story and teachings of Kabir and Dadu have undergone is not merely the work of those who were anxious to secure for their heroes high lineage and a link with Hinduism; it is symptomatic of the general movement of separation that became common in both Islam and Hinduism in later centuries. As the Muslims grew more orthodox, they turned away from men such as Kabir and Dadu, while the Hindus accepted them as saints, but forgot their Islamic origins. In order to conform to the requirements of the Hindu *bhakti* tradition, they have undergone a transformation that at times necessitates a falsification of history. Two poet-saints who are clearly in the Hindu *bhakti* tradition but show traces of Islamic influence are Namadeva and Tukaram, the great religious figures of the Maratha country. Namadeva, who lived in the late fourteenth or early fifteenth century, used a number of Persian and Arabic words, suggesting that even at this early time the influence of Islam

[2] K. M. Sen, *Medieval Mysticism in India* (London, 1936), p. viii.

was felt by a man, in a remote area of the country, whose only concern seems to have been with religion. The writings of Tukaram (1598–1649), the greatest of the Marathi poets, contain many obvious references to Islam, such as the following:

First among the great names is Allah, never forget to respect it.
Allah is verily one, the prophet is verily one.
There Thou art one, there Thou art one, There Thou art one, O friend.
There is neither I nor thou.[3]

In general the attitude of the Marathas to Muslim saints was one of respect, the most vivid example of this being the great faith Shivaji's grandfather had in Shah Sharif of Ahmadnagar. In honor of the saint he gave his sons the names of Shahji and Sharifji. While a full study of the religious and social ferment of Maharashtra in the fifteenth and sixteenth centuries has yet to be made; it seems certain that the new religious life did not take the form of a Hindu revivalism that emphasized the separation of the Hindus from Islam. Antagonism toward Muslims came later, and, as was the case with the Sikhs, had definite antecedents in particular historical events. The creative spiritual and literary movement provided the basis on which the Maratha nation could be built, and its emergence as the great antagonist of Muslim power in India was based on political, not religious, factors. The evidence from the songs of Namadeva and Tukaram strongly suggests that they were not reacting in any hostile fashion to Islam. For this reaction one must look to Chaitanya and the Vaishnavite movement in Bengal.

Chaitanya (1485–1533) of Bengal represents an aspect of the *bhakti* movement that is very different from that seen in the lives and teachings of Kabir and his successors. Chaitanya's concern, unlike that of Kabir, was not with bringing people to an understanding of a God beyond all creeds and formulations; it was to exalt the superiority of Krishna over all other deities.[4] It was, in other words, a revivalist, not a syncretic, movement, a return to a worship of Vishnu under one of his most appealing forms, the loving ecstatic Krishna. The attitude

[3] Quoted in Tarachand, *The Influence of Islam on Indian Culture* (Allahabad, 1946), p. 228.
[4] M. T. Kennedy, *The Chaitanya Movement* (Calcutta, 1925), pp. 92–93.

of Bengal Vaishnavites toward Islam was the antithesis of the attitude advocated by Kabir and Nanak. Conscious of the appeal being made by Islam, they did not try to reform Hinduism by adopting any of the attractive features of the rival faith. Instead, they emphasized precisely those features, such as devotion to Krishna, which were most anti-pathetic to the Islamic spirit. Another difference between Chaitanya's movement and that of Kabir is the attitude toward caste. While it is true that Chaitanya made disciples from all classes, one does not find the same note of condemnation of caste as one does in Kabir. Accord-ing to some students of the period, this indicates the essential differ-ence between the two aspects of *bhakti* in the fifteenth and sixteenth centuries: only where Hinduism was directly influenced by Islam was there evidence of concern for social inequities.[5]

Because of the interest that is attached to such great names as that of Kabir there is a tendency to think of the movement of interaction between the two faiths as mainly from Islam to Hinduism. This was not true, however, for Muslim society was deeply influenced by its contacts with Hinduism. Some contacts had been made even before Islamic rule was established in India; for example the probable Hindu element in certain forms of Islamic mysticism, and the intellectual interchanges that had taken place after the conquest of Sind in the seventh and eighth centuries. During the sultanate, changes of a quite different order were apparent.

One of these concerns the lives of converts to Islam. Here the important point to keep in mind is that when one sees Hindu prac-tices followed by Indian Muslims, it is not a case of Hindu influence, but simply of incomplete change from the old way of life. Indian Muslims did not start with orthodox Islam, but began by accepting a few basic features, and only in the course of time, particularly during the last two centuries, have they become more orthodox. The process is less complete in the lower classes, or those groups which, like the Khojas, adopted a somewhat composite form of religion. More than religious beliefs, Indian Islam retained certain characteristic features of Hindu society which, if not religious in themselves, certainly had

---

[5] T. K. Raychaudhuri, *Bengal under Akbar and Jahangir* (Calcutta, 1953), pp. 94–95.

been given religious sanction. One of these was the place given to caste, with converts clinging to some memory of their former status in a hierarchical society, while what may be called Muslim castes developed as Indian Muslims classified themselves as Sayyid, Shaikh, Mughal, or Pathan. This structure was never very rigid; as Bernier commented, anyone who put on a white turban called himself a Mughal. An old saying makes the same point: "Last year I was a Julaha (weaver); this year a Shaikh; and next year if the harvest be good, I shall be a Sayyid." And in the mosque the Islamic ideals of brotherhood and equality remained triumphant.

Muslims in India also adopted the Hindu practices of early marriages and of objection to widow remarriage. Some social ceremonies connected with births, deaths, and marriages may also be traced to Hindu origin. Some writers think that reverence for *pirs,* or saints, and their graves, a marked feature of popular Indian Islam, is a carry-over of Hindu practices. This interpretation overlooks the fact, however, that even outside India *pirs* and their tombs are objects of great attention and veneration.

The main influence of Hinduism on Islam, however, is probably seen not so much in these specific instances as in a general softening of the original attitude of the conquerors, particularly the Turks, in religious matters. This softening is to be seen partly as a movement of Hindu attitudes toward the universe into Islamic thought; it is also partly a recognition of the position of Islam in India. More striking than the amount of interaction that took place in the first three centuries of Muslim rule was the fact that there was not more. The impression one gains is that there was never a very conscious attempt to create understanding, except on the part of Kabir and Nanak, and that the contacts between the two great religions were, on the whole, remarkably superficial as far as the total life of the country was concerned. Writing in 1030, before the full tide of conquest had begun, Al-Biruni spoke of how the Hindus differed from the Muslims in every respect, and, because of the raids by Mahmud of Ghazni, "cherish the most inveterate aversion toward all Muslims." [6] Nearly three centuries later another traveler, Ibn Battuta, remarked that

[6] E. C. Sachau, *Alberuni's India* (London, 1914), I, 22.

Hindus and Muslims lived in entirely separate communities. For Hindus, there could be no intermarriage with Muslims nor even inter-dining. "It is the custom among the heathen of the Malabar country," he remarked, "that no Muslim should enter their houses or use their vessels for eating purposes. If a Muslim is fed out of their vessels, they either break the vessels or give them away to the Muslims." [7]

It is against this background that one must see the greatness of the achievements of men like Kabir and Nanak and, at the same time, the almost insurmountable barriers to a genuine rapprochement. The tenacity with which attempts continued to be made to establish links between the two religions is a dominant theme in the cultural history of the Mughals, the new group who entered India at the beginning of the sixteenth century.

[7] Mahdi Husain, *The Rehla of Ibn Battuta* (Baroda, 1953), p. 182.

Part Two

The Mughal Period, 1526-1858

Chronology and Dynasties, 1526-1858

The Mughal Empire

1526	First Battle of Panipat: Mughals defeat the Lodis.
1526–1530	Reign of Babur.
1530	Accession of Humayun.
1540–1555	The Sur dynasty.
1556	Second Battle of Panipat: Humayun regains power.
1556–1605	Reign of Akbar.
1605–1627	Reign of Jahangir.
1627–1658	Reign of Shah Jahan.
c.1646–1680	Rise of the Marathas under Shivaji.
1658–1707	Reign of Aurangzeb.
1713–1719	Reign of Farrukhsiyar.
1719–1748	Reign of Muhammad Shah.
1720–1740	Maratha expansion under Baji Rao I.
1739	Sack of Delhi by Nadir Shah.
c.1720–1750	Establishment of Hyderabad, Oudh, and Bengal as independent states.
1757	Battle of Plassey: Clive defeats nawab of Bengal. Ahmad Shah Abdali sacks Delhi.
1759–1806	Reign of Shah Alam II.
1761	Third Battle of Panipat: Afghans and Mughals defeat Marathas.
1765	Diwani of Bengal granted to East India Company.
1774–1785	Warren Hastings, Governor-General.
1775–1782	First Anglo-Maratha war.
1798–1805	Lord Wellesley, Governor-General.
1803	Delhi taken by the British.
1806–1837	Reign of Akbar Shah II.
1837–1858	Reign of Bahadur Shah II.
1843	British take Sind.
1849	British annex Punjab.
1856	Annexation of Oudh.
1857–1858	Mutiny and revolt.
1858	British India placed under the Crown. Bahadur Shah deposed.

X. The Establishment of the Mughal Empire

WHILE there is continuity in the history of Indo-Islamic civilization, with the foundation of the Mughal empire in the second quarter of the sixteenth century a political and cultural watershed was reached. The era of the sultanate (from 1206 to 1526) is often referred to as the medieval period of Indian history, partly because of correspondence in time to the conventional classification of European history, and partly because of certain analogies in spirit of the two historical epochs. But it is also the Middle Ages of Indian history in that it divides ancient India and modern India. While it is true, as has been shown in the preceding chapters, that the seeds of the new life which bloomed so vigorously in the sixteenth and seventeenth centuries were planted during the seemingly barren years of the sultanate, nevertheless the Mughal empire has a different atmosphere from the preceding era. It can be argued that the beginning of modern Indian history is to be dated not from the establishment of British hegemony in the early nineteenth century, but from the coming of the Mughals in 1526.

One obvious reason for the different tone and spirit of the Mughal empire is the greater continuity of administration. For three hundred years the same dynasty ruled from Delhi, and for half of this period, from 1556 to 1707, four rulers in direct succession maintained control. This is a remarkable achievement in the dynastic history of any great country, but it is particularly astonishing when measured against the rapid overthrow, not just of rulers, but of dynasties, in the sultanate period. Undoubtedly this dynastic stability contributed to the rich and varied cultural life of the period. The basic reason for the different tone of the two periods is, however, the success of Akbar, the third of the Mughal rulers, in creating an enduring system of administration. Whatever evaluation may be put on the role of individuals as creative forces in history, it is difficult to escape the conclu-

sion that to quite an extraordinary degree Akbar was responsible for many of the features that characterize the Mughal period.

The beginnings of Mughal rule followed a familiar pattern: an adventurous chieftain in the mountainous areas to the northwest, attracted by possibilities of wealth and power during a period of internal weakness in India, gathered his forces for a sudden descent upon the Punjab.[1] Babur was ruler of a kingdom centered on Kabul when he invaded India in 1526, but his original territory was the little principality of Farghana in Turkistan. A Chaghatai Turk, he claimed descent from both of the great Central Asian conquerors, Timur and, more remotely, Chingiz Khan. It was this connection with the great Mongol invader that gave the dynasty the misleading appellation of "Mughal" or "Mongol." This is especially ironic, since Babur himself had an intense dislike for the Mongols. While it is too late to change the long-accepted nomenclature, it is worth remembering that the Mughal dynasty was Turkish in origin, and the cultural tradition which Babur imported into India was the one which had flourished on the banks of the Oxus. Timur attracted a large number of poets, musicians, and philosophers to his brilliant court, and built and embellished his capital, Samarqand, in a truly magnificent style. After Timur's death in 1405 these cultural traditions were more than maintained by his descendants, who made their capitals centers of art and learning that drew upon the whole Islamic world. This was the atmosphere in which Babur grew up, and which he and his successor were to transplant to Lahore, Delhi, and Agra. Babur himself was a writer of great distinction, and his autobiography is considered one of the great monuments of Turkish prose.

Babur had established himself in Kabul in 1504, after he had been driven out of Farghana by the westward movement of the Uzbegs, and when he found that he was prevented from expansion towards Persia by the rise of a new dynasty there, he turned his attention to India. There the revival of Hindu power and the virtual independence of the Muslim governors provided him with an opportunity to attack the

---

[1] *Memoirs of Zehir-ed-Din Muhammed Babur,* trans. by J. Leyden and W. Erskine, rev. by Sir Lucas King (2 vols.; London, 1921), provides a firsthand account of Babur's reign.

sultanate with the assurance that he would not be met by any united resistance. In 1525 he captured Lahore, the capital of Punjab, whose ruler was in virtual rebellion against the sultan, and then made plans for an attack on Delhi. The decisive encounter with the sultan, Ibrahim Lodi, took place on the historic battlefield of Panipat on April 21, 1526. It is probable that Babur had fewer than 12,000 men, in contrast to at least 100,000 in the army of the sultan, but he had the decisive advantages of fine artillery and disciplined, well-led troops. The sultan had neither, and before evening he and 15,000 of his soldiers were dead, and the road was open to Delhi and Agra. After Babur had taken these, he swept on to capture the other great centers of North India—Gwalior, Kanauj, and Jaunpur. His strongest opposition came from the famous Rana Sanga, the Rajput ruler of Mewar, who had collected a great force of Hindu chieftains and a few Muslim nobles. The two armies met at Khanua, a village near Agra, on March 16, 1527, and although the rana was a far better leader than the sultan, his bravery was no match for Babur's superior tactics and modern weapons. Rana Sanga's defeat meant the end of Rajput hopes for a restoration of Hindu power; also it freed Babur's army for mopping-up operations against the Afghan supporters of the sultan in the outlying provinces. By 1529 he was master of the Gangetic plain as far as Patna in Bihar, but he died in the following year before he could complete the conquest of North India. Even so, the territory that he bequeathed to his son, Humayun, included Afghanistan, the Punjab, the fertile Ganges plain, and a rim of forts along central India.

Humayun was twenty-three when he succeeded his father, and while he had experience as a military commander, he lacked his father's vigor and toughness. These qualities were needed, for he was faced with a hostile combination of his own jealous relatives, including his three younger brothers, and the Afghan nobles who were not reconciled to their loss of power. He soon found himself fighting his enemies on two widely separated fronts. In the west, Bahadur Shah, the ruler of Gujarat, which had been independent of Delhi for over a century, provided shelter for his enemies; in the east, his authority was challenged by the Afghan chieftains, under Sher Khan

Sur. He was able to carry out a successful attack on Bahadur Shah's territories, but he had to abandon his gains to move against the threat to his power from Sher Khan Sur in Bihar.

Sher Khan Sur was one of the most colorful of the numerous Afghans who had created places for themselves in the outlying provinces. The son of a petty Afghan jagirdar in Bihar, he had gone at an early age to Jaunpur, where he acquired an excellent knowledge of the Arabic and Persian classics. He entered the service of the governor of Bihar, but apparently seeing the likelihood of a Mughal triumph in North India, he joined the army of Babur when he invaded India. After Babur's death he took advantage of the disturbed conditions to assert his own supremacy over Bihar. This, however, did not satisfy him, and at the end of February, 1536, he appeared at the gates of Gaur, the capital of Bengal, and retired only after receiving a large payment. Next year he marched eastward again and entered Gaur in triumph, but on the return of Humayun from Gujarat, he withdrew toward Bihar to fight the Mughals in the area he knew best. In 1539 Humayun, who had occupied Gaur, was caught in unfamiliar territory during the monsoon, and as he tried to withdraw his forces toward Agra, Sher Khan blocked his communications and defeated him at Chausa on the Ganges. The two armies met again at Kanauj, in 1540, but the Mughal army was so demoralized that on Sher Khan's advance they fled in panic. Humayun's last chance of making a stand against the Afghans was gone. He fled toward Rajputana and Sind, and at one time turned toward Qandahar where his brother Kamran was in power, but he received no help and had to seek refuge with the shah of Persia. For the next fifteen years he wandered through the Indian borderlands, quarreling with his brother and seeking support for a return to India, but it was not until 1555, a year before his death, that he was able to enter Delhi again.

Sher Khan Sur proclaimed himself ruler of North India in 1539 after the battle of Chausa with the title of Sher Shah Adil, and he quickly conquered Malwa, Rajputana, and Sind. To guard against a Mughal invasion, he built a strong line of forts in the northwest Punjab.

Although he reigned for only six years, and his successors lost control ten years after his death, Sher Shah's rule is one of the more

significant Islamic administrations in Indian history. His deep knowledge of earlier history and his practical experience with the working of the system evolved by the Delhi sultans enabled him to utilize what was good in the past and to improve and add to it. In this way he paved the way for the final phase of Muslim administration under Akbar and the later Mughals. For example, he undertook administrative reforms which had been introduced originally by Ala-ud-din Khalji, such as a powerful standing army officered by the nobles of the sultan's choice, and improved on them, leaving his successors with a more efficient state service.

The principal reforms for which Sher Shah is remembered are those connected with land revenue administration. The agency which he built up, and which with further improvements under Akbar and the British continues to the present day, fulfilled many functions. It was entrusted with the recovery of government dues, collection of data regarding the villages and the holdings of the cultivators, and the general economic situation. In this reform Sher Shah was able to draw upon his experience of the detailed administration of a *pargana* of his father's *jagir*. The fundamental change made by Sher Khan was the use of actual measurement, rather than an estimation, of the cultivated land as the basis for revenue assessment. The land was to be measured every year, and then one fourth or one third of the average produce was to be taken as revenue. Allowance was to be made for soils of different degrees of productivity.

The revenue system depended upon careful organization, and Sher Shah attempted to create an administrative structure that would be under continual supervision from the capital. Here again he was drawing upon the experience of the past, which had shown the dangers of too much power in the hands of governors. The smallest administrative unit was the *pargana,* or group of villages, and for each of these Sher Shah appointed a shiqqdar, who was responsible for the general administration, including the preservation of law and order, an amin, who supervised assessment and collection of revenue, a treasurer, and two clerks to keep accounts, one in Persian, and the other in Hindi. The next unit was a *sarkar,* or a revenue district, which had a chief shiqqdar and a chief munsif, "whose duty it was to see that the

revenue was collected in full, but that the cultivators were not oppressed."

Sher Shah's desire for a centralized administration is also reflected in his attempt to link the various parts of his empire by an efficient system of roads. Of his four great roads, one connected Sonargaon (near modern Dacca) in Bengal, through Agra, Delhi, and Lahore, with the Indus; others connected Agra and Mandu; Agra, Jodhpur, and Chitor; and Lahore and Multan. Fruit trees were planted on both sides of the roads and at short intervals caravansaries were set up with separate lodgings for Muslims and Hindus, with servants to supply food to the travelers of each religion. Safety was ensured by making the officials of the adjacent villages responsible for incidents on the roads passing through their areas. Trade along the highroads was encouraged by the abolition of all tolls, with custom duties levied only on the frontiers. Although Sher Shah was rigidly orthodox, Hindus held high positions in his army, and Todar Mal, who later gained renown under Akbar, was originally in his service. One of his best-known generals was Brahmajit Gaur, whom he sent in pursuit of Humayun, and Raja Ram Singh of Gwalior is also said to have been in his service. His army included a contingent of Rajputs.

Islam Shah, who succeeded Sher Shah in 1545, made an effort to preserve the institutions of his father. He kept the fortifications in good repair, increased the number of caravansaries, and ordered the compilation of a detailed statement of government regulations, extracts of which were read every Friday in meetings of government officials of each area. He was, however, unable to keep his rebellious nobles in check, and religious unrest among his subjects further undermined his power.

The religious ferment of Islam Shah's reign was part of a widespread movement. At this time the millennium of the migration of the Prophet of Islam from Mecca was approaching, and many people believed in the imminent appearance of a Mahdi who would convert the whole world to Islam and fill the earth with equity and justice. Sayyid Muhammad, a leading scholar and saint of Jaunpur, encouraged this expectation and later claimed to be the Mahdi. Those who accepted his claims and followed his injunctions were known as

Mahadwis. The Mahadwi movement gradually lost its importance in northern India, but it flourished longer in the south, and Mahadwi doctrines have been held by some important persons in Hyderabad Deccan (including the late Nawab Bahadur Yar Jang). Even in northern India, the struggle which it generated and the conflict which ensued between the court jurists and the Mahadwi notables had their effect on the religious history of Akbar's day.

Sayyid Muhammad Jaunpuri died in Farah, in modern Afghanistan, in 1504; but his doctrines were kept alive by his enthusiastic followers. In Sher Shah's reign, Shaikh Alai, son of a leading religious teacher of Bengal, established himself at Bayana near Agra, where he came under the influence of Shaikh Abdullah, an Afghan follower of Sayyid Muhammad. The two leaders confined their preaching, marked by rigid puritanism and asceticism, to the poor. They kept no property and encouraged others to do the same, and admonished anyone who committed irreligious acts. The group carried arms and permitted no interference with their actions by officials. This defiance brought them into conflict with the established government, in particular Makhdum-ul-Mulk, an important office-holder in the state, who strongly objected to the new cult and used his influence with Islam Shah to punish those who believed in its doctrines. Shaikh Alai and Shaikh Abdullah had many powerful friends, but their unwillingness to acknowledge any superior secular authority, including a refusal to salute even the emperor, gave Makhdum-ul-Mulk an opportunity to have them both flogged. The bitterness and animosity engendered by the strife between the sect's leaders and the government help to explain, in part at least, the growing confusion and disorder of Islam Shah's reign.

Quarrels over the succession at the time of Islam Shah's death in 1554 provided the opportunity for which Humayun, now established as ruler of Kabul, had long been waiting. Just prior to this he had finally freed himself of his brother's opposition, and he was able to move against India without fear of an attack from the rear. He took the great key cities of the north, Lahore and Delhi, in a series of campaigns in 1555, but bad luck pursued him before he had a chance to consolidate his gains. In January, 1556, he was killed in a fall on

the stairs of his library in Delhi. To his young son Akbar he left the royal title and a foothold in Hindustan, but little security against the members of the Sur family and their supporters. To make good the claims of Babur's descendants to the throne of Delhi was to be the work of Akbar, not of the unfortunate Humayun.

While Humayun's career as an Indian ruler was brief and insecure, his contribution to the cultural synthesis of the Mughal period was of very considerable importance, for from his reign dates the increasing Persian influence on Islamic civilization in India. During years of exile at the court of Shah Tahmasp of Persia he had come in contact with the artists who were making Tabriz a great cultural center. Two of them, Mir Sayyid Ali and Khwajah Abdus Samad, apparently were given offers of employment by Humayun, and in 1550 both of them joined him at Kabul, which he had occupied prior to his reconquest of India. Humayun entrusted the two artists with various commissions including the preparation and illustration of the famous Persian classic, *Dastan-i-Amir Hamzah,* portions of which have survived. They accompanied Humayun to Agra, and were retained later by Akbar as his court painters. By training local talent and attracting other artists from abroad, a school of painting was established which was to be one of the glories of the Mughal empire.

To the Perso-Turkish culture Akbar added other elements such as Indo-Muslim music, Hindu philosophy, and Hindi literature which had received little official support at Delhi during the sultanate, although they had flourished in the regional kingdoms. With this broadened basis, Mughal culture assumed a pattern which has left a permanent mark on the cultural life of the subcontinent.

XI. The Age of Akbar

ONLY Ashoka, who had ruled eighteen centuries before, vies with Akbar for the title of the greatest of Indian kings, and if weight is given to initial difficulties encountered and overcome, the claim must surely go to Akbar. The great Mauryan had received intact a great heritage from his predecessor; what Akbar had received from his father was little more than a disputed title as emperor of Hindustan. Akbar, who had been born in 1542 while his father was in flight from the victorious Surs, was only thirteen when he was proclaimed emperor in 1556. In the eight months he had spent in India before his death Humayun had succeeded in regaining control of the Punjab, Delhi, and Agra, but even in these areas his hold was precarious, and when the leaders of the Sur family recovered Agra and Delhi, the fate of the boy king seemed certain.

Akbar had a great asset in the regent, Bairam Khan, who had been Humayun's faithful friend in his days of adversity. One of the ablest soldiers of the time, he was the real ruler of the Mughal inheritance for the first four years of Akbar's reign. His first great triumph came at Panipat on November 5, 1556, when he defeated the Sur armies under the command of their Hindu general, Himu. He led a vigorous pursuit of the enemy, and recaptured Delhi and Agra, the key fortresses of the north; then he moved on to extend control over the rest of Hindustan. Having reduced the great fortress of Gwalior and annexed the rich province of Jaunpur, he was planning the conquest of Malwa when he suddenly fell from power.

While the young king spent his time hunting and watching elephant fights, Bairam Khan had extended his authority in the kingdom. In so doing, he had antagonized many of the nobles, and when he appointed a member of the Shia sect as sadr-ul-sadur, the chief religious post in the government, he became even more obnoxious to them. Furthermore, the young emperor, at the age of eighteen, wanted to take a more active part in managing affairs. Urged on by his foster mother,

Maham Anaga, and his relatives, Akbar decided to dispense with the services of the great minister. He sent a suitably worded message to Bairam and fixed a *jagir* for him, but Bairam Khan, after a half-hearted show of defiance, left for Mecca and was murdered on the way by a man who bore him a private grudge. Akbar married his widow, and his son, Abdul Rahim eventually became one of the chief nobles.

During the next few years, Akbar's foster mother and her family were supreme. This tutelage came to an end, however, in 1562, when Akbar, enraged at the repeated excesses and cruelty of Maham Anaga's son, Adham Khan, had him thrown from the palace terrace. Maham Anaga did not long survive her son's death, and henceforth the emperor was master of his affairs.

Meanwhile some of the features for which Akbar's reign was famous were becoming manifest. The policy of vigorous conquest started under Bairam Khan was maintained. In 1560 Malwa was annexed, and four years later Akbar conquered Gondwana. Even more important than these victories was his policy toward his Hindu subjects, which was adopted practically from the beginning of his active assumption of kingship. The first of his marriages to Rajput princesses (one of the landmarks in the development of his religious policy) took place early in 1562. There is nothing to show that the Rajput princesses had to renounce Hinduism; presumably, as in the case of a Muslim marrying a Christian or a Jew, these marriages were considered valid without change of religion. These alliances were only one aspect of broadening religious horizons, for far-reaching administrative changes accompanied them. One of these was that the relatives of the Rajput wives, like Raja Bhagwan Das and Raja Man Singh, were appointed to high posts and became partners of the Mughals in the administration of the country. Then in 1564 Akbar abolished the pilgrim tax, earning the gratitude of the large number of Hindus who flocked to various places of pilgrimage. The following year he took a more important step—the abolition of the *jizya*. These measures enabled Akbar to gain the active collaboration of the fighting classes of Hindu India and the goodwill of the Hindu population.

Akbar now turned his attention to the conquest of Rajputana. In 1567 he reduced the fortress of Chitor, and this was soon followed

by the surrender of Ranthambhor. Gujarat was annexed in 1573. Akbar now was free to turn his attention to Bengal, which since the days of Sher Shah had been the happy hunting ground of Afghan adventurers driven out of northern India. Although Tanda, then the capital of Bengal, was occupied early in 1574, and the Afghan ruler of Bengal was decisively defeated in March, the Mughal conquest of the area was not complete for several years.

Akbar's expansionist policy from this time on could be carried out by his commanders under his general direction, and he was able to indulge his personal interests nearer the seat of his government, including the building of his new capital. His children had died in infancy, and he approached Shaikh Salim, a saint who lived at Sikri, near Agra, to pray for a male child and his long life. Early in 1561 he sent his pregnant wife to the monastery of Shaikh Salim, and it was here that his successor to the throne was born, and was named Salim after the saint. Akbar was so grateful to the saint that in 1571 he started building a capital at Sikri, known as Fathpur, or "Victory City." In 1575 he erected the famous House of Worship near the tomb of Shaikh Salim, who had died the meanwhile. It was in this building that Akbar spent his time in religious pursuits. He remained preoccupied with these controversies for many years and did not leave the capital on a military campaign until 1581, when the Punjab was invaded by his brother, Mirza Hakim, to whom the territories centering on Kabul had passed at their father's death. Akbar pursued Mirza Hakim to Kabul, but left him in control of the area until his death in 1585.

This expedition was the beginning of a long period of concern over the northern marches of the empire. For thirteen years Akbar had to remain in the north, with Lahore as his virtual capital, dealing with a threat from beyond the mountains. This came from the Uzbegs, the tribe that had driven Babur out of his home in Central Asia. They had been organized under Abdullah Khan, a capable leader, and were a danger to the northwestern frontiers of Akbar's empire. The tribes on the border were also restless, partly on account of the hostility of the Yusufzais of Bajaur and Swat, and partly owing to the activity of a new religious leader, the founder of the Raushaniya sect,

who preached that plundering the property of those who did not believe in his doctrines was lawful. Mughal forces sent against the Yusufzais met with disaster in February, 1586, when the inept commander, Raja Birbal, lost his life. It took two years to pacify the area.

Akbar was not able to leave Lahore until the death of Abdullah Khan in 1598 removed the Uzbeg danger, but the long stay had been fruitful. Kashmir was added to the Mughal empire in 1586; Sind followed in 1593. There Mirza Jani Beg, the ruler of Thatta, after his defeat at the hands of Abdul Rahim, became a Mughal mansabdar and was appointed governor of his old territory. In 1594 Baluchistan, with the coastal region of Makran, was added to the empire, and in the following year Qandahar was surrendered by its Persian governor.

These conquests, by bringing the whole of the northwest under Mughal rule, greatly reduced the danger of invasion from Central Asia. Akbar was free, therefore, to extend his empire to the Deccan. The opposition to Mughal expansion came from the Muslim rulers of the regional kingdoms established in the fourteenth and fifteenth centuries. Akbar sent envoys to them in 1591, asking them to recognize his suzerainty, and when they refused, the imperial troops marched upon Ahmadnagar, the capital of one of the important sultanates. For some time the heroic leadership of a princess, Chand Bibi, saved the city, but in 1599 Akbar appeared in person and Ahmadnagar fell. In January, 1601, after the key fortress of Asirgarh had capitulated, the conquered territories of Ahmadnagar and Khandesh were organized as a province of the Mughal empire.

Akbar returned to Agra in May, 1601, his career of conquest over. His last years were troubled by unhappy relations with his son, Prince Salim, who had the royal favorite, Abul Fazl, assassinated by the robber chief, Bir Singh Bundhela, in 1602. Akbar fell ill in August, 1605, and the physicians were not able to diagnose the disease properly. There was a strong suspicion that his illness was due to a secret irritant poison, possibly diamond dust. He died on January 7, 1606.

Akbar was the real builder of the Mughal empire, and he laid down the principles and policies which, but for occasional modifications and minor adjustments, remained the basis of the Mughal administrative system. This will be dealt with in a separate chapter, but a few

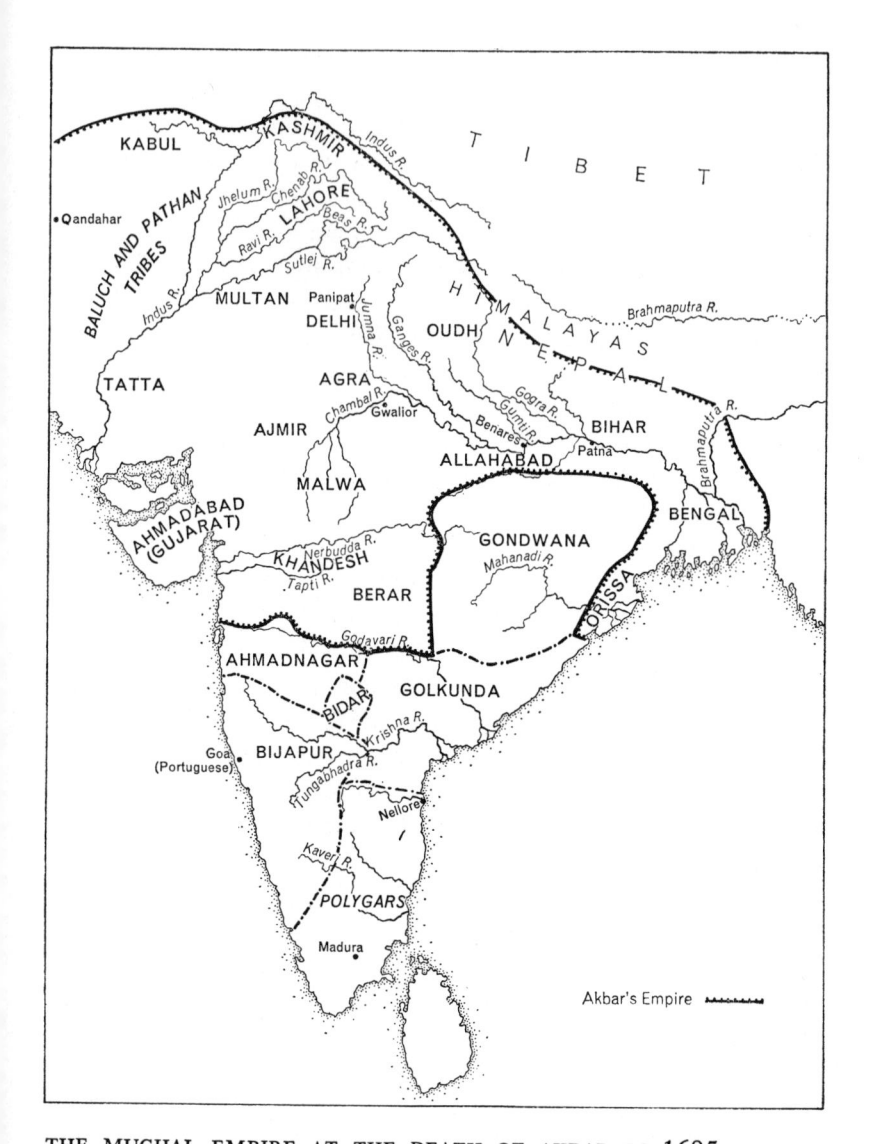

THE MUGHAL EMPIRE AT THE DEATH OF AKBAR IN 1605

From: *An Historical Atlas of the Indian Peninsula* (Oxford University Press, Bombay, 1961).

of the policies particularly associated with Akbar may be mentioned here.

Foremost among these was his treatment of the Hindu population. For understanding the significance of his policy of toleration, it is important, however, to see his actions against the background of previous movements in the same direction, and not as a complete innovation. Hindus had long been employed in positions of responsibility—even Mahmud of Ghazni, the great "destroyer of idols," had a contingent of Indian troops under Indian officers—and no Muslim ruler had succeeded in dispensing with the services of Hindu officials on the level of local administration. There were, however, great difficulties to be overcome before general participation was possible. From the side of the early Turkish rulers, there had been prejudice not only against Hindus, but even against Indian converts to Islam. Under the Khaljis a change took place, and henceforth converts found employment in high office. This change led to a more general employment of Hindus, and during Sher Shah's reign (1538–1545) a number of Hindus held important military posts. But this exclusion of Hindus had not been entirely the result of Islamic attitudes: many Hindus had strong objection to service under a Muslim ruler. Furthermore, until Hindus were willing to learn Persian, the court language, their widespread employment in government was not possible. By the fifteenth century, when it was apparent that the Muslim rule was permanent, many Brahmans had begun to learn Persian, and their movement into government service began.

Thus by Akbar's time many of the traditional difficulties had been removed, and he was able to take full advantage of the changes in outlook on both sides. One example of this was his enunciation of the principle of *sulahkul,* or universal tolerance, by which he accepted responsibility for all sections of the population, irrespective of their religion. Through his marriages with leading Rajput families, Hindus became members of the ruling dynasty, and Hindu women practiced their faith within the palace confines. The abolition of *jizya* was a more widespread indication of his policy, making the common people aware of the changing climate of opinion. That two of his most famous officials, Man Singh, viceroy of Kabul and Bengal, and Todar

Mal, his revenue minister, were Hindus, was an indication not of his desire to show his tolerance but his freedom to choose able associates wherever they might be found. Beyond these administrative acts, Akbar showed his sympathies with Hindu culture by patronizing the classical Indian arts, providing scope once more for painters, musicians, and dancers of the old tradition. Perhaps the most striking of his activities in this area is the creation of the post of *kavi rai,* or poet laureate, for Hindi poets. The adaption of Hindu elements in architecture is demonstrated in many of Akbar's buildings, notably at Fathpur Sikri. There and elsewhere he showed regard to Hindu religious leaders.

The detailed measures which Akbar took to build up an efficient system of administration are no less indicative of a great constructive genius. He adopted what was vital in Sher Shah's administrative system and greatly increased its effectiveness. He insisted on maintaining a high level of administration, and for this purpose drew on talent from all available sources—the Mughals, the Uzbegs, the Rajputs, and other Hindus like Raja Todar Mal, and, of course, the Turanis and the Persians. By a judicious selection of personnel, their training in different fields, and by providing suitable opportunities to them, he was able to build up an efficient officers' cadre. Satisfactory arrangements for assessment and recovery of land revenue, and their integration in the general administrative system set the pattern for revenue administration which has been followed ever since. Akbar also preferred payment of cash salaries to the grant of *jagirs.* These measures, coupled with the general improvement in education and a brilliant spurt of expansion and conquest, enabled him to build up an efficient administrative machinery, centralize administration, and unify the country to an extent which had not been possible hitherto for any length of time.

In an earlier chapter we have outlined the basis of Indo-Muslim polity as laid down by Iltutmish, and its transformation at the hands of Balban, who introduced elements of the ancient Iranian concept of monarchy and centralized system of government. The pattern adopted by Balban became the norm for Muslim India (with only minor changes of policy), and was adopted by subsequent rulers.

The Mughal theory of kingship as it emerged under Akbar, while rooted in the basic pattern laid down by Balban, has important features of its own. In the Mughal system the king remained all-powerful, but he was not an autocrat of Balban's type. The most authoritative exposition of the Mughal theory of rulership is that provided by Abul Fazl, Akbar's closest companion, in his introduction to *Ain-i-Akbari*. The first two paragraphs dealing with the need for a king to maintain order and suppress crime and injustice echo Balban's views on the subject. Then Abul Fazl emphasizes the divine elements in kingship:

Royalty is a light emanating from God, and a ray from the sun, the illuminator of the universe, the argument of the book of perfection, and the receptacle of all virtues. Modern language calls it *farr-i-izidi* (the divine light), and the tongue of antiquity called it *kiyan-i-khura* (the sublime halo). It is communicated by God to kings without the intermediate assistance of anyone, and men, in the presence of it, bend the forehead of praise toward the ground of submission.[1]

He lists these further requisite elements of Mughal kingship:

A paternal love toward the subjects. Thousands find rest in the love of the king and sectarian differences do not raise the dust of strife. In his wisdom, the king will understand the spirit of the age and shape his plans accordingly.
A large heart. The sight of anything disagreeable does not unsettle him nor is want of discrimination for him a source of disappointment. His courage steps in. His divine firmness gives him the power of requittal, nor does the high position of an offender interfere with it. . . .
A daily increasing trust in God. . . .
Prayer and devotion.

There is much that is rhetorical in the analysis of the court historian, but the course of the Mughal history and pronouncements of various rulers show that during Mughal rule an attempt was made to approximate to this ideal, with the concept of paternal government constantly emphasized by Akbar and his successors. This concept of kingship was similar to the old indigenous notion of the ruler being the *Mai Bap* (Mother and Father) of the people, and it is not im-

---

[1] Abul Fazl, *Ain-i-Akbari,* trans. by H. Blockmann et al. (Calcutta, 1927–1941), I, 3.

possible that Akbar and Abul Fazl were influenced by Indian political ideas. Akbar's views were also supported and strengthened by references in Muslim philosophical and mystical writings to the ruler as "the shadow of God," and Abul Fazl makes repeated use of these sources. But whatever the origin of their inspiration, by softening the autocracy of the absolute monarch, Akbar and Abul Fazl transformed its very nature. The Mughal badshah (emperor) was not an autocratic sultan, or even a traditional Commander of the Faithful; in theory at least he was a father of his people and a trustee of their welfare. The ideal was obviously not always achieved, and Aurangzeb's reign was marked by far-reaching deviations, but by and large the *Mai Bap* concept was accepted by the rulers and the ruled.

Writers and Scholars

While Akbar's own great abilities go far in explaining his success as a ruler, he was fortunate in the very high quality of the men who surrounded him. Among these were such notable administrators as Amir Fathullah Shirazi, Man Singh, Todar Mal, Khwaja Mansur, and scholars like Nizam-ud-din Bakshi and the historian Badauni. The persons who most vividly represent the caliber of his servants, however, were Abul Fazl (1551–1602) and his elder brother, Faizi (1545–1595). They were members of a distinguished family of scholars, and were held in high esteem by Akbar because of their intellectual gifts, their loyalty to him, and the similarity of their views on religion. Abul Fazl was the court chronicler, the drafter of the emperor's correspondence, and his personal confidant. The animosity of the other courtiers because of his favored position was given a religious coloring when he became the spokesman for Akbar's unorthodox religious policy, and in his last years they succeeded in keeping him away from the capital.

Both brothers were writers of distinction but Abul Fazl clothed his ideas in an ornate and verbose style. It is Faizi's writings that give us more indication of the intensity of the conflict which tore the hearts and minds of the intellectuals of the age. He was introduced at the court in September, 1567, when he was a young man of twenty. He gave

expression to his feelings in the first *Qasida* which he wrote in praise
of Akbar:

> How shall I write of the time when the barge of my heart
> Was tossing on the billows of the tempest?
> A quickening spring visited my word-garden,
> A youthful morning came to my spirit's tulip,
> While I was disturbed, thinking by what argument
> I could remove doubts about absolute verities.
> Why is this diversity practiced in Islam?
> Wherefore ambiguities in the words of the Quran?
> Why did false witness shoot out the tongue in the tribunal
> Of pride and hypocrisy, and claim belief?
> If such be the religion of Islam in this world,
> Scoffers can have a thousand smiles at the Musulman faith.

His inner conflicts form a recurrent theme in Faizi's poetry.
In a later quatrain he says:

> O God! What can I do, except lament on your path.
> One particle did not receive illumination, what can I do?
> I long to move towards the heights
> But You Yourself have given me a feeble might, what can I do!

And again,

> O God, through Your grace, grant me hope untainted by fear.
> Teach me that knowledge, in which lies your pleasure.
> The darkness of intellect keeps me in conflict;
> Give me the light of resignation from the lamp of *raza* [resignation].

His other common theme was exultation in the joy of living and in
the new possibilities opening before men. Here he was mirroring the
hopes and ambitions of a great age. In one of his *ghazals* he cries:

> Glad tidings for the world that a new day has dawned!
> And one who shines brighter than the sun has been born.
> The luckless ones of the night of separation have awakened
> As an auspicious dawn beautified the world.
> You who want a glimpse of the sun of good fortune,
> Open your eyes and see, a new sun has arisen.
> The wanderers of the path of *taqlid* [tradition] were perplexed;
> Thank God that a guide has appeared for this caravan!

Faizi! How long can there be the distant gloom of the night of separation?
Wake up, glimpses of the auspicious dawn are visible.

In these verses the purport of the poet is unmistakable but his language is vague. Elsewhere he is more direct. In a poem he rejects the
literal acceptance of the Quranic verses relating to heaven and hell
and endorses the Mutazila viewpoint treating them as metaphorical.
The idea that there is need for a new spiritual approach finds expression in such verses as these:

Come, so that we may turn our faces toward the arch of light,
We lay the foundation of a new Kaba with the stones from Sinai.

It is not surprising that some of Faizi's contemporaries accused him
of heresy. Yet if as a restless intellectual, aware of the new currents
moving within Indian Islam, he expressed dissatisfaction with the
rigidities of orthodoxy, in his prose commentary on the Quran he is
completely orthodox.

Literary gifts have secured a high place for Abul Fazl and Faizi
in the cultural history of Islamic India, but the greatest scholar of the
age was Amir Fathullah Shirazi. Badauni called him "the most
learned man of his times," and Abul Fazl declared: "If the books of
antiquity should be lost, the Amir would restore them." Only Abul
Fazl, Faizi, and Birbal had a higher place in Akbar's esteem.

Shah Fathullah was born and educated in Shiraz at a time when it
was witnessing a revival of learning after the effect of the Mongol
holocaust and Timur's invasion had spent itself. His teachers included
Amir Ghiyas-ud-din Mansoor Shirazi, the well-known philosopher,
and Jamal-ud-din Mahmud, a pupil of the celebrated Jalal-ud-din
Dawwani.[2] Hearing of Fathullah's reputation as a sage and an intellectual, the ruler of Bijapur invited him to come to his capital, and
from there in due course Akbar took him to Fathpur Sikri. Among

[2] Dawwani (1427–1501) occupies an important place in the intellectual history of the subcontinent. His pupils included Abul Fazl Gazruni, under whom
Shaikh Mubarik, the father of Abul Fazl and Faizi, studied at Ahmadabad, as
well as Fathullah Shirazi's teacher. Many of his religious works became textbooks and the subject of commentaries during the Mughal period. His most
famous work is *Akhlaq-i-Jalali,* which is still prescribed as a textbook for certain
examinations in India and Pakistan. It has been translated into English by
W. F. Thompson under the title, *The Practical Philosophy of the Muslim
People.* It contains considerable elements of Greek thought and ethics.

other assignments, he collaborated with Todar Mal in the creation of a system of revenue administration. He eventually became the head of the department for religious affairs, with responsibility for making grants to religious schools and seminaries.

According to Badauni, Fathullah was "thoroughly versed in all those sciences which demand the exercise of the reasoning faculty, such as philosophy, astronomy, geometry, astrology, geomancy, arithmetic, the preparation of talismans, incantations, and mechanics, and in this department of learning he was such an adept that he was able to draw up an astronomical table as soon as the emperor demanded one from him. He was equally learned in Arabic traditions, interpretation of the Quran, and rhetoric, and was the author of some excellent works." [3] He completed Dawwani's commentary on the important work of logic, *Tahzib-ul-Mantaq,* and wrote an exegesis of the Quran. His lasting contribution, however, was as an educator. He brought about extensive changes in the curriculum of the schools by introducing the works of recent Iranian scholars, including Dawwani, Sadr-ud-din, Ghias-ud-din Mansur, and Mirza Jan. Some works of the later Iranian philosophers and scholars had been introduced earlier in the days of Sikandar Lodi but they did not gain general currency. Now the fruits of the new philosophical era of Iran were sponsored by someone who had studied them under the Iranian masters and who was in charge of the department dispensing state patronage to educational institutions. This dual advantage played an important part in the success of the new education.

There were, however, other factors which facilitated the new trends in education. In Akbar's time there was a general emphasis on reason, intellect, and philosophy, and works connected with these subjects were encouraged. Furthermore, there were a number of other scholars besides Fathullah who had migrated from Persia. Among these was Hakim Abul Fath Gilana, Akbar's court physician, who wrote a commentary on Avicenna. Scholars from Samarqand and Bukhara also encouraged the study of logic. The efforts of these scolars and Akbar's own preferences combined to give an impetus to the spread of

---

[3] Abdul Qadir Badauni, *Muntakhab-ut-Tawarikh,* trans. by G. S. A. Ranking, W. H. Lowe, and Sir Wolseley Haig (Calcutta, 1884–1925), III, 216.

education which placed learning on a new footing in Islamic India. *Maqulat,* or mental sciences, became so important in the Mughal empire that a century later, when the educational curriculum was standardized, these traditional studies, and not the Islamic subjects such as *tafsir* and *hadith,* occupied the place of honor in the syllabus. These new disciplines were formal in nature, but their study in the Mughal period stimulated intellectual interest, facilitated mental discipline of the pupils, and provided the intellectual basis for the splendid Mughal cultural life.

XII. Religion at Akbar's Court

OF ALL the aspects of Akbar's life and reign, few have excited more interest than his attitude toward religion. There is every indication that he began his rule as a devout, orthodox Muslim. He said all the five prayers in the congregation, often recited the call for prayers, and occasionally swept out the palace mosque himself. He showed great respect for the two leading religious leaders at the court, Makhdum-ul-Mulk and Shaikh Abdul Nabi. Makhdum-ul-Mulk, who had been an important figure during the reign of the Surs, became even more powerful in the early days of Akbar. Shaikh Abdul Nabi, who was appointed sadr-ul-sadur in 1565, was given authority which no other holder of the office (the highest religious position in the realm) had ever enjoyed. Akbar would go to his house to hear him expound the sayings of the Prophet, and he placed his heir, Prince Salim, under his tutorship. "For some time the Emperor had so great faith in him as a religious leader that he would bring him his shoes and place them before his feet." [1]

Further indication of Akbar's orthodoxy and of his religious zeal was shown in his devotion to Khwaja Muin-ud-din, the great Chishti saint whose tomb at Ajmer was an object of veneration. He made his first pilgrimage to the tomb in 1565, and thereafter he went almost every year. If there was a perplexing problem or a particularly difficult expedition to undertake, he would make a special journey to pray at the tomb for guidance. He always entered Ajmer on foot, and in 1568 and 1570, in fulfillment of vows, walked the entire way from Agra to Ajmer.

It was probably devotion to Khwaja Muin-ud-din that was responsible for Akbar's interest in Shaikh Salim Chishti, a contemporary saint who lived at the site of what was to become Akbar's capital at Fathpur Sikri. It was there that he built the *Ibadat Khana,* the House

[1] Abdul Qadir Baudauni, *Muntakhab-ut-Tawarikh,* trans. by G. S. A. Ranking, W. H. Lowe, and Sir Wolseley Haig (Calcutta, 1884–1925), III, 127.

of Worship, which he set apart for religious discussions. Every Friday after the congregational prayers, scholars, dervishes, theologians, and courtiers interested in religious affairs would assemble in the *Ibadat Khana* and discuss religious subjects in the royal presence.

The assemblies in the *Ibadat Khana* had been arranged by Akbar out of sincere religious zeal, but ultimately they were to drive him away from orthodoxy. This was partly the fault of those who attended the gatherings. At the very first session there were disputes on the question of precedence, and when these were resolved, a battle of wits started among the participants. Each tried to display his own scholarship and reveal the ignorance of the others. Questions were asked to belittle rivals, and soon the gatherings degenerated into religious squabbles. The two great theologians of the court, Makhdum-ul-Mulk and Shaikh Abdul Nabi, arrayed on opposite sides, attacked each other so mercilessly that Akbar lost confidence in both of them. His disillusionment extended to the orthodoxy they represented.

Of the two, Makhdum-ul-Mulk was a powerful jurist and had received the title of Shaikh-ul-Islam from Sher Shah Suri. He used his position for two main purposes: to persecute the unorthodox and to accumulate fabulous wealth. Badauni says that when he died, thirty million rupees in cash were found in his house, and several boxes containing gold blocks were buried in a false tomb.

Shaikh Abdul Nabi, although not personally accused of graft, is said to have had corrupt subordinates. He was a strict puritan, and his hostility toward music was one of the grounds on which his rival attacked him in the discussions in the House of Worship. The petty recriminations of the ulama disgusted the emperor, but probably a deeper cause for his break with them was an issue that is comparable in some ways to the conflict between the church and the state in medieval Europe. The interpretation and application of Islamic law, which was the law of the state, was the responsibility of the ulama. Over against this, and certain to come in conflict with it, was Akbar's concentration of all ultimate authority in himself. Furthermore, with Akbar's organization of the empire on new lines, problems were arising which the old theologians were unable to comprehend, much less settle in a way acceptable to the emperor.

One such problem brought matters to a climax in 1577. A complaint was lodged before the emperor by the qazi of Mathura that
a rich Brahman in his vicinity had forcibly taken possession of building material collected for the construction of a mosque and had used
it for building a temple. "When the qazi had attempted to prevent
him, he had, in presence of witnesses, opened his foul mouth to curse
the Prophet, . . . and had shown his contempt for Muslims in
various other ways." [2] The question of suitable punishment for the
Brahman was discussed before the emperor, but, perplexed by conflicting considerations, he gave no decision. The Brahman languished
in prison for a long time. Ultimately Akbar left the matter to Shaikh
Abdul Nabi, who had the offender executed. This led to an outcry,
with many courtiers like Abul Fazl expressing the view that although
an offense had been committed, the extreme penalty of execution was
not necessary. They based their opinion on a decree of the founder
of the Hanafi school of Islamic law. Abdul Nabi's action was also
severely criticized by the Hindu courtiers and by Akbar's Rajput
wives. [3]

Akbar was troubled not only by this incident but by the general
legal position which gave so much power to the ulama that he was at
their mercy on such vital issues. He explained his difficulties to
Shaikh Mubarik, the father of Faizi and Abul Fazl, who had come
to the court on business. The shaikh, who was liberal minded and independent in his views, had suffered at the hands of Makhdum-ul-
Mulk. He stated that according to Islamic law, if there was a difference of opinion between the jurists, the Muslim ruler had the authority and the right to choose any one view, his choice being decisive.
He drew up a brief but important document, the arguments of which
were supported by quotations from the Holy Quran and traditions
of the Prophet. It read as follows:

Whereas Hindustan has now become the center of security and peace,
and the land of justice and beneficence, a large number of people, especially learned men and lawyers, have immigrated and chosen this country
for their home. Now we, the principal ulama, who are not only well
versed in the several departments of the law and in the principles of

[2] Badauni, III, 128.   [3] Badauni, III, 129.

jurisprudence, and well acquainted with the edicts which rest on reason
or testimony, but are also known for our piety and honest intentions, have
duly considered the deep meaning, first, of the verse of the Quran: "Obey
God and obey the Prophet, and those who have authority among you";
and secondly, of the genuine tradition: "Surely, the man who is dearest
to God on the day of judgment is the imam-i-adil; whosoever obeys the
Amir obeys Thee; and whoever rebels against him rebels against Thee";
and thirdly, of several other proofs based on reasoning or testimony; and
we have agreed that the rank of a sultan-i-adil is higher in the eyes of
God than the rank of a mujtahid. Further, we declare that the King of
Islam, Amir of the Faithful, Shadow of God in the world, Abul Fath
Jalal-ud-din Muhammad Akbar Padshah Ghazi (whose kingdom God
perpetuate), is a most just, most wise, and a most God-fearing king.
Should, therefore, in the future, a religious question come up, regarding
which the opinions of the mujtahids are at variance, and His Majesty, in
his penetrating understanding and clear wisdom, be inclined to adopt, for
the benefit of the nation, and as a political expedient, any of the conflicting opinions, which exist on that point, and issue a decree to that
effect, we do hereby agree that such a decree shall be binding on us and
on the whole nation.

Further, we declare that should His Majesty think it fit to issue a new
order, we and the nation shall likewise be bound by it, provided always
that such order be not only in accordance with some verse of the Quran,
but also of real benefit to the nation; and further, that any opposition on
the part of his subjects to such an order passed by His Majesty shall in-
volve damnation in the world to come, and loss of property and religious
privileges in this life.

This document has been written with honest intentions, for the glory
of God and the propagation of Islam, and is signed by us, the principal
ulama and lawyers, in the month of Rajab of the year nine hundred and
eight-seven.[4]

The document has been referred to as the "Infallibility Decree of
1579," with the implication that it gave to Akbar unlimited powers
in both the spiritual and temporal spheres. This is an erroneous reading for the king's authority was confined to measures which were "in
accordance with some verse of the quran" and were of "real benefit
for the nation." The modern Islamic scholar, Abul Kalam Azad, has
argued that the central thesis of the document was in line with traditional Islamic political theory. "The *khalifa* of the day and those in

⁴ Badauni, II, 279–80.

charge of affairs, and their advisers have the right of *ijtihad* (independent judgment) at all times and in all ages, and its denial has been
responsible for all the misfortunes of Islam." [5]

But the limitations laid down in the declaration of 1579 were not
observed by Akbar, and in practice it became an excuse for the exercise of unrestrained autocracy. Soon the gatherings of the *Ibadat
Khana* were exposed to new and more hostile influences. Before
long, in addition to the Muslim scholars, Hindu pandits, Parsi mobeds
and Jain sadhus began to attend the gatherings. They expressed their
own points of view, and the emperor, ever open to new ideas, was
attracted by some of their practices. A more serious complication
arose when the emperor invited Jesuits from Goa to the discussions.
They did not confine themselves to the exposition of their own beliefs, but reviled Islam and the Prophet in unrestrained language.

When the news of these discussions and the new decrees promul-
gated by the emperor became known, there was serious disaffection
among the Muslims. The first to criticize the new developments was
Mullah Muhammad Yazdi, the Shia qazi of Jaunpur, who declared
in 1580 that the emperor had ceased to be a Muslim and the people
should rise against him. Even some courtiers like Qutb-ud-din Khan
Koka and Shahbaz Khan Kamboh criticized the emperor in the court.
Akbar sent for Mullah Muhammad Yadzi and Muiz-ul-Mulk, the
chief qazi of Bengal, and had them put to death by drowning. His
punitive action against others did not prevent open rebellion from
breaking out in 1581. Akbar's enemies did not confine themselves to
sporadic outbursts and regional risings, but made a serious attempt to
dethrone him and place his brother Mirza Muhammad Hakim, ruler
of Kabul, on the throne. Akbar's brilliant diwan, Khawaja Shah
Mansur, was executed for alleged conspiracy with Mirza Hakim, who
got as far as Lahore, but being no match for Akbar, was driven back
to Kabul.

The historian Vincent Smith, in his biographical study of Akbar,
declares that the emperor, after he had returned from his successful
expedition against the rebels, called a formal council to promulgate

[5] Abul Kalam Azad, *Tazkirah* (Calcutta, 1919), p. 20.

his new religion the *Din-i-Ilahi*.[6] This reading of the evidence is, however, almost certainly erroneous. The Jesuits apparently had not heard of any such proclamation. In fact, Father Monserrate, who accompanied Akbar to Kabul and back, thought that the emperor had grown more cautious in the expression of his views. On the return journey Akbar performed prayers in the customary Muslim manner in a mosque near Khyber, was reluctant to have religious discussions with the Jesuits, and during one debate in which Muslim spokesmen appeared likely to lose, Akbar took their side and brought his own knowledge into play.[7] Not only Smith, but most European historians, have assumed that Akbar abandoned Islam. Hindu writers, on the other hand, have generally held that although he followed a tolerant policy, he lived and died a Muslim. Muslim historians are about equally divided on the question. These conflicting judgments partly reflect the inevitable differences that result from assessing a complex personality, but they are due also to conflicting contemporary accounts and, in no small degree, to erroneous translations of the relevant Persian texts.

The foundation for the misunderstanding of Akbar's religious history was laid by Blochmann in the introduction to his translation of Abul Fazl's *Ain-i-Akbari;* here he set the pattern for relying on Badauni, Akbar's enemy, rather than Abul Fazl, his friend, for studying Akbar's religious history. The crucial question about Akbar's religious activity is whether he established a new religion or a new spiritual order. Badauni's account is clearly intended to give the impression that Akbar no longer respected Islam and, indeed, actively persecuted it.[8] The expressions used by both Abul Fazl and Badauni in this connection, however, are *iradat* or *muridi* (discipleship) but Blochmann habitually translates these expressions as "divine faith," thus converting a religious order (or even a bond of loyalty) into a

[6] Vincent Smith, *Akbar the Great Mogul* (London, 1917), p. 213.
[7] Sir Edward Maclagan, *The Jesuits and the Great Mogul* (London, 1932), p. 35; *The Commentary of Father Monserrate, S.J.,* trans. by J. S. Hoyland (London, 1922), pp. 154–60, 180; and C. H. Payne, *Akbar and the Jesuits* (London, 1925), pp. 32–34.
[8] Badauni, II, 200–1, 255–61.

new religion. He translated the expression *ain-i-iradat gazinan,* which correctly means "Rules for the (royal) disciples," as the "principles of divine faith," and gives the subsection the heading, "ordinances of the divine faith," although there is no such heading in the original text.[9]

The sharp difference between the viewpoints of Abul Fazl and Badauni is obvious, but our study of the subject has revealed a surprisingly large area of common ground between them, and if the present divergence of opinion about Akbar's religion is to be resolved, more attention will have to be given to what is common ground between these two principal sources of our information. It appears that modern historians, fascinated by the wit and sarcasm of Badauni, have paid scant attention to Abul Fazl's informative sections on Akbar's religion contained in his *Akbar-Nama* and *Ain-i-Akbari.* Akbar's regulations which were not of an ephemeral or tentative character have been preserved in the voluminous *Ain-i-Akbari,* and it would be illogical to suppose that important royal orders, which were to be given general currency in the empire, would have been omitted. Since the *Ain*'s accounts of Akbar's religious innovations and of the practices of the royal disciples contain much that would shock an orthodox Muslim, there is no reason to suppose that regulations for the *Din-i-Ilahi* would not have been included. Judging by its contents and the public nature of the information which is sought, the *Ain* appears to be the most dependable source of information regarding Akbar's religious regulations and spiritual practices.

According to *Ain-i-Akbari* the emperor discouraged people from becoming his disciples, but the person whom he accepted for initiation approached him with his turban in his hand and put his head on the emperor's feet. This was to express that the novice had "cast aside conceit, selfishness—the root of so many evils." The emperor then stretched out his hand, raised up the disciple and replaced the turban on his head. . . . The novice was given a token containing the ruler's symbolic motto *Allah-u-Akbar* (God is Great). When the disciples met each other, one would say, *"Allah-u-Akbar"* and the

[9] Abul Fazl, *Ain-i-Akbari,* trans. by H. Blockmann et al. (Calcutta, 1927–1941), I, 175.

other responded, *"Jall-u-Jallaluhu."* "The motives of His Majesty in allowing this mode of salutation," Abul Fazl wrote, "is to remind men to think of the origin of their existence and to keep the Deity in their fresh, lively and grateful remembrance." [10] The disciples were to endeavor to abstain from flesh and not to make use of the same vessels as butchers, fishermen, and bird catchers. Each disciple was to give a party on the anniversary of his birthday and to bestow alms. The dinners customarily given after a man's death were to be given by a disciple during his lifetime.

For students of history, general orders intended for compliance by all are more important than the regulations framed for the royal disciples. According to Abul Fazl, the kotwals were asked to ensure that no ox or buffalo or horse or camel was slaughtered, and the killing of all animals was prohibited on many days of the year—including the whole month of Aban—except for feeding the animals used in hunting and for the sick.

Akbar interested himself in the reform of marriage customs. He abhorred marriages before the age of puberty and also considered marriages between near relations highly improper. He disapproved of large dowries, but admitted that they acted as a preventative to rash divorces. "Nor does His Majesty approve of everyone marrying more than one wife; for this ruins the man's health, and disturbs the peace of the home." Circumcision before the age of twelve was forbidden. The kotwals were to "forbid the restriction of personal liberty and the selling of slaves," and a woman was not to be burned on her husband's funeral pyre without giving her consent. Government officers were not to consider homage paid to the sun as worshiping fire. A governor was expected to accustom himself to night vigils and to partake of sleep and food in moderation. He was to pass the dawn and evening in meditation and pray at noon and midnight. Nauroz, the Parsi New Year, was to be celebrated officially, with the kotwal keeping a vigil on that night.

It was true that Akbar adopted and prescribed for his disciples and even others many practices which were borrowed from alien creeds, but precedents for this may be found in the lives of many Sufi

[10] Abul Fazl, I, 175.

saints who continue to be considered Muslims in spite of wide departures from traditional Islam. For all of his innovations, Islamic texts or precedents, genuine or spurious, were cited by his courtiers. But while Akbar did not claim to be a prophet or to establish a new religion, Islam lost its privileged position and many of his practices and regulations differed widely from the normal Muslim practices. It is not surprising that by many Muslims he was—and is—regarded as having gone outside the pale of Islam. Writing of the proclamation of 1579, Abul Fazl very ably summed up the popular misconceptions concerning Akbar, noting that he was accused by the "ill-informed and the unfair," of claiming divinity, or at least prophethood, of being anti-Muslim, a Shia, and partial to Hinduism.[11] While Abul Fazl answered these criticisms, he admitted that Akbar's policy and some of his regulations facilitated the task of his enemies. Possibly Akbar sincerely believed that the powers conferred on him by ulama in 1579 authorized him to initiate his regulations, and the court flatterers pandered to this belief by citing precedents in Islamic history. That they caused serious misgivings and resentment among orthodox Sunni Muslims was to be expected.

In any assessment of Akbar's religious policy, it is important to see that it had two quite distinct aspects. On the one hand were the political and administrative measures which he took to broaden the basis of his government and secure the goodwill of all his subjects. For this policy of religious tolerance and of giving an adequate share in the administration to all classes there can be nothing but praise, and it became a part of the Mughal political code. In themselves, these measures involved nothing more than what Muhammad ibn Qasim, the Arab conqueror of Sind, had adopted eight centuries before with full concurrence of the ulama of Damascus. Zain-ul-Abidin introduced similar measures in Kashmir without a murmur on the part of Muslims. They were adopted by Akbar in the very beginning of his reign—mainly between 1662 and 1665—at a time when the ulama were dominant at the court, without offending Muslim opinion.

An aspect of Akbar's religious policy that began several years after

[11] Abul Fazl, *The Akbarnama,* trans. by H. Beveridge (London, 1909), III, 390–400.

the acrimonious debates of the House of Worship was on a different footing. His attempt to set himself up as a jagat guru, the spiritual leader of the people, was a political mistake. Akbar's Hindu well-wishers like Raja Bhagwan Das and Raja Man Singh left him in no doubt about their dislike of his religious innovations. The only prominent Hindu who became his disciple was Birbal, regarded by succeeding generations as the court jester. Muslims were greatly offended and a reaction began against Akbar's policy which was to destroy much that he had created.

Akbar's failure was also due to forces operating outside the court. At this time a great Hindu religious revival was sweeping the country. It commenced in Bengal, but under Chaitanya's successors, Mathura in northern India became the great center of resurgent Hinduism. It was there that the great crisis had arisen over the wealthy Brahman who had taken building material collected for the construction of a mosque, and used it for building a Hindu temple. It is possible that this particular incident occurred in connection with the large-scale Vaishnava temple-building operations which were going on at Mathra at this time. Among the temple-builders was Raja Man Singh, Akbar's great Hindu general. The defiant spirit which had been inculcated by the new movement can be seen in the Brahman's action.

With such developments in the country, possibly with the support of his Hindu officers, Akbar's efforts at religious syncretion were doomed to failure. In fact, as we shall see, the new aggressive attitude of the Hindu revivalists and the offense which the emperor's religious innovations gave to the Muslims led to a reaction which was to destroy even the existing basis of harmony.

XIII. The Orthodox Reaction

THE OLD spiritual orders of Islam in India adopted the practice of keeping out of affairs of state, but toward the end of Akbar's reign a new religious group, following quite different traditions, entered the subcontinent. This was the Naqshbandi movement, which was introduced into India under the leadership of Khwaja Baqi Billah. The order's intention of seeking to influence temporal rulers is indicated in the statement of one of its leaders: "If I were after spiritual prominence, no disciple would be left with the other saints. But I have another mission—to bring comfort to the Muslims. To achieve this, I have to associate with the worldly rulers, gain influence over them and thereby fulfill the objects of the Muslims." [1]

Khwaja Baqi Billah was born at Kabul in 1563, and after completing his scholastic education there and at Samarqand he visited several saints for spiritual training. Ultimately he was initiated in the Naqshbandi order by a leading saint of Bukhara, who asked him to make India the center of his work. Khwaja Baqi Billah came first to Lahore, where he spent more than a year before moving to Delhi. Partly owing to his great spiritual powers, and partly because he represented the order belonging to the native land of the ruling family, he acquired a prominent position in the religious life of the capital. He was particularly active as a link between the various nobles who were displeased with Akbar's religious innovations. One of these was Shaikh Farid, who, according to Jesuit accounts, extracted a promise from Jahangir, Akbar's heir, to uphold Islam in the kingdom.[2] Other nobles who had great regard for the khwaja included Qulich Khan,

[1] For fuller commentaries on religious movements, see S. M. Ikram, *Ab-i-Kausar, Rud-i-Kausar,* and *Mauj-i-Kausar* (Karachi, 1958).

[2] C. H. Payne, *Akbar and the Jesuits* (London, 1926), pp. 204 and 248. The accuracy of this account is denied by I. M. Habib in "The Political Role of Shaikh Ahmad Sirhindi and Shah Waliullah," *Proceedings of the Twenty-Third Session of the Indian History Congress, 1960* (Calcutta, 1961), Part I, pp. 209–23. The view given in the text, however, is the one usually accepted. See *Cambridge History of India* (Cambridge, 1928), IV, 152.

the devout viceroy of Lahore, Abdul Rahim Khan-i-Khanan, the commander-in-chief of the Deccan, and Khan-i-Azam, the deputy of the realm. In some of the khwaja's letters there are references to Sadr Jahan (the head of the religious endowments under Akbar) coming to him for spiritual training. The khwaja died in 1603, but before his death the Naqshbandi order had been firmly established in India.

Khwaja Baqi Billah's most prominent disciple was Shaikh Ahmad, popularly known as Mujaddid Alif Sani (reviver of Islam during the second millennium). He was born at Sirhind on June 26, 1564, and was educated there and at Sialkot. He established himself at Sirhind, but he was soon attracted to Akbar's capital, Fathpur Sikri. Here he moved in the most distinguished intellectual circles, and seems to have favorably impressed Abul Fazl and his versatile brother, Faizi. Shaikh Ahmad's views and temperament had little in common with those of the two brothers (though he himself passed through a period of youthful free-thinking and at one time wrote verses with the poetic surname of Kufri, the "heretic"), but they had enough respect for each other's learning to be able to carry on this intellectual comradeship in spite of the difference in views. The shaikh is even stated to have helped Faizi in the completion of his commentary on the Quran.

He visited Delhi in 1599 and went to see Khwaja Baqi Billah, who asked him to spend a few days in his hospice. Within two days Ahmad requested the khwaja to take him into discipleship. After having initiated Shaikh Ahmad into various stages of spiritual development under the Naqshbandi order, the khwaja wrote: "Shaikh Ahmad is . . . rich in knowledge and vigorous in action. I associated with him for a few days, and noticed truly marvelous things in his spiritual life. He will turn into a light which will illuminate the world."

Shaikh Ahmad returned to Sirhind, convinced that he had a major role to play in the religious life of the times. He twice visited Delhi during the lifetime of the khwaja, who deputed him to work at Lahore. After the khwaja's death, he retired to Sirhind, which remained the main seat of his activities. He carried on his work partly through personal guidance and oral instructions, but he had discovered his literary gifts, and believed that he could also fulfill his mission by writing letters on religious and public subjects to important personages

of the day. Khwaja Baqi Billah had, by his warm praise and encouragement, made Shaikh Ahmad aware of his potentialities. He
had also facilitated the achievement of his task by providing him
useful contacts with persons in key positions in the state. Shaikh
Ahmad was able to make full use of these opportunities. A profound
scholar, a master of polemics, and possessing a polished and forceful
literary style, he began sending letters to important nobles bemoaning
the sad state into which Islam had fallen in India and reminding them
of their duty.[3] The rhetoric and appeal of these letters kindled a religious fervor which, although it took some time to bear fruit, profoundly affected the history of Islam in India by strengthening the
position of the orthodox in places of power.

But Shaikh Ahmad's letters touched on more than just religious
revival, and it was this that placed him in serious difficulties. Some of
his letters stated that in his trances he saw that at one time he had
gone ahead of all the Companions of the Prophet. The theologians
criticized these claims, and asked Emperor Jahangir to take action.
The wazir, Asaf Khan, who was a Shia, could not have been fond of
the anti-Shia views of Shaikh Ahmad, and he is said to have pointed
out the political dangers inherent in the growing influence and organization of Shaikh Ahmad. In 1619, through the governor of Sirhind,
he was summoned to the emperor's court and asked to explain his
statements. The shaikh behaved at the court with great dignity and
courage. He made it clear that there could be no question of his
considering himself superior to the Companions of the Prophet, and
gave an explanation of the relevant entry in his letters. The emperor
seemed to be satisfied with this, but he took offense when somebody
pointed out that the shaikh had not performed the *sijdah* (deep
obeisance), which Akbar had prescribed for everybody coming in the
royal presence. The shaikh's reply that he was not prepared to perform the *sijdah* before any human being seemed to be open defiance,
and he was imprisoned in Gwalior fort.

After about a year the shaikh was released from the fort, presented
with a dress of honor and a thousand rupees for expenses and given
an option of accompanying the royal camp or returning to Sirhind.

[3] Shaikh Ahmad, *Maktubat-i-Iman-i-Rabbani* (Lucknow, 1877).

The shaikh preferred to remain in the royal camp, and this enabled him to visit the whole of the empire, and even establish friendly contacts with the emperor. It appears that Jahangir came to hold the shaikh in great respect; in his autobiography he twice refers to having made large offerings to the saint, and among the shaikh's letters there is one addressed to the emperor. In another letter the shaikh gave a detailed account of a lengthy conversation he had with the emperor on religious subjects, with the emperor apparently taking a great interest.

Shaikh Ahmad was in the royal camp for nearly three years. His letters written during this period contain few biographical details, but the entries in Jahangir's autobiography suggest that during this period the easy-going Jahangir was unusually religious. It would not be surprising if the emperor's orthodox mood were due to the shaikh's presence in the camp. For example, in describing the conquest of Kangra and his visit there in early 1622, Jahangir says: "I went to see the fort of Kangra, and gave an order that the qazi, the Chief Justice, and other learned men of Islam should accompany me and carry out in the fort whatever was customary, according to the religion of Muhammad. Briefly . . . by the grace of God, the call to prayer and the reading of the *khutba* and the slaughter of a bullock, which had not taken place from the commencement of the building of the fort till now, were carried out in my presence. I . . . ordered a lofty mosque to be built inside the fort." [4] It is more than probable that Shaikh Ahmad was one of "the learned men of Islam" who accompanied Jahangir to Kangra. Soon after, the saint's health began to fail, and with the emperor's permission he returned to Sirhind. Here he lived in seclusion, devoting himself to charity and prayers until his death on December 10, 1624.

Shaikh Ahmad was the most forceful and original thinker produced by Muslim India before the days of Shah Waliullah and Iqbal. Indeed he occupies a high place in the religious history of the entire Muslim world, for his exposition of *tawhid-i-shahudi* was a distinct contribution to Islamic thought. Perhaps even more important was the atti-

---

[4] *Memoirs of Jahangir*, trans. by Alexander Rogers and H. Beveridge (London, 1909), II, 161 and 223.

tude of vigorous self-confidence and self-assertion which he contributed to Muslim thinking, the like of which had been seen rarely since the days of Ibn Taimiya in the eighth century.

The white heat of revivalist fervor which one finds in his writings is not visible among early members of his order, the Naqshbandi. In spite of Shah Waliullah's emphasis on moderation (see Chapter XIX), the Mujaddidiya revival, associated with the shaikh, ultimately superseded other branches of the Naqshbandi order, not only in the subcontinent but in the Ottoman empire as well. This is remarkable considering that the main order was of Central Asian and Turkish origin. The influence of the Mujaddidiya seems to have been a factor in creating those forces which ultimately led to the rise and widespread acceptance of Wahhabism.

In discussing Akbar's religious policy, reference was made to the circumstances which made its failure inevitable. The inability of the Hindus and Muslims to evolve a common spiritual brotherhood was the result of the basic fact that to the Hindus the Muslims were (and are) untouchables. This attitude of the Hindus, nourished by the revivalistic fervor of the Vaishnava Gosains of Mathura, became more marked during Akbar's era of toleration. The writings of the shaikh, which reveal the anguish he felt at the low position of Islam under Akbar and even later, also militated against the success of Akbar's policy. In fact, it would not be wrong to say that the swing of religious policy from Akbar to Aurangzeb was in some measure due to the influence and teachings of Shaikh Ahmad.

His forceful and eloquent letters addressed to the leading nobles at Jahangir's court calling on them to rise in defense of Islam and uphold the dignity of their religion have great power and effectiveness. These letters were meant not only for the individuals to whom they were addressed; they were really "open letters" and were no less forceful than the poems with which Byron tried to engender enthusiasm for the cause of Greek independence, or with which Hali tried to reawaken Indian Muslims. Copies of them were supplied to the shaikh's disciples and admirers, and given wide circulation.

Some Naqshbandi writers state that Aurangzeb became a disciple of Khwaja Muhammad Masum, son and successor of Shaikh Ahmad,

but even though Aurangzeb's contemporary, the satirist Nimat Khan Ali, refers to it in his *Wiqaya,* the connection is not certain, since it is not mentioned in the historical accounts of the reign. The official history of the period, however, does refer to his visits to the emperor's court, where he received high honors and rich gifts. After his death, his son, Shaikh Saif-ud-din, came to stay at the royal capital and apparently was in close contact with Aurangzeb. The court history speaks of his being a formal witness at the wedding of Prince Azam Shah. Next year, on June 3, 1669, the emperor visited the saint at his residence for one hour late at night, and then returned to the palace.[5]

Even more remarkable than these historic links between Aurangzeb and Shaikh Ahmad's family is the fact that almost all the steps which are associated with Aurangzeb's religious policy had been advocated so forcefully by the shaikh in his letters. Shaikh Ahmad had seen those days when, according to him, "non-Muslims carried out aggressively the ordinances of their own religion in a Muslim state and the Muslims were powerless to carry out the ordinances of Islam; if they carried them out, they were executed." He had described with great anguish those tragic days those who believed in the Holy Prophet were "humiliated and powerless, while those who denied his prophethood enjoyed high position, and used to sprinkle salt on the wounds of the Muslims with ridicule and taunts."

These developments had filled Shaikh Ahmad with anger and hatred against Akbar and the non-Muslims. What had troubled him even more was that with Akbar's withdrawal of patronage from Islam, and an aggressive religious revival among the Hindus, non-Muslims had started persecuting Islam. "The non-Muslims in India," he wrote, "are without any hesitation demolishing mosques and setting up temples in their place. For example, in Kurukshetra there was a mosque and the tomb of a saint. They have been demolished and in their place a very big temple has been erected." Hindus were even interfering with Muslim observances. "Moreover, non-Muslims openly carry out their observances, but Muslims are powerless to carry out

[5] Saqi Mustad Khan, *Maasir-i-Alamgiri,* trans. by Jadunath Sarkar (Calcutta, 1947), pp. 49 and 53.

openly many of the Islamic injunctions. During Ekadashi, Hindus fast and strive hard to see that in Muslim towns no Muslim cooks or sells food on these days. On the other hand, during the sacred month of Ramadan, they openly prepare and sell food, but owing to the weakness of Islam, nobody can interfere. Alas, the ruler of the country is one of us, but we are so badly off!"

Shaikh Ahmad was convinced that the considerations shown to Hindus in Akbar's reign had emboldened them, and that this policy must be reversed. In a number of his letters he expressed regret at the abolition of *jizya* and urged its revival. In another letter he demanded the abolition of the ban on cow slaughter. He called upon the Muslim nobles not to associate with non-Muslims and unorthodox Muslims, including Shias. In a letter to Shaikh Farid, one of the chief nobles, he went so far as to say that the company of Muslim nonconformists was worse than that of non-Muslims. Once the preacher at the principal mosque of Samana did not follow the Sunni practice of mentioning all the four caliphs in his Id sermon; Shaikh Ahmad immediately wrote an open letter to the religious leaders of the city, rebuking them for the neglect of their duties, and for their failure to deal "aggressively and offensively" with that "unjust preacher."

Shaikh Farid and other leaders did not accept the extremist point of view, and in some of his letters Shaikh Ahmad has expressed his disappointment with Farid's failures and omissions. But his warnings and his denunciations had their effect, and there is no doubt that he had a wide following in the highest places. Is it a mere coincidence that the attitude which Aurangzeb had toward Shias—at least during his early days—was identical with that of Shaikh Ahmad?

Elsewhere in India other saints and prophets were upholding orthodoxy with scarcely less vigor and success than Khwaja Baqi Billah and Shaikh Ahmad. On the northwest frontier Sayyid Ali Shah Tirmiz, known as Pir Baba, and his disciple Akhund Darweza took as their special task the uprooting of the heretical Raushaniya sect which flourished in the mountains. Pir Baba's descendants wielded great influence among the Pathan tribesmen, and three centuries later provided a rallying point against the Sikhs and the British.

Signs of religious activity of a somewhat different nature, but con-

ducive to the strengthening of the forces of orthodox Muslim were visible at about the same time in Bengal. The religious history of Muslim Bengal is as yet unwritten, but there are indications that after the vigor and energy displayed by Chaitanya and his prominent disciples, and particularly the vigorous expression which their devotions and religious yearnings found in the new Bengali literature, Islamic influences in the area gradually weakened, especially outside the principal cities. This happened partly because the waves of the immigrant Sufis and preachers had subsided, but the lack of knowledge of Persian and Arabic among the general populace also prevented the propagation of Islam. At the same time, a vigorous new Bengali literature was coming into existence, often under the patronage of the Muslim rulers. This was concerned largely with the stories of the *Ramayana* and the *Mahabharata,* and the Muslim masses, not well-versed in any language other than Bengali, heard the Bengali poems and stories connected with these themes or saw them acted at Hindu festivals under the patronage of the Hindu landlords. Their mental background thus became more Hindu than Islamic.

As a counter-measure to the popular Bengali Hindu literature, marked literary activity among Bengali Muslims took place at the end of the sixteenth and the beginning of the seventeenth century, with a special emphasis on the writing of lives of the prophets and other saints in the language of the people. Sayyid Sultan, a leader of this movement, gave the reasons for the literary activity in his *Wafat-i-Rasul:*

All the Bengalis do not understand Arabic;
None understands the words of your religion.
Everyone remains satisfied with [Hindu] tales.
I, the despised and sinful, am in the midst of these people.
I do not know what Ilahi [God] will ask me in the afterlife.
If He asks, "Having been in their midst, why did you not tell them about the religion?" and blames me for this fault, I will have no power to give a proper reply. Considering this, I have composed *Nabi-vamsa* [a history of the Prophet's family] for the benefit of the ignorant people.
For this reason many people blame me for having polluted this religious book.

When the learned read from the books, which are in Arabic, and do
   not translate them into Hindustani [i.e., Bengali], how can our people
   follow?
In whatever language God has given one birth, that alone is his highest
   treasure.

Thus, as men like Shaikh Ahmad appealed to the upper classes to
maintain the Faith through their political power, men like Sayyid
Sultan took the Prophet's message to the common people. Both appeals explain the resurgent power of Islam in the century following
Akbar's experiments.

XIV. The Age of Splendor

AKBAR'S only surviving son, Prince Salim, succeeded to the throne on November 3, 1605, under the title of Jahangir. To prove his desire to end the bitterness that had divided the court when he had made an unsuccessful attempt to usurp power during the last years of his father's reign, he granted a general amnesty to all his former opponents. Abdur Rahman, the son of Abul Fazl (Akbar's friend who had been murdered at Jahangir's instigation), was promoted to higher rank. The nobles who had endeavored to have Jahangir's son, Khusrau, made Akbar's successor were allowed to retain their ranks and *jagirs.*

Despite his attempts at conciliation, Jahangir was soon faced with the task of suppressing a revolt led by Khusrau, who had fled to the Punjab. The revolt was quelled without great difficulty with Khusrau brought back in chains, but it led, incidentally, to one important development. Khusrau had received help from Arjan Dev, the guru or leader of the Sikhs. After Khusrau's defeat, Arjan Dev was summoned to the court to answer for his conduct. Sikh historians say that the enmity of Chandu Lal, the Hindu diwan of Lahore, who had a family quarrel with the guru, was responsible for his troubles. When the guru was unable to give any satisfactory explanation for his part in the rebellion, he was put to death. He might have ended his days in peace if he had not espoused the cause of the rebel, but this punitive action against him marked the beginning of a long and bitter conflict between the Sikhs and the Mughal government.

An event of Jahangir's private life that was to have great significance for his reign was his marriage to Nur Jahan in 1611. She was the widow of a Persian nobleman, Sher Afghan, a rebellious official of Burdwan who met his death while resisting arrest at the hands of Qutb-ud-din Khan Koka, the viceroy of Bengal.

Nur Jahan was taken to the court, and three years later, at the age of forty, she became the royal consort. A capable woman, she acquired such an ascendency over her husband that she became in effect

the joint ruler of the kingdom. Coins were struck in her name, and Jahangir used to say that he had handed her the country in return for a cup of wine and a few morsels of food. Nur Jahan's relatives soon occupied the chief posts of the realm. Her brother, Asaf Khan, became the prime minister, and his daughter, Mumtaz Mahal, the Lady of the Taj, married Prince Khurram, who succeeded his father as Shah Jahan. The influence of the gifted but masterly queen and her relatives was not entirely beneficial, but they were all capable people and until toward the end of the later part of Jahangir's reign, they administered the empire efficiently. Their influence attracted a large number of brilliant soldiers, scholars, poets, and civil servants from Iran who played an important role in the administration and the cultural life of Mughal India.

One of the most fruitful achievements of Jahangir's reign was the consolidation of Mughal rule in Bengal. This province had been incorporated in the empire under Akbar, but the governors of Akbar's time had not attempted to bring the existing local chiefs—Hindu and Muslim—under the full control of the central government. The imposition of Mughal power and the crushing of local resistance was largely the work of Jahangir's foster-brother, Shaikh Ala-ud-din, entitled Islam Khan, who was viceroy of Bengal from 1608 to 1613. He employed all possible methods—force, reward, and diplomacy—to terminate the independence of the powerful zamindars. He also enlarged the territorial limits of the empire by subjugating Cooch Behar in 1609 and Kamrup in 1612. In 1612 he shifted his capital from Rajmahal to Dacca, a singularly appropriate choice in view of the menace of Magh raids on the eastern rivers. Islam Khan died in 1613, and after an interval of four years, during which his incompetent brother was in charge of the area, his good work was continued by another capable viceroy, Ibrahim Khan Fath-i-Jung. He devoted the six years of his viceroyalty (1617–1623) to consolidating the gains already made and died fighting loyally against Prince Khurram when he revolted against his father the emperor and tried to seize the government of Bengal.

Outside Bengal, the main military events of Jahangir's reign were the victory over the Rajputs of Mewar in 1615, the reassertion of the Mughal authority in the Deccan, and the capture of Kangra in 1620.

Two years later the Mughals lost the great fort of Qandahar to the Persians, and in spite of efforts made during Jahangir's and Shah Jahan's reigns, they were never able to recover it. This was also a time of internal difficulties. Hitherto, Nur Jahan, Asaf Khan, and Prince Khurram had cooperated in controlling the affairs of the country, and Khurram had been the leader of victorious expeditions in Rajputana and the Deccan. Nur Jahan, however, had now attained complete ascendency over the emperor and tried to promote the claims of his youngest son, Prince Shahryar, to whom her daughter by Sher Afghan was married. This brought her into conflict with Prince Khurram, who revolted in 1623. He became master of Bengal and Bihar for a brief time, but was ultimately defeated and obliged to retire to the Deccan. In the end he asked his father's pardon and was reconciled in 1626.

Jahangir died in the following year on his way back from Kashmir and was buried at Shahdara, a suburb of Lahore. Through a relay of messengers, Asaf Khan sent word to Prince Khurram, his son-in-law, who was still in the Deccan, and the succession was secured without much difficulty. Prince Shahryar, Nur Jahan's son-in-law, was captured and blinded; Nur Jahan herself retired from the world she had dominated, living quietly until her death sixteen years later.

Owing to his likable personality, the brilliance of his court, and his friendliness toward foreigners, Jahangir has been favorably treated, especially by English writers. There are, however, certain aspects of his administration which cast a shadow on his regime and darken the course of the later Mughal history. The extension of the Mughal dominion came practically to a halt in his reign, and the empire suffered a serious blow in the loss of Qandahar. In spite of vast imperial resources, no serious attempt was made to bring the great unconquered areas of the Deccan under the empire. A contemporary Dutch writer commenting on this said: "The probable explanation is to be found in the sloth, cowardice, and weakness of the last emperor, Salim, and in the domestic discords of his family." [1] There is little reason to doubt the essential truth of this harsh judgment.

A significant change took place in the composition of the nobility

---

[1] Joannes de Laet, *Empire of the Great Mogul*, trans. by J. S. Hoyland (Bombay, 1928), p. 246.

and the holders of high office during the years of Nur Jahan's ascend-ency. Akbar had made good use of the indigenous element—such men as Abul Fazl, Faizi, Todar Mal, Shaikh Farid, Man Singh, and Bhagwan Singh come to mind—and had maintained a due balance between the Irani and Turani elements. Under Jahangir this balance was upset, and the Iranis became all-powerful. This was facilitated by the early death of Shaikh Farid and by the stigma attached to Man Singh, the Rajput leader, and to Khan-i-Azam, the premier Turani noble, because of their association with Khusrau. Held in check, the Irani element was a source of strength, but this ceased to be the case in the eighteenth century, when its political role during the decline of the empire weakened the realm.

Even more objectionable was the mushroom growth of bureaucracy and the resultant increase in government expenditure. No large ter-ritory was added to the empire, but the number of mansabdars, which under Akbar numbered about eight hundred, was increased to nearly three thousand in Jahangir's reign. The author of *Maasir-ul-Umara,* himself a financial expert, in dealing with the fiscal history of the Mughal period, said: "In the time of Jahangir, who was a careless prince and paid no attention to political or financial matters, and who was constitutionally thoughtless and pompous, the fraudulent officials, in gathering lucre, and hunting for bribes, paid no attention to the abilities of men or to their performance. The devastation of the country and the diminution of income rose to such a height that the revenue of the exchequer-lands fell to five million rupees while ex-penditure rose to fifteen million, and large sums were expended out of the general treasury." [2]

Jahangir must bear the ultimate responsibility for this state of affairs, but the immediate cause was the dominance and policy of Nur Jahan. She was a woman of noble impulses and good taste who spent large sums in charity, particularly for the relief of indigent women, and worked hard to relieve the drabness of Indian life. Many innovations which enhanced the grace and charm of Mughal culture can be directly traced to her, and her influence led to the maintenance of a magnificent court. But all this strained the royal resources.

[2] *Maasir-ul-Umara,* trans. by Henry Beveridge (Calcutta, 1911–1952), I, 579.

The lavish style of living introduced at the royal court was initiated by the nobility, and an era of extravagance, with its concomitants of corruption and demoralization among officers of the state, was inaugurated. This corroded the structure of the Mughal government. A contemporary Dutch account sharply criticized Nur Jahan and her "crowd of Khurasanis" for what it was costing the state to maintain "their excessive pomp" and complained that the foreign bureaucrats were particularly indifferent to the condition of the masses.[3] To Nur Jahan herself belongs the doubtful honor of introducing the system of *nazars* or gifts to the court—corruption at the royal level. Asaf Khan emerges in the pages of Sir Thomas Roe's account of his negotiations at the Mughal court as exceedingly greedy for such gifts.[4]

The era of extravagance which was ushered in during Jahangir's reign was fed from two other sources. One was the change in the prevalent philosophy of life. The old Indian emphasis on plain living and the excellence of limitation of wants was not consistent with the way of life introduced by Muslim rulers in the subcontinent, but (coupled with the Sufi philosophy) it was not without a certain influence. In Akbar's days in particular, with emphasis on the spiritual side of things, it is easy to trace a certain idealism, an other-worldliness, and the ability to rise above purely materialistic values, in spite of the elaborate grandeur of a great empire. The Irani newcomers were alien to this approach and under their influence the gracious living became the *summum bonum,* the goal of human existence.

The other factor responsible for increased extravagance was the vast opportunity for spending provided by the new commercial contacts with Europe. By now the fame of the Mughal empire had spread to distant lands, and in Jahangir's day embassies came to his court from European countries. England sent Captain Hawkins in 1608, and Sir Thomas Roe, the ambassador of James I, came to conclude a commercial treaty in 1615. By September, 1618, he was able to obtain a *farman* signed by Prince Khurram as viceroy of Gujarat which gave facilities for trade, but owing to the prince's opposition,

[3] Brij Narain and S. R. Sharma, trans. and eds., *A Contemporary Dutch Chronicle of India* (Calcutta, 1957), pp. 92–93.
[4] William Foster, ed., *The Embassy of Sir Thomas Roe to India* (London, 1926).

did not allow a building to be built as a residence. The new trade, which will be noted more fully later, brought out some pathetic propensities in the Mughal nobility. Costly toys were devised to please the taste of the court. In this Jahangir led the way. He was described as "an amateur of all varieties and antiquities, and displayed an almost childish love of toys." One traveler tells how he presented the emperor with "a small whistle of gold, weighing almost an ounce, set with sparks of rubies, which he took and whistled therewith almost an hour." [5]

The Reign of Shah Jahan

The charge made against Jahangir—that he had been too slothful to extend the empire—could not be made against his son, Prince Khurram, who ascended the throne as Shah Jahan on February 6, 1628. Although under him the splendor and luxury of the court reached its zenith, he revived the expansionist policy of Akbar and widened the frontiers of the empire to include territories that had so far escaped Mughal domination.

Before he could bring new areas under his sway, however, he had to meet a number of threats within the existing empire. One came at the very beginning of his reign, on the death of Bir Singh Bundela, the favorite of Jahangir and murderer of Abul Fazl; his son revolted and tried to establish himself as an independent chieftain in Bundelkhand. This revolt was put down quickly. More serious was one in the south led by Khan Jahan Lodi, a former viceroy of the Deccan, who gained some support from Hindu chieftains. He fought Shah Jahan's troops for three years but was finally killed in 1631. Another threat came from the Portuguese who had been permitted by the last independent king of Bengal to settle at Hugli. They had received commercial privileges, but they began to abuse their position through their relations with the Portuguese at Chittagong, who indulged in piracy in the Bay of Bengal and on Bengal rivers. Another cause for

[5] S. M. Edwardes and H. L. O. Garrett, *Mughal Rule in India* (Delhi, 1956), p. 269.

dispute was that the Portuguese had fortified their settlement at Hugli and, owing to their command of the sea and superiority in the use of firearms, the Mughal authorities "could not but conceive great fears," to quote a contemporary Portuguese account, "lest His Majesty of Spain should possess himself of the kingdom of Bengal." Shah Jahan, who had become particularly aware of the problem in the course of his wanderings in Bengal during his revolt against his father, gave orders in 1631 to Qasim Khan, viceroy of Bengal, to drive them out. As the Portuguese were well-organized, elaborate measures were necessary. They offered stiff resistance, but Hugli was captured in 1632, and the garrison was severely punished. This was followed by the reconquest of Kamrup (1637–38), which had been lost to the Ahom ruler of Assam in the previous reign.

In the Deccan, Shah Jahan was faced by the opposition of the virtually independent Muslim ruler of Ahmadnagar. Akbar had succeeded in annexing Khandesh, Berar, and a part of Ahmadnagar, but the ruler of Ahmadnagar took advantage of Jahangir's preoccupation with the rebellion of Shah Jahan to reassert his independence. Shah Jahan, having acted as governor for the area, knew the Deccan well and adopted a vigorous policy. In 1633 the last king of the Nizam Shahi dynasty of Ahmadnagar was captured, and the famous fort of Daulatabad fell into the hands of the Mughals. Three years later Shah Jahan went to the Deccan himself and compelled the rulers of Golkunda and Bijapur to acknowledge the Mughal suzerainty and to pay tribute. He appointed his son Aurangzeb as viceroy of the Deccan. Under him were the four provinces of Khandesh, Berar, Telingana, and Daulatabad. In 1638 Aurangzeb added Baglana to the empire.

Having attained his goal in the Deccan, Shah Jahan turned his attention to the northwest. The Mughals had not reconciled themselves to the loss of Qandahar, and in 1638 Shah Jahan's officers persuaded Ali Mardan Khan, the local Persian governor, to hand over the fort to the Mughals and enter their service. Ali Mardan Khan was a capable officer and proved a great acquisition to the empire. While governor of Kabul and Kashmir he erected many magnificent buildings. The recovery of Qandahar was only temporary, however, for

the Persians regained the fort in 1648. Attempts made by the Mughals in 1649, 1652, and 1653 to dislodge them were all unsuccessful.

Shah Jahan's efforts to interfere in the affairs of Central Asia were equally fruitless. In 1645 conditions at Bukhara were disturbed, and Shah Jahan took this opportunity to send an army under Murad, who entered Balkh in 1646. Aurangzeb, who was appointed governor, fought bravely to hold his own against the Uzbegs, but he found it impossible to hold the country, and evacuated Balkh in 1647.

Despite Shah Jahan's failures in Central Asia, he was singularly successful in dealing with the northwest frontier. This area had given trouble in the days of Akbar, mainly because of the opposition of the Yusufzais and the followers of the Raushaniya sect. Shah Jahan's chief official in the area, Saíd Khan, who was appointed governor of Kabul, dealt with Abdul Qadir, the Raushaniya leader, in an effective way.

He dispersed the hostile tribesmen with heavy casualties, but by tact and firmness he persuaded Abdul Qadir and his mother to surrender on promise of safe-conduct. Abdul Qadir died shortly thereafter, but his mother with other relatives and Raushaniya leaders appeared before the emperor at Delhi. "They were kindly treated, and sent with rank and dignity to the Deccan provinces, where they were allowed to gather round them their adherents in the empire's service." [6]

Aurangzeb, who was the viceroy of the Deccan from 1636 to 1644, had placed the affairs of the newly conquered territory on a satisfactory basis, but the viceroys who succeeded him were unable to administer the area effectively. A large number of soldiers and officials belonging to the Deccani kingdoms who had been displaced fomented unrest, cultivation was neglected, and revenues diminished. Aurangzeb was sent back to the Deccan in 1653 and worked arduously to restore order and good government. He introduced the land revenue system which Akbar had adopted in the north, and with the adoption of a regular system of land revenue, cultivation was extended and revenue increased.

Aurangzeb's relations with his eldest brother, Dara Shukoh, who had gained great power at the capital with their father, were not

[6] Olaf Caroe, *The Pathans* (London, 1958), p. 229.

happy. His requests for additional funds received little attention and many other difficulties were placed in his way. He was hampered even in his dealings with the rulers of the Deccan. They failed to pay the annual tribute regularly and, after obtaining the approval of the court, Aurangzeb demanded from the ruler of Golkunda a part of his territory to cover his tribute. He marched on Golkunda and laid siege to the fort, but the sultan made representations to Delhi and Aurangzeb was ordered to pardon him.

Lack of harmony between the viceroy of the Deccan and the authorities at Delhi became even more manifest in the case of Bijapur. In 1657 disorder broke out in that kingdom, and after obtaining the permission from the emperor, Aurangzeb set out to conquer Bijapur. Bidar and Kalyani were captured and the Bijapur army was decisively defeated, but again Dara Shukoh and Shah Jahan interfered. Aurangzeb was ordered to withdraw.

Shah Jahan fell seriously ill in 1658 and was unable to attend to affairs of state for so long a time that there were even rumors of his death. His sons, feeling that his end was near, began to assert their claims. Dara Shukoh, the eldest, viceroy of the Punjab and Allahabad, had been treated practically as heir-apparent, and toward the end of Shah Jahan's reign, the administration of the state had been left largely to him. His brothers, who also were in charge of vast territories—Aurangzeb as viceroy of the Deccan, Shah Shuja in charge of Bengal and Murad, ruler of Gujarat—contested Dara's claims. On hearing of their father's illness and Dara Shukoh's assumption of the administration of the imperial affairs, Shuja and Murad claimed the succession, but the ever-cautious Aurangzeb bided his time. He corresponded with Shuja and Murad, and all three brothers started moving toward the capital from their respective territories. The forces of Murad and Aurangzeb met near Ujjain in Central India and continued toward Agra. Dara sent Jaswant Singh to oppose them, but he was defeated and the victorious armies of the allies reached Samugarh, near Agra. Here Dara, with the bulk of the imperial army, gave them battle, but he was no match for Aurangzeb in generalship, and the battle ended in his complete defeat.

Aurangzeb entered Agra and was invited by Shah Jahan to meet

him, but his well-wishers, Khalil Ullah Khan (who had originally been sent by Shah Jahan as an intermediary and later switched allegiance to Aurangzeb) and Shayista Khan informed him that there was a plot to have him arrested and assassinated. Shah Jahan was so closely allied with Dara that Aurangzeb refused to trust him. A point had been reached where there could be no turning back; Aurangzeb therefore placed his father under restraint and assumed the imperial authority on July 21, 1658.

In the meanwhile, Murad, who had shown resentment at the growing power of Aurangzeb, was arrested and imprisoned in the fort of Gwalior. Some three years later, after an attempt at escape, Aurangzeb decided that alive he was dangerous. A complaint was lodged by the son of a former diwan of Gujarat whom Murad had put to death, and, obtaining a legal decree, Aurangzeb had Murad executed on December 4, 1661.

Dara fled to the north, but after wandering in the Punjab, Sind, Gujarat, and Rajputana, he was captured and put to death in 1659. Shuja, after the initial setback, reorganized his forces and moved toward Allahabad. Aurangzeb met him at Khajuha and decisively defeated him. He took refuge in Arakan, where the Magh chief had him assassinated.

Thus ended the grim struggle for the throne, and Aurangzeb, who was already exercising royal powers, held a grand coronation ceremony in 1659. Shah Jahan recovered from his illness and though there was an exchange of bitter letters between him and his son, ultimately he became reconciled to Aurangzeb's assumption of power. When he died in 1666, his daughter, Jahan Ara Begum, who was with him throughout his internment, presented Aurangzeb with a letter of pardon written by Shah Jahan.

Shah Jahan, whose reign ended on such a sad note, was perhaps the most magnificent of the Muslim rulers of India. His empire extended over an area greater than that of any of his Mughal predecessors. Largely due to the financial ability of his wise wazir, Saadullah Khan, the royal treasury was full. Because of this, Shah Jahan was able to embark on a great building program in Delhi and Agra and to encourage the other arts, particularly music and painting.

Shah Jahan wanted to earn the title of *Shahanshah-i-Adil,* the Just Emperor. He took a personal interest in the administration of justice and tried to be like a father to his subjects. During the first few years he seems to have been under the influence of religious revivalists, although later, under Sufi influences, he became more tolerant. The apathy and indifference that had characterized Jahangir's attitude disappeared, and the regime was marked by attempts to approximate the administration to orthodox Islamic law—including the creation of a department to look after new converts to Islam.

But if the developments of the period are closely studied, a major Hindu revival is also noticeable in the reign of Shah Jahan. In Jahangir's time the rebellion of his son Khusrau, who had a Rajput mother, drove the Rajput nobility into the background, and after his marriage with Nur Jahan, Persians became supreme in the state. Shah Jahan's reign was marked not only by the predominance of the indigenous Muslim elements but also by the dominating position of Rajputs in the army and Hindu officials in the imperial secretariat. Rai Raghunath officiated for some time as diwan, while Rai Chandra Bhan Brahman was in charge of the secretariat. The explanation seems to be that by now Hindus were in a position to take advantage of the opportunities offered by the Mughal polity, and with the increasing influence of their patron, Dara, they made rapid headway.

Akbar had based his policy of equal treatment for all subjects on laws of natural justice; in Shah Jahan's time the Muslim scholars advocated it on the basis of Islamic law and principles. Shah Muhibullah of Allahabad wrote in a letter to Dara Shukoh that the Holy Prophet had been referred to as *Rahmat-ul-lil-Alimin*—a blessing to all the worlds and not only to Muslims. Mulla Abul Hakim, the greatest scholar of the day, gave a ruling that according to Islamic law a mosque could not be set up on the property of another, and that the conversion of a Jain temple into a mosque by Prince Aurangzeb was unauthorized.

Such discussions remind one of the controversies of Akbar's time, but as they were without Akbar's excesses and innovations, the Hindu case gained more general support. But it also awakened anxieties, and the support which Aurangzeb was able to get against Dara Shukoh

was probably due not only to Dara's arrogance and tactlessness but also to a feeling among the Muslim nobility—especially among the Persian nobles, who had lost their privileged position—that their interests were not safe.

Involved in this was not just the problem of increasing Hindu influence but also what may be called an "Indian-Irani" controversy. In the rebellion against his father, Shah Jahan's main collaborator had been Mahabat Khan, whose opposition to Nur Jahan and Irani nobles was well known. It is true that after his accession, Shah Jahan maintained his father-in-law Asaf Khan, an Irani, as the prime minister, but his two successors—Fazil Khan and Saadullah Khan—were of indigenous origin. Irani influence seems to have decreased in the secretariat. This Irani-Indian competition in the administrative sphere found an echo in the literary controversies of the day. Munir, a well-known poet of Lahore, complained of the airs assumed by Irani writers, and Shaida, another prominent poet of the day, challenged contemporary Irani poets, rated high by the Irani nobles on points of Persian language and style, to compete with him.

These developments indicate that by now indigenous elements, benefiting by the spread of learning and orderly government in the country, were able to assert their claims in administrative and literary fields. Shah Jahan's own vision was not narrow or parochial. The way in which the Taj Mahal was built is indicative of his policy. At one time it was thought that it had been designed by a Venetian architect, but this view has been abandoned. The Taj represents the culminating point of the development of Indo-Muslim architecture. Particulars of those who took part in the production of this incomparable masterpiece indicate that no effort was spared to obtain the services of specialists in every phase of the work: craftsmen from Delhi, Lahore, Multan; a calligraphist from Baghdad and another from Shiraz to ensure that all the inscriptions were correctly carved; a flower-carver from Bukhara; an expert in dome construction, Ismail Khan Rumi, who, by his name may have come from Constantinople; a pinnacle-maker from Samarqand; a master-mason from Qandahar; and lastly, an experienced garden designer. The chief supervisor who coordinated

the entire work was Ustad Isa, according to one account an inhabitant of Shiraz whose family had settled in Lahore.

Shah Jahan's reign represents the golden age of the Mughal empire, but as some students have pointed out, the artistic productions of the period give an impression of over-ripeness and a certain loss of vigor. Mughal civilization had reached its climax and was moving toward its declining phase. But the resolute vigor of Aurangzeb, a man of iron will, held the structure together for another half a century and gave it new support, so that the end came very gradually.

A special word must be said of Dara Shukoh, who, except for Aurangzeb, is the best-known of Shah Jahan's four sons. That he was not the paragon of virtue his partisans would have him is indicated by the statement of the French traveler Bernier that he had poisoned Saadullah Khan, Shah Jahan's able prime minister.[7] And his interference with Aurangzeb's efforts to extend the empire in the south shows his inability to rise above personal enmity. But as a figure in the religious history of India he holds a unique place, and it is for this that he is remembered.

When he was nineteen, Dara had recovered from a serious illness after having visited Mian Mir, a famous saint who lived at Lahore. From this time on, his faith in the power of saints and his interest in religion were firmly established. In 1640 he became a disciple of Mullah Shah, one of Mian Mir's successors. In the meanwhile he had already completed a book containing biographies of Sufi saints. A biography of Mian Mir and his principal disciples followed two years later. He also wrote brief Sufi pamphlets, one of which was a reply to those who criticized Dara for his heterodox statements. In order to justify himself, he collected a number of utterances and statements similar to those attributed to him by celebrated Sufis.

In *Majma-ul-Bahrain* (The Mingling of Two Oceans), which was completed in 1655, Dara Shukoh tried to trace parallels between Islamic Sufism and Hindu Vedantism. In the introduction he says that after a deep and prolonged study of Islamic Sufism and Hindu

---

[7] François Bernier, *Travels in the Mogul Empire, A.D. 1656–1668,* trans. by A. Constable (London, 1914), p. 23.

Vedantism he had come to the conclusion that "there were not many differences, except verbal, in the ways in which Hindu monotheists and Muslim Sufis sought and comprehended truth." Here he sounded a note that was to become the hallmark of many Hindu thinkers in the nineteenth and twentieth centuries. None of his books is without interest, but his translation of the *Upanishads,* which he made with the help of Sanskrit scholars, had a particularly interesting history. It was completed in 1657, just before his disastrous struggle for the throne. A French traveler, Anquetil Duperron, translated Dara Shukoh's Persian version of the *Upanishads* into Latin. It was this version, which was published in two volumes in 1801 and 1802, that fell into the hands of Schopenhauer. His enthusiasm for the new world of speculation profoundly influenced many others, including Emerson and other Transcendentalists in the United States.

In India itself Dara Shikoh's work had a considerable influence. *Majma-ul-Bahrain* was translated into Sanskrit by a Hindu scholar, and Hindu protegés of Dara Shukoh gave expression to ideas of Islamic Sufism in moving Persian verse. Among the distinguished people whom Dara attracted were the celebrated poet and Sufi, Sarmad; the unknown author of that remarkable history of religions, *Dabistan-i-Mazahib;* and Muhandis, the son of Ustad Isa, the architect of the Taj. Indeed, Dara Shukoh seems to have been a center of an entire literary, spiritual, and intellectual movement, but with his defeat by Aurangzeb, the liberal group also lost its cohesion and potency.

XV. Aurangzeb

AURANGZEB, the third son of Shah Jahan, was born on October 24, 1618, at Dohad, on the frontier of Gujarat and Rajputana. Industrious and thorough, he had distinguished himself as an able administrator during the years that he spent in the Deccan and other provinces of the empire. He was also a fearless soldier and a skillful general, and because of the hostile influence at court of his brother Dara, he had had to learn all the tactics of diplomacy. As emperor, he ruled more of India than any previous monarch, but in a court that had become a byword for luxury, he lived a life of austere piety. Yet of all India's rulers, few pursued policies that have excited more controversy among successive generations. In large measure, this is the result of his religious policies, for it was these that have colored men's evaluation of his reign.

Even as a young man, Aurangzeb was known for his devotion to the Muslim religion and observance of Islamic injunctions, and in some of his letters written during the struggle for the succession he claimed that he was acting "for the sake of the true faith and the peace of the realm." As soon as he was securely on the throne, he introduced reforms which could make his dominion a genuine Muslim state. After his second (and formal) coronation on June 5, 1659, he issued orders which were calculated to satisfy orthodoxy. He appointed censors of public morals in all important cities to enforce Islamic law and he tried to put down such practices as drinking, gambling, and prostitution. He forbade the cultivation of narcotics throughout the empire, and in 1664 he issued his first edict forbidding *sati* or the self-immolation of women on funeral pyres. He also repeatedly denounced the castration of children so they could be sold as eunuchs. In the economic sphere he showed a determined opposition to all illegal exactions and to all taxes which were not authorized by Islamic law. Immediately after his second coronation he abolished the inland transport duty, which amounted to ten percent

of the value of goods, and the *octroi* on all articles of food and drink brought into the cities for sale.

Although these measures were partly responsible for Aurangzeb's later financial difficulties, they were popular with the people. But gradually the emperor's puritanism began to manifest itself, and steps were taken which were not so universally approved. In 1668 he forbade music at his court and, with the exception of the royal band, he pensioned off the large number of state musicians and singers. The festivities held on the emperor's birthday, including the custom of weighing him against gold and silver, were discontinued, and the mansabdars were forbidden to offer him the usual presents. The ceremony of *darshan,* or the public appearance of the emperor to the people, was abandoned in 1679.

During the long struggle for the throne the central authority had tended to lose administrative control over the distant parts of the empire, and after he had defeated his rivals, Aurangzeb started to reorganize the civil government. He had used the need of revitalizing the instruments of imperial power as a justification for his seizure of the throne, and his intention of making good his promise was soon felt throughout the empire.[1] The provincial governors began to expand the borders of the empire, and local authorities, who had grown accustomed to ignoring orders from Agra, the imperial capital, discovered that the new regime could act swiftly against them.

The Eastern Borders

Aurangzeb's earliest conquests were in the eastern parts of the empire. In the years when he had been fighting with his brothers for the throne, the Hindu rulers of Cooch Behar and Assam, taking advantage of the disturbed conditions in the empire, had invaded the imperial dominions. For three years they were not attacked, but in 1660 the time came for restitution. Mir Jumla, the viceroy of Bengal, was ordered to recover the lost territories. He started from Dacca in November, 1661, and occupied the capital of Cooch Behar after a few weeks. The kingdom was annexed, and the Muslim army left for

[1] Jadunath Sarkar, *History of Aurangzib* (Calcutta, 1916), III, 246.

Assam. The capital of the Ahom kingdom was reached on March 17, 1662, and the raja was forced to sign a humiliating treaty.

The Mughals received a heavy tribute, and annexed some forts and towns in the cultivated districts near the frontier of Bengal, but their army had suffered great hardships. The aged Mir Jumla died on his way back to Dacca and was succeeded as viceroy by Shayista Khan. The new viceroy took action against the Arakan pirates, who, with the help of Portuguese adventurers and their half-caste offspring, had made the area unsafe. They carried their depredations to Dacca, the provincial capital. "As these raids continued for a long time, Bengal became day by day more desolated. Not a house was left inhabited on either side of the rivers lying on the pirates' track from Chittagong to Dacca." [2] Shayista Khan made thorough preparations, built a powerful flotilla, won over some of the European collaborators of the pirates by inviting them to Dacca, and in January, 1666, attacked the king of Arakan. He captured the island of Sondip in the Bay of Bengal, and after defeating the Arakanese fleet, compelled the king of Arakan to cede Chittagong, the pirates' stronghold. Chittagong, which was renamed Islamabad, proved a valuable addition to the empire.

The Mughal interest in Bengal had steadily increased. Since Shah Jahan's days, the viceroy was usually either a leading noble of the realm or a member of the royal family. Through the organization of the *mansabdari* system, and with an elaborate system of supervision, close contact with the imperial capital was maintained. Bengal became the most peaceful area of the empire, with its revenues the mainstay of Aurangzeb's army.

The conquest and settlement of a great part of what is now East Pakistan was essentially a Mughal achievement—in a great measure of Aurangzeb's reign. The area east of the Brahmaputra, commonly called Bang, was one of the three well-marked regions of the former province of Bengal (Varind, Radh, and Bang). Owing to its geographical situation, climate, terrain, and the ethnic origin of the population, it had remained isolated from the rest of the subcontinent. The

[2] R. C. Majumdar and Jadunath Sarkar, *History of Bengal* (Dacca, 1943–1948), II, 378.

force of Aryan colonization and Aryan culture had spent itself before it reached this area. The people, who were related to the Mongoloid races, had retained their ancient religious customs. Without written languages, they had not shared in earlier literary movements. Even during the Hindu rule the influence of the Hindu scholars and priests of Western Bengal was confined to the large towns and rich monasteries. After the Muslim conquest even this ceased. The people east of the Tista and the Brahmaputra were Hindus and remained Hindus, but they had no learned priesthood to maintain the purity of the tradition. During Aurangzeb's reign this isolation of the eastern area was finally broken, for once the menace of the pirates had disappeared, the jungles could be cleared and colonization begun. The Eastern Bengalis remained the butt of satire in Bengali literature (as rough, uncouth people) up to the nineteenth century, but they were no longer separated from the main stream of Indian history.

The Northwestern Frontier

Operations in the east were barely over when trouble started on the northwest frontier of the empire. In 1667 a Yusafzai leader named Bhaku (who had supported Dara Shukoh against Aurangzeb in the struggle for the throne) rebelled. The faujdar of Attock defeated Bhaku, and with the help of reinforcements from Lahore and Kabul gradually subdued the area. The area remained quiet for some time, but in 1672 trouble broke out again. Many tribes combined in opposition to the authorities, and they had a stroke of good fortune when Muhammad Amin Khan, the governor of Kabul, decided to risk an engagement with the rebels with a poorly equipped contingent. His forces were annihilated, and he was barely able to escape to Peshawar with a few of his senior officers. On hearing of the disaster the emperor degraded Muhammad Amin Khan and transferred him to another area, but the officers who were sent to replace him quarrelled among themselves and failed to make much progress. In July, 1674, Aurangzeb himself went to Hasan Abdal, a convenient half-way station between Rawalpindi and Peshawar, and stayed there for over a year directing the operations. He took officers with him who knew the

area, and by the use of force and diplomacy was able to restore peace.

Among the tribal leaders who opposed Aurangzeb was the famous Pushtu poet Khushal Khan Khattak. He was the chief of the Khattak tribe, which since the days of his great grandfather had guarded the road from Attock to Peshawar against the hostile Yusufzais, and had the right to levy tolls on this highway. Khushal had fought with distinction in Mughal armies, and had sided with Aurangzeb against Dara Shukoh. But differences arose between him and Aurangzeb, mainly because of the abolition of all tolls within the empire. Khushal's family had collected tolls on the Indus since Akbar's time, and he resented the loss of income. Apparently to prevent him making trouble, he had been imprisoned for two years. This made him a bitter enemy of Aurangzeb, and on his release he incited the Pathan tribesmen to rebel. He had only a small measure of success. Some Afridi chiefs joined him, but the more numerous Yusufzais refused to side with him. An era of Mughal-Afghan cooperation was opening —owing to the success of Mughal diplomacy and the failure of the Raushaniya movement—and even some of his sons, notably Bahram, opposed him. Khushal died broken-hearted in 1689, but he had left one enduring legacy—a body of forceful poetry in which he had expressed his hatred of the Mughals.

Despite the trouble with Khushal, Aurangzeb's reign finally saw a complete transformation in Mughal-Afghan relations. Amir Khan, the Mughal governor of Kabul and Peshawar established such order on the frontier between 1678 and 1698 that his wife maintained control of the area for some time after his death.

The Sikhs

The Sikhs, who ultimately were to play an important part in the weakening of the empire, caused Aurangzeb some difficulties, but he dealt with them in an effective, though harsh, manner. The Sikh religion as founded by Guru Nanak (1469–1539) was a part of a general religious movement to bring Hinduism and Islam closer together. In the early years, the relations of the Sikhs with the Muslims had been friendly, especially since, as the Brahmans resented the growth

of the new movement, the Sikhs had looked to the Muslims for support. Akbar himself had visited the third guru and made him a present of the land in Amritsar on which the Golden Temple was built.

Soon, however, there was conflict between the Sikhs and the Mughal authorities. Probably the basic reason was that the peasants of central Punjab had a militant tradition, and when new religious doctrines that emphasized the individual's relationship with God and society were adopted, a clash with established authority was inevitable. The first trouble came during Jahangir's reign when Guru Arjun had given assistance to the revolt led by Prince Khusrau. The guru died under torture, but one of his last instructions to his son, Guru Har Govind, was to maintain an army. This was the turning point in Sikh history. They now began to organize themselves on semi-military lines, and there were further conflicts with the Mughal government. Guru Har Govind had "so completely sunk the character of a religious reformer into that of a conquering general, that he had no scruple in enlisting large bands of Afghan mercenaries." [3] In 1628 the Sikhs defeated a Mughal force which had been sent against them, but they were ultimately defeated, and Har Govind had to flee to the hills. The succession of gurus was maintained, however, through an agreement with the Mughals.

The ninth guru, Tegh Bahadur, who came to the *gaddi* in 1664, served in the Mughal army on the Assam frontier for some years, but later returned to eastern Punjab and settled down at Anandpur. He called himself Sacha Badshah (True King), and started levying tribute from the local population. The imperial forces defeated him, and he was taken to Delhi and put to death by Aurangzeb in 1675. His successor was Guru Govind Singh, who concentrated his energies on establishing a Sikh kingdom in the hilly areas of east Punjab.

It was Govind Singh who gave the Sikhs their very distinctive symbols—the uncut hair, the steel bangle, the sword—that established their identity as a separate people. The real sufferers from the growing military strength of the Sikhs, who had enrolled a large number

[3] Sarkar, III, 357.

of Pathans in their ranks, were the Hindu rajas of the Punjab hills. Many bloody battles were fought between them and the guru. At last they complained to the Mughal governor, who passed on the complaint to Aurangzeb. On the rajas undertaking to bear the cost of an expedition, Aurangzeb agreed to send forces to assist them in besieging Govind Singh in his stronghold at Anandpur. The guru himself escaped, but his children were executed.

During his flight from the Mughal forces, Guru Govind Singh addressed Aurangzeb in a long Persian poem, known as *Zafar Nama*. This poem contained bitter complaints against the Mughal emperor, but as its appeal was in the name of humanity and of Islam, it provided a basis for mutual understanding. According to certain Sikh accounts, Aurangzeb invited the guru to visit him in the Deccan. Evidence on this point is not conclusive, but it is certain that after this Guru Govind Singh was allowed to live in peace. After Aurangzeb's death his son Bahadur Shah, who was the viceroy of the Punjab before ascending the throne, was on excellent terms with the guru. Later the relations of the Mughals with the Sikhs sharply deteriorated owing to the emergence of Banda, a Hindu religious mendicant, as the leader of the Sikhs.

The Marathas

Far more serious opposition to Aurangzeb came from the Deccan, where the Marathas were beginning their long struggle with the Mughal empire. A people of whose earliest history little is known, the Marathas as a dynamic force in Indian history owe much to the *Bhakti* movement. By giving birth to a new literature, enriching the local language, and popularizing a religious cult which made a powerful emotional appeal to all sections of the people, the movement had infused a new life in this society. The growing self-awareness of the Marathas was also helped by the fact that the Muslim conquest of the Deccan was far less complete than that of northern India. Hindus held many offices in the revenue and finance departments of the Muslim rulers of Golkunda and Bijapur, and at times even the highest

ministerial appointments were filled by Deccani Brahmans. Life in the
hill forts of the Western Ghats, never easily accessible and practically
cut off from the world during the monsoon, did not appeal to the
Muslim officers, and Maratha chiefs and soldiers were employed in
large numbers in garrisoning these forts.

Since Maratha statesmen and warriors controlled various departments of the Muslim states of Ahmadnagar, Golkunda, and Bijapur,
the conflicts of the Mughals with these states provided them with an
opportunity to advance their sectional interests. Amongst Maratha
statesmen who rose to prominence during the days of Shah Jahan was
Shahji, who served under the sultans of Ahmadnagar and Bijapur
and had large estates at Poona. His importance may be judged by the
fact that in 1635 he set up a Nizam Shahi boy as the nominal sultan
of the kingdom of Ahmadnagar, and reoccupied in his name the
whole of the western portion of the old dominion as far as the sea.
Shah Jahan was able to deal with him, and Shahji, after making his
submission to the Mughals, sought service with the ruler of Bijapur.
Shahji's son, Shivaji, more than fulfilled the dreams of his father.
Shivaji's mother lived at Poona, and he spent his early days in the
spurs and valleys of the Ghats, which were to be his battlefield. He
attached to himself a number of young men and in the disturbed conditions of the Deccan started taking control of hill fortresses. For a
long time these aggressive proceedings were ignored at Bijapur, but in
1659 a strong contingent of ten thousand cavalry was sent against him
under Afzal Khan. Shivaji lured Afzal to a private conference and
then killed him with his dagger. The leaderless troops of Bijapur were
routed by Shivaji's soldiers, who lay in ambush.

The following year Shivaji came in conflict with the Mughal rulers.
In 1660 Aurangzeb appointed Shayista Khan, his maternal uncle and
a veteran general, viceroy of the Deccan, with instructions to suppress
the activities of Shivaji. He gained a few victories and recaptured
several forts, but on April 5, 1663, the Marathas made a night attack
on his encampment at Poona, and although the viceroy escaped, his
son was killed. Shayista Khan was recalled by Aurangzeb, who then
sent Dilir Khan and Raja Jai Singh, with his son, Prince Muazzam,

to the Deccan. The imperialist generals forced Shivaji to sue for peace. In 1666 he attended the court at Agra, but insulted at being given the rank of mansabdar of only five thousand horsemen, he made his displeasure public. He was kept under surveillance, but he escaped and reached the Deccan. On his return Shivaji formally assumed the title of maharaja in June, 1674, and as Aurangzeb was busy in the northwest, he was not disturbed. After his death in 1680, the mad cruelty of his unworthy son Shambhuji forcibly attracted the attention of the Mughal ruler. In 1682 Shambhuji raided Burhanpur and perpetrated such cruelties on the Muslim population that the qazis there sent a manifesto to Aurangzeb upbraiding him. The Mughal emperor, who was concerned about the developments in the Deccan since his rebel son, Prince Akbar, had taken refuge at Shambhuji's court, decided to go south. He reached Aurangabad in the third week of March, 1682, and the last twenty-five years of his life were to be spent in that part of the subcontinent.

Bijapur and Golkunda, which often gave shelter to the Maratha raiders, were annexed in 1686 and 1687, and Shambhuji was captured and executed in early 1689, but this did not mean the end of Aurangzeb's troubles in the Deccan. Aurangzeb brought up Shambhuji's son, Shahu, at the court and treated him with great consideration, but his younger brother, Rajaram, took over the Maratha leadership. On his death in April, 1700, his widow, Tara Bai, carried on the struggle.

The Mughals achieved many successes against the Marathas, but these proved temporary. Often the forts, won at great cost and after prolonged effort, would be lost through the treachery or the incompetence of the Muslim commanders. But even though Aurangzeb had conquered most of the Maratha forts, he was unable to suppress the powerful roving Maratha bands which challenged Mughal authority whenever they got an opportunity. In 1699, they carried their first raid in Malwa. Four years later they disrupted the communications between northern and southern India, and in 1706 they sacked Baroda. After Aurangzeb's death, the Marathas became a major factor in the downfall of the Mughal empire.

Religious Policy

While Aurangzeb was extending the empire in the east and south, and consolidating his position on the northwest marches, he was also concerned with the strengthening of Islam throughout the kingdom. His attempt to conduct the affairs of state according to traditional Islamic policy brought to the fore the problem that had confronted every ruler who had attempted to make Islam the guiding force: the position of the Hindu majority in relation to the government. In 1688, when he forbade music at the royal court and took other puritanical steps in conformity with strict injunctions of Muslim law, he affected both Hindus and Muslims. When *jizya,* abolished for nearly a century, was reimposed in 1679 it was the Hindus alone who suffered.

By now Aurangzeb had accepted the policy of regulating his government in accordance with strict Islamic law and many orders implementing this policy were issued. A large number of taxes were abolished which had been levied in India for centuries but which were not authorized by Islamic law. Possibly it was the unfavorable effect of these remissions on the state exchequer which led to the exploration of other lawful sources of revenue. The fact that, according to the most responsible account, the reimposition of *jizya* was suggested by an officer of the finance department would seem to show that it was primarily a fiscal measure.[4] The theologians, who were becoming dominant at the court, naturally endorsed the proposal and Aurangzeb carried it out with his customary thoroughness.

Another measure which has caused adverse comment is the issue of orders at various stages regarding the destruction of Hindu temples. Originally these orders applied to a few specific cases—such as the temple at Mathura built by Abul Fazl's murderer, to which a railing had been added by Aurangzeb's rival, Dara Shukoh. More far-reaching is the claim that when it was reported to him that Hindus were teaching Muslims their "wicked science," Aurangzeb issued orders to all governors "ordering the destruction of temples and schools and totally

[4] S. R. Sharma, *The Religious Policy of the Mughal Emperors* (Bombay, 1962), p. 153; see also note on p. 175.

prohibiting the teaching and infidel practices of the unbelievers." [5] That such an order was actually given is doubtful; certainly it was never carried out with any thoroughness. However, it is incontestable that at a certain stage Aurangzeb tried to enforce strict Islamic law by ordering the destruction of newly built Hindu temples. Later, the procedure was adopted of closing down rather than destroying the newly built temples in Hindu localities. It is also true that very often the orders of destruction remained a dead letter, but Aurangzeb was too deeply committed to ordering of his government according to Islamic law to omit its implementation in so significant a matter. The fact that a total ban on the construction of new temples was adopted only by later jurists, and was a departure from the earlier Muslim practice as laid down by Muhammad ibn Qasim in Sind, was no concern of the correct, conscientious, and legal-minded Aurangzeb.

As a part of general policy of ordering the affairs of the state in accordance with the views of the ulama certain discriminatory orders against the Hindus were issued, for example imposition of higher customs duties, 5 percent on the goods of the Hindus as against 2 percent on those of Muslims. These were generally in accordance with the practice of the times but they marked a departure not only from the political philosophy governing Mughal government, but also from the policy followed hitherto by most Muslim rulers in India.

Aurangzeb has often been accused of closing the doors of official employment on the Hindus, but a study of the list of his officers shows this is not so. Actually there were more Hindu officers under him than under any other Mughal emperor. Though this was primarily due to a general increase in the number of officers, it shows that there was no ban on the employment of the Hindus.

That Aurangzeb's religious policy was unpopular at the time is true, but that it was an important factor, as usually charged, in the downfall of the empire is doubtful. The Hindu uprisings of his reign seem to have had no wide religious appeal, and they were supressed with the help of Hindu leaders. Their significance comes in the following reigns, when the rulers were no longer able to meet opposition as effectively—and as ruthlessly—as had Aurangzeb. His religious policy

[5] Z. Faruki, *Aurangzeb and His Times* (Bombay, 1935), p. 117.

aimed at strengthening an empire already overextended in Shah Jahan's time; that it failed in its objective is probably true, but the mistake should not be made of assuming that the attempt was a major element in the later political decay. It should be seen, rather, as part of an unsuccessful attempt to stave off disaster. Seen in this light, his religious policy is one element, but not a causal one, save in its failure to achieve its intended goal, among the many that have to be considered in seeking an understanding of Aurangzeb's difficulties.

The East India Company

The behavior of the English East India Company was another element that has to be added to the complex situation created by internal rebellion, the activities of the Sikhs, and the long drawn-out war with the Marathas. The East India Company opened its first factory, or trading post, at Surat on the west coast in 1612, and in the next half century established a chain along the coast. Trouble first arose in Bengal, where Shayista Khan was trying to introduce some order and regard for the Mughal government in place of the lax administration of his predecessor, Shah Shuja. The foreign settlements of the Portuguese, the Dutch, and the British, emboldened by their superiority on the sea, had become truculent, and in distant regions considered themselves subject to no checks from the Mughal government. Shah Shuja, partly out of his general indifference to financial considerations and partly to gain support in the coming struggle for the throne, was particularly generous to the foreign traders. To the English factory which was opened at Hugli in 1651, he gave an order in 1652 permitting open trade in Bengal on a payment of three thousand rupees annually in lieu of customs dues. In the succeeding years the Company's trade multiplied many times, but, insisting on the authority of Shuja's order, it refused to increase its contribution or pay any of the normal taxes. When Shayista Khan objected, difficulties arose between him and the English. The attitude of the Company's officers may be judged from a letter addressed to London in 1665:

"Your Worship must consider that these people are grown more powerful than formerly, and will not be so subject to us as they have

been, unless they be a little beaten by us, that they may understand, if they impede us by land, it lieth in our power to requite them by sea. . . . In fine . . . your affairs will be quite ruined if this Nabob [Shayista Khan] lives and reigneth long." [6]

The first attempt by the English to wage war against the Mughals was made in 1686 when Sir Josia Child, the powerful governor of the East India Company, persuaded the government to send a small fleet to India to seize and fortify Chittagong. The expedition was an utter failure, and, far from gaining any territory, English traders were expelled from all their factories in Bengal. Meanwhile on the west coast, the English had also angered Aurangzeb. English pirates operating out of Bombay were seizing ships taking pilgrims to Mecca; among them was the *Ganj-i-Sawai* owned by the emperor himself. They were also minting coins in Bombay with a superscription containing their own king's name. Aurangzeb ordered the seizure of the Surat factory and the expulsion of all Englishmen from his dominions. He relented because of the English control of the pilgrim trade in the Arabian Sea and, also, it appears, because they had a powerful advocate at court in the wazir, Asad Khan. After levying a fine of one and a half lakhs of rupees Aurangzeb allowed them to return to their factories, and, for the next fifty years, the English merchants refrained from any further attempts to establish themselves as a territorial power.

The Enigma of Aurangzeb's Purposes

In the background of all these events—the struggle for the throne, the annexations of great territories in the South, the wasting struggle with the Marathas, the pacification of the northwest frontier, the consolidation of Mughal power in Bengal, the contemptuous treatment of the East India Company—stands the enigmatic figure of Aurangzeb, surely the most controversial personality in the history of Islamic rule in India. Held responsible by some for the downfall of the Mughal empire, by others he is praised for maintaining as long as he did the unity of his vast realm.

[6] William Foster, ed., *The English Factories in India 1660–1664* (Oxford, 1923), p. 401.

So far as Aurangzeb's personal qualities are concerned, however, there is general admiration. R. C. Majumdar writes: "Undaunted bravery, grim tenacity of purpose, and ceaseless activity were some of his prominent qualities. His military campaigns gave sufficient proof of his unusual courage, and the manner in which he baffled the intrigues of his enemies shows him to have been a past master of diplomacy and statecraft. His memory was wonderful, and his industry indefatigable." [7] "He never forgot a face he had once seen or a word that he had once heard." Apart from his devotion to duty, his life was remarkable for its simplicity and purity. His dress, food, and recreations were all extremely simple. He died at the age of ninety, but all his faculties (except his hearing) remained unimpaired.

A well-read man, he kept up his love of books till the end. He wrote beautiful Persian prose. A selection of his letters (*Ruq'at-i-Alamgiri*) has long been a standard model of simple but elegant prose. According to Bakhtawar Khan, he had acquired proficiency in versification, but agreeable to the word of God that "Poets deal in falsehoods," he abstained from practicing the art. He understood music well but he gave up this amusement in accordance with Islamic injunctions.

It is his general attitude to culture that explains why the Mughal court, which under Shah Jahan had been the great center of patronage for the arts, ceased to be so in Aurangzeb's reign. He disbanded the court musicians, abolished the office of the poet-laureate, discontinued the work of the court chronicler, and offered little encouragement to painters. On grounds of both economy and fidelity to the Islamic law he criticized the Taj Mahal, the tomb of his mother, remarking: "The lawfulness of a solid construction over a grave is doubtful, and there can be no doubt about the extravagance involved." [8]

Although Aurangzeb's attitude toward the arts was one of disapproval, his reign was not culturally barren. Large-scale building activity ceased, but this was as much a reflection of a treasury depleted by war as deliberate policy. Other forms of artistic life flour-

[7] R. C. Majumdar et al., *An Advanced History of India* (London, 1958), p. 509.

[8] Quoted in Abdullah Chughtai, *Fanun-i-Latif Ba-ahd-i-Aurangzeb* (Lahore, 1957), p. 42.

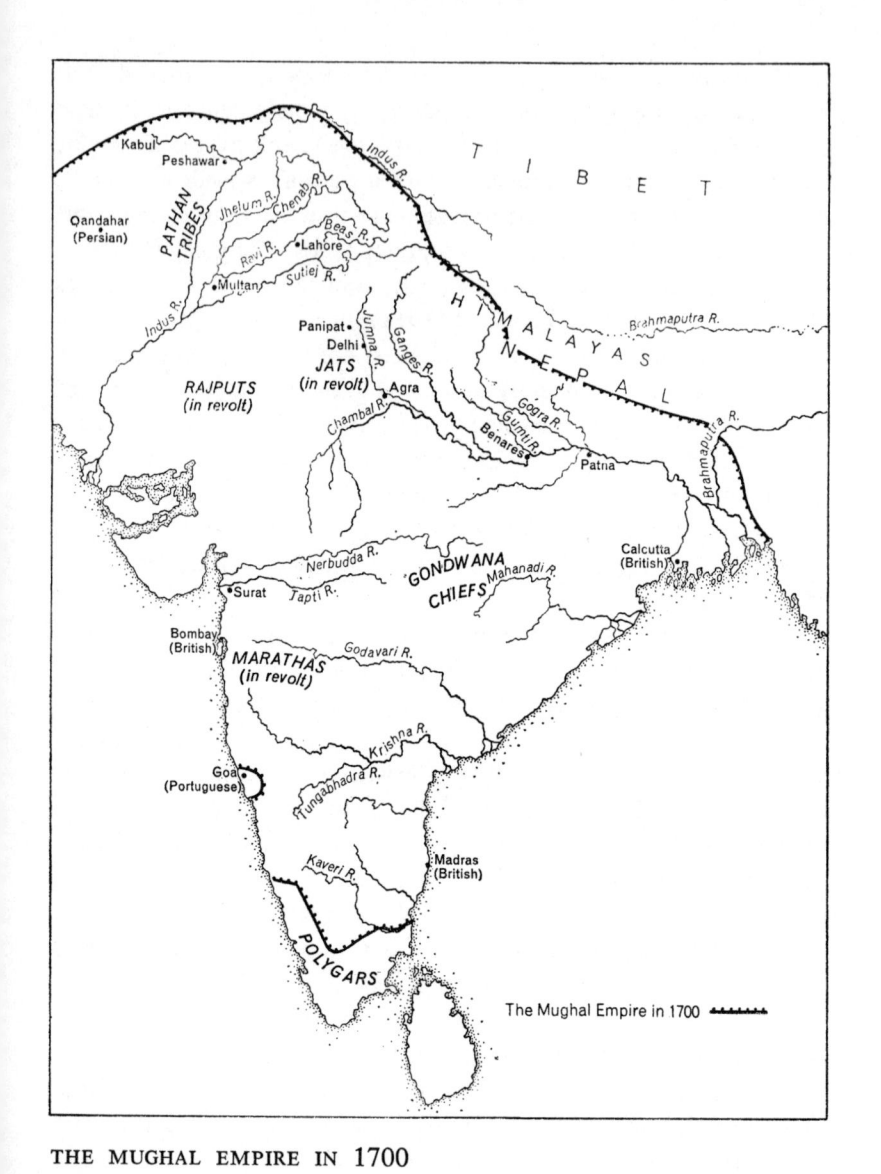

THE MUGHAL EMPIRE IN 1700

From: *An Historical Atlas of the Indian Peninsula* (Oxford University Press, Bombay, 1961).

ished, partly because they had taken firm foot in Indian soil, and partly because the great nobles made up to some extent for the lack of royal patronage. In the case of poetry, where self-expression yields better results without compliance with a patron's wishes or moods, the abolition of the court patronage and the weakening of the court tradition led to some welcome new developments. The greatest Persian poet of the period, Bedil, turned away from the polished love lyrics of the old court poets and concentrated on metaphysical poetry. Often his fancy ran riot. Many of his metaphors are quaint and far-fetched, and his meaning is frequently obscure, but he is unmatched for profundity of thought and originality of ideas and similes. He is highly popular in Afghanistan and Tajikistan, where his poetry appeals to the serious readers in the same way as does the great *Masnavi* of Rumi. He paved the way for Ghalib, who followed him in aiming at originality and depth of thought, but adopted the polished diction of Mughal court poets.

Perhaps even more important was Wali (d.1707), originally a writer of Deccani, who became the first major poet of modern Urdu. This replacement of Deccani by Urdu was a direct result of Aurangzeb's conquest of the Muslim kingdoms of the south. So long as the kingdoms of Golkunda and Bijapur existed and patronized the poets and writers of Deccani, "it was fully in vogue and its peculiarities immune from criticism and sneers." When this source of patronage dried up and the Hindustani-speaking officers became dominant in the south, the writers of Deccani had to adjust to a new situation. They were forced to shed their peculiarities of dialect, themes, and treatment while the speakers from the north saw the literary possibilities of the spoken language. The two streams of literary tradition mingled, and gave birth to modern Urdu.

These developments owed little to Aurangzeb's deliberate efforts. The cultural activities for which he was directly responsible were the spread of Islamic learning and general diffusion of education. His reign was marked by the extensive grant of patronage and stipends to scholars and students. There were no religious leaders of the caliber of Shah Waliullah or Shaikh Ahmad Sirhindi, but there is no doubt that the foundation of the Islamic religious revival in the eighteenth and nineteenth centuries were laid at this time. The Islamic academic

curriculum, known as *Dars-i-Nizamiya,* was begun in his reign, and the emperor was personally responsible for the grant of extensive buildings, known as Farangi Mahal of Lucknow, to the family of Mulla Nizam-ud-din, after whom *Dars-i-Nizamiya* is named. Most of the books included in the *Dars-i-Nizamiya,* other than those of foreign origin, were written during Aurangzeb's reign. They were mainly the work of two scholars patronized by the emperor—Mir Zahid, the qazi of Kabul, and Muhibullah Bihari, the qazi of Allahabad. Compilation of the comprehensive legal digest, known as *Fatawa-i-Alamgiri,* was also initiated by the emperor.

In turning from Aurangzeb's influence on culture to his work as a statesman, we find that his achievements are obvious but his final years were clouded by difficulties. The strong kingdoms of Golkunda and Bijapur, for long centers of Muslim power in the south, were conquered in less than a year, but the entire might of the Mughul empire was pitted against the Marathas for twenty years, without resulting in decisive gains. And in the struggle the Marathas gained a new confidence and soon moved from the defensive in the Deccan to an offensive in the north.

In the financial field, Aurangzeb's achievements were even less distinguished. When he died, the imperial treasury was almost empty. He left barely 12 crores of rupees—not very much more than the inheritance of a great Mughal noble like Asaf Khan. Towards the end of his reign, the imperial finances were in such straits that the diwan anxiously waited for the receipt of the Bengal revenue, so that the expenses of the Deccan campaign could be met.

It is a tribute to Aurangzeb's control over the affairs of the empire that no major upheaval occurred in the north during his prolonged absence in the Deccan, but there are clear indications of many minor disturbances and a general slackening of administration. In Bengal, for example, Sobha Singh, a petty chief of Midnapur district, joined an Afghan chief to defeat the Hindu zamindar of Burdwan. They also seized the fort and city of Hugli and plundered the cities of Nadia, Murshidabad, Malda, and Rajmahal. The emperor removed Ibrahim Khan, the governor (though, it appears, soon to appoint him to Allahabad), and the rebellion was effectively put down, but it exposed the insecure state of the administration. As this disturbance

enabled the English and other foreigners to fortify their settlements at Calcutta and elsewhere, its effects were far-reaching.

The basic cause of Aurangzeb's failures did not lie in his own weakness, but in the quality of men at his disposal. Aurangzeb's misfortune was that he began to rule when two generations of unparalleled prosperity had sapped the moral fiber of the Mughal aristocracy. The Mughals were no longer the hardy soldiers and resourceful improvisers of the days of Babur and Akbar. Aurangzeb constantly bemoaned the scarcity of good officers. In one of his letters he says, "My great grandfather [Akbar] had many faithful servants. He entrusted them with the work of gaining successful victories and of performing many affairs, and in the time of my father [Shah Jahan] there came forward many brave and faithful servants, well-behaved officers and able secretaries. Now I want one competent person, adorned with the ornament of honesty, for the Diwani of Bengal; but I find none. Alas! alas! for the rarity of useful men."

A growing weakness of the Mughal officials was that they shirked arduous and difficult assignments. For them the continuous stay in the Deccan, away from the attractions of the capital, was such a calamity that they would probably have preferred the Maratha victory to such an exile. One of Aurangzeb's leading nobles used to say that he would distribute a lakh of rupees in charity if he could see the capital once again. Such ease-loving generals fared badly against the hardy Marathas. They took years to conquer small hill-forts, and many of these forts conquered after long sieges would be quickly lost owing to the sloth and negligence of the officers in charge.

Treachery was rampant in the Mughal army, and the royal princes were sometimes the cause. During the seven-year siege of Ginji, Prince Kam Bakhsh, who was in charge of the operations along with Zulfiqar Khan, was placed under arrest as he was about to join the Marathas with his troops. During the siege of Satara the Marathas bribed Prince Azam to ensure that the provisioning of their garrison would not be interfered with, and the fort which at the commencement of the siege had provisions to last only for two months was not conquered for six months. With such instruments at his disposal, it is little wonder that Aurangzeb's policies were not successful.

The causes of some of Aurangzeb's difficulties were beyond his con-

trol. Others, especially the financial and the administrative ones, arose out of his personal character and its reflection in his basic policies. In making his decision to run his government according to Islamic law, he did more than reverse Akbar's religious policy: he gave up the age-old policy, followed since the inception of the Muslim rule in India, and which had been openly proclaimed by Balban, Ala-ud-din Khalji, and Sher Shah, of subordinating legal and ecclesiastical considerations to practical requirements of administration. Aurangzeb was inspired by high motives, but the policy created many problems.

His financial difficulties were partly due to the wholesome remission of some eighty taxes, and partly to his refusal to levy any tax, not specifically authorized by *shariat*. He failed to see, as even Firuz Tughluq had, that such a policy was inconsistent with military expansion and large-scale warfare. In the administrative field, also, he was opposed to taking any action or imposing any penalty, except in strict accordance with the Islamic law. This resulted in precedence being given to the qazis, which was not liked by many of Aurangzeb's officers. Some of Aurangzeb's ablest generals found the attention given by the emperor to rigid legal procedure irksome. Firuz Jang, the conqueror of Golkunda (whom the emperor held so dear that once when he fell ill and was forbidden melons, Aurangzeb himself gave up this fruit), put to death one Muhammad Aqil on a charge of highway robbery, without formal trial by a qazi. Aurangzeb sternly rebuked him, and asked his wazir to write to the noble that if the heirs of the slain refused to accept the blood-money permitted by law he would have to pass an order of retaliation against him.[9]

There is something truly noble in a ruler reminding his ablest general that he would have to face the full rigors of the law for an unlawful action, and there can be nothing but admiration for Aurangzeb's endeavors to uphold the law and proper judicial procedure. But in the seventeenth century the administrators found this meticulous emphasis on legal procedure and the prominent position of the qazis a hindrance. The contemporary historian Khafi Khan has attributed the imperfect success of Aurangzeb, in spite of his great ability and immense industry, to his reluctance to go beyond Islamic law. "From reverence

[9] Inayat-Ullah Khan, *Akham-i-Alamgiri,* trans. by Jadunath Sarkar as *Anecdotes of Aurangzib* (Calcutta, 1912), p. 91.

for the injunctions of the Law, he did not make use of punishment and without punishment the administration of a country cannot be maintained. Dissensions rose among his nobles through rivalry. So every plan and project that he formed came to little good; and every enterprise which he undertook was long in execution and failed in its objective." [10]

Perhaps the time to make a final assessment of Aurangzeb has not yet arrived. More than five thousand of his letters are extant, but only a handful have been published, and until this rich material is studied, a proper appraisal of his personality is not possible. At present, evidence about him is fragmentary and contradictory, and his personality was more complex than either his admirers or critics are willing to acknowledge. In the context of conflicting evidence the tendency for each group is to emphasize the elements supporting its point of view. These verdicts are liable to be modified in the light of the vast material which remains to be utilized and all judgment of Aurangzeb, at this stage, can only be provisional.

Whatever view is taken should not obscure, however, Aurangzeb's solid and abiding achievements. He greatly enlarged the Mughal empire and much of what he accomplished has endured. A large part of what is East Pakistan today was either conquered or consolidated during his reign. In the Deccan he annexed vast areas which were to remain centers of Mughal culture and administration for more than two centuries. He selected and promoted administrators whose work constitutes a landmark in the history of the regions entrusted to them —Shayista Khan and Murshid Quli Khan in Bengal, and Nizam-ul-Mulk in the Deccan. He tried to reduce the Irani preponderance in administration and attracted some gifted Turani families to the service of the Mughals. He also trained a body of men who were to sustain the empire through a period of foreign invasions and repeated internal struggles for the succession. Viewed in this light, Aurangzeb can be seen not as the instigator of policies that led to ruin but as the guardian of the Islamic state in India.

[10] H. M. Elliot and John Dowson, *The History of India as Told by Its Own Historians* (London, 1867–1877), VII, 386–87.

XVI. Mughal Administration

BEFORE following the fate of the Mughal empire under Aurangzeb's successors in the eighteenth century, it will be useful to outline the main features of administration under the four great emperors. The most prominent features of the administrations of the different rulers have already been noted, but a general view is necessary in order to understand the Mughal contribution.

The Central Government

First of all, it should be recognized that the Mughals drew heavily on the past, for the organization of their government was on essentially the same lines as that of the sultanate. The principal officers of the central government were four: 1) diwan; 2) mir bakhshi; 3) mir saman; and 4) sadr. The first of these dignitaries, the diwan, often called the wazir (the chief minister), was mainly concerned with revenue and finance, but as he had a say in all matters where any expenditure was involved, the work of other departments also came under his control. All the imperial orders were first recorded in his office before being issued, and the provincial governors, district faujdars, and leaders of expeditions came to him for instructions before assuming their duties. All the earning departments were under his direct control, and could spend only what was allotted to them by the diwan.

The mir bakhshi performed those duties which had been the responsibility of the ariz-i-mamalik during the earlier period. Owing to the organization of the civil services on military lines, his power extended far beyond the war office, and some foreign travelers called him the lieutenant-general or the captain-general of the realm. The main departure from the sultanate was in respect to work relating to state *karkhanas*, stores, ordinance, and communications, now so important that the dignitary dealing with it, called the mir saman, ranked

as an important minister often senior in rank to the sadr. The sadr (or, more fully, sadr-i-jahan) was, as in the earlier period, director of the religious matters, charities, and endowments.

Occasionally a higher dignitary, superior to the wazir and other ministers was also appointed. He was called the vakil, and functioned like the naib (deputy) of the sultanate period. This appointment, as under the sultanate, was sporadic, depending on the wish of the monarch and the requirements of the situation. During the reigns of Akbar, Jahangir, and Shah Jahan, a period of ninety-seven years (1560–1657), there were ten vakils whose terms of service totaled about thirty-nine years. Ibn Hasan, the author of the *Central Structure of the Mughal Empire,* argues that the post was primarily for show and honor, with the vakil as the head of the nobility but not of the administration.[1] To a large extent this is true, and normally the vakil was less effective than the wazir, who controlled the purse, but theoretically the vakil was the king's deputy and even the wazir referred to him whatever was "beyond his own ability." Abul Fazl calls him "the emperor's lieutenant in all matters connected with the realm and the household," adding that "although the financial offices are not under his immediate superintendence, yet he receives the returns from heads of all financial offices and wisely keeps abstracts of their return." [2]

The splendor and stability of the Mughal rule was due to a succession of very capable rulers who attempted to build up an efficient administrative system, choosing their principal officers on the basis of merit. The most famous diwan under Akbar was Raja Todar Mal, who for a time acted as the chief minister of the realm, but the contribution of Khwaja Mansur and Mir Fathulla Shirazi to the building up of Akbar's revenue administration was perhaps equally great. Under Jahangir, Itimad-ud-Daula, the father of Nur Jahan, who was a diwan even before his daughter married the emperor, remained the chief wazir and diwan until his death. He was succeeded by his son, Asaf Khan, who became the vakil just before the death of Jahangir.

[1] Ibn Hasan, *The Central Structure of the Mughal Empire* (London, 1936), pp. 138–39.
[2] Abul Fazl, *Ain-i-Akbari,* trans. by H. Blockmann et al. (Calcutta, 1927–1941), I, 5.

Itimad-ud-Daula and Asaf Khan were able, efficient officers. Asaf Khan maintained his position until his death, but his successors were selected on the basis of their scholarship and technical efficiency. Allami Afzal Khan remained Shah Jahan's diwan for ten years, and the office was held from the nineteenth to the thirtieth years of Shah Jahan's reign by the celebrated Saadulla Khan who, like his predecessor, had won his post because of his learning, wisdom, and resourcefulness.

The diwan, who can perhaps be called the finance minister, had under him two principal officers, called diwan-i-tan and diwan-i-khalsa, who were in charge of salaries and state lands respectively. It is interesting that all the assistants of the diwan-i-khalsa under Shah Jahan's reign were Hindus, and five out of the seven under the diwan-i-tan belonged to the same community. Raja Raghunath Rai, who had been diwan-i-khalsa for some years, became sole diwan in the thirty-first year of Shah Jahan's reign, and maintained this position until his death, during the reign of Aurangzeb. Aurangzeb's principal wazir, who held office for thirty-one years, was Asad Khan, originally his mir bakhshi. Next to him, the most famous mir bakhshi of the Mughal period was Shaikh Farid, who played a decisive role in the enthronement of Jahangir.

The organization of public services was perfected during Akbar's reign, and was based on the *mansabdari* system, borrowed originally from Persia. Every important officer of state held a *mansab* or an official appointment of rank and emoluments, and, as members of an imperial cadre, were liable for service anywhere in the empire. In 1573–74 Akbar classified the office holders in thirty-three grades, ranging from commanders of ten to commanders of ten thousand.[3] The principal categories of Mughal mansabdars, however, were three: those in command of ten to four hundred were commonly styled mansabdars (officers); those in command of five hundred to twenty-five hundred were amirs (nobles); and those in higher ranks belonged to the category of umara-i-kibar or umara-i-izam (grandees). The highest amir in the third category was honored with the title of amir-

[3] S. M. Edwardes and H. L. O. Garrett, *Mughal Rule in India* (Delhi, 1956), pp. 164–65.

ul-umara. In the eighteenth century this title was usually given to the mir bakhshi. Until the middle of Akbar's reign, the highest rank which any ordinary officer could hold was that of a commander of five thousand; the more exalted grades between commanders of seven thousand and ten thousand were reserved for princes of royal blood. Toward the end of his reign and under his successors these limits were relaxed.

Originally each grade carried a definite rate of pay, out of which the holders were required to maintain a quota of horses, elephants, beasts of burden, and carts. But even in Akbar's days and in spite of safeguards introduced by him, the number of men actually supplied by the mansabdars rarely corresponded to the number indicated by his rank, and under Akbar's successors greater latitude was allowed. The mansabdars were paid either in cash or by temporary grant of *jagirs*. Theoretically, the mansabdars received enormous salaries, which appear all the more excessive when it is realized that they did not normally maintain all the troops expected of them. It was probably an awareness of this that led Shah Jahan to introduce the practice of paying salaries to the mansabdars for only four months of the year instead of twelve, the implication being that the actual income for part of the year was equivalent to what the emperor had originally intended for the whole year.[4] Even with this reduction, the mansabdars lived extravagantly. The tendency to luxurious expenditure was undoubtedly heightened by the mansabdar's knowledge that on his death, his whole property would be taken over by the state, pending satisfaction of any outstanding claims by the treasury. But while there may have been little incentive to save within the system, the high scale of salaries enabled the state to attract the ablest and most ambitious individuals from almost the whole of southern and western Asia.

Appointment to the ranks of mansabdars was made by the emperor, usually on the recommendation of military leaders, provincial governors, or court officials. In addition to the mansabdars, there was a class known as ahadis, who though holding no official rank, were employed in posts in the palace. They were usually young men of good families, who were not fortunate enough to secure a *mansab* on

[4] Edwardes and Garrett, p. 170.

their first application. Given an opportunity to show their worth, they could then be promoted to the ranks of mansabdars. These mansabdars have been compared to the Civil Service during British rule in that they formed an all-India cadre of officials, liable to transfer anywhere in the empire and providing the personnel for all major offices. The existence of a single imperial cadre undoubtedly gave a cohesion and unity to the Mughal empire that was lacking during the sultanate.

Provincial Administration

Provincial administration was greatly improved under Akbar, and in this respect the Mughal period differs substantially from the sultanate. The boundaries of the provincial units were more definitely fixed and a uniform administrative pattern, with minor modifications to suit local conditions, was developed for all parts of the empire. Further, drawing upon the experiments introduced by Sher Shah, the provincial administration was strengthened, and each province was provided with a set of officials representing all branches of state activity. By the introduction of a cadre of mansabdars, liable to be transferred anywhere at the behest of the central government and by the introduction of other checks, the control over the provinces was made more effective.

The principal officer was the governor, called sipah salar under Akbar and nazim under his successors, but popularly known as subahdar and later only as subah.[5] Next to him in official rank, but not in any way under his control, was the provincial diwan, who was in independent charge of the revenues of the province. He was usually a mansabdar of much lower status than the governor, but he was independent of the governor's control and was directly under the imperial diwan.

The next provincial functionary was the bakhshi, or the paymaster. He performed a number of duties, including, occasionally, the functions of the provincial newswriter. The diwan-i-buyutat was the provincial representative of the khan-i-saman, and looked after roads

[5] Parmatma Saran, *The Provincial Governments of the Mughals* (Allahabad, 1941).

and government buildings, supervised imperial stores, and ran state workshops. The sadr and the qazi were entrusted with religious, educational, and judicial duties.

The faujdar and the kotwal were the two other important provincial officials. The faujdar, who was the administrative head of the *sarkar* (district), was appointed by the emperor but was under the supervision and guidance of the governor. The kotwals were not provincial officers, but were appointed by the central government in the provincial capitals and other important cities, and performed a number of executive and ministerial duties similar to the Police Commissioners during British rule in Bombay, Calcutta, and Madras. The ports were in charge of the mir bahr, corresponding to the modern Port Commissioner, but with powers over customs also.

The Mughals interfered very little with the local life of the village communities, for they had no resident functionary of their own in the villages. The muqqadam was normally the sarpanch (head of the village *panchayat,* or council) and these *panchayats* continued to deal with local disputes, arrange for watch and ward, and perform many functions now entrusted to the local bodies.

Finances

The tax structure of the Mughal empire was relatively simple in its theoretical formulation, however much it was complicated by changing needs and local circumstances. Both revenue and expenditure were divided between the central and the provincial government. The central government reserved for itself land revenue, customs, profits from the mints, inheritance rights, and monopolies. Land revenue was the most important source of income, as it has been throughout Indian history, and more than doubled in value between the reigns of Akbar and Shah Jahan. The principal items of expenditure for the central government were defense, the general civil administration of the empire (including the religious organizations), maintenance of the court and the royal palace, and the cost of buildings and other public works. The provincial sources of income were the assignments of land revenue granted to the provincial governor and his officials as a remuneration

for their services, a variety of local taxes and cesses, transit dues and duties, and fines and presents.[6]

The Mughal revenue system was based on the division of the empire into *subas* or governorships, *sarkars* or districts, and *parganas,* consisting of number of villages which were sometimes styled *mahals.* (These were replaced during British rule by the somewhat large *tehsils* or *talukas.*) The revenue staff had also to perform miscellaneous administrative duties, including the keeping of the public peace, and recruitment of the military forces. The *suba* was modeled after the central imperial structure. The *sarkar* was in charge of the faujdar, or military commander, who combined the functions of the modern district magistrate and superintendent of police. The revenue work in the *sarkar* was looked after by the amalguzar, who would correspond to the modern afsar-i-mal (revenue officer).

The levy of land revenue was based on survey settlements calculated after a detailed measurement and classification of the cultivated areas. The nature of the crops grown and the mean prevailing market prices were also taken into consideration in fixing the final assessment. This assessment system, evolved after many experiments, became the basis of the survey settlement of the British period. Akbar's revenue system in most areas was *raiyatwari,* the revenue being collected directly as far as possible from the individual cultivator, and was payable in cash. Akbar introduced the system in the greater part of northern India, and during the viceroyalty of Aurangzeb, it was extended to the Deccan. The revenue system as evolved under Akbar was thoroughly sound, but the government demand was heavy and amounted to one-third of the produce. Abul Fazl tried to justify it by referring to the abolition of many miscellaneous cesses and taxes, but it is not certain whether all the cesses abolished by royal order were given up by subordinate officials. In the settlement of the Deccan during Aurangzeb's viceroyalty, the state share was reduced to one-fourth.[7]

Mughal emperors, particularly Akbar and Aurangzeb, continued

[6] Edwardes and Garrett, pp. 194–95.
[7] W. H. Moreland in *Cambridge History of India* (Cambridge, 1928), III, 468.

to make cautious experiments and improvements in the land-revenue
system. The basic data was collected by detailed measurement of land
and assessment of the yield and estimates of productivity of each
pargana or assessment area. When sufficient data had been collected
the system of group assessment was introduced, with the alternatives
of measurement and sharing being held in reserve.

That the Mughal rulers wanted the revenue system to operate fairly
is evident from the guidance to collectors of revenue given in the *Ain-
i-Akhari*. "The Collector was directed to be the friend of the agri-
culturist; to give remissions in order to stimulate cultivation . . .
to grant every facility to the raiyat, and never to charge him on more
than the actual area under tillage; to receive the assessment direct from
the cultivator and so avoid intermediaries; to recover arrears without
undue force; and to submit a monthly statement describing the condition of the people, the state of public security, the range of market
prices and rents, the conditions of the poor and all other contingen-
cies." [8]

The specifications were high—at least on paper, but anyone who
studies the procedure for giving relief to the raiyats in case of hardships, the general instructions to the collectors, and the details of the
assessment system and mode of recovery is bound to be struck by the
professional competence of men like Todar Mal, Shah Mansur, and
Amir Fathullah Shirazi, as well as the statesmanlike benevolence
motivating the state's basic policy. The British paid special attention
to revenue administration, and introduced many significant improvements, but it can be said without injustice that on certain points the
Mughal system compared favorably with the one that evolved over
a long period in British India. As an example, one may take the
assessment of lands newly brought under cultivation or reclaimed
after having fallen out of cultivation. A variety of scales of assessment
was applied to such lands, such as a low initial rate, rising to the full
amount after five years. The collector was also able to vary the revenue demands to encourage wasteland being cultivated. Regulations
under the British were neither so liberal nor so flexible for this particular kind of cultivation.

[8] Edwardes and Garrett, pp. 204–5.

Another important difference between the British and the Mughal systems was the position of the village accountant, or patwari. Throughout the Mughal period the patwari, who was responsible for the maintenance of the financial records, was an employee of the village, not of the revenue administration. Under the British system, however, he became an employee of the government. This altered his relationship to the people, because previously he had been an agent for the people, but now he became an instrument of government. This was one factor that led to the weakening of village autonomy.

The Mughal theory and practice of revenue administration must be seen as the essential elements underlying the later administrative structure of India. The great memorial to Mughal rule is not so much the great architectural monuments that fill the subcontinent, but the governments of the great successor states, India and Pakistan, which following the model of the period of British rule, have maintained an administrative pattern that derives from the Mughals. "The District system with the district officer as head of the public services and general factotum or Poo Bah, the erection of an administrative hierarchy upon the basis of land revenue collection, and the development of an involute maze of office procedure, these features of Mughal rule were all accepted as the foundation of British rule; and, indeed, to an astonishing degree, in India and Pakistan today local administration is Mughal in spirit." [9]

Military Organization

The weakest part of Mughal administration was the military organization, precisely the area where one might have expected the most efficient centralized control. But instead of a large standing army, the emperors depended upon four different classes of troops for the maintenance of order and the defense of the empire's borders. There were, first of all, the soldiers supplied by the mansabdars; the number a mansabdar was expected to provide upon the demand of the emperor were specified in his warrant of appointment or were indicated by his rank. Another class of troops under the command of a mansabdar

[9] Hugh Tinker, *India and Pakistan* (London, 1962), p. 16.

was known as dakhili, whose services were paid for by the state. A third class were the ahadis, or "gentlemen troopers," drawing higher pay than those in the ordinary service; according to the *Ain-i-Akbari,* they might get as much as five hundred rupees a month in contrast to the seven or eight rupees of the regular troopers. Finally, the chiefs who had been permitted to retain a degree of autonomy were required to provide contingents under their own command.

The artillery was paid wholly out of the imperial treasury. Recognizing its importance, Akbar had given it his special attention, but his efforts to secure from the Portuguese some of their better pieces were unsuccessful. European gunners were employed later on in appreciable numbers, but no permanent improvement was effected. During the eighteenth century the Mughal army shared in the decline of the other imperial institutions, and little advantage was taken of technical improvements in weaponry. When Nadir Shah invaded India in 1739 the *jazair* or swivel guns employed by his troops were superior to anything the Mughals could bring against them.

There are no existing statistical records of the strength of the Mughal army. The best estimate is probably that of Sir Jadunath Sarkar, who concluded from evidence from the reign of Shah Jahan that in 1648 the army consisted of 440,000 infantry, musketeers, and artillery men, and 185,000 cavalry commanded by princes and nobles. The army could still count on the personal valor of the commander of an individual contingent, but pitted against disciplined European soldiers, or hardy, resourceful Maratha horsemen, it did not prove effective. The loose organization of the army, the paucity of officers, the failure to build up a well-knit and active pyramidical organization, reduced the efficiency of the army. There were no uniforms, and discipline was poor, particularly in lower ranks. The cavalry was the only branch which was considered respectable and fit for a gentleman to join, while the ordinary "Indian foot soldier was little more than a night watchman and guardian over baggage." [10] The Mughal practice of taking along a great number of camp followers, including occa-

[10] William Irvine, *The Army of the Mughals,* p. 57, quoted in Edwardes and Garrett, p. 178.

sionally the families of the soldiers and the royal harem, made the army a very cumbersome, slow-moving organization.

Descendants of a people who knew nothing of the sea, the Mughals had little success in creating a navy. They had no large fighting vessels, and the ships that they maintained were primarily for the furtherance of the commercial operations of the state. After the conquest of Gujarat, the Mughal army reached the shores of the Indian Ocean, but Akbar failed to build a navy. He tacitly acquiesced in the Portuguese supremacy by making no effort to challenge their authority, and by taking out licenses from them for the ships which he sent to the Red Sea. To deal with the pirates in the Bay of Bengal, and also for the purpose of communication over the vast river system of Bengal, a river flotilla was maintained at Dacca. Under Akbar it consisted of 768 small armed vessels and boats, estimated to cost about 29,000 rupees a month. It was not effective against the Magh and Portuguese pirates, but it was reorganized under the efficient administration of Mir Jumla and Shayista Khan, and in 1664 the latter was able to inflict a decisive blow against the pirates.[11]

A few years later Aurangzeb had an opportunity to make at least tentative arrangements for the defense of the seas along the west coast of India. A coastal chieftain known as the sidi of Janjira had provided protection for the ships and ports of the sultan of Bijapur. When the sidi's territories were attacked by Shivaji, however, the sultan did not come to his assistance, and in 1670 the sidi offered his services to Aurangzeb. Since Aurangzeb needed all the help he could get in the Deccan, he took the sidi into his service, placing him under the Mughal governor of Surat, and subsidizing his fleet. The sidi was assisted by another fleet based on Surat, and in every way treated as an official of the empire, but the Mughal command of the sea was too slight to make supervision of so independent a force possible. In course of time his descendants established themselves as the rulers of the state of Janjira south of Bombay.

[11] R. K. Mookerji, *Indian Shipping: A History* (Bombay, 1912).

The Judiciary

The judicial system of the Mughals was very similar to that of the sultanate. It became more systematic, particularly under Aurangzeb, but as compared with the judicial structure of British India, it was very simple, being based on a different approach to many categories of disputes. Normally no lawyers were allowed to appear. The disputes were speedily settled, often on the basis of equity and natural justice, though of course, in the case of Muslims the injunctions and precedents of Islamic law applied where they existed. Many crimes—including murder—were treated as individual grievances rather than crimes against society. The complaints in such cases were initiated by the individuals aggrieved, rather than by the police, and could be compounded on payment of compensation. The aim of the judicial system was primarily to settle individual complaints and disputes rather than to enforce a legal code, as is indicated by the fact that the criminal court was normally known as the diwan-i-mazalim, the court of complaints.

All foreign travelers have commented on the speedy justice of the Mughal courts and the comparatively few cases coming before them. The latter was partly due to the general prejudice against litigation, but even more to the fact that a large number of disputes, particularly those affecting the Hindus, were settled by the village and caste *panchayats,* and did not come before the official courts. The Hindus were not debarred from taking cases before the qazi or the governor —and frequently did so where other arrangements did not prove effective—but normally they had their own arrangements for settling their disputes. Badauni has recorded that according to Akbar's orders the cases of Hindus were to be decided by the Hindu judges and not by the qazis. The Jesuit Father Monserrate says that "Brachmane (Brahmans) governed liberally through a senate and a council of the common people"—referring presumably to the administration of justice by these agencies. Local usage and custom ruled in most rural areas, and, according to one estimate, perhaps not one person out of a hundred in the Punjab, for example, was governed by the provisions of either the classic Hindu or Muslim law.[12]

[12] George C. Rankin, *Background to Indian Law* (Cambridge, 1946), p. 16.

The judicial courts provided by the Mughals were principally of two types—secular and ecclesiastical. Except during the reign of Aurangzeb, the principal courts for settlement of disputes were presided over by the emperor, the governors, and other executive officers. Akbar used to spend several hours of the day disposing of judicial cases, and governors followed the same procedure in the provinces. In the *Ain-i-Akbari* we find the instructions issued to a governor detailing the judicial procedure he should follow.

Apart from the secular courts and the *panchayats,* the principal agency for the settlement of disputes was the qazis' court. The qazi, being the repository of Muslim law, attended the hearing of cases by the executive authority, whether governor, faujdar or kotwal, and assisted the latter in arriving at a decision consonant with Quaranic precepts. Presumably the civil disputes of Muslims were, as a rule, left to the qazis to be settled according to the canon law. When both parties in a dispute were Hindus, the point at issue was referred to Hindu pandits for an opinion. This principle was supported by the *Fatawa-i-Alamgiri,* the authoritative digest of Islamic law, where it is held that "Dhimmis . . . do not subject themselves to the laws of Islam either with respect to things which are merely of religious nature, such as fasting or prayer, or with respect to such temporal acts, as though contrary to [Islam], may be legal by their own, such as sale of wine or of swine's flesh, because we [Muslim jurists] have been commanded to leave them at liberty in all things, which may be deemed by them to be proper according to the precepts of their own religion." [13] These provisions presumably related to religious matters. In the case of Muslims, the secular types of criminal suits went to the kotwal, while the religious and civil cases, such as concerning inheritance, marriage, divorce, and civil disputes went to the qazis' courts.

The death penalty normally had to be confirmed by the emperor, but there seem to have been departures from the rule. A Dutch resident of India states that fines represented the normal mode of settling all disputes in Mughal India. Capital punishments and mutilations were frequent, and there are records of impaling, dismember-

---

[13] N. E. B. Baillie, *A Digest of Moohummudan Law* (London, 1875), I, 174.

ment, and other cruel punishments. They were, however, limited in their incidence and were inflicted only under the royal orders. Furthermore they were confined to those cases where an example was to be made of the individual concerned. Imprisonment was not a method of punishment that appealed to the Mughals. It was seldom used as a sentence in private cases, though it was sometimes resorted to for preventive purposes. Whipping was commonly used. The Muslim punishment of parading the offender in an ignominious condition seems to have been frequently used as it coincided with the Hindu tradition as well.

The assessments made by two acute British observers on Mughal government as they saw it in a period of decline may serve as summary of the Mughal achievement as administrators. Luke Scrafton, who was resident for the East India Company at the capital of Bengal in 1758, declared that until the invasion of Nadir Shah in 1739 "there was scarce a better administered government in the world. The manufactures, commerce, and agriculture flourished exceedingly; and none felt the hand of the oppression but those who were dangerous by their wealth or power." [14] Mughal government was despotic, and official corruption increased from the reign of Jahangir, but on the whole, the judgment of the English historian, Sidney Owen seems just: "Whatever its defects, it was . . . a grandly conceived, well-adjusted, and beneficent structure of government. . . . Taxation was light; and its most productive source, the land revenue, was moderately assessed, and equitably adjusted. Foreign commerce was protected and favoured; and the English East India Company throve, and multiplied its factories, under the shadow of the Imperial authority. The judicial system, though what we should consider crude and capricious, as well as too often corruptly exercised, was not liable like our own to the tedious delays which have been its reproach, and which have so much tended to obstruct, and even defeat, the course of justice. And the right of appealing to the Emperor from inferior tribunals, though too generally a futile privilege, was sometimes really remedial, and probably was a standing check to judicial iniquity. Much the same may be said as to the provincial Governors." [15]

[14] Luke Scrafton, *Reflections on the Government of Indostan* (London, 1770).
[15] Sidney J. Owen, *The Fall of the Moghul Empire* (London, 1912), pp. 1–4.

XVII. Economic and Social Developments under the Mughals

IT WAS the normal policy of the Timurid rulers, both in their original Central Asian homelands and in India, to encourage trade. As in much else, Sher Shah Suri during his brief reign (1538–1545) set a pattern that was followed by the later Mughals, especially Akbar, when he encouraged trade by linking together various parts of the country through an efficient system of roads and abolishing many inland tolls and duties. The Mughals maintained this general policy, but their rule was distinguished by the importance which foreign trade attained by the end of the sixteenth century. This was partly the result of the discovery of the new sea-route to India, but, even so, progress would have been limited if conditions within the country had not been favorable.

Trade and Industry

Both Akbar and Jahangir interested themselves in the foreign sea-borne trade, and Akbar himself took part in commercial activities for a time. The Mughals welcomed the foreign trader, provided ample protection and security for his transactions, and levied a very low custom duty (usually no more than $2\frac{1}{2}$ percent ad valorem). Furthermore, the expansion of local handicrafts and industry resulted in a reservoir of exportable goods. Indian exports consisted mainly of manufactured articles, with cotton cloth in great demand in Europe and elsewhere. Indigo, saltpeter, spices, opium, sugar, woolen and silk cloth of various kinds, yarn, asafoetida, salt, beads, borax, turmeric, lac, sealing wax, and drugs of various kinds, were also exported. The principal imports were bullion, horses, and a certain quantity of luxury goods for the upper classes, like raw silk, coral,

amber, precious stones, superior textiles (silk, velvet, brocade, broad-cloth), perfumes, drugs, china goods, and European wines. By and large, however, in return for their goods Indian merchants insisted on payment in gold or silver. Naturally this was not popular in England and the rest of Europe, and writers on economic affairs in the seventeenth century frequently complained, as did Sir Thomas Roe, that "Europe bleedeth to enrich Asia." The demand for articles supplied by India was so great, however, and her requirements of European goods so limited, that Europe was obliged to trade on India's own terms until the eighteenth century, when special measures were taken in England and elsewhere to discourage the demand for Indian goods.

The manufacture of cotton goods had assumed such extensive proportions that in addition to satisfying her own needs India sent cloth to almost half the world: the east coast of Africa, Arabia, Egypt, Southeast Asia, as well as Europe. The textile industry, well established in Akbar's day, continued to flourish under his successors, and soon the operations of Dutch and English traders brought India into direct touch with Western markets. This resulted in great demand for Indian cotton goods from Europe, which naturally increased production at home. Even the silk industry—especially in Bengal—was in flourishing condition. Bernier wrote: "There is in Bengal such a quantity of cotton and silk, that the kingdom may be called the common storehouse for these two kinds of merchandise, not of Hindoustan or the Empire of the Great Mogol only, but of all the neighbouring kingdoms, and even of Europe." [1]

Apart from silk and cotton textiles, other industries were shawl and carpet weaving, woolen goods, pottery, leather goods, and articles made of wood. Owing to its proximity to sources of suitable timbers, Chittagong specialized in shipbuilding, and at one time supplied ships to distant Istanbul. The commercial side of the industry was in the hands of middlemen but the Mughal government, like the earlier sultans, made its own contribution. The emperor controlled a large number of royal workshops, busily turning out articles for his own

---

[1] François Bernier, *Travels in the Mogul Empire, A.D. 1656–1658,* trans. by A. Constable (London, 1914), p. 439.

use, for his household, for the court, and for the imperial army. Akbar took a special interest in the development of indigenous industry. He was directly responsible for expansion of silk weaving at Lahore, Agra, Fathpur-Sikri, and in Gujarat. He opened a large number of factories at important centers, importing master weavers from Persia, Kashmir, and Turkistan. Akbar frequently visited the workshops near the palace to watch the artisans at work, which encouraged the craftsmen and raised their status. It is said that he took such an interest in the industry that to foster demand he "ordered people of certain ranks to wear particular kinds of locally woven coverings . . . an order which resulted in the establishment of a large number of shawl manufactories in Lahore; and inducements were offered to foreign carpet-weavers to settle in Agra, Fathepur Sikri, and Lahore, and manufacture carpets to compete with those imported from Persia." [2] In course of time, the foreign traders established close contracts with important markets in India and new articles which were more in demand in Western Europe began to be produced in increasing quantities. Among the foreign inventions that excited Akbar's interest was an organ, "one of the wonders of creation," that had been brought from Europe.[3]

Urban Life

All foreign travelers speak of the wealth and prosperity of Mughal cities and large towns. Monserrate stated that Lahore in 1581 was "not second to any city in Europe or Asia." Finch, who traveled in the early days of Jahangir, found both Agra and Lahore to be much larger than London, and his testimony is supported by others. Other cities like Surat ("A city of good quantity, with many fair merchants and houses therein"), Ahmadabad, Allahabad, Benares, and Patna similarly excited the admiration of visitors.[4] The new port towns of

[2] S. M. Edwardes and H. L. O. Garrett, *Mughal Rule in India* (Delhi, 1956), p. 265.
[3] Abdul Qadir Badauni, *Muntakhab-ut-Tawarikh*, trans. by G. S. A. Ranking, W. H. Lowe, and Sir Wolseley Haig (Calcutta, 1884–1925), II, 299.
[4] *The Commentary of Father Monserrate, S.J.*, trans. by J. S. Hoyland (London, 1922); for other travelers, see William Foster, ed., *Early Travels in India* (London, 1921).

Bombay, Calcutta, Madras, and Karachi developed under British rule, but they had their predecessors in Satgaon, Surat, Cambay, Lari Bunder, and other ports.

The efficient system of city government under the Mughals encouraged trade. The pivot of urban administration was the kotwal, the city governor. In addition to his executive and judicial powers, it was his duty to prevent and detect crime, to perform many of the functions now assigned to the municipal boards, to regulate prices, and in general, to be responsible for the peace and prosperity of the city. The efficient discharge of these duties depended on the personality of the individual city governor, but the Mughals tried to ensure high standards by making the kotwal personally responsible for the property and the security of the citizens. Akbar had decreed (probably following Sher Shah Suri's example of fixing the responsibility on village chiefs for highway robberies in their territory) that the kotwal was to either recover stolen goods or be held responsible for their loss. That this was not only a pious hope is borne out by the testimony of several foreign travelers who state that the kotwal was personally liable to make good the value of any stolen property which he was unable to recover. The kotwals often found pretexts to evade the ultimate responsibility, but in general they took elaborate measures to prevent thefts.

Most of this flourishing commerce was in the hands of the traditional Hindu merchant classes, whose business acumen was proverbial. Their caste guilds added to the skills in trade and commerce that they had learned through the centuries. Not only were their disputes settled by their *panchayats,* but they would frequently impose pressure on the government by organized action. Foreign visitors record that the governors and kotwals were very sensitive to this, and in spite of hardships inseparable from a despotic system of administration, the business communities had their own means of obtaining redress. Bernier, writing during Aurangzeb's time, declared that the Hindus possessed "almost exclusively the trade and wealth of the country." [5] If Muslims enjoyed advantages in higher administrative posts and in the army, Hindu merchants maintained the monopoly in trade and

[5] Bernier, p. 225.

finance that they had had during the sultanate. A Dutch traveler in the early seventeenth century was struck by the fact that few Muslims engaged in handicraft industries, and that even when a Muslim merchant did have a large business, he employed Hindu bookkeepers and agents.[6] Banking was almost exclusively in Hindu hands. In the years of the decline of the Mughals, a rich Hindu banker would finance his favorite rival claimant for the throne. The role of Jagat Seth of Murshidabad in the history of Bengal is well known. Even the "war of succession" out of which Aurangzeb emerged victorious was financed by a loan of five and a half lakhs of rupees from the Jain bankers of Ahmadabad.[7] Here one sees a contrast with British rule, when the British monopolized not only the higher civil service posts but also controlled most of the major industries as well as the great banks and trading agencies.

Rural Conditions

Conditions in the rural areas during the Mughal period were much the same as at present, with one important difference—the Muslim rulers had scarcely disturbed the old organization of the villages. The *panchayats* continued to settle most disputes, with the state impinging very little on village life, except for the collection of land revenue, and even this was very often done on a village basis rather than through individuals, with the age-old arrangements being preserved. The incidence of land revenue was substantially higher under the Mughals and in Hindu states like Vijayanagar than in British India, but the administration was more flexible, both in theory and in practice, in its assessment and collection. Apart from the remission of land revenue when crops failed, there was reduction in government demand even when bumper crops caused prices to fall. For example, between 1585 and 1590 very large sums had to be written off because a series of exceptionally good harvests had resulted in a surplus, and peasants could not sell their crops. The state also advanced loans to the cul-

[6] Quoted in L. S. S. O'Malley, *Modern India and the West* (London, 1941), p. 5.
[7] M. S. Commissariat, *Studies in the History of Gujarat* (Bombay, 1935), pp. 69–76.

tivators and occasionally provided seed as well as implements for digging wells. Loans advanced to the cultivators for seeds, implements, bullocks, or digging of wells were called *taqavi*—an expression which has continued in modern land revenue administration.

Health and Medical Facilities

A feature noticed by many foreign travelers was the good health of the local inhabitants. Fryer, writing of the mortality among the English at Bombay and the adjacent parts, says that "the country people lived to a good old age, supposed to be the reward of their temperance." Bernier also speaks of "general habits of sobriety among the people," though this did not apply to a few cases among the upper classes or the royal family. The European travelers found "less vigour among the people than in the colder climates, but greater enjoyment of health." From their accounts, even the climate would appear to have been healthy. "Gout, stone complaints in the kidneys, catarrh . . . are nearly unknown; and persons who arrive in the country afflicted with any of these disorders soon experience a complete cure." The Mughal emphasis on physical fitness and encouragement of out-of-door manly games also raised the general standard of health. The ideal was that everyone was to be trained to be a soldier, a good rider, a keen *shikari,* and able to distinguish himself in games. Ovington found that the English at Surat were "much less vigorous and athletic in their bodies than Indians." It is possible that the drinking habits of the Europeans made them an easy prey to ill-health in the tropics.[8]

Public hospitals had been provided in Muslim India, at least since the days of Firuz Tughluq (1351–1388), and though it would be ridiculous to compare them with the arrangements introduced by the British, the system seems to have been extended during the Mughal period. Jahangir states in his autobiography that on his accession to the throne he ordered the establishment, at government expense, of hospitals in large cities. That this order was actually made effective

[8] In addition to works mentioned in footnotes 1 and 4, see John Fryer, *A New Account of East India and Persia,* ed. by William Crooke (3 vols.; London, 1909–1915); Edward F. Oaten, *European Travellers in India* (London, 1909); and other works in the Hakluyt series.

is shown by the records of salaries paid by the government and of grants for the distribution of medicine.[9]

The supply of local physicians was not plentiful and judged by the demand for European doctors, particularly surgeons, they were apparently not equal to all demands. The general health of the inhabitants suggests, however, that the medical services were not completely inadequate, and the local physicians were able to deal with normal problems. As early as 1616 they knew the important characteristics of the bubonic plague and suggested suitable preventive measures. According to an account in *Iqbal Nama,* which was written in Jahangir's reign: "When the disease was about to break out, a mouse would rush out of its hole, as if mad, and striking itself against the door and the walls of the house, would expire. If immediately after this signal the occupants left the house and went away to the jungle, their lives were safe. If otherwise, the inhabitants of the village would be spirited away by the hands of death." [10] As modern scholars have pointed out, this observation includes two facts about the plague whose significance has been corroborated by modern science: the association of the death of rodents with the disease, and the necessity of evacuating the infected quarter.[11]

A crude form of vaccination against smallpox seems to have been employed by Eastern doctors, for it was vaguely realized that the introduction of a mild form of cowpox prevented the virulent form of smallpox. An article in the *Asiatic Register* of London for 1804 contained a translation of a memorandum by Nawab Mirza Mehdi Ali Khan describing from personal observations the method adopted by a Hindu medical practitioner of Benares. A thread drenched in "the matter of a pustule on the cow" was placed on the arms of a child to cause an easy irruption, thus avoiding a virulent attack of smallpox.

In ancient times, the use of medicines had been well developed among the Hindus, but dissection was considered to be irreligious. The Muslims, who did not have this restriction, performed a number of operations. As Elphinstone pointed out: "Their surgery is as re-

[9] Parmatma Saran, *The Provincial Governments of the Mughals* (Allahabad, 1941), pp. 419–40.
[10] Mutamid Khan, *Iqbal Nama,* quoted in Edwardes and Garrett, p. 279.
[11] Edwardes and Garrett, p. 279.

markable as their medicine especially when we recollect their ignorance of anatomy. They cut for the stone, couched for the cataract,
and extracted the feotus from the womb, and in their early works
enunciate no less than one hundred and twenty-seven surgical
works." [12] According to Manucci, Muslim surgeons could provide
artificial limbs.

Social Customs

The marriage customs of Hindus and Muslims had many similari-
ties. Early marriages were much in vogue amongst the Hindus, with
seven considered the proper age for a girl to be married. To leave
a daughter unmarried beyond twelve years of age was to risk the displeasure of one's caste. The Muslims also betrothed their children
between the ages of six and eight, but the marriage was generally not
solemnized before they had attained the age of puberty.

Among the wealthier classes polygamy and divorce are said to
have been very common. The custom of secluding women, known as
purdah, was very strictly observed. Marriage negotiations were undertaken by the professional broker or the friends of either party. The
marriage ceremonies were more or less the same as they are at
present, and the character of the average Indian or Pakistani home
and the socio-ethical ideas which influence it have not undergone any
fundamental change. The son's duty to his parents and the wife's
duty to her husband were viewed almost as religious obligations.
"Superstitions played a prominent part in the daily life of the people.
Charms were used not merely to ensnare a restive husband but also
to secure such other ends as the birth of a son or cure of a disease.
The fear of the evil eye was ever present . . . and the young child
was considered particularly susceptible. . . . People believed in all
sorts of omens." [13] Astrologers were very much in demand, even at
the Mughal court.

The Muslim aristocrats lived in great houses decorated with rich

[12] Quoted in P. N. Chopra, *Some Aspects of Society and Culture during the
Mughal Age* (Agra, 1955), p. 152, n. 10.
[13] T. K. Raychaudhuri, *Bengal under Akbar and Jahangir* (Calcutta, 1953),
p. 189.

hangings and carpets. Their clothing was made of finest cotton or silk, decorated with gold, and they carried beautiful scimitars. There was a considerable element of ostentatious display involved in this, however, for their domestic arrangements did not match the outward splendor of their dress and equipment. Manucci, a keen observer, refers to Pathans who came to court "well-clad and well-armed, caracolling on fine horses richly caparisoned and followed by several servants," but when they reached home, divested themselves of "all this finery, and tying a scanty cloth around their loins and wrapping a rag around their head, they take their seat on a mat, and live on . . . rice and lentils or badly cooked cow's flesh of low quality, which is very abundant in the Mogul country and very cheap." [14]

The courtly manners and the elaborate etiquette of the Muslim upper classes impressed foreign visitors. In social gatherings they spoke "in a very low voice with much order, moderation, gravity, and sweetness. . . . Betel and betelnut were presented to the visitors and they were escorted with much civility at the time of departure. Rigid forms were observed at meals. . . . Dice was their favourite indoor game. Polo or *chaugan*—for which there was a special playground at Dacca—elephant-fights, hunting, excursions and picnics, were also very popular." [15] The grandees rode in *palkis,* preceded by uniformed mounted servants. Many "drove in fine two-wheeled carts, carved with gilt and gold, covered in silk, and drawn by two little bulls which could race with the fastest horses."

The Position of the Hindus

The Hindu upper classes undoubtedly shared in the material culture of the Mughals, for, as already noted, they had a virtual monopoly of trade and finance. Furthermore, they had long held many high posts in the government. The contrast between the position of Hindus under the Mughals and of Indians in general under the British was often made by Indian historians during the period of the nationalist movement. Thus a Hindu historian writing in 1940 could argue that

[14] Nicolo Manucci, *Storia do Mogor,* trans. by William Irvine (London, 1906–1908), II, 453.
[15] Raychaudhuri, pp. 200–3.

"under Shah Jahan Hindus occupied a higher status in the government than that occupied by the Indians today." [16]

The vitality of the Hindus was shown in more than their ability to maintain footholds within administrative and commercial life. Widespread religious movements, having, as we have seen, their roots partly in the vivifying contacts of Hinduism with Islam, had produced a religious enthusiasm among the masses that was transforming the older Brahmanical religion.

Although Muslim historians ignore this religious revival among the Hindus, there is enough evidence to indicate its importance during Mughal rule. The new regional literature of Bengal and Maharashtra, which owed much to the new movement, is a clear mirror of what was taking place in Hindu society. In Bengal, there was not only the rise of a new literature, but numerous temples were built during the late seventeenth century.[17] The significance of this phenomenon becomes clear if it is remembered that practically throughout the second half of the seventeenth century, Aurangzeb was on the throne. His alleged ceaseless campaign of temple destruction obviously could have been neither thoroughgoing nor universal.

The developments in intellectual life were even more marked. The rise of Navadipa as a great center of Sanskritic learning, and the vogue of navyanyaya (new logic) belong to this period.

In relation to Islam, Hinduism exhibited a new vigor, greater self-confidence, and even a spirit of defiance. Hinduism is not generally thought of as a missionary religion, and it is often assumed that during Muslim rule conversions were only from Hinduism to Islam. This is, however, not true. Hinduism by now was very much on the offensive and was absorbing a number of Muslims.[18] When Shah Jahan returned from Kashmir, in the sixth year of his reign, he discovered that Hindus of Bhadauri and Bhimbar were forcibly marrying Muslim girls and converting them to the Hindu faith. At death these women were cremated according to the Hindu rites. Jahangir had tried to stop this practice but with no success, and Shah Jahan also issued orders de-

---

[16] S. R. Sharma, *The Religious Policy of the Mughal Emperors* (London, 1940), p. 101. This statement does not appear in the 1962 edition.

[17] Raychaudhuri, p. 155.

[18] For a fuller account, see Sharma, pp. 90–92, 165–74.

claring such marriages unlawful. Four thousand such conversions are said to have been discovered. Many cases were also found in Gujarat and in parts of the Punjab. Partly to deal with such cases, and partly to conform to his early notions of an orthodox Muslim king, Shah Jahan established a special department to deal with conversions. After the tenth year of his reign, he seems to have ceased trying to prevent the proselytizing activities of the Hindus. There are several later cases of the conversion of Muslims, not recorded by the court historians. A number of Muslims—including at least two Muslim nobles, Mirza Salih and Mirza Haider—were converted to Hinduism by the vairagis, the wandering ascetics of the Chaitanya movement, which had become a powerful religious force in Bengal. There were also cases of conversions from Islam to Sikhism. When Guru Hargovind took up his residence at Kiratpur in the Punjab some time before 1645, he is said to have succeeded in converting a large number of Muslims. It was reported that not a Muslim was left between the hills near Kiratpur and the frontiers of Tibet and Khotan. His predecessor, Guru Arjan, had proselytized so actively that he incurred Jahangir's anger, and, as Jahangir mentions in his autobiography, the Hindu shrines of Kangra and Mathura attracted a number of Muslim pilgrims.

The Hindu position was so strong that in some places Aurangzeb's order for the collection of *jizya* was defied. On January 29, 1693, the officials in Malwa sent a soldier to collect *jizya* from a zamindar called Devi Singh. When he reached the place, Devi Singh's men fell upon him, pulled his beard and hair, and sent him back empty-handed. The emperor thereupon ordered a reduction in the *jagir* of Devi Singh. Earlier, another official had fared much worse. He himself proceeded to the *jagir* to collect the tax, but was killed by the Hindu mansabdar. Orders to destroy newly built temples met with similar opposition. A Muslim officer who was sent in 1671 to destroy temples at the ancient pilgrimage city of Ujjain was killed in a riot that broke out as he tried to carry out his orders.

Muslim historians, in order to show the extreme orthodoxy of Aurangzeb, have recorded many reports of temple destruction. On a closer scrutiny, however, there seem to be good grounds for believ-

ing that all the reports were not correct, and that quite often no action was taken on imperial orders. We read, for example, about the destruction of a certain temple at Somnath during the reign of Shah Jahan and again under Aurangzeb. It is likely that in this and in many similar cases, the temple was not destroyed on the first order. According to accounts by English merchants, Aurangzeb's officers would leave the temples standing on payment of large sums of money by the priests.[19] However, new temples whose construction had not been authorized were often closed.

If the situation is closely examined, it appears that the complaint of Shaikh Ahmad that under Muslim rule as it existed in India, Islam was in need of greater protection than other religions does not appear to have been completely unfounded. Aurangzeb tried, of course, to reverse this trend, and some other rulers also had occasional spells of Islamic zeal, either from political or religious causes. But by and large, it is perhaps fair to say that during Muslim rule, Islam suffered from handicaps which almost outweighed the advantages it enjoyed as the religion of the ruling dynasty. This paradox becomes understandable if the basic Muslim political theory is kept in mind under which the non-Muslim communities, so long as they paid certain taxes, were left to manage their own affairs. This local and communal autonomy severely circumscribed the sovereignty of the Muslim state, and in most matters the caste guilds and the village *panchayats* exercised real sovereignty, which they naturally utilized to safeguard their creed and way of life. It was this power which enabled them to evade, or even defy, unwelcome orders from the capital. A curious light on the situation is thrown by the penalties and economic losses which a Hindu had to suffer on the adoption of Islam. Practically until the end of Muslim rule, a Hindu who became a Muslim automatically lost all claim to ancestral property.[20]

This extraordinary position was a natural result of the application of Hindu law, which, according to the Muslim legal system, governed Hindu society even under Muslim government, and under which apostacy resulted in disinheritance. Shah Jahan, who began as an

[19] Sharma, pp. 138–39.
[20] M. L. Roychoudhury, *The State and Religion in Mughal India* (Calcutta, 1951), p. 346.

orthodox Muslim, tried to redress the balance by issuing orders that "family pressure should not prevent a Hindu from being admitted to Islam" and laid down that a convert should not be disinherited. Whether these orders could overcome the subtle but solid pressure of the joint family system and the power of the caste *panchayats* must remain a matter of speculation. The question, however, of handicaps or advantages of one community against another is not of fundamental significance. The important fact is that during normal times conditions of tolerance prevailed. This was of special interest to European visitors, almost all of whom commented on the concessions enjoyed by non-Muslims under Muslim rule. The Jesuits were critical of this policy of tolerance, declaring the destruction of Hindu temples by Muslims "a praiseworthy action," but noting their "carelessness" in allowing public performance of Hindu sacrifices and religious practices. When Akbar granted the followers of the Raushaniya sect the freedom to follow their religion, Monserrate sadly commented that "He cared little that in allowing everyone to follow his own religion he was in reality violating all religions." [21]

Even in Aurangzeb's reign a cow could not be slaughtered in important places like Surat, and attempts made by some English merchants to obtain beef led to riots. According to one account: "In Surat the Hindus paid a fixed sum to the Mohammadans in return for sparing the cows. In 1608 a riot was caused at Surat by a drunken sailor Tom Tucker who killed a calf. Similar occurrences at Karwar and Honavar led to outbreaks, in one of which the whole factory was murdered." [22] But nothing brings out the Mughal administration's respect for the susceptibilities of the Hindus as well as the experience of the Portuguese missionary traveler, Manrique. "In a village where he stopped for the night, one of his followers, a Musalman, killed two peacocks, birds sacred in the eyes of Hindus, and did his best to conceal the traces of his deed by burying their feathers. The sacrilege was, however, detected, the whole party arrested, and the offender sentenced to have a hand amputated, though this punishment was eventually commuted to a whipping by the local official,

[21] *Commentary of Father Monserrate*, pp. 12, 27, and 142.
[22] Philip Anderson, *The English in Western India* (London, 1956), pp. 107–8.

who explained that the emperor had taken an oath that he and his successors would let the Hindus live under their own laws and customs and tolerate no breach of them." [23]

Although the Mughals interfered little with Hindu customs, there was one ancient practice which they sought to stop. This was *sati,* or the custom of widows, particularly those of the higher classes, burning themselves on their husbands' funeral pyres. Akbar had issued general orders prohibiting *sati* and, in one noteworthy case, personally intervened to save a Rajput princess from immolating herself on the bier of her husband. Similar efforts continued to be made in the succeeding reigns. According to the European traveler Pelsaert, governors did their best to dissuade widows from immolating themselves, but by Jahangir's orders were not allowed to withhold their sanction if the woman persisted.[24] Tavernier, writing in the reign of Shah Jahan, observed that widows with children were not allowed in any circumstances to burn, and that in other cases governors did not readily give permission, but could be bribed to do so.[25] Aurangzeb was most forthright in his efforts to stop *sati*. According to Manucci, on his return from Kashmir in December, 1663, he "issued an order that in all lands under Mughal control, never again should the officials allow a woman to be burnt." Manucci adds that "This order endures to this day." [26] This order, though not mentioned in the formal histories, is recorded in the official guidebooks of the reign.[27] Although the possibility of an evasion of government orders through payment of bribes existed, later European travelers record that *sati* was not much practiced by the end of Aurangzeb's reign. As Ovington says in his *Voyage to Surat:* "Since the Mahometans became Masters of the Indies, this execrable custom is much abated, and almost laid aside, by the orders which *nabobs* receive for suppressing and extinguishing it in all their provinces. And now it is

[23] O'Malley, p. 22.

[24] Francisco Pelsaert, *Jahangir's India,* trans. by W. H. Moreland and Peter Geyl (Cambridge, 1925), p. 79.

[25] Jean Tavernier, *Travels in India,* trans. by Valentine Ball (London, 1925), II, 163–64.

[26] Manucci, II, 97.

[27] Jadunath Sarkar, *History of Aurangzib* (Calcutta, 1916), III, 92.

very rare, except it be some Rajah's wives, that the Indian women burn at all." [28]

Any generalization about Indian history is dangerous, but the impression one gains from looking at social conditions during the Mughal period is of a society moving towards an integration of its manifold political regions, social systems, and cultural inheritances. The greatness of the Mughals consisted in part at least in the fact that the influence of their court and government permeated society, giving it a new measure of harmony. The common people suffered from poverty, disease, and the oppression of the powerful; court life was marked by intrigue and cruelty as well as by refinement of taste and elegant manners. Yet the rulers and their officials had moral standards which gave coherence to the administration and which they shared to some extent with most of their subjects. Undeniably, there were ugly scars on the face of Mughal society, but the sixteenth and seventeenth centuries had a quality of life that lent them a peculiar charm. The clearest reflection of this is seen in the creative arts of the period.

[28] John Ovington, A Voyage to Surat (London, 1929), p. 201.

XVIII. The Mughals
and the Arts

THE GREATNESS of the Mughal achievement in the political unification of India was matched by the splendor and beauty of the work of the architects, poets, historians, painters, and musicians who flourished in the period. The resemblances of the Mughal empire to the Bourbon monarchy in France during the same period have often been noted, and in India, as in France, a literate and refined court gave a recognizable style and manner to a wide variety of arts.

Education

Before turning to the arts themselves, something must be said of the vigorous educational activity at the capitals—both Delhi and Agra —and in such great provincial cities as Sialkot, Lahore, Ahmadabad, and Burhanpur. Without these centers, the cultural achievements of the Mughal period would scarcely have been possible. During Akbar's reign the "mental sciences"—logic, philosophy, and scholastic theology—had taken on new importance. About the same time, we notice a very considerable improvement in the teaching of the religious sciences. Akbar's conquest of Gujarat opened up ports like Cambay and Surat to those scholars from northern India who wished to go to the great religious center of Hejaz for further study. That the standard of learning in these subjects rose as a consequence is evidenced by the career of scholars like Shaikh Abdul Haq Muhaddis (1551–1642). The extensive study of *hadith,* in which Indian scholars were to distinguish themselves in the eighteenth century, began because of this contact with Arabia.

Bernier, the French traveler who was in India during Aurangzeb's reign, deplored the deficiencies of the educational system. To prove his point, he quoted Aurangzeb's reproaches against his tutor for having

wasted time on grammar and metaphysics, while ignoring geography, history, and politics.[1] No attempt was made to control education, even though the state gave large grants of rent-free lands to ulama for setting up *madrasas.* There were no regular examinations, and no organization for maintaining standards. Yet Mughal education had its special values, for Muslim education did not decay in the eighteenth century with the decline of Muslim political authority. The reduced calls made by the state employment on Muslim manpower left more men free to devote themselves to academic and literary work. A number of educational institutions and foundations, including the colleges established by Ghazi-ud-din Khan Firuz Jang, Sharaf-ud-daulah, and Raushan-ud-daulah in Delhi belong to this period.

The standardization of the educational curriculum was accomplished in the eighteenth century. The *Dars-i-Nizamiya,* named after Mulla Nizam-ud-din (d.1748) provided instruction in grammar, rhetoric, philosophy, logic, scholasticism, *tafsir* (commentary on the Quran), *fiqh* (Islamic jurisprudence), *hadith,* and mathematics. This curriculum has been criticized for containing too many books on grammar and logic and in general for devoting too much attention to formal subjects and too little to useful secular subjects like history and natural sciences or even religious subjects like *tafsir* and *hadith.* But it provided good mental discipline, and its general adoption was responsible for the widespread interest in intellectual and philosophical matters. In the period in which it was systematized it was perhaps reasonably adequate for the average student. Those wishing to specialize or pursue a particular branch of knowledge went to the experts in that subject. The needs of the students specially interested in religious subjects were better served at institutions like *Madrasa-i-Rahimiya,* the forerunner of the modern seminary of Deoband, where *tafsir* and *hadith* were the principal subjects of study, but for those needing a general education to qualify for the posts of munshis, qazis, or religious preachers, *Dars-i-Nizamiya* provided a satisfactory basis until modern times.

Bernier, despite his criticism of the educational system, has left

---

[1] François Bernier, *Travels in the Mogul Empire A.D. 1656–1668,* trans. by A. Constable (London, 1914), pp. 155–57.

evidence that at least two intellectuals of the Mughal court tried to learn about Western philosophy. One of them was Fazil Khan, the prime minister, whom Bernier taught "the principal languages of Europe, after he had translated for him the whole philosophy of Gassendi in Latin, and whose leave he could not obtain, until he had copied for him a select number of best European books, thereby to supply the loss he should suffer of his person." The other was Danishmand Khan who supported Bernier for a number of years. "My Nawab, Agha Danishmand Khan, expects my arrival with much impatience," Bernier wrote. "He can no more dispense with his philosophical studies in the afternoon than avoid devoting the morning to his weighty duties as Secretary of State for Foreign Affairs and Grand Master of the Horse. Astronomy, geography, and anatomy are his favorite pursuits, and he reads with avidity the works of Gassendy and Descartes." [2] Colonel Sleeman, who knew India in the first half of the nineteenth century better than almost any other Englishman, paid high tribute to the quality of Muslim education in India. He wrote:

Perhaps there are few communities in the world among whom education is more generally diffused than among Mohammadans in India. He who holds an office worth twenty rupees a month commonly gives his sons an education equal to that of a Prime Minister. They learn, through the medium of Arabic and Persian languages, what young men in our colleges learn through those of Greek and Latin—that is, grammar, rhetoric, and logic. After his seven years of study, the young Mohammadan binds his turban upon a head almost as well filled with the things which appertain to these branches of knowledge as the young man raw from Oxford—he will talk as fluently about Socrates and Aristotle, Plato and Hippocrates, Galen, and Avicenna (alias Sokrat, Aristotalis, Aflatun, Bukrat, Jalinus, and Sina).[3]

Nor was education confined only to men. Many Muslim women were patrons of literature and themselves writers. The memoirs of Gulbadan Begum, Akbar's aunt, are well known, and his fostermother, Maham Anga, endowed a college at Delhi. Akbar's wife

[2] Bernier, pp. 352–53.
[3] William Sleeman, *Rambles and Reflections of an Indian Official* (London, 1844), II, 283.

Salima Sultana, the famous Empress Mumtaz Mahal, and Aurangzeb's sister, the Princess Jahan Ara Begum, were poetesses of note, as was his daughter, Zeb-un-Nissa.

The spread of knowledge and intellectual development is linked up with the growth of libraries. Printing was not introduced in northern India till after the end of the Muslim rule, but hundreds of katibs (calligraphists) were available in every big city, and no Muslim noble would be considered cultured, unless he possessed a good library. The royal palaces contained immense libraries. According to Father Manrique, the library of Agra in 1641 contained 24,000 volumes, valued at six and a half million rupees.

Literature

Persian was the language of Mughal intellectual life. Since the Ghaznavid occupation of Lahore in the beginning of the eleventh century, Persian had been the official language of the Muslim government and the literary language of the higher classes, but with the advent of the Mughals it entered a new era. Hitherto Persian had reached India mainly from Afghanistan, Turkistan, and Khorasan, and had many common features with Tajik. With the establishment of closer relations between India and Iran after Humayun's visit to that country, and the arrival of a large number of distinguished Iranis in the reign of Jahangir and later Mughal rulers, the linguistic and literary currents began to flow from Iran itself. Shiraz and Isfahan now replaced Ghazni and Bukhara in literary inspiration, with considerable refining of the language as a result.

A large number of prominent Irani poets, including Urfi, Naziri, Talib, and Kalim migrated to India, and at times the level of Persian literature was higher in Mughal India than in Iran. Unluckily the style of poetry, which was popular in both countries at this time, was the subtle and involved type made popular by Fighani of Shiraz. This school of poetry culminated in Bedil, the best known poet of Aurangzeb's reign. His similes and metaphors are often obscure, but his poetry is marked by great originality and profundity of thought. From love, the traditional preoccupation of Persian poets, he turned to the

problems of life and human behavior, and in certain circles (particularly in Afghanistan and Tajikistan) he ranks high as a philosophical poet. But the two poets who outshone all others in a distinguished group were Faizi and Ghalib. Faizi (1547–1595), whose genius matured before the large-scale immigration of poets from Iran and the introduction of the "new" school of poetry, was the brother of Abul Fazl. As Akbar's poet-laureate, his poetry mirrors a triumphant age. Ghalib (1796–1869), who was attached to the court of the last Mughal emperor, Bahadur Shah, began in the style of Bedil, but soon outgrew it and came under the spell of the immigrant Irani poets—Urfi, Naziri, Zahuri, and Hazin. His maturer work epitomizes all that is best in the different schools of Mughal poetry—profundity and originality of Bedil's thought combined with the polished diction of Urfi and Naziri. He wrote largely of love and life, but the deep, melancholy note in his poetry reflects the sad end to which the Mughal empire was drawing in his day.

Next to poetry, history and biography were most extensively cultivated during the Mughal period. Historians include Abul Fazl (1551–1602), whose comprehensive *Akbar Nama* is one of the most important historical works produced in India; Badauni (1540–1615), who wrote with bias and even venom, yet who was a consummate artist, a master of the telling phrase, and capable of evoking a living picture with a few deft strokes; the intelligent and orderly Firishta; Khafi Khan; and the author of *Siyar-ul-Mutakhkhirin,* the last of the great Mughal historical works.[4] Among biographical works, Babur's autobiography, originally written in Turkish, but soon translated into elegant Persian by Abdul Rahim Khan-i-Khanan, is the best. There were, however, other biographical works, including the comprehensive *Ma'asir'ul-umara* dealing with the Mughal nobility, and numerous biographies of saints, poets, and statesmen. A very interesting historical work written during Aurangzeb's reign is *Dabistan-i-Mazahib,* which has been translated into English under the misleading title, "School of Manners" but which is really a "History of Religions."

[4] Selections from the writings of many of these historians are found in H. M. Elliot and John Dowson, *The History of India as Told by Its Own Historians* (London, 1867–1877).

The author, who belonged to the band of the writers and thinkers around Dara Shukoh, gives considerable first-hand information about non-Muslim sects.[5]

The Persian literature produced in India is of interest not only for its intrinsic worth but also for the influence it exercised on the formation and shaping of regional literatures, especially those cultivated by the Muslims. In addition to vocabulary and general influence on thought, it contributed a number of literary genres to the regional languages, provided models for the writers, and supplied themes for many major literary works. Indeed, apart from Islam itself, the Persian literary heritage has been the most important basis of the cultural unity of Muslim India.

It is characteristic of the Mughals that, next to Persian, the language which received the greatest patronage at court was Hindi. The practice started in Akbar's day of having a Hindi kavi rai (poet-laureate) along with the Persian malik-ul-shuara. Already Muslim poets such as Jaisi and Kabir had enriched the Hindi language. Among Hindus, the greatest Hindi poet of Akbar's days was the famous Tulasidas, whose career was spent far from the worldly courts. There were, however, well-known Hindi poets amongst Akbar's courtiers. Raja Birbal (1528–1583) was the kavi rai, but the works of Akbar's famous general, Abdul Rahim have been better preserved. A skillful writer in Hindi, Abdul Rahim furthered the development of the language by extending his patronage to a number of other poets who used it. The title of *kavi rai* continued to be conferred even in Aurangzeb's time, and two of his sons, Azam and Muazzam, who ascended the throne as Bahadur Shah, were known to be patrons of Hindi literature. It is interesting to observe that during the later Mughal period Hindi poets like Bihari followed the same ornate style which was popular with the contemporary Persian poets.

Until the decline of the empire Urdu literature received scarcely any encouragement at the Mughal courts, but it was systematically nourished in the south by the Sufi saints and the Deccani kings.

---

[5] *The Dabistan or School of Manners,* trans. by David Shaw and Anthony Troyer (3 vols.; Paris, 1843).

Nusrati, a poet attached to the court of Bijapur, wrote *masnavis* (or narrative poems) in a language remote from modern Urdu but within its tradition. The first collection of Urdu lyrics was written by Sultan Muhammad Quli Qutab Shah (r. 1581–1611), the king of Golkunda and founder of the city of Hyderabad. Modern Urdu poetry really began, however, with Wali (1667–1741), who came in contact with the spoken Urdu of the Mughal camp during the long campaigns of Aurangzeb in the Deccan. He blended the Deccani and Gujarati idioms with the polite and more sophisticated language of the north, and following the traditions of standard Persian literature, he produced poetry which set a literary fashion in Delhi. He transferred to Urdu poetry ideas and images with which readers of Persian poetry were familiar, and thus enriched, Urdu could replace Persian poetry. Although a proportion of Wali's verse is in Deccani idiom, a good proportion is in polished Urdu.

Once Urdu was adopted as the medium of literary expression by the writers of the metropolis, its development was rapid, and it soon replaced Persian as the court language and principal literary language of Muslim India. The process of change-over to the new literary language was facilitated by certain other factors. The invasion of Delhi by the Persian monarch Nadir Shah in 1739 and the massacres perpetrated by his army must have led to a revulsion of feeling against everything Persian—including the language. An acute literary controversy of the period further hastened the process. Hazin, a major Persian poet who came to India to escape Nadir Shah, was subjected to great hardship in the unsettled conditions prevailing at that time, and in a controversy with Arzu, the foremost local writer of Persian verses, expressed his contempt for the Persian poetry written in India. Some local writers sided with him, but the general effect of the controversy must have been to set people thinking about the advisability of writing in Persian.

Thus the ground was prepared for literary change-over. What was needed was the appearance of talented writers in the new language to give it a literary status. This was provided by Mazhar (1699–1781), Sauda (1717–1780), the Sufi poet Dard (1719–1785), and above all Mir (1724–1808)—popularly known as the four pillars of classical

Urdu poetry. Both Sauda and Mir had been trained by Arzu to write in Urdu rather than in Persian.

The encouragement which the growth of regional languages and literatures received in the regional Muslim kingdoms has already been outlined. Muslim rulers, unhampered by any religious devotion to Sanskrit, freely patronized Bengali, Kashmiri, Hindi, Deccani, and other languages of the people. This trend was most powerful in the regional kingdoms which grew up after the weakening of the Delhi Sultanate. Persian continued as the court language in these kingdoms but local languages were freely patronized and became respectable vehicles of literary expression.

The literary trend under Mughal rule was not exactly in the same direction. The establishment of a well-organized central government at Delhi, with cohesive control over the outlying regions, resulted in greater linguistic unification, and the influence of Persian became far more dominant. Mughal rule, however, indirectly assisted the regional literatures. Apart from the direct patronage of Hindi at the Delhi court, the conditions in the country helped the regional literatures. The general peace and tranquillity, greater prosperity, particularly in urban areas, the more general diffusion of education, and the patronage of literature by the Mughal emperors and the nobility, led to extensive literary activity, from which the regional literatures benefited. By now they had developed so much that they could not wither away by want of direct court patronage, and the general prosperity in the country was enough to sustain them. The result was that a marked literary activity in the regional languages continued along with the cultivation of Persian, and particularly in the later part of Mughal rule there was a great outburst of literary activity in Bengali, Deccani, Hindi, Sindhi, Pushto, Kashmiri, and other regional languages.

Architecture

Architecture, which had already achieved a high level of development under the sultanate, reached the pinnacle of its glory under the Mughals. Although Babur's stay in India was brief, and he was preoccupied with the conquest of the country, he found time to summon

from Constantinople pupils of the great Ottoman architect Sinan, to whom he entrusted the construction of mosques and other buildings. Time has dealt harshly with buildings constructed in his reign and that of Humayun, and only four minor ones have survived. These buildings exhibit no trace of local influence and are distinctly foreign.

Akbar's most ambitious project was his new capital and the numerous buildings at Fathpur Sikri, the seat of the imperial court from 1569 to 1584. Some of the buildings there are dominated by the Hindu style of architecture, reflecting the emperor's regard for the Hindu tradition. But Persian influences were equally strong in his day, as can be seen in the magnificent tomb for Humayun built early in 1569 at Delhi. Akbar's efforts were not confined to tombs, mosques, and palaces, but included fortresses, villas, towers, sarais, schools, and reservoirs or tanks. He built two major fortresses at Agra and Lahore. The Lahore fort, which was built on the banks of the Ravi, at about the same time as that at Agra, was planned and constructed on practically the same grand scale. The buildings within the Lahore fort were greatly altered by Shah Jahan and later by the Sikhs, but much remains in the original form. A striking feature of the fort is the carved decoration, representing living things. This may indicate merely the predominance of Hindu craftsmen, and a lax overseer, but more likely it can be ascribed to Akbar's own predilections.

Akbar's death in 1605 was followed by a pause in building activities of the Mughals. His successor, Jahangir, was less interested in architecture than in painting and gardens. Akbar's tomb at Sikandar and some other buildings were constructed during his reign, but Jahangir's greatest contribution was in laying out the large formal gardens which adorn many cities of Kashmir and the Punjab. The Mughal garden is a regular arrangement of squares, usually in the form of terraces placed on a slope (for easy distribution of water), with pavilions at the center. Artificial pools with numerous fountains form an important part of the plan and the flagged causeways are shadowed by avenues of trees. Babur and Akbar had made a beginning in this direction, but during Jahangir's reign a number of lovely gardens came into existence, such as the Shalamar Bagh and the Nishat in Kashmir. Jahangir's beautiful mausoleum at Shahdara near Lahore was prob-

ably planned by the emperor himself, but it was completed in the next reign, by his widow Nur Jahan. It suffered serious damage in the reign of Ranjit Singh, when the marble pavilion in front of the building, which offered a central point of interest, was removed. It cannot be fairly judged after the spoliation by the Sikhs, and in any case it lacks many noble features of the Taj Mahal, but even now it is a beautiful building, decorated by inlaid marbles, glazed tiles, and painted patterns. Not far from Jahangir's resting place Nur Jahan lies buried in a very unpretentious tomb.

Shah Jahan was the greatest builder amongst the Mughals. One secret of his success was the liberal use of the marble. He replaced many sandstone structures of his predecessors in the forts of Agra and Lahore and other places with marble palaces. This change in the material itself facilitated a corresponding change in architectural treatment. Rectangular forms gave way to curved lines, and the art of the marble cutter gave a new grace and lightness to the decoration. The style of Shah Jahan's principal edifices is basically Persian but is distinguished by the lavish use of white marble, minute and tasteful decoration, particularly open-work tracery which ornaments the finest buildings, giving them their distinctive elegance. Among the more famous of his buildings are the Pearl Mosque and the Taj Mahal at Agra, the Red Fort and Jama Masjid at Delhi, palaces and gardens at Lahore, a beautiful mosque at Thatta in Sind, a fort, palace, and mosque at Kabul, royal buildings in Kashmir, and many edifices at Ajmer and Ahmadabad.

Aurangzeb was not a great builder but among buildings of merit erected in his reign is the great Badshahi Mosque of Lahore, completed in 1674. Its construction was supervised by Fidai Khan Kuka, Master of Ordnance, whose engineering skill and experience enabled him to design and erect a building of great size and stability. It is one of the largest mosques in the subcontinent, if not in the world. There is a great dignity in its broad quadrangle leading up to the facade of the sanctuary. Its ornamentation is boldly conceived, but perhaps representing Aurangzeb's puritanical taste, this is sparingly introduced. For this reason the building suffers in comparison with the Great Mosque at Delhi.

After Shah Jahan Mughal architecture declined even at the capital, although some interesting buildings were erected from time to time. The tomb of Safdar Jang at Delhi, built in 1783, is indicative of the decline in the architectual standards, which was to become more manifest in the hybrid structures exhibiting European and Mughal influences at Lucknow.

Painting

As patrons of painting the Mughals gave the world a legacy of enduring beauty. The particular styles of painting which developed in India had their origin in the courts of the relatives of the Mughals at Herat and elsewhere. Babur himself, although he had some painters in his service, made no efforts to foster the art in his newly won empire.

To Humayun must go the credit for the founding of the Mughal school of painting. During his wanderings in Persia and what is now Afghanistan he came across painters who had studied under Behzad, and persuaded Khwaja Abdul Samad and Mir Sayyid Ali, the pupil of Behzad, to join his court at Kabul in 1550. They accompanied him to Delhi, forming the nucleus of the Mughal school.

This school was properly developed under Akbar, who organized it with his usual zeal. It was under his direct supervision, and the more prominent of the hundred or so painters were granted ranks in the governmental structure as mansabdars or ahadis. The painters worked in a large building at Fathpur Sikri, and, according to Abul Fazl, "the works of all painters are weekly laid before His Majesty by the daroghas (supervisors) and the clerks; he then confers rewards according to the excellence of workmanship or increases the monthly salaries."

Khwaja Abdul Samad was the head of the establishment and was known by the title of shirin qalam (or sweet pen), referring to his skill in calligraphy. Later he became master of the mint (1577) and subsequently was appointed diwan at Multan.

There was a small number of Persian artists, and, in course of time, a preponderance of Hindus. They had had previous training in wall-

painting and joined with the Persian painters between 1570 and 1585 in decorating the walls of Akbar's new capital. They were quick to learn the principles and techniques of Persian art, and the joint efforts of Persian and Indian artists soon led to the rise of the distinct style of Mughal painting. The foreign artists included Khwaja Abdul Samad, Farrukh Beg, and Khusrau Quli. Among the Hindus Basawan Lal and Daswant were preeminent. Occasionally many artists collaborated in the painting of a single picture, the leading artists sketching the composition and other painters putting in the parts at which they were expert.

Akbar's artists specialized in portraiture and book illustration. The emperor's album containing likenesses not only of Akbar and the royal family but of all the grandees of the realm has been lost, but many examples of book illustrations of the period have survived: *Razm Nama* at Jaipur, *Babur Nama* in the British Museum, and the *Akbar Nama* in the Victoria and Albert Museum.

Akbar's traditions were maintained by Jahangir, who was proud both of his artists and his own critical judgment. "As regards myself," he wrote in his *Memoirs,* "my liking for painting and my practice in judging it have arrived at such a point that when any work is brought before me, either of deceased artists or those of the present day, without the names being told me, I say on the spur of the moment that it is the work of such and such a man. And if there be a picture containing many portraits, and each face be the work of a different master, I can discover which face is the work of each of them. If any other person has put in the eye and eyebrow of a face, I can perceive whose work the original face is, and who has painted the eye and eyebrows." [6] The main remnants of Jahangir's principal picture albums are in the State Library of Berlin, while another album, which was taken away by Nadir Shah during his sack of Delhi, is in the Imperial Library at Tehran.

A special skill developed by Indian painters in Jahangir's time was the production of extremely faithful copies of paintings. The emperor appreciated gifts of paintings from foreign visitors, and Sir Thomas

---

[6] *Memoirs of Jahangir,* trans. by Alexander Rogers and H. Beveridge (London, 1909), II, 20–21.

Roe records that once when he presented a painting in the morning, by the evening several copies had been prepared by the native artists. They were such accurate copies that Roe had some difficulty in spotting the original. Jahangir's best known painters were Agha Raza of Herat and his son Abul Hasan; the Kalmuck artist, Farrukh Beg; Muhammad Nadir and Muhammad Murad, both of Samarqand; Ustad Mansur, the leading animal painter; Bishan Das; Manohar; and Govardhan. These and many others were constantly in attendance on the emperor at the capital and during his travels. They were commissioned to paint any incident or scene that struck the emperor's fancy. When a Mughal embassy visited Persia it was accompanied by the painter Bishan Das who painted for Jahangir the likenesses of the Safavid king and his courtiers. The court painters have left a record of the public men of note that is probably unequalled for fidelity and artistry. It is regrettable that these portraits have not yet been utilized as a source material for social history.

Under Shah Jahan painting, like all the other arts, continued to flourish. He reduced the number of court painters, keeping only the very best and forcing others to seek the patronage of the princes and the nobles, but the art did not suffer by this. Dara Shukoh was a patron of painting, and nobles like Zafar Khan, the governor of Kashmir, who had a beautiful anthology of the works of the living poets prepared, illustrated with their paintings, employed many artists. Other painters set up studios in the bazaars. An interesting feature of the period, typical of the general predominance of the indigenous elements in various spheres—in the secretariat, literature, and music —was that only one Persian artist was employed by Shah Jahan. The preponderance of the Hindus among court painters is indicative of the emancipation of the local school from dependence on Iran as well as the importance of Hindus in all spheres of life. The excellence of Mughal painting depended not only on the taste of individual ruler but on his prosperity, and with the disintegration of the empire, the artists migrated from the capital to other centers like Oudh and Hyderabad, where artistic standards quickly declined.

Music

Mughals patronized music lavishly, and in this Akbar led the way. Abul Fazl gives the names of nearly forty prominent musicians and instrumentalists who flourished at Akbar's court. The principal artists came from Gwalior, Malwa, Tabriz (in Iran), and Kashmir.

The most famous musician of the period was Tansen. According to some Muslim chroniclers, he was brought up in the hospice of Shaikh Mohammad Ghaus of Gwalior, but Hindu tradition describes him as a disciple of Swami Haridas. It is not certain whether he formally adopted Islam, but his son, Bilas Khan, was certainly a Muslim. "A singer like him," wrote Abul Fazl, "has not been in India for the last two thousand years." He was not very popular with conservative Hindu musicians, who held him responsible for the deterioration of Hindu music. He is said to have falsified the *ragas.*[7]

Although Tansen made some changes, the variety of music most extensively cultivated at Akbar's court was the ancient *dhrupad.* The same tradition was continued by Bilas Khan, the inventor of *bilas todi.* Music received great encouragement under Shah Jahan. He had thirty prominent musicians and instrumentalists at his court who were generously rewarded for good performances. The stately *dhrupad* continued its sway, though there was a marked tendency towards beautification and ornamentation. The *khiyal,* or ornate, school of music was beginning to assert itself.

Aurangzeb had himself studied music, but his deepening puritanism led him to abandon it on religious grounds. In 1688, he disbanded the large band of musicians attached to the royal court. A famous story is told of how the court musicians, seeking to draw the emperor's attention to their distressing condition, filed past his balcony carrying a gaily dressed corpse upon a bier and chanting mournful funeral songs. When the emperor asked what it was, they told him that music had died from neglect and that they were taking its corpse to the burial ground. He replied at once: "Very well, make the grave deep, so that neither voice nor echo may issue from it." [8]

[7] A. H. Fox-Strangways, *The Music of Hindostan* (Oxford, 1914), p. 84.
[8] Herbert Popley, *The Music of India* (Calcutta, 1921), p. 20.

While during Aurangzeb's reign music ceased to enjoy royal patronage, its popularity with the upper classes was firmly established, and a number of books on the history and theory of Indo-Muslim music were written during this period. One of the most famous was the *Rag-darpan* (The Mirror of Music), written by Fakirullah (Saif Khan), who was at one time governor of Kashmir. It purports to be a translation of *Man-Kauthal* written at the court of Raja Man Singh of Gwalior, but contains much additional information derived from other sources. With the reaction against Aurangzeb's puritanism under his grandson Jahandar Shah and his great-grandson Muhammad Shah Rangila, music had an unprecedented vogue. In conformity with court tastes, the *khiyal* came into its own. The *khiyal* developed slowly, and drew from many sources. Literally the term means, "thought," "imagination," "phantasy," and technically stands for imaginative or romantic music. As the Arabic origin of the word signifies, this music developed after the advent of the Muslims, but traditionally its themes echo the Hindu legends of Krishna and his Gopis. Probably the court musicians, catering to the interest of their patrons, found it expedient to adapt the legends and treatment which had been developed by musicians and Bhagats of the Krishna cult. This variety of music did not gain a firm footing at the Delhi court until the decline of the Mughal empire, and is closely associated with the court of Muhammad Shah Rangila (r. 1719–1748).

With the weakening of the Mughal empire and the setting up of provincial governments, music was encouraged in provincial capitals, and just as Lucknow became the refuge of Urdu poets, musicians in northern India flocked to the court of the nawab-wazirs of Oudh. At Lucknow, music underwent some important changes. With the breakup of the empire and the loss of the patronage of a formal court, the musicians had to cater to popular tastes. As a result, the quality and the variety of music underwent a subtle change, with two forms of popular music originating in Lucknow. One of these was *thumri,* love music that makes a sensuous appeal through repetition of words and musical phrases. The theme is human love, not a symbolic representation of divine longing as in the older music. The other form, *tappa,* found inspiration in folk music, a source that had pre-

viously been ignored by court musicians.[9] Through such developments as these, the music of the courts became part of the life of the ordinary people of North India.

[9] S. A. Halim, *The Muslim Year Book of India,* 1948–1949 (Bombay, 1949), p. 118.

XIX. A Century of Political Decline: 1707-1803

CULTURAL and artistic achievements did not come to an end with Aurangzeb's death in 1707, and for a century and more, the Mughals dominated the cultural life of North India. In political life, one visible sign of the enduring power of the empire was the eagerness of every usurper of territory to gain recognition from Delhi. Another was that until 1835, the East India Company, which had become the effective successor to Mughal power, still minted coins in the emperor's name. In general, however, the eighteenth century saw a progressive decline in Mughal political control.

The Struggle for Succession

After Aurangzeb's death, the usual war of succession followed, with his eldest surviving son, Muazzam, the subedar of Kabul, who was the first to reach Agra, being successful. He ascended the throne as Bahadur Shah. A mild and forbearing man, he tackled the problems confronting him with tolerable competence. Rebellious chieftains in Rajputana troubled him but were overcome without much difficulty. His longest campaign was against Banda, a leader of the Sikhs. Govind Singh, the last Sikh guru, after years of bitter fighting against Aurangzeb, had entered into friendly relations with Bahadur Shah, accepting the position of mansabdar in the Mughal army. His assassination in 1708 ended this period of amity. Govind Singh's successor as temporal leader of the Sikhs was Banda, who returned to the Punjab declaring he was Guru Govind Singh miraculously brought back to life. In response to his call for disciples many zealous Sikhs assembled and marched in arms to Sonepat, some twenty-five miles north of Delhi. There the faujdar, who was utterly unprepared, was routed. This success emboldened Banda. Accompanied by forty thousand

men he set out to establish his power in the north. The town of Sadhaura, near Ambala, was captured, and the Muslim inhabitants were
cruelly treated. He then moved against Sirhind, whose governor,
Wazir Khan, was held responsible for the execution of Govind Singh's
children. Banda's army pillaged the city for four days, and the
whole Muslim population was slaughtered.

The situation became so serious that Bahadur Shah himself moved
against Banda, and on December 4, 1710, he forced the evacuation
of Sadhaura. The Sikhs then moved to the strong fort of Lohgarh,
where Banda had issued coins in his own name. Bahadur Shah captured Lohgarh, but Banda escaped. Sirhind was reoccupied in January, 1711, and Banda took shelter in the hills.

After a halt at Sirhind, Bahadur Shah moved to Lahore. His stay
here was marked by the one major controversy of his reign. Soon
after his accession to the throne, he had given orders that the title
wasi should be used after the name of Hazrat Ali in the Friday
prayers. This usage, indicating that Ali was the testamentary successor to the Prophet, and considered by the Sunnis to be a Shia
innovation, was bitterly resented. During his stay in Lahore Bahadur
Shah tried to persuade the local ulama to accept the change, but without success. He then ordered his chief of artillery to have the new
form of prayer recited from the pulpit of the Badshahi Masjid on
April 22, 1711. When he found that a vast crowd, ready for violent
resistance, had gathered in the streets of Lahore, he gave way and in
the end the old form in use in the days of Aurangzeb was recited.
Seven leading ulama of Lahore were sent, however, to the state prison
in the Gwalior fort. The episode indicates the limitations imposed on
the emperor by the ulama, but the punishment given the leaders shows
that resistance, even if successful, could be dangerous.

Bahadur Shah died on February 27, 1712. His favorite son, Azim-
ush-Shan, expected to succeed him, but a powerful general, Zulfiqar
Khan, the son of Aurangzeb's wazir, Azad Khan, formed an alliance
with Azim's three brothers against him. They agreed to partition the
empire among them, with Zulfiqar Khan as their common minister. In
the battle that followed Azim was drowned in the Ravi, and Zulfiqar
threw aside the two youngest princes in favor of the worthless Ja-

handar Shah. Zulfiqar became the all-powerful minister, and the emperor, infatuated with his concubine Lal Kunwar and relieved by Zulfiqar from all responsibilities of the state, spent his time in frivolous amusements.

Disaster was not long in coming. Muhammad Farrukhsiyar, the second son of Azim-ush-Shan, and deputy governor of Bengal, had not reconciled himself to Jahandar Shah's enthronement and when he heard of his father's death, he proclaimed himself emperor at Patna in April, 1712. He interested the two powerful Sayyid brothers, Husain Ali and Hasan Ali, in his fortunes, and having collected an army the allies moved towards the capital. They defeated Jahandar Shah at Samugarh on January 6, 1713. Jahandar Shah fled from the battlefield, hidden in the howda of Lal Kunwar. Entering Delhi surreptitiously at night, he sought help from Zulfigar and Asad Khan. Realizing that Jahandar was of no more use, Zulfigar and Asad Khan tried to gain favor with the new power by imprisoning him. Jahandar was murdered in prison, but Zulfigar also was put to death two days later.

Farrukhsiyar's reign (1713–1719) saw a general deterioration in the power of the central government, but in one area its authority was strongly asserted. Bahadur Shah had not succeeded in overcoming the menace of the resurgent power of the Sikhs. Early in his reign, Farrukhsiyar appointed Abdus Samad Khan as governor of Lahore with instructions to destroy Banda, who had taken refuge in the hills and used them as a base for raids on the countryside. Abdus Samad finally penned him up in the fort of Gurdaspur. Banda's followers offered fanatical resistance, but all their attempts to escape failed, and the garrison was forced to surrender unconditionally on December 17, 1715, after an eight-month siege. Banda was taken to Delhi and put to death. Stern vengeance was wreaked on his followers, but the peace of the area was ensured for a generation or more.

Farrukhsiyar owed his throne to the Sayyid brothers, and he rewarded them with the highest offices in the realm. He soon found their power galling, but a number of ineffectual attempts to get rid of them only worsened his position. Husain Ali left Delhi in 1715, as viceroy of the Deccan, but before leaving he warned the emperor that

if ever his brother was harassed at Delhi he would promptly return to the capital. Matters came to a head in 1718 when Hasan Ali, believing he was in danger, asked his brother to come to Delhi. A peculiarly sinister feature of Husain Ali's return was that he was accompanied by eleven thousand Maratha troops as well as by his own army. Maratha support had been bought for a heavy price— among other concessions they were promised one-fourth of the revenue from the Deccan. The emperor was imprisoned and blinded in February, 1719; two months later he was strangled to death. Two of the puppets placed on the throne by the king-making Sayyids died within a year, but a third, Raushan Akhtar, a grandson of Bahadur Shah, who became emperor in 1719 as Muhammad Shah, reigned for thirty years. In its duration, his reign recalls that of his great predecessors, but possibly even they could not have prevented the decline that was now obvious in the imperial power.

The power of the Sayyids was broken early in the reign of the new emperor when two of the opposing factions at the court, the Irani nobles and the Turani, formed an alliance against them. Both brothers were killed in 1720, one by an assassin and the other in battle. For a short time the wizarat was held by Muhammad Amin Khan, one of the Turani nobles who had helped overthrow the Sayyids, but after his death in 1721, an important new figure appeared on the Delhi scene.

This was Chin Qilich Khan, another of the Turani nobles who had been an enemy of the Sayyids. He is best known in history by his title, Nizam-ul-Mulk. An able administrator and soldier who had been governor of the Deccan provinces, Nizam-ul-Mulk was made wazir of the empire in 1722. His experience in the office illustrates the increasing weakness of the administration and the reason it could not meet the challenges of the time. His advice to the gay young sovereign to reform the court was not followed, and his attempts to bring about changes in the administration were met by obstruction and indifference. He was especially anxious to stop the farming of imperial revenues, a practice that was diverting much of the resources that should have come into the central treasury, to reimpose *jizya,* and to eradicate bribery. This call to return to the austerity of the

court of Aurangzeb had little chance of being heeded in Delhi in the eighteenth century, and Nizam-ul-Mulk left Delhi late in 1723 for Hyderabad. There he established the power which he was able to transmit to his descendants as the largest of the Indian states.

After Nizam-ul-Mulk's departure from Delhi the Marathas became an increasingly grave menace to the empire. By 1732 they had partially occupied Gujarat, had partitioned Bundelkhand, and temporarily overrun Mewar in Rajputana. Muhammad Shah moved against them in 1733, but the imperial army never went beyond Faridabad, sixteen miles south of Delhi. The Marathas continued to advance, and although they suffered defeats, in 1737 under one of their greatest leaders, Baji Rao I (r. 1720–1740), they reached Delhi itself. They looted the suburbs but when they heard that the whole Mughal army was approaching the capital, they retired southwards.[1]

It was the Maratha danger that led to the recall of Nizam-ul-Mulk to Delhi in 1737. He was received by the wazir outside the capital with great honor, and during the winter months was engaged in a series of negotiations and skirmishes with Baji Rao and his troops. In return for concessions in Central India, the Marathas withdrew from the north, but Nizam-ul-Mulk had scarcely returned to Delhi when a new danger, invasion from the northwest by Nadir Shah, was threatening the empire.

External Threats —

In Persia, the ruling Safavid king had been driven out by an Afghan soldier, whose father had freed Qandahar—long an object of dispute between the Mughals and the Safavids—from the Persians. He conquered Herat and Khurasan, and in 1722 occupied Isfahan, the capital. It seemed likely that Persia would disappear as a state, since the Russians were also interested in expanding into the area, but a remarkable soldier named Nadir Quli, acting in the name of the Safavid dynasty, drove out both the Afghans and the Russians. In 1736 he ascended the throne as Nadir Shah, and wishing to regain Qandahar from the Afghans, appealed to the Mughal emperor, Mu-

[1] G. S. Sardesai, *New History of the Marathas* (Bombay, 1958), II, 166–67.

hammad Shah, for assistance. He was particularly anxious to have the emperor close the border of the Mughal province of Kabul so that fugitives from Qandahar could not escape him.

Delhi sent favorable replies, but nothing tangible was done to prevent the Afghans crossing into Kabul, and Nadir Shah sent another envoy to Muhammad Shah for an explanation. When the envoy could not get an audience with Muhammad Shah, Nadir Shah began to make preparations to enter Mughal territory. After defeating the Afghans at Qandahar, he moved toward Ghazni and Kabul, which he captured in June, 1738. From there he continued to Peshawar and Lahore, which he occupied in 1739 after minor local resistance. From Lahore he addressed a letter to Muhammad Shah complaining of gross discourtesy, adding that he was coming to Delhi to punish the royal counsellors who were responsible for the insult. Muhammad Shah with a large force marched to stop the invader at Karnal, but the Indian army (to which Rajput chiefs had refused to send any contingents) was outmaneuvered. In a skirmish between the Irani scouts and the fresh troops which were being brought to join the main Indian army, Burhan-ul-Mulk, the subedar of Oudh, was captured, and Khan-i-Dauran, the commander-in-chief, was fatally wounded. Although the main body of the Indian army had not been involved in action, the battle of Karnal was over, with disastrous results for the Mughal empire.

The catastrophe begun on the battlefield was completed by treachery and poor statesmanship. Burhan-ul-Mulk, who had been taken to the Persian camp, persuaded Nadir to leave Muhammad Shah on the throne of Delhi and to retire from India on payment of an indemnity of twenty million rupees. Burhan-ul-Mulk hoped, however, to be made commander-in-chief in place of Khan-i-Dauran, but Muhammad Shah conferred the office on Nizam-ul-Mulk. Burhan-ul-Mulk was so furious that he now advised Nadir Shah not to be contented with twenty millions, but to move on Delhi. The Persian king decided to leave the question of indemnity open until he reached the capital.

Further suffering was brought about by the rashness of the citizens of Delhi. Nadir Shah's troops were quartered in different parts of the

city, when a rumor spread that the Persian king had been assassinated. This led to a massacre of nearly nine hundred Persian soldiers, who were moving about unarmed. Nadir took vengeance by ordering a general massacre of the citizens of Delhi. This continued for a whole day, resulting in the slaughter of nearly thirty thousand persons. The massacre stopped by evening, but the looting continued. In addition to the seizure of Shah Jahan's wonderful Peacock Throne and a large stock of jewelry from the imperial treasury, levies were imposed on nobles, and the wealthy citizens were plundered.

On May 16, Nadir Shah retired from Delhi laden with a greater booty than any previous conqueror had ever taken. He left Muhammad Shah on the throne of Delhi, but annexed all territory west of the Indus, including the province of Kabul. He later stipulated that a sum of twenty lakhs out of the revenue of four districts of Gujarat, Sialkot, Pasrur, and Aurangabad (in the Punjab) which had hitherto been reserved for meeting the administrative cost of the province of Kabul should be paid into the Persian treasury.

Nadir's defeat of the Indian army and massacre and plunder of the capital destroyed the prestige of the Mughal government and ruined it financially. This emboldened the Sikhs and the Marathas, and even the provincial governors became defiant. Addressing Muhammad Shah in a letter from Kabul, Nadir Shah had stated that he had occupied his northwestern territory "purely out of zeal for Islam" so that in case "the wretches of the Deccan" again moved towards Hindustan, he might "send an army of victorious Qizilbashes to drive them to the abyss of Hell." [2] He had, in fact, given a death wound to the Mughal empire.

Nadir's invasion of India was a stunning blow, but after a period of helpless stupor, Muhammad Shah tried to reorganize his government. According to contemporary accounts, "the emperor and the nobles turned to the management of state affairs and gave up all sorts of uncanonical practices," but this phase was short-lived. Nadir Shah, by his attempts to influence Muhammad Shah against Nizam-ul-Mulk and to buttress the influence of the Irani faction, had further

[2] Quoted in Muhammad Latif, *The History of the Panjab* (Calcutta, 1891), p. 200.

aggravated the internal conflicts at the court which had contributed to Mughal weakness. Muhammad Shah's reign did not, however, close without at least one victory. In March, 1748, the Mughal army defeated Ahmad Shah Abdali, who had succeeded to the eastern territories of Nadir Shah's empire, near Sirhind. This was the last victory the Mughals were to win against a foreign invader.

Disintegration of the Empire

Muhammad Shah died in 1748, a few weeks after this last victory. His long reign had seen a growing paralysis in imperial power, of which the most visible symptom was the establishment of hereditary viceroyalties in the major provinces of the empire. The pattern was one that had been seen before in India history: as the central power weakened, either as a cause or result, the outlying provinces assumed independent status. These states were the administrative units of the Mughal empire, but they were also the traditional "nuclear" regions of Indian history, defined by geography, language, and past traditions.

The provincial governors long continued to demonstrate the symbolic function of the Mughal emperor by their desire to gain his recognition for their rule, but from the time of Muhammad Shah they sought such recognition after, not before, their seizure of power. In the Punjab, largely because of the intervention of external forces from the northwest, independent kingdoms were not formed in the middle of the eighteenth century, but elsewhere the process of disintegration of central authority was complete. In the Deccan, Oudh, Bengal, and to some extent in Rohilkhand, large principalities, over which the central government of Delhi had only nominal authority, came into existence. By depriving the empire of financial resources, even though they continued to send an annual tribute to Delhi, and by reducing the possibility of united action, these kingdoms lessened the chances of the empire's survival when attacks came from without.

The most important of the new principalities was Hyderabad, made up of six *subas* of the Deccan, which at this time had a revenue of sixteen crores of rupees, compared with seventeen crores from the other twelve provinces of the Mughal empire. As already noted the

founder of the state was Nizam-ul-Mulk, who had been made viceroy of the Deccan by Farrukhsiyar in 1714 and wazir of the empire by Muhammad Shah in 1722. On his return to the Deccan in 1724, he began to build up a strong state, although still offering assistance to the emperor. At his death in 1748, he passed on a well-administered state that continued to be a center of Muslim culture in the Deccan for two centuries.

In Bengal, power passed into the hands of two remarkable men, Murshid Quli Khan and Alivardi Khan. Under these able administrators Bengal was among the most peaceful and prosperous areas of India, and paid an annual tribute of ten million rupees to the Delhi court.

In the Punjab the Sikhs used Nadir Shah's invasion in 1739 as an opportunity to attack Mughal authority, but the able governor, Zakariya Khan, crushed them. After his death in 1745 the province passed out of effective Mughal control.

Sind does not figure greatly in Mughal history, and authority had always tended to reside in the hands of local chiefs. The most important of these belonged to the Kalhara family, descendants of the disciples of a sixteenth-century spiritual leader. Through the course of the next hundred years they built up great land holdings, and by the beginning of the eighteenth century were recognized as governors of a large area of Upper Sind. Muhammad Shah completed the process in 1736 by conferring on the chief of the Kalharas a title that acknowledged his control of the whole province of Sind.

Cultural Life

Against this picture of a disintegrating empire must be set the undoubted fact that Muhammad Shah's reign was a time of very considerable cultural activity. Urdu, which had gained admission in the literary and cultural circles of the metropolis only a few years before the beginning of Muhammad Shah's reign, was a fully developed literary language at its end. A new school of music grew up around the Mughal court, and the names of Sadarang and his brother occupy a high place in the evolution of *khiyal,* which was to supersede all

other varieties of the Hindustani music. Indian dancing, freed from the atmosphere of the temple, became an art ministering to human pleasure. A new style of painting, closely related to the rise of Urdu literature, brought fresh vigor to the tradition of pictorial art.[3] Indian astronomy also reached a new level of excellence in this period, as indicated by the magnificent astronomical instruments at Delhi and Ujjain. The creator of these works, Maharaja Jai Singh of Jaipur, was Muhammad Shah's governor in Malwa from 1728 to 1734.

Most significant of all the cultural activities of Muhammad Shah's reign was the beginning of the work of Shah Waliullah (1703–1762), the greatest Islamic scholar India ever produced. That the political disintegration of Islamic power in the eighteenth century was not accompanied by a religious collapse was largely due to his work, and, more than anyone else, he is responsible for the religious regeneration of Indian Islam.

Shah Waliullah received his training from his father, who as a theologian, Sufi, and philosopher combined in his own person these three main strands of Indian Islam. He was in his teens when he started teaching in his father's *madrasah*. He continued this for twelve years, after which he left for Arabia for higher studies and for performing the Hajj. He was in Arabia for nearly fourteen months pursuing his studies under famous teachers at Mecca and Medina.

During his stay at Mecca, Shah Waliullah saw a vision in which the Holy Prophet informed him that he would be instrumental in the organization of a section of the Muslim community. Friends urged him to stay in Hijaz, and not to return to the unsettled conditions of India, but he was convinced that his mission was to work there. He returned to Delhi in 1732, and began what was to be his life's work. He had been a teacher before he went to Arabia, and while he resumed his occupation, he no longer followed the traditional methods of instruction. He trained pupils in different branches of Islamic knowledge, then entrusted them with the teaching of the students, while he devoted himself to writing. Before his death in 1762, he had completed practically a library of standard works in all branches of

[3] Hermann Goetz, *The Crisis of Indian Civilization in the Eighteenth and Early Nineteenth Century* (Calcutta, 1939).

"Islamic sciences" of the type particularly suited to the Indian conditions.

Shah Waliullah's most important single work was his translation of the Quran into simple Persian, the literary language of Muslim India. Translations had been attempted earlier, but either they were incidental to a voluminous commentary, or did not gain wide acceptance. After some opposition Shah Waliullah's translation became popular, either because of the translator's eminence in religious circles, or because his translation was connected with a broad-based movement, aimed at bringing the knowledge of the Quran within the reach of the average, literate Indian Muslim. Shah Waliullah's action, which involved not only scholarship, but imagination and great moral courage, smoothed the way for others. Within sixty years his two sons prepared their Urdu translations—one completely literal and following the Arabic sentence-structure, and the other idiomatic and in accordance with Urdu usage. Not only did his sons follow his example, but, in course of time, so did scores of others, and it is because of his initiative that, outside the Arabic-speaking countries, Muslims in India and Pakistan have taken the lead in the study and propagation of the Quran.

Not less important was his balanced understanding and fair-minded approach to different religious questions. In his day Indian Islam was rent by controversies and conflicts between the Shia and the Sunni, the Sufi and the Mullah, the Hanafi and the Wahhabi, the Mujaddidi and the Wahdat-al-Wajudi, and the Mu'tazali and the Asha'ari. To Shah Waliullah, *adl,* (justice, equity) was the prime virtue and the basis of civilized existence, and he studied the writings of all schools of thought, trying to understand the attitudes of each of them. He then wrote authoritative volumes expounding what was just and acceptable to different points of view. In this way, by working out a system of thought on which all but the extremists could agree, he helped to provide a spiritual basis for national cohesion and harmony.[4]

Shah Waliullah's success was also due to his able and devoted

[4] For a brief selection from Shah Waliullah's writings, see Wm. Theodore de Bary et al., *Sources of Indian Tradition* (New York, 1958), pp. 455–62.

successors. One of his grandsons was the great reformer Shah Ismail Shahid. Three of his sons were leading scholars and writers, including Shah Abdul Aziz, who dominated Delhi religious life for nearly fifty years. The brothers taught and trained a large body of men who carried the message of Shah Waliullah to all parts of India. Their students and successors organized *jihad* against persecution of Islam by the Sikhs in the northwest, brought about a revival of Islam in Bengal, and were held in equal veneration by Sir Sayyid Ahmed Khan, the leader of the Aligarh movement, and Maulana Muhammad Qasim, the founder of the Deoband seminary.

While Islam is not organized along national lines, owing to historic, racial, linguistic, and geographic factors, a variety of schools and viewpoints have gained prominence in different Muslim countries. In Iran, for example, the Shia form of Islam is the national religion, while in the desert of Najd, Wahhabi puritanism is dominant. Similarly different countries have adopted, according to their peculiar developments, different schools of law—the Shafii, the Hanbali, the Maliki, and the Hanafi. If the beliefs, the legal traditions, and the religious tendencies of modern Muslim India and Pakistan were to be examined from this point of view, it would be seen that the foundation of the religious structure which is dominant there was laid by Shah Waliullah.

Shah Muhammad's Successors

Looking at Shah Muhammad's reign, the author of the late eighteenth-century history, *Siyar-ul-Mutakhkhirin,* declared: "In his reign the people passed their lives in ease, and the empire outwardly retained its dignity and prestige. The foundations of the Delhi monarchy were really rotten, but Muhammad Shah by his cleverness kept them standing. He may be called the last of the rulers of Babur's line, as after him the kingship had nothing but the name left to it." [5] The records of the last fifty years of the century suggest no reason for challenging this melancholy verdict. After Muhammad Shah's death,

[5] Ghulam Husain Khan, *Seir-ul-Mutaqheerin,* trans. by Raymond Mustapha (Calcutta, 1902), III, 281. The quotation is translated differently in this edition.

Prince Ahmad Shah (r. 1748–1754), the hero of the battle of Sirhind, ascended the throne, and although he was a well-meaning and active young man, he could effect no improvement in government affairs. His appointment of Safdar Jang as wazir was especially unfortunate. An opportunist whose measures helped to destroy the Mughal empire, Safdar Jang seems to have been motivated by two aims. One was to humiliate any relatives of his predecessors in the wizarat; the other was to drive out all Afghans from positions of authority.

Safdar's policy brought him in conflict with the principal Turani families, but his initial difficulties came from the royal favorites headed by the chief eunuch, Javed Khan, and the emperor's mother. Safdar Jang had Javed Khan assassinated in August, 1752, but then the emperor started favoring Ghazi-ud-din, a grandson of Nizam-ul-Mulk, and a clever, but completely unscrupulous, youth of eighteen. Safdar Jang lost the support of the emperor, and in May, 1753, though still the wazir of the realm, rebelled against his master. Ghazi-ud-din organized the opposition to Safdar Jang, and with his usual lack of scruples, whipped up Shia-Sunni and Afghan-Irani differences to gain supporters. Safdar was defeated and forgiven, but realizing that the best field for the satisfaction of his ambitions was away from the capital, withdrew to Oudh. Ghazi-ud-din was now all-powerful at the capital. This was dramatically attested when the emperor, who had soon become estranged from him, sought to have him removed from the court. With the help of the Maratha chiefs, Ghazi-ud-din made himself wazir and in June, 1754, deposed the emperor.

The man placed on the throne in 1754 as Alamgir II was a son of Jahandar Shah. A man of good intentions, his adoption of Aurangzeb's title was an indication of his desire to follow in his great predecessor's footsteps, but the situation in the empire was beyond his control. The Marathas, who had grown more powerful because of their collaboration with Ghazi-ud-din, now dominated the whole of northern India. In 1758 they occupied Lahore and drove out Taimur Shah, the son and viceroy of the Afghan ruler, Ahmad Shah Abdali. This was the high-water mark of the Maratha expansion. "Their frontier extended on the north to the Indus and the Himalaya, and in

the south nearly to the extremity of the peninsula; all the territory within those limits which was not their own, paid tribute." The whole of this great power was wielded by one hand, that of the Peshwa, who talked of placing Bishvas Rao on the Mughal throne.[6]

Maratha dreams, however, received a shattering blow. The expulsion of Taimur Shah provoked the wrath of Ahmad Shah Abdali, who was joined in the war against the Marathas by the principal Muslim nobles of North India. The main battle was fought at Panipat on June 14, 1761. This was the most desperate of the three historic battles of Panipat (the first fought by Babur in 1526 and the second by Humayun in 1556), and its results were of great significance for Indian history. The Marathas were completely defeated, and while their chiefs retained power in Central India, the centralizing power of the Peshwa was destroyed. Panipat meant that whoever succeeded the Mughals on the throne of Delhi, it would not be the Marathas. Ahmad Shah Abdali's own design of building up an Afghan empire in India was frustrated by the impetuosity of his soldiers, who hated the heat of the plains and clamored for an immediate return to Kabul with their plunder. Since they had been away from their homes for a long time and were on the verge of mutiny, Ahmad Shah had to abandon his dreams and return to his own country.

Ghazi-ud-din had put Alamgir II to death in 1759, replacing him with a puppet, but after the battle of Panipat, Ahmad Shah nominated a son of Alamgir II as emperor, with the title of Shah Alam (1761–1803). In the struggles that followed Ghazi-ud-din lost power and fled from the capital. The administration of the shrunken empire —by now reduced to little more than the area around Delhi—was in the hands of Najib-ud-daula. It was he who had organized the Muslim confederacy that defeated the Marathas at Panipat, and he remained loyal throughout his life to the Mughal emperor. This was all the more remarkable since Shah Alam was absent from Delhi almost continuously until 1772. Najib's main task was to maintain order in the Mughal domain around Delhi. After the battle of Panipat the Marathas were quiescent for some time, but the Jats and the

[6] Mountstuart Elphinstone, *History of India* (London, 1905), p. 276.

Sikhs began to threaten the integrity of the remaining imperial territories. Najib defeated the Jats and killed their leader, Suraj Mal, but he was less successful with the Sikhs. They were kept from creating too much trouble, however, by an internal split between two groups.

Rise of British Power

Meanwhile, far-reaching developments had taken place outside the capital. Alivardi Khan, the able governor of Bengal died on April 10, 1756, and was succeeded by his grandson, Mirza Muhammad, better known as Siraj-ud-daula. The disruptive forces which had been kept under check by Alivardi got out of hand and overwhelmed the government. Alivardi's commander-in-chief, Mir Jafar, to whom his half-sister was married, started plotting against Siraj-ud-daula and for a short time was removed from the command. Another reason for weakness was the existence of the East India Company, which had established at Calcutta not only a commercial, but a political center. A third was the attitude of the Hindu zamindars, bankers, and officials who, always influential in Bengal, had grown very powerful since the days of Murshid Quli Khan.

Alivardi Khan made no distinction between the Hindus and the Muslims. He had gained his position with the support of the Hindu notables, and they shared the government with him. This had not reconciled them to a Muslim ruler; or perhaps they recognized that a new power might soon overthrow his rule, and they wanted to be on the winning side. In any case, as an official of the East India Company had written two years before Alivardi's death: "[Hindu] rajas and inhabitants were disaffected to the Moor government and secretly wished for a change and opportunity of throwing off their tyrannical yoke." [7] These three forces sealed the fate of Siraj-ud-daula. The familiar story of British activities need not be told here, but the role of the treacherous Mir Jafar, generally held responsible for the fate of Siraj, was comparatively a minor one. More significant was the alliance of the Hindu merchants with the East India Company. This

[7] Quoted in S. C. Hill, *Bengal in 1756–1757* (London, 1903), III, 328.

new alignment, as much as any single factor, must be taken into account in explaining the end of Muslim rule in Bengal.

The battle fought at Plassey, a few miles outside Murshidabad, has been called by a modern British writer "the most miserable skirmish ever to be called a decisive battle." [8] An army, of which the commander-in-chief had been won over and took no part in the battle can hardly offer spirited contests. Siraj-ud-daula's Hindu paymaster, Mir Madan, however, was loyal to the nawab, and fell in action. Clive's spirited leadership and British organization, coupled with the help they received from the powerful local elements, resulted in the rout and flight of Siraj-ud-daula. On June 28, 1757, Clive installed Mir Jafar on the *masnad* of Murshidabad and four days later Siraj-ud-daula was executed.

The legal position in Bengal had not changed with the British victory at Plassey for the nawab was still in charge of the administration. But the officials of the East India Company expected him to do their bidding, and a clash was inevitable if a nawab sought to impose policies counter to British interests. The clash came when Nawab Mir Qasim, who had succeeded the incompetent Mir Jafar, tried to collect internal revenue from the English traders. According to an agreement, only the East India Company itself was to be free from the tax; in practice, every company servant traded on his own account and refused to pay any duty. In desperation, since his revenues were disappearing, Mir Qasim abolished all internal duties, thus removing the English advantage over the Indian traders. The British refused to accept this, and Mir Qasim left Bengal to organize an attack on the British.

Support of a half-hearted kind came from Emperor Shah Alam and Shuja-ud-daula, the wazir of Oudh who had followed the general pattern of the time by establishing himself as a semi-independent ruler. The Mughal and the British forces met at Buxar in October, 1764, and while the British suffered fairly heavy losses, they won a clear victory. The results of the battle of Buxar were more far-reaching than those of Plassey. Even before the battle the British had attempted to facilitate military task by diplomatic means, and the newly

[8] Philip Woodruff, *The Men Who Ruled India* (New York, 1954), I, 100.

crowned Shah Alam was only a fugitive from Delhi, but the East India Company had gained a victory against what appeared to be the combined army of the emperor and the rulers of Bengal and Oudh. It gave greater prestige to British arms than had the earlier victory over a provincial government. It also altered Shuja-ud-daula's course of action. Henceforth dependence on the British became a cardinal point of his policy, and Oudh was, for all practical purposes, drawn into the orbit of the British influence. Most important of all, Emperor Shah Alam was forced to give the East India Company the *diwani,* or civil government, of Bengal, Bihar, and Orissa in return for the districts of Allahabad and Kora and an annual payment of two and a half million rupees. This provided the legal basis for British rule in Bengal.

Emperor Shah Alam remained in Allahabad for some years after the battle of Buxar, but he returned to Delhi in 1772, after the death of his wazir, Najib-ud-daula, who had been the actual ruler of the city for a decade. Motivated either by his own greed for money, or under the influence of the Marathas, who were supporting him for their own ends, Shah Alam attacked Zabita Khan, the powerful son of Najib-ud-daula, who was the leader of the Rohilla Afghans who had established themselves to the east of Delhi. In one punitive expedition against the family stronghold of Ghausgarh, Zabita Khan's relatives were treated with great cruelty. According to tradition, his son, Ghulam Qadir, was castrated and made to serve as page in the palace at Delhi, but a few years later, Ghulam Qadir was able to exact a terrible revenge.

Affairs in the capital were following a tortuous course, with the nobles intriguing against each other for the spoils of the decaying empire. One able administrator, Najaf Khan, succeeded for a time in organizing a small effective army to maintain order, but he eventually succumbed to the debilitating atmosphere.

Without any able or loyal followers, the emperor took a momentous step. In 1785 he invited the great Maratha chieftain Mahadaji Sindhia of Gwalior to take charge of the Delhi administration. Appointed commander-in-chief and supreme regent (*wakil-i-mutliq*) of the empire, Sindhia tried to get the cooperation of Ghulam Qadir in

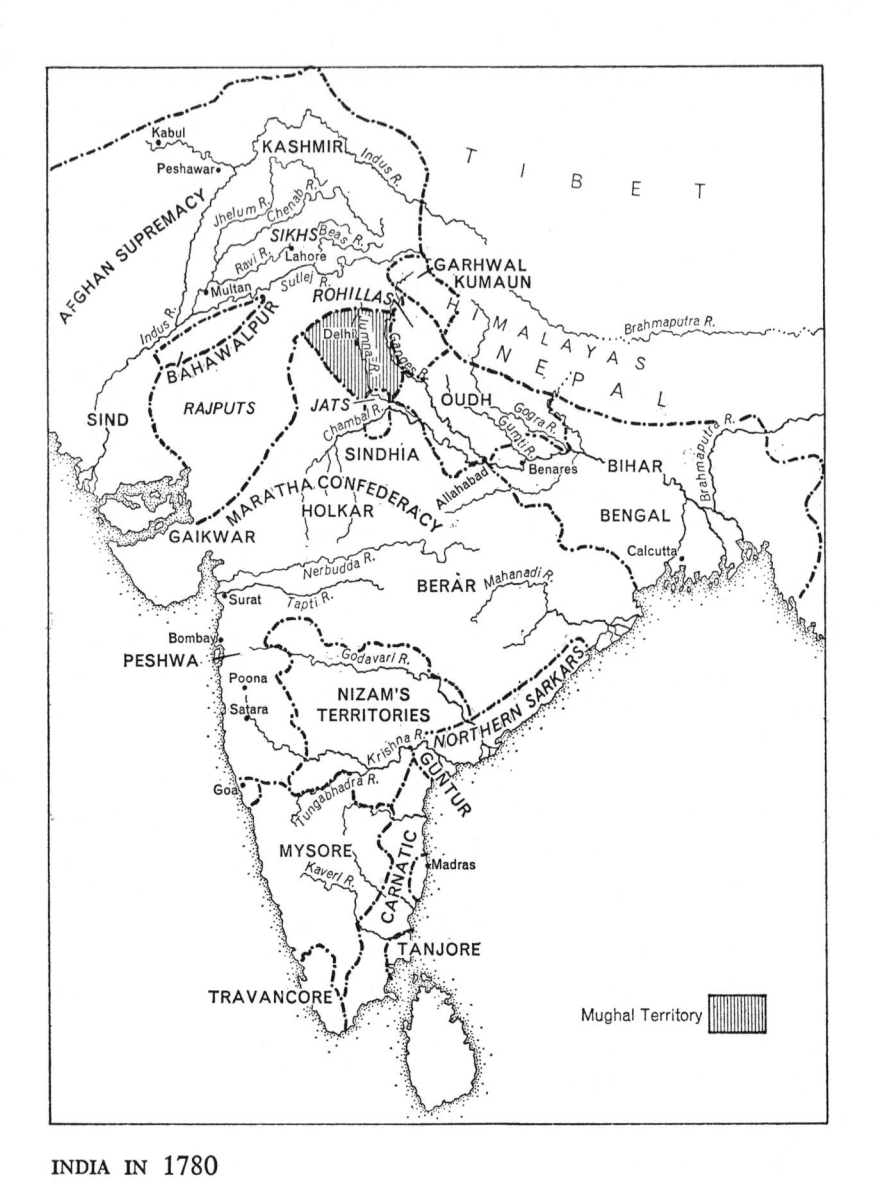

INDIA IN 1780

From: *An Historical Atlas of the Indian Peninsula* (Oxford University Press, Bombay, 1961).

dealing with the Sikhs, but Ghulam Qadir, waiting for a chance to repay the humiliation he and his family had suffered at the hands of Shah Alam, had no desire to strengthen the emperor's rule.

His opportunity came in 1787 when Sindhia was defeated by the Rajputs. Ghulam Qadir entered Delhi in September, 1787, and forced the emperor to appoint him mir bakhshi or paymaster, and regent. He was driven out of Delhi by the emperor's supporters, but entered the city again the following year, deposed Shah Alam, and blinded him.

A drunken ruffian, Ghulam Qadir, behaved with gross brutality to the emperor and his family. Three servants and two water-carriers who tried to help the bleeding emperor were killed. According to one account, Ghulam would pull the beard of the old monarch, and say: "Serves you right. This is the return for your action at Ghausgarh." Servants were tortured and made to reveal the hidden treasures, and the entire palace was ransacked to find the buried wealth.

After ten horrible weeks during which the honor of the royal family and prestige of the Mughal empire reached its lowest ebb, Ghulam Qadir left with the booty for his stronghold. Sindhia's officers hunted him down and captured him in December, 1788. He was put to death with tortures which equalled his own fiendish cruelties.

When Delhi was retaken by the Marathas, the blind Shah Alam was enthroned again. While his action reconciled the people to Sindhia's rule, it meant that Delhi was being drawn into the great struggle then taking place between the Marathas and the British.

An account of that struggle and of British expansion is outside the scope of this chapter, for the British did not defeat Mughal India, but its successor states, both Muslim and Hindu. Conquest was cautiously achieved. Periods of rapid expansion alternated with long periods of consolidation. Military action was effectively aided by diplomatic activity. Local differences and jealousies were most skillfully exploited. The Company's forces were normally able to depend on the direct or indirect cooperation of the commander or at least some of the major leaders of the troops confronting them. At Plassey it was Mir Jafar; at Buxar the differences between Shuja-ud-daula and Mir Qasim were fully exploited. In fact, British success owed as

much to diplomatic skill and the demoralized state of Indian society as to valor and military organization.

The great period of expansion initiated during the governor-generalship (1798–1805) of Lord Wellesley saw Delhi and the Mughal emperor pass under British sway. But even as late as 1798 this absorption did not seem inevitable, for an attempt was made to create a confederacy of the Afghan king, the wazir of Oudh, and a number of Maratha chiefs, to strengthen the position of the emperor. Wellesley took the plan seriously enough to stir up trouble between the Persian and the Afghan courts so that the Afghan ruler would not be able to give any attention to India.[9]

More important for the fate of the Mughals was Wellesley's war with the Marathas in 1803. In a two-pronged attack, they were defeated in the Deccan and North India. Sindhia's defeat meant the capture of Delhi, and with this the Mughal empire, long a dependent of the Marathas, passed into British control. Yet after a century of decline, the Mughal emperor still remained a symbol of greatness that was not easily defaced. To many British, his continuance seemed absurd, at best an empty pageant. Yet as events were to show in 1857, even the last flickering shadow of Mughal greatness still appeared to be a possible center of power.

Causes of the Mughal Decline

Before turning to these last years of the Mughal emperor, it may be useful to summarize what appear to have been certain general causes of Mughal decline, leaving aside such specific causes as external invasions and internal rebellions. One feature of Islamic power in India, as elsewhere, was the failure to make progress in certain vital fields. For example, even Akbar failed to see the possibilities in the introduction of printing. The scarcity of books resulted in comparative ignorance, low standards of education, and limitation of the subjects of study. Because of this, the governing classes were ignorant of the affairs of the outside world. The position becomes clear if we

[9] H. W. C. Davis, "The Great Game in Asia," *Proceedings of the British Academy*, XII (1926), 230.

compare the books on India printed in Europe during the eighteenth century with the knowledge of the West current in India. The interest on the part of Europeans that led travelers like Bernier to make reports on their travels finds no parallel in Mughal India. So far from being concerned with Europe, the Mughals, after *Ain-i-Akbari,* made no real addition to their knowledge even of their own dominions.

The stagnation visible in the intellectual field was visible also in the military sphere. Babur had introduced gunpowder in India, but after him there was no advance in military equipment, although the organization and discipline of forces had been completely revolutionized in the West. The Portuguese had brought ships on which cannons were mounted, and had thus introduced a new element which made them masters of the Indian Ocean. What was a fortified wall round the country became a highway, and opened up the empire to those countries which had not remained stagnant. Mughal helplessness on the sea was obvious from the days of Akbar. Their ships could not sail to Mecca without a safe-conduct permit from the Portuguese. Sir Thomas Roe had warned Jahangir that if Prince Shah Jahan as governor of Gujarat turned the English out, "then he must expect we would do our justice upon the seas." The failure of the Mughals to develop a powerful navy and control the seas surrounding their dominions was a direct cause of their replacement by an European power having these advantages.

On land no real progress or large-scale training of local personnel in the use of artillery was made in Mughal India, and the best they could do was to hire foreigners for manning the artillery. The military weakness resulting from this was obvious, and was clearly visible to foreign observers. Bernier wrote in the early years of Aurangzeb's reign: "I could never see these soldiers, destitute of order, and marching with the irregularity of a herd of animals, without reflecting upon the ease with which five-and-twenty thousand of our veterans from the army in Flanders, commanded by Prince Condé or Marshal Turenne would overcome these armies, however numerous." [10] With this condition of the Mughal army, the downfall of the empire was only a question of time.

[10] François Bernier, *Travels in the Mogul Empire A.D. 1656–1668,* trans. by A. Constable (London, 1914), p. 55.

Another factor which contributed to the fall of the Mughal empire was the moral decay of the ruling classes. This was partly due to the affluent standard of living maintained by monarchs like Shah Jahan and queens like Nur Jahan. Ostentatious luxury became the ambition of everyone who could afford it, and the puritanical Aurangzeb's attempts to arrest the tide were without success. The evil had gone too far and was only driven underground to reappear, within ten years of the emperor's death, in the uncontrolled orgies of his grandson Jahandar Shah. Perhaps Aurangzeb's extreme asceticism and self-denial only intensified the reaction of the nobility. Many a Maratha hill fortress captured after long and dreary siege were lost because the Mughal commander, unwilling to spend the monsoon months in his lonely perch, came down to the plains, while the hardy Marathas, awaiting for the opportunity, moved in.

The moral decline of the nobility showed itself in lack of discipline, laziness, evasion of duties, and even treacherous conduct. It also made them rapacious and heartless in dealing with the public. The extravagant standards that the Mughal bureaucrats tried to maintain were not possible without corruption, extortion, and the enrichment of the officers at the expense of the state and the people. These evils increased as Mughal authority weakened, but their seed had been sown in earlier days and were a natural result of the efforts of the officers to maintain standards beyond their means.

These were the basic factors responsible for the downfall of the Mughal empire, but others were contributory. The fact that after the death of Aurangzeb no ruler of real vigor and resourcefulness came to the throne made recovery of the lost position almost impossible. Even Aurangzeb's long life was an asset of doubtful value in its last stages. He drove himself hard and resolutely, conscientiously performing his duties, but at the age of ninety he was subject to the laws governing all human machines. When he died, his son and successor Bahadur Shah was already an old man of sixty. He began well but was on the throne for barely six years, and with his death a disastrous chapter opened in Mughal annals.

Directly related to the troubles of this period was the absence of a well-defined law of succession to ensure the continuity of government. The result was that each son of a deceased king felt that he had

an equal claim to the crown, and succession to the throne was in-
variably accompanied by bloody warfare. The disaster was compounded when the imperial princes, who were often viceroys governing vast territories, started making secret pacts with soldiers to ensure
their support for the time when the fateful struggle would begin. Soon
not only the imperial army but forces external to the empire—the
East India Company, the Marathas, the Sikhs—were being used by
claimants for the throne of Delhi as well as for control of the provincial kingdoms. The results were fatal.

XX. The Beginning of
a New Era: 1803-1857

WE CONCLUDE our account of Muslim civilization in India with the
exile of the last Mughal emperor from Delhi in 1858, and not with
the British assumption of overlordship of Delhi in 1803, partly because even in 1803 large areas of the subcontinent were outside the
control of the East India Company, and partly because the Company
retained the legal fiction of Mughal sovereignty until 1857. At Delhi
the Mughal ruler received all the courtesies of a king, and the Company paid him large sums of money, which were claimed on his behalf
as the tribute paid by the Company by virtue of past arrangements
and treaties. It was argued that "the Company was administering territories for him, as the Marathas had in constitutional theory done before the Company; that the Company's authority was derived from
his *farmans* in so far as it was covered by the *farmans,* and was mere
illegal usurpation in so far as it was not so covered." [1] Against the
background of actual military and political power these claims were
mere pretensions, but legally and constitutionally the Delhi house had
not been set aside from the position they had occupied when they
granted the *diwani* to the Company in 1765. The Mughal ruler was
designated shahinshah, and later padshah, in official correspondence.
He continued to bestow titles of honor until 1828; coins continued to
be issued in his name until 1835. It seemed in 1803 that the British
representative was stepping into the shoes of Sindhia. Special arrangements were made for the administration of Delhi, where Muslim law
was used in criminal cases. "Within the walls of the Red Fort the
king retained his ruling powers. The inhabitants of the Fort *bazar* were
his direct subjects, and the members of the imperial family who lived
within enjoyed diplomatic immunity. The etiquette of the court was
maintained, the sonorous titles and the language of the great Mughals

[1] The best statement of this argument is found in F. W. Buckler, "The Political Theory of the Indian Mutiny," *Transactions of the Royal Historical Society,*
4th series, V (1922), 71–100.

continued, and the Resident attended the durbar in the Diwan-i-Khas regularly as a suitor. He dismounted like any other courtier . . . and was conducted on foot . . . to the imperial presence where he stood respectfully like the rest." [2]

Shah Alam died in 1806. His successor was Akbar II. With the consolidation of British power, a tendency grew to treat the Mughal emperor more and more as a pensioner of the East India Company, while he insisted on the privileges accorded at the time of the conquest of Delhi. The differences between Akbar Shah and the Company came to a head when a meeting between Lord Hastings, the governor-general and the emperor could not be held because Akbar insisted that Hastings should appear as a subject and present the usual *nazr* or gift. He also refused to allow the governor-general a chair on the same level as his own at the time of the interview. Hastings refused a meeting on these terms, and soon after the emperor's privileges were curtailed. The ruler of Oudh (hitherto called wazir) and the nizam of Hyderabad were encouraged to adopt royal titles. While the nizam declined to do so out of regard for the Mughal emperor, the ruler of Oudh accepted the suggestion. To present his case in London, Akbar Shah appointed the celebrated Bengali reformer, Ram Mohan Roy, who was planning a visit to England, as the Mughal envoy to the Court of St. James, conferring on him the title of raja. Ram Mohan Roy submitted an ably drafted memorial on behalf of the Mughal ruler, but nothing came of his mission.

When Akbar II died in 1837, his successor, Bahadur Shah (r. 1837–1858) refused to give up the claims put forward by his father. The East India Company gradually limited his powers and privileges, however, and when his heir-apparent died in 1856, the claims of the next surviving son were recognized on the condition that his title would only be prince or shahzada and not shah or king.

Whatever may have been the disputes between the emperor and the Company, there is no doubt that in some ways the position of the Mughal ruler improved with the British occupation of Delhi. There was peace and order, and the royal family was not exposed to those vicissitudes and uncertainties which it had suffered prior to the

[2] Percival Spear, *Twilight of the Mughals* (Cambridge, 1951), p. 38.

reoccupation of Delhi by Sindhia in 1788. Their financial position also improved, for income from the emperor's lands increased because of the greater general security. Even so, the emperor's income did not exceed 600,000 rupees a year, out of which he had to feed a horde of dependents. But the respect and the position which he enjoyed was out of all proportion to his material resources.

Cultural and Religious Vitality

The Mughals had learned the art of maintaining dignity in the most unpropitious circumstances, and the tawdry Mughal court became the cultural center of Muslim India. The court once again began to attract the most distinguished Muslim noblemen, ulama, and men of letters.

In particular the great Ghalib, who epitomised in his personality and works the splendor and humanity of Mughal culture adorned his court, sang verses on the age-old themes of love and life, and recited eulogies which easily surpassed anything written by the court poets of Akbar and Jahangir. The influence of the court in the early years of the nineteenth century was felt throughout India, for Mughal manners and etiquette became the standard almost everywhere. As Percival Spear has pointed out, such an influence was of great importance in giving cohesion to Indian life. "The fall of the dynasty was a serious cultural loss, and inaugurated that period of nondescript manners and indefinite conduct from which India suffers today." [3]

Second only to Delhi as a center of Islamic culture, and in many ways more cosmopolitan, was Lucknow, the capital of the rulers of Oudh. To some extent it was the heir of the older centers of Islamic culture in the Gangetic plain, Budaun and Jaunpur, but it also drew upon the great Hindu tradition that lived on in Benares and the surrounding region. It was also an asylum in the eighteenth century for refugees fleeing Delhi before the invasion of Nadir Shah, Ahmad Shah, and the Marathas. Furthermore, it was open to Western influences, and one of the interesting developments was the introduction of opera, a form of music quite unknown in India.

[3] Spear, p. 83.

One important difference between Delhi and Lucknow was that the former was a religious as well as cultural center. This was not the case with Lucknow, for while it had learned ulama, their influence was scholastic and intellectual, not spiritual, with more attention paid to form than to content. This tendency reflected itself in all the arts of Lucknow. Lucknow poetry, for example, was rich in ornament and followed elaborate rules of prosody, but had little depth of thought or feeling. "Delhi was less careful about words and gave more attention to thought and subject." [4] The emphasis at Lucknow on the formalities of court etiquette, purity of language, and appropriate enunciation added a distinct strand to Indo-Muslim civilization.

An interesting development of the period was the foundation of Delhi College in 1825. It was housed in the magnificent building of the madrassa founded in the eighteenth century by Nazim-ul-Mulk's son Ghazi-ud-din Khan I, and its development was greatly facilitated by the donation of 170,000 rupees in 1829 by a native of Delhi. It had European principals from the beginning and marked a new experiment in education, with English as well as Oriental sections. The first head of the Arabic Department was a favorite pupil of Shah Abdul Aziz. An even more remarkable person was the second head, Maulana Mamluk Ali, who also had studied under members of Shah Waliullah's family. He headed the Arabic Department from about 1833 until his death in 1851. He found very little time for literary work and devoted himself exclusively to teaching both at Delhi College and at his own residence. Among his private pupils were Sir Syed Ahmad Khan, the founder of Aligarh College. His nephew, Maulana Muhammad Qasim, who is generally regarded as the founder of the seminary at Deoband, studied with him for several years at Delhi, and for a brief period was enrolled as a student at Delhi College. This link between Delhi College and the two most important institutions of modern Muslim India led to the observation that, "After the Mutiny, Sir Syed Ahmad Khan took the English section of the Delhi College to Aligarh, and Maulana Muhammad Qasim took the Arabic section to Deoband." Of course this statement is correct only in a figurative and limited sense, but it may well explain many modern features of the seminary

[4] T. G. Bailey, *A History of Urdu Literature* (Calcutta, 1932), p. 60.

at Deoband, of which the founder was a nephew of Maulana Mamluk Ali, and his son was the first principal.

Of even more significance than the artistic and cultural life of the great Islamic cities were the vigorous spiritual movements of the time. The spiritual leader of Delhi, and indeed of all Islamic India, during the first half of the nineteenth century was Shah Abdul Aziz (1746–1823), the son and successor of Shah Waliullah. Shah Abdul Aziz was the most learned Islamic theologian in India, and his views on Muslim law were accepted by all parties among the Sunnis. Unlike most Muslims during this period, he recognized the value of learning English, and displayed no bitterness toward the conquerors. But he was a teacher and thinker rather than a leader, and the most vital Islamic movement of the period was headed by his disciple, Sayyid Ahmed Brelvi. While the spiritual basis of the new movement was found in Shah Waliullah's works, it was Sayyid Ahmed's organizing ability and knowledge of military affairs that gave it the impetus to overcome the apathy of many Muslims.

Sayyid Ahmed Brelvi had begun life as a soldier in the army of Nawab Amir Khan, the founder of Tonk state, but when the nawab came to terms with the British in 1806 he gave up military service and went to Delhi to study under Shah Abdul Aziz. His spiritual powers and organizing ability greatly impressed his teachers, and his reputation increased when Shah Abdul's nephew, Shah Ismail, and his son-in-law, Maulvi Abdul Hai, became Sayyid's disciples. Both of them were distinguished scholars and their example was followed by many others. In 1818, with the help of his two disciples, Sayyid Ahmed wrote *Sirat-i-Mustaqim,* which, apart from a mystical portion, is largely a summary of the reforms which Shah Waliullah had urged. About this time Sayyid Ahmed started to preach in public, and although he used simple words and images, soon made a great reputation for himself.

His activities were not confined to Delhi, and during a visit to Rampur some Afghan travelers complained to him about the Sikh persecution of Muslims in the Punjab. He expressed a desire to conduct a holy war against them, but he knew that war required elaborate preparations and, in any case, he wished to perform the *Hajj* before

undertaking *jihad*. His journey to Calcutta on the way to Mecca was marked by enthusiastic demonstrations. At Patna so many people became his disciples that he appointed four caliphs, or spiritual vice-regents, to look after them. At Calcutta the crowds flocked to him in such numbers that he could not follow the usual custom in making disciples by the laying on of hands, but had to stretch out his turban for people to touch.

At Mecca, Sayyid Ahmed must have gained fuller knowledge of the Wahhabis, the puritan sect that had been in control of the Holy Places some years earlier, and their teaching undoubtedly strengthened his resolve to carry on *jihad* against the Sikhs. He arrived in the Pathan area in December, 1826, just when the tribesmen had suffered grievously from raids by Sikh armies. Gathering the tribesmen, Sayyid Ahmed attacked the Sikh stronghold of Akora with such success that the Sikhs withdrew. He carried the war into the plains, occupying Peshawar for two months, and won support from many of the tribal chieftains. But difficulties arose between his companions and the tribal chiefs. After the conquest of Peshawar Sayyid Ahmed wanted to introduce an Islamic system of government, but the tribal chiefs realized that this would work against their authority. His hold was further weakened by opposition to social reforms that he had introduced and the hostility of the Sikhs and their allies, the Barakzais. In November, 1830, he was forced to relinquish Peshawar in favor of Sultan Muhammad, the old governor, on the promised payment of a fixed tribute. The biggest blow came when his deputies in Yusufzai villages were killed by the tribesmen themselves. Accompanied by a few faithful companions he left for Hazara, where after a few months of desultory warfare he was killed at Balakot by a Sikh contingent in May, 1831.

The Islamic Revival in Bengal

Although Sayyid Ahmed's military efforts ended in a disaster and many of his companions died on the battlefield, his meteoric career left a lasting impression in distant corners of the subcontinent. The scene of his activities on the Afghan frontier continued to attract

mujahids (militant spiritual leaders), who gave considerable trouble to the Sikhs and later to the British. The effect of Sayyid Ahmed's activities in the eastern part of the country was even more far-reaching. During his leisurely trip to Calcutta and his long sojourn in that city, he had enrolled a number of disciples—many of them from distant areas in what is now East Pakistan—who continued his work. Some of them joined him in the *jihad* on the frontier, and many continued to send men and money to the mujahids, who kept up the struggle until the second half of the nineteenth century. But perhaps even more important was the extension of Shah Waliullah's reform movement in areas which had been cut off from Delhi for generations, and which, through these disciples, were now brought closer with the spiritual centers of Muslim India.

Islam had been spread in Bengal by the Sufi missionaries in the thirteenth and the fourteenth centuries, but a vigorous Hindu revival under the Vaishanavite leaders had infused new religious life into the Hindus. Assam and the neighboring hill areas were converted to Hinduism. Through its literary expression it also influenced Muslim society. The stream of Muslim missionaries to the area had dried up, and there was a general ignorance of Islam amongst the masses. A local popular religion grew up, thinly veiling Hindu beliefs and practices. Bengal Muslims who were schooled in their religion were steadfast in their observance of Islamic injunctions, but in distant villages, isolated by rivers and streams, there were serious obstacles to the spread of Islamic knowledge.

The nineteenth century saw a new movement of Islamic revival in Bengal.[5] This was largely the work of local reformers and scholars who took advantage of new conditions and the facilities of steamship travel to Arabia. The first of these was Haji Shariat Ullah, who was born of poor parents in the village of Daulatpur and received his early education at a religious seminary at Dacca or Faridpur. He went on pilgrimage to Mecca sometime around 1802, when he was about eighteen years old, and did not return until about 1820. While he was in Arabia he was influenced by Wahhabi doctrines, which he

[5] A. R. Mallick, *British Policy and the Muslims in Bengal, 1757–1858* (Dacca, 1961), pp. 66–91.

preached to the people of his native district on his return. He denounced the superstitions and corrupt beliefs which had been developed by long contact with the Hindus. He also opposed the prevalent
procedure of the Sufi initiation, and replaced the expressions *piri-
muridi,* which suggested a complete submission, by the relationship
between ustad (teacher) and shagird (pupil). Because of his insistence on *tauba,* or repentance for past sins, his followers called
themselves *tawbar* Muslims. They were also known as "Faraizis" because of their insistence on the performance of *faraiz,* the obligations
imposed by God and the Prophet. Haji Shariat Ullah was persecuted
by zamindars who feared his emphasis on a common Islamic brotherhood, but he managed to continue his ministry until his death.

Even more influential was his son, Haji Muhammad Mohsin (more
properly known as Dudhu Miyan), whose name became a household
word in the districts of Faridpur, Pabna, Baqarganj, Dacca, and
Noakhali. He was born about 1820, and visited Arabia at an early
age. On his return he took up the leadership of the movement started
by his father. He divided East Bengal into circles, and appointed a
caliph, as spiritual leader, to look after his followers in each circle.
Under him the movement became the spearhead of the resistance of
the Muslim peasantry of East Bengal against Hindu landlords and
European indigo planters. He especially denounced the custom of
forcing Muslim peasants to contribute to the maintenance of Hindu
shrines. He was harassed by lawsuits all his life and was repeatedly
jailed. He died in 1860.

The doctrines preached by Haji Shariat Ullah and Dudhu Miyan
for some forty years brought permanent changes in the spiritual life of
Bengal, but the influence of their group gradually declined. Apart from
the conflict with landlords, Dudhu Miyan's policy brought his group
in conflict with other Muslims, especially as he used violence to get
people to join his sect. The main religious dispute, however, centered
around the observance of Friday prayers. To the ordinary believer, the
ceremonial performance of the customary prayers was of great importance, but the Faraizis taught that the continuance of Friday
prayers in India was unlawful. This was because the country was no
longer *dar-ul-Islam,* or land of the faithful, but, because of conquest

by the Christians, had become *dar-ul-harb,* land of infidels. The quarrel became particularly acrimonious because the Faraizis treated all Muslims who did not share their interpretation of the religious situation as kafirs, or infidels.

Aside from the Faraizis, the religious revivalists who had the greatest influence in East Bengal were four disciples of Sayyid Ahmed Brelvi. One of these was Maulvi Imam-ud-din, who was born in Hajipur in Bengal, but who was educated in Delhi under Shah Abdul Aziz, the son of Shah Waliullah. He became a disciple of Sayyid Ahmed Brelvi at Lucknow in 1824, and was with him at Calcutta during his triumphal journey to Arabia. At that time he had brought large numbers of people from his village to be initiated into the new movement by Sayyid Ahmed. He went to Arabia with Sayyid Ahmed, and later took part in the *jihad* on the frontier. After the disaster at Balakot, he returned to his home district, Noakali, and converted many of its inhabitants to the doctrines of his master. Another of Sayyid Ahmed's disciples had a similar success in the Chittagong district. A third member of the group, Maulvi Inayat Ali of Patna, spent nearly ten years in central Bengal, building mosques and appointing qualified teachers. His great interest, however, was in the *jihad* which Sayyid Ahmed had started on the frontier. He died there in 1858.

The fourth of the great reformers was Maulvi Karamat Ali (d.1873), who devoted his life to the preaching of Islam in East Bengal. A superb organizer, for forty years he moved up and down the rivers with a flotilla of small boats, carrying the message of Islamic regeneration and reform from the Nagas of Assam to the inhabitants of the islands in the Bay of Bengal. His flotilla was often compared to a traveling college: one boat was for the residence of his family, another was reserved for the students and disciples accompanying him, while the third was for lectures and prayers. Maulvi Karamat Ali revitalized Islamic life in East Bengal, and it has been said that at the time of his death there was scarcely a village in Bengal that did not contain some of his disciples.

Maulvi Karamat Ali shared with the Faraizi leaders of East Bengal an abhorrence of all un-Islamic practices, but he violently disagreed

with their position that, because of the British conquest, the Friday prayers could no longer be observed. He argued that India had not become *dar-ul-harb,* but that even if it had, Muslims should still carry on all those observances which characterized *dar-ul-Islam.* This question of whether or not India had ceased to be *dar-ul-Islam* continued to be debated among Muslims, but the great majority of Bengal Muslims continued to celebrate Friday prayers. Only a very small group remained steadfast to the teaching of Haji Shariat Ullah that India was *dar-ul-harb;* they did not offer Friday prayers in the traditional manner until after the establishment of Pakistan in 1947.

The significance of this religious revival in Bengal in the nineteenth century has generally been overlooked, but there is no doubt that it gave new life to Islam. The emphasis on strict religious observances the denunciation of participation in Hindu practices, and the call to an austere life safeguarded the community in a time of political weakness. These particular "puritan" aspects of the reform movement have led it to be confused with the Wahhabi movement of Arabia, but there were important differences in spirit. The four great reformers derived their inspiration from Shah Waliullah, and they avoided the fanatic extremism usually associated with the true Wahhabis. They were more forward looking, more concerned with spiritual improvement, than were the Arabian group. Above all, they were influenced by the mysticism of Indian Islam, and Shah Waliullah himself had adopted a conciliatory attitude towards the teachings of the Sufis. For the Wahhabis, on the other hand, the Sufis posed a threat to Islamic truth that could not be tolerated. What the Wahhabis and the disciples of Shah Waliullah shared in common was an emphasis on the ancient purity of the Islamic way of living, untainted by alien accretions.[6]

The Indian Revolt, 1857–1858

The course of these religious movements, in common with almost every aspect of Indian life, was affected by the most spectacular event

[6] Wm. Theodore de Bary et al., *Sources of Indian Tradition,* pp. 461–62. For a discussion of the relation of Indian religious movements to Wahhabism, see W. W. Hunter, *The Indian Musalmans* (London, 1871), and I. H. Qureshi, *The Muslim Community of the Indo-Pakistan Subcontinent* ('sGravenage, 1962).

in the history of nineteenth-century India, the uprising of 1857. The causes of this outbreak have been a matter of endless dispute ever since. The range of opinion varied then, as it still does, from those who see it as a simple mutiny by disgruntled soldiers to those who see it as a nationalist war for an independent India. That the general cause was the distrust awakened by the rush of social change initiated by the British and that this took the particular form of a fear that the changes presaged an attempt by the British to convert the people to Christianity, there can be little doubt. This fear was used by those who had been displaced from power by the British to rally support for one last desperate effort to regain what they had lost.

As far as Islamic civilization was concerned, the immediate result of the uprising was to cast suspicion on the Muslim community. As the rulers who had been overthrown, it was assumed that they would be the ringleaders in the war. Tangible proof of this was the assumption by Emperor Bahadur Shah of leadership of the revolt at Delhi. That his control was only nominal was plain enough, but his name still awakened echoes of past glory throughout India. Furthermore, in the great center of revolt, the Muslim kingdom of Oudh, the leaders were mainly Muslim, drawn from the ranks of the zamindars embittered by the recent British seizure of the state.

Evidence of the British feeling that the Muslims had a special responsibility for the uprising was shown when Delhi was recaptured. Accounts, some true and some false, of cruel massacres of British women and children by the mutineers had so enraged British officers that they forgot all considerations of justice and equity and indulged in an orgy of vengeance. The city was subjected to a punishment such as it had not undergone even in its dismal history during the eighteenth century. The massacre of Nadir Shah and the lootings by Marathas, Jats, and Afghans had continued for only a few days, but in 1857 the ordeal lasted for months. The entire population was driven out of the city, and in the absence of owners, the houses were broken into, their floors dug up, and contents removed or destroyed.

Next to suffer were the city buildings. The principal mosques were occupied by the British troops. One proposal was to sell the Grand Mosque of Shah Jahan. Another was to convert it into a barracks for the main guard of European troops. Muslims were not allowed to

use it until five years later. Some parts of the Fatehpuri Masjid, the second largest in the city, remained in non-Muslim hands till 1875. The beautiful Zinat-ul-Masjid, built by Aurangzeb's daughter, was only restored to the Muslims by Lord Curzon at the beginning of the twentieth century. The royal palace and the fort suffered even more. The palace proper, the residence of the royal family, was razed and all the gardens and courts were completely destroyed. "Not one vestige of them now remains . . . The whole of the haram courts of the palace were swept off the face of the earth to make way for a hideous British barrack, without those who carried out this fearful piece of vandalism, thinking it even worthwhile to make a plan of what they were destroying or preserving any record of the most splendid palace in the world." [7] There was considerable damage to the public buildings also. The more important ones were retained, but the contents of the palace were looted, and even structural decorations were removed.

Perhaps an even greater loss was the destruction and dispersal of the royal library, where rare works had been accumulated since the days of Babur and Akbar. While it must have already been damaged during the depredations of the eighteenth century, it was still a great library at the time of the mutiny. The contents were looted and scattered to all corners of the earth, so that we find some leaves of one royal album at Patna, a few in Berlin, some more in the National Library of Paris, though the major portion found its way to the public and private libraries of England.

The Hindu population was allowed to return to the city in January, 1858, and Muslims were allowed a few months later, but the destruction of buildings continued for a long time. The large areas between the Jama Masjid and the fort, which are now covered by an extensive park, were originally the principal residential quarters of the Mughal nobility, and contained the large Akbarabadi Mosque, where Shah Waliullah's successors used to teach. All these buildings were razed and the entire area cleared, so that there should be a suitable field of fire beyond the walls of the fort to house the British garrison.

[7] James Fergusson, *A History of the Indian and Eastern Architecture* (New York, 1899), II, 311–12.

In course of time peace and order returned. The civil authorities, many of whom were unhappy at what was going on, were at last able to assert themselves. Canning, the governor-general, was of a kindly disposition, and although the press cried for vengeance, gradually good sense prevailed, and by slow stages a return to civil administration was effected. Delhi recovered but it was now a small appendage of the Punjab. The grand edifices built by a succession of the Mughal monarchs remained as a reminder of what once had been, but they were an empty shell. The Delhi of the Mughals had perished for ever.

Out of the tragedy came at least one good result. The enforced dispersal of scholars meant that Lahore now replaced Delhi as the cultural center of Muslim India. Urdu was firmly rooted as the language of culture in the land of the five rivers. Similarly, although Delhi ceased to be a place of learning, those who had drunk at this fountainhead and had imbibed the spirit of Shah Waliullah and Shah Abdul Aziz established great centers of learning at Deoband and Aligarh, not far from the old capital.

Ghalib (1796–1869), the greatest of Urdu poets, saw the whole tragedy enacted before his eyes, but he was convinced that there were possibilities for new life in the destruction of the world he had loved. He had long forseen the breakup of the old system, before the mutiny he had written:

They gave me the glad tidings of the dawn in the dark night.
They extinguished the candle and showed me the rising sun.
The fire-temple got burnt; they gave me the breath of fire.
The idol-temple crumbled down and they gave me the lamentation of the
    temple-gong.
They plucked away the jewels from the banners of the kings of Ajam.
In its place they gave me the jewel-scattering pen.
They removed the pearl from the crown, and fastened it to wisdom.
Whatever they took away openly, they returned to me in secret.

The mutiny led to a careful reassessment of the administration and a reorientation of many policies. Developments in the political field paved the way for the later political struggle and the final independence. The control of the subcontinent by the East India Company was transferred to the British government, which for the first time took

direct responsibility for the administration of the area. This meant the replacement of an indirect rule by direct government administration. The old expansionist policy at the expense of the native administered territory was totally abandoned. No Indian state was later annexed, and Hyderabad, which was marked for an early annexation in the days of Dalhousie, escaped that fate. In religious matters the British had learned a bitter lesson, and henceforth they treated local religious sentiments with a respect that was not always visible in the first half of the nineteenth century.

In the political field a beginning was made which was to have far-reaching consequences. Even before the embers of the great revolt had died out, and while martial law was yet in force, Sayyid Ahmed Khan, a sincere friend and fervent admirer of the British, whose loyalty had been tested in the great struggle itself, sat down to analyze the causes of the revolt. With his sturdy common sense and characteristic fearlessness he pointed out in a remarkable book that the basic cause of the revolt was the government's ignorance of the views of the vast population directly affected by its legislative and administrative measures.[8] This criticism, coming from a friend, and reinforced by the observations of many Englishmen, led to remedial action. The Indian Councils Act of 1861 provided for the appointment of Indians to the governor-general's council for the first time. It marked the beginning of the association of the native population with the upper administrative councils of the subcontinent, an association which gradually expanded under the pressure of public opinion, and ultimately led to the complete transfer of political control in 1947.

Seeds of Separatism

The twilight of the Mughals might seem, in view of the changes that followed, to have ended with a movement towards the progress and unity of the subcontinent. But in fact the seeds of separatism, which were to bear fruit in 1947, had already been sown. Some of the causes of this spirit of division between Muslim and Hindu can be traced to the changes taking place in the nineteenth century. The

[8] Sayyid Ahmed Khan, *The Causes of the Indian Revolt* (Calcutta, 1860).

mutiny of 1857 was one answer to these changes; a more complex one was the growth of communalism.

In the first half of the nineteenth century many innovations and reforms were introduced by the British. Some of these, such as the printing press, the telegraph, the railways, were the results of scientific progress in the West, which in course of time became available to other parts of the world. Other steps—the introduction of English education, suppression of *sati*—were the work of administrators impelled by a desire to bring about social change. The establishment of institutions of a kind unfamiliar to Indian society, such as the Asiatic Society with its work of editing and publishing the great works of both the Hindu and Muslim traditions, led to a new knowledge of the past. The role of this enterprise on the intellectual revival in the subcontinent cannot be overemphasized.

The general effect of these developments was healthy, forming a valued part of the heritage of India and Pakistan. All the new measures were not, however, so beneficial, and some of them have created stupendous problems. Even the literary and linguistic activity at Fort William College in Calcutta, which had an important share in the rise of the new Indian languages, did not prove an unmixed blessing. The bifurcation of the common spoken language of the Hindus and Muslims of northern India into two separate languages was partly the result of the attempts made at the college to create "literary" languages. Not only was the polite spoken language of northern India (Urdu-Hindustani) cultivated at that institution, but with the help of Lalluji Lal and other Sanskritists, practically a new language was created in the form of the modern Hindi. This was not the form of the language spoken by the Hindus or the evolution of any regional dialect, but a new, artificial language. As Keay says in his *History of Hindi Literature,* modern Hindi, "was produced by taking Urdu and expelling from it words of Persian or Arabic origin, and substituting for them words of Sanskrit or Hindi origin." [9] A somewhat similar process can be seen in the creation of modern Bengali. That in the eighteenth century Bengali was characterized by the presence of a large number of nonindigenous words is suggested by the comment

[9] F. E. Keay, *A History of Hindi Literature* (Calcutta, 1920), p. 88.

made by Nathaniel Halhed in the preface to his Bengali grammar in 1778. "Those persons are thought to speak the compound idiom with most elegance," he wrote, "who mix the greatest number of Persian and Arabic nouns." [10] This *do-bhashi,* or bilingual, form of Bengali fell into disrepute in the nineteenth century, and a highly Sanskritized vocabulary became the norm of excellence.

Other aspects of the language policy adopted by the East India Company had even more important consequences. In 1829 it was announced that it was "the wish and the admitted policy of the British Government to render its own language gradually and eventually the language of public business throughout the country," and in 1834, English replaced Persian in government offices. The reasons for this step can be understood, but the British claim of having given cultural consolidation to India would have had a firmer basis, if, along with English, an indigenous language had been given at least a secondary place throughout the country. This might have been Hindustani which, in its various forms, was understood throughout much of the subcontinent. Instead of one common language, an entire plethora of vernaculars was encouraged. Urdu, Hindi, Bengali, Gujarati, Sindhi —all seemed to get similar attention. Apart from ballads and simple verse, many of these had no literature, and the Mughals had refused to give them any official status. Now they were officially recognized. Prose works in them were systematically sponsored, and in course of time, a literature in each developed. Thus the cultural unity of the subcontinent of India became dependent on English, and the seeds of the present language problem of India and Pakistan were sown.

The British policy with regard to religious communities has also been a subject of criticism and controversy. The gradual evolution of a common legal system (outside the limited spheres of the personal law of the Hindus and the Muslims) and the impartial administration of justice on modern Western lines were perhaps the most substantial boon conferred on India by the British. In the administrative field, however, political considerations and historical factors intervened, and to many historians it has seemed that out of self-interest, the British sought to rule by dividing Hindus from Muslims. As al-

[10] Nathaniel Halhed, *A Grammar of the Bengali Language* (Hoogly, 1778).

ready pointed out, the battle of Plassey was won by a combination of the officers of the East India Company and the Hindu merchant princes of Murshidabad, and for many years it seemed to be a sensible precaution to seek the support of the majority community, the Hindus, against the Muslims. This policy found a spokesman on the highest level in Lord Ellenborough, governor-general from 1842 to 1844, who wrote: "I cannot close my eyes to the belief that the [Muslim] race is fundamentally hostile to us and therefore our true policy is to conciliate the Hindus." [11] The same idea had occurred to another British observer a few years earlier. It was desirable, he thought, that "the Hindoos should always be reminded . . . that their previous rulers were as much strangers to their blood and to their religion as we are, and they were notoriously far more oppressive masters than we have ever shewn ourselves." [12]

This same spirit was reflected in the preface to the great collection of Muslim histories made by Sir Henry Elliot, *The History of India Told by Its Own Historians*. The intrinsic merit of the Muslim histories might be small, but, he argued, by showing Islamic rule in its true light, it would make "our native subjects more sensible of the immense advantages accruing to them under the mildness and equity of our rule." Those who "rant about patriotism and the degradation of their present position" would learn from reading the history of Islamic rule how in another time "their ridiculous fantasies would have been attended, not with silence and contempt, but with the severer discipline of molten lead and empalement." [13] Elliot's work has been severely criticized by modern historians on the ground that the bias he displays in the preface prevented him making a selection that presents Islamic rulers in a true light. The work was more than a private scholarly enterprise; it received official support for publication, and became the source for most of the historical works produced on the Muslim period. While it would be difficult to document the effect

[11] Quoted in B. D. Basu, *The Rise of the Christian Power in India* (Calcutta, 1931), p. 830.
[12] Reginald Heber, *Narrative of a Journey through the Upper Provinces of India* (London, 1828), I, 89.
[13] H. M. Elliot and John Dowson, *A History of India as Told by Its Own Historians* (London, 1867–1877), I, preface.

of Elliot's work on communal relations in India, it is reasonable to suppose that the picture it gave to Indian students of Islamic India helped to strengthen the growing Muslim-Hindu antagonism of the nineteenth century.

Yet while some British policies led to a worsening of communal relations, it is only fair to note that they would not have had much effect if the soil had not been congenial. During the eighteenth and early nineteenth centuries, the relations between the Hindus and Muslims were generally peaceful, but it was because of the dominance of a third power, and not because of the integration of the two social groups. The two communities had coexisted—generally in harmony, often in friendship, occasionally in conflict—but had never coalesced. Indeed, as R. C. Majumdar, the Indian historian, has said, between Hindus and Muslims, "the social and religious differences were so acute and fundamental that they raised a Chinese wall between the two communities, and even seven hundred years of close residence (including two of common servitude) have failed to make the least crack in that solid and massive structure, far less demolish it." It was this dividing wall which led, in 1947, to the partitioning of the subcontinent.

XXI. Conclusion

LOOKING BACK over the ten centuries of Muslim rule that we have briefly surveyed, it is possible to identify four main strands that have given Indo-Islamic culture its characteristic texture. The first of these is the Islamic religious inheritance, including those aspects specifically rooted in an Arabic tradition; the second was the Turkish origin of many of the rulers; the third was the pervasive influence of Persian culture; and finally there was the indigenous environment, both in India and in Afghanistan, into which Islam came. There has been a tendency to overlook this indigenous component, but its influence is deep rooted and all-pervading. The predominantly non-Muslim environment in which Indo-Muslim culture developed and the heritage of an ancient civilization did not leave Islam untouched. Furthermore, the vast majority of the Muslims were either Hindu converts, which shows not only in numerous usages and practices carried over from the ancestral Hindu society, but also in unconscious reactions and mental attitudes. The vigorous Islamic revival of later centuries has tended to overshadow the indigenous element. While the Turkish rulers and aristocracy contributed much in the sphere of government, law, dress, and food, and the Persian element was prominent in literature, fine arts, mysticism, and philosophy, essentially the two basic components which gave the civilization its peculiar flavor were the Indian and the Islamic. It represents the creative efforts and reactions of a Muslim society in a predominantly non-Muslim area.

This peculiar situation has resulted in developments which distinguish the course of Muslim civilization in India from those in countries where the population is predominantly Muslim. The dissimilarity between two main elements of Indo-Muslim civilization has resulted in a curious phenomenon. At times the attractions of the native element proved powerful, and there was a large-scale assimilation of indigenous elements, as under Akbar, Dara Shukoh, and in the writings of Kabir. At other times, there was a vigorous reaction against

non-Muslim elements, resulting in greater repugnance towards them than was traditional in the history of Islam. In this connection, it is significant that puritanical Wahhabism, with its emphasis on the purity of Islam, had considerable influence in India. Furthermore, the continuing presence of a large non-Muslim element has been a persistent challenge for missionary effort in which Indian Muslims distinguished themselves, even in recent times.

The local situation has resulted in a fundamental conflict, as symbolized in the two sons of Shah Jahan, Aurangzeb and Dara Shukoh. This situation has resulted in tensions and occasionally in conflicts, but outside somewhat narrow circles, the long-term result of two heterogeneous elements constituting Indian Islam has been a growth of forbearance and toleration of conflicting practices and beliefs. This toleration extended not only towards non-Muslims, but also to the minority sects of Islam. Perhaps in no country outside Iran, where Shiaism is the state religion, has Shia genius had such an opportunity for making a contribution in the realm of literature, administration, and statecraft. This has been possible because of the normal prevalence of an attitude of toleration. This forbearance, subject to the deep attachment to Islam, was extended to European civilization as well.

For understanding the Muslim approach to the problems of the subcontinent it is worth remembering that though revivalist thinkers, like Hazrat Mujaddid Alif Sani in Mughal times and Iqbal in the twentieth century, have exercised a powerful influence, the religious teacher with the greatest following and influence has been Shah Waliullah, perhaps the most catholic and broadminded of religious reformers of the modern Muslim world. A position similar to that of Shah Waliullah in the religious sphere has been occupied by Ghalib in recent times in the literary field. He has been universally popular with Hindus and Muslims, and his poetry reflects a personality of broad sympathies, deep humanity, and liberal views. Amir Khusrau who laid the foundation of the Indo-Muslim cultural tradition in the pre-Mughal period had the same characteristics. In their writings and in the lives of those whom they influenced, may be found the true spirit of Islamic India during the period which has been covered in this book.

Glossary and
Suggested Readings

Glossary

AMALGUZĀR. A revenue collector, usually the head of a district or parganā (q.v.).

ĀMIL. Under the Mughals, a revenue collector, but the term had more general application during the sultanate.

AMĪN. A revenue assessor, who decided the government's share of the produce of the land.

AMĪR. During the sultanate, a designation for officers of the third rank. Later, amīr and the plural, umarā, were used for "noblemen" in general, and to indicate officials of high rank.

AMĪR-I-AKHŪR. Commander of the cavalry.

AMĪR-I-DĀD. The law officer who carried out the decisions of the judges. Appeals from a qāzī's (q.v.) judgment could be made to him, and he investigated complaints made against high officials.

AMĪR-I-HĀJIB. An official of great prestige who superintended all court ceremonies, regulated protocol, and controlled contacts between the ruler and his subjects. "Lord Chamberlain" is the usual translation.

AMĪR-I-MAJLIS. The official who arranged the social and cultural contacts of the sultan.

AMĪR-UL-UMARĀ. Literally, chief of nobles. This was a title conferred by a ruler, rather than an office.

ĀRIZ (or dīwān-i-arz). The department of government under the sultanate concerned with maintaining the army. Usually translated "War Office" or "Ministry of War."

ĀRIZ-I-MUMĀLIK. The official during the sultanate responsible for the administration of the army, including recruiting, payment of salaries, supplies, and transportation. The office was similar to that of the mīr bakshī under the Mughals. See bakhshi.

BĀDSHĀH. See pādshāh.

BAKSHĪ. Under the Mughals, the official who kept the army records and

paid the troops. The chief paymaster in the central administration was known as the mīr bakhshī, and there were subordinate bakhshīs in the provinces.

BARĪD. Official in charge of intelligence and newsgathering. The barid-i-mumālik was the head of the central office, and his agents sent in reports from all over the country. This system was of great importance in controlling local governments.

BHAKTI. In Hinduism, devotion offered to a deity, with an emphasis on love and self-surrender.

CALIPH (khalīfa). A representative or successor; the title adopted by the rulers of the Islamic community indicating, that as successors of Muhammad, they were both spiritual and temporal leaders. After the destruction of the Abbāsid caliphate in 1258, the title was held by various rulers, including the Ottoman sultans. The office is referred to as the caliphate or khilāfat.

CRORE (kror). Ten millions or one hundred lakhs (q.v.).

DĀR-UL-HARB. "Abode of War." A land ruled by infidels that might, through war, become the "Abode of Islam," dār-ul-Islām. In the nineteenth century, some Muslims argued that India had become dār-ul-harb because of British rule.

DĀR-UL-ISLĀM. "Abode of Islam." A country where Islamic laws are followed and the ruler is a Muslim.

DECCAN. India south of the Vindhya Mountains, but more particularly the interior plateau.

DĪWĀN. *1.* A ministry or department; but under the Mughals it meant specifically the financial or revenue ministry (dīwanī). *2.* In the provincial administration, the diwan had judicial power in civil cases as well as having control of revenue collection. *3.* The term was also applied to the royal court and the council that advised the ruler. *4.* The word is also used for the collected works of a poet.

DĪWĀN-I-ARZ. See āriz.

DĪWĀN-I-KHĀLSĀ (khālisa). The office in charge of the lands reserved as sources of revenue for the state.

DĪWĀN-I-MAZĀLIM. A court presided over by the ruler in which petitions were received, complaints against officials were heard, and to which appeals could be made from other courts.

DĪWĀN-I-TAN. The office responsible for payment of salaries.

DOĀB. "Two rivers." The land lying between two rivers, particularly the area between the Ganges and the Jamna.

DURBĀR (darbār). The court of a ruler, or an audience granted by him.

FARMĀN (firmān). An order issued by a ruler.

FAUJDĀR. In the early period, the word was applied to a military officer, but under the Mughals, it meant the head of a district. Later it was used for a police official.

FIQH. Islamic jurisprudence, or the science of interpreting the Shariat (q.v.). There are four orthodox schools: Hanafī, Hanbalī, Mālikī, and Shāfiī. The sources of fiqh are the Qurān, hadith, ijmā, and quiyās (q.v.).

GADDĪ (gādī). The cushion or seat on which a ruler sits, hence, "throne."

GHANĪMAH. The spoils of war. In original Islamic practice, four-fifths of all the captured goods went to the army, and a fifth was taken for pious purposes. Under the sultanate, the state took four-fifths and one-fifth was given to the soldiers.

GHAZAL. A short poem, usually on a theme dealing with love.

HADĪTH (hadis). A saying or reported action of Muhammad that is not found in the Qurān, but that is accepted as a source of fiqh (q.v.).

HAJJ. Annual pilgrimage made to Mecca; every Muslim is supposed to make the journey at least once in a lifetime.

HANAFĪ. A school of Islamic jurisprudence. See fiqh.

HANBALĪ. A school of Islamic jurisprudence. See fiqh.

HINDŪSTĀNI. *1*. Any native of North India (Hindūstān). *2*. The term was applied to the Indian converts to Islam. *3*. As an adjective, is used to describe the products of the fusion of Islamic and Hindu influences; e.g., Hindūstāni music.

IJMĀ. The consensus of the Islamic community as a source of law. See fiqh.

IMĀM. A leader of the Islamic community. Among the Shīas (q.v.), the descendants of Alī.

INĀM. A gift or reward; particularly applied to lands which were granted rent-free.

IQTĀ. A form of grant made by the sultans. The grantee had rights of revenue collection but not property rights, which were retained by the state. This tenure corresponded to the jāqīr (q.v.) of the Mughals.

JĀGĪR. The term used during Mughal rule for iqtā tenures. The holder of land under the jāgīr system was known as a jāgīrdār. The assignment of land was usually made for a lifetime, and it was not inheritable. Jāgīr tenures were different from inām (q.v.) in that they carried an obligation to perform services for the state.

JIHĀD. A righteous war against unbelievers.

JIZYA. Tax paid by zimmīs (q.v.) in a Muslim society.

KAVI RAI. "Prince of Poets," or poet-laureate. A title used by the Mughals.

KHALĪFAH. See caliph.

KHĀLSĀ. See dīwān-i-khālsā.

KHĀN. A Turkish title. Under the sultanate, it designated a particular rank in the military service, but it was frequently used to indicate ethnic affiliations (e.g., the Pathans) or by anyone claiming its connotation of "brave" and heroic."

KHARĀJ. Originally, the tribute paid by conquered populations, but in India it came to mean simply the land tax, or the proportion of the produce claimed by the state.

KHUTBA. Sermon delivered in the mosque on Fridays. Mention in it of a ruler's name was a declaration of a claim for sovereignty.

KHWĀJA. A Persian title of respect. In the sultanate it was used for the official in each province who kept the revenue accounts.

KOS. A land measure, varying in different parts of India from one mile to two.

KOTWAL. A term applied to various local officials, but usually to the officer who was responsible for police functions in a town or rural area.

LAKH. One hundred thousand.

MADRASA. A school for Islamic studies, usually associated with a mosque.

MALIK. Under the sultanate, a title indicating a military rank, but later used as a general title of honor. Also used for a person who owns land.

MĀLIKĪ. A school of Islamic jurisprudence. See fiqh.

MANSAB. A rank in the Mughal army based on the number of horsemen the officer was supposed to bring into the field. Mansabdārs, the holders of the rank, were graded from those responsible for ten horses up to those who were responsible for ten thousand.

MAUND. A measure of weight, roughly equal to eighty pounds, but varying greatly in different areas.

MĪR BAKHSHĪ. See bakhshi.

MĪR SĀMĀN. The official in charge of the imperial household stores, the workshops for producing goods for the palaces, and the arsenals.

MLECCHA. Sanskrit term for a non-Indian meaning "barbarian," often used for the Muslim invaders.

MOHALLA. A subdivision of a city.

MUHTASIB. The overseer of public morality.

MUJTAHID. A man who through learning and piety is able to undertake the interpretation and application of the Islamic law in such a way that his judgments should be followed by others.

MULLAH. A teacher of the law and doctrines of Islam.

MUSHRIF. The officer responsible for keeping the account of state income during the sultanate.

MUSTAUFĪ. The official responsible for expenditure and for the auditing of accounts.

NĀIB. A deputy, lieutenant, or assistant, as in the title, nāib wazīr.

NAWĀB. Originally used for the viceroy or governor of a province of the Mughal empire, but later used simply as a title.

NĀZIM. Term used for a provincial governor, particularly indicating his function as administrator of the criminal law.

NIZĀM. A governor, particularly the viceroy of the Deccan.

PĀDSHĀH. King, emperor. A title used by the Mughal rulers.

PANCHĀYAT. A traditional Indian village court (made up of five elders) that judged petty cases and controlled local affairs.

PARGANĀ. A subdivision of the basic administrative unit, the sarkār, made up of a number of villages.

PESHWĀ. The Chief Minister of the Marātha rulers. The office became hereditary, and in the eighteenth century the peshwā was virtually an independent ruler.

PĪR. The head of a Sūfī order; later, a Sūfi saint.

QASĪDA. A long, usually panegyric, poem, or ode.

QĀZĪ. The judge who administered Islamic law. Qāzī-i-mumālik was the chief judge of the kingdom.

QIYĀS. One of the sources of fiqh (q.v.); the process of applying hadīth (q.v.) to new situations by the use of analogy.

QURĀN (Koran). For Muslims, the Word of God. The fundamental source of fiqh (q.v.) and all rules governing human relationships.

RAĪYAT (ryot). Cultivator, peasant.

RAĪYATWĀRĪ. A system of revenue assessment and collection in which the government officials dealt with the actual cultivator, not an intermediary.

RUPEE (rupiya). A silver coin introduced by Sher Shah in 1542 which became the standard unit of the Indian currency system. In 1800 it was worth about two shillings.

SADR (sadar). Chief or supreme. A term especially used in connection with the chief religious offices. The sadr-ul-sadūr advised the Mughal emperor on religious matters, controlled religious endowments, and had oversight of educational institutions.

SĀHIB. An honorific applied to titles and names, e.g., Sāhib-i-barīd was the chief barīd (q.v.), or intelligence officer.

SANAD. A charter or grant.

SARKĀR (sircār). A subdivision of a sūbah or province. The word is also used to mean simply "the government."

SARPANCH. The head of a panchāyat (q.v.).

SATĪ. "A true wife." By extension, the term was used for a woman who immolated herself on her husband's funeral pyre.

SAYYID (said, syed). A chief. Also a name used by those who claim descent from Husain, the son of Muhammad's daughter, Fatima.

SEPOY (sipāhī). A soldier.

SHĀFIĪ. A school of Islamic jurisprudence. See fiqh.

SHAIKH. "Old man." A term used for a Sūfī (q.v.) who guided disciples. Also used to denote a caste or class among Indian Muslims.

SHARĪAT (Sharīa). The law of Islam, comprising all the rules that govern life.

SHĪA. The Muslim sect that asserts the leadership of Islam is hereditary in the descendants of Alī, the son-in-law of the Prophet. It is the dominant group in Iran, and is well represented in India.

SHIQQ. In the sultanate, the administrative district corresponding to the later sarkār (q.v.).

SIPĀH-SĀLĀR. A military rank during the sultanate, but under Akbar the name was used for a provincial governor.

SŪBAH. The term for the provinces into which the Mughal empire was divided. The sūbadār was the governor. This word was later used for the administrator of a smaller district.

SŪFĪ. An Islamic mystic. Sūfism, with its emphasis on the possibility of unity with the divine, was of special importance in winning converts to Islam in India.

SULTĀN. King, ruler. In its early usage, the term implied dependence on the caliph (q.v.). The Delhi sultāns sought recognition from the Abbāsid caliphate, and even after its destruction they maintained a nominal connection with the Egyptian ruler who claimed to be the caliph.

SUNNĪ. An inherent of the majority, or "orthodox," Islamic sect that accepted the Abbāsid rulers as caliphs, in contrast to the Shīas (q.v.).

"Sunna" means the custom or traditions associated with Muhammad, and its usage implies that the Sunnī follow the canonical tradition.

TAFSĪR. Explanation. The commentaries on the Qurān and the science of its interpretation. Tafsīr was an important branch of learning in the madrasas (q.v.).

TĀLUKA (Tāluq). A name for a subdivision of a province in the late Mughal empire.

TAWHĪD. "Asserting oneness." A theological term that refers to the oneness of God.

TEHSĪL (tahsil). The collection of land revenue. Later applied to a subdivision of a district.

ULAMĀ. Learned men, plural of ālim. Used particularly for those learned in Islamic studies, or for the theologians who were guardians of Islamic custom.

UMARĀ. Nobles. Plural of amīr (q.v.).

URDŪ. Literally, camp. The "camp-language" that grew up through an infusion of Persian, and some Arabic and Turkish, words into Hindī, the language of the Delhi region.

VAKĪL. See wakīl.

WAHHĀBĪ. Follower of the community founded by Abdul Wahhāb (1703-1787) in Arabia. The aim of the Wahhābīs is to purify Islam of all innovations and to return to the strict observances of Islamic law. It is the dominant sect in Saudi Arabia. The beliefs of the Wahhābīs, especially the strong emphasis on the removal of all non-Islamic practices, had considerable influence in India in the nineteenth century.

WAKĪL (vakīl). The office of the wakīl or wakīl-i-dār under the sultanate was concerned with the management of the royal household. In the Mughal period, however, the wakīl or wakīl-i-sultānat, was the chief minister, the post formerly held by the wazīr (q.v.).

WAQF. An endowment, usually in the form of lands, for the upkeep of a mosque, madrasa, or some other religious enterprise.

WAZĪR. The chief minister of the Delhi sultans. Under the Mughals,

the title was sometimes used for the official in charge of revenue and finance.

WIZĀRAT. The office of the wazir.

ZAKĀT. A tax collected from Muslims for charitable purposes.

ZAMĪNDĀR. Literally, "a landholder," from zamīn, land. Under the Mughals, he was a revenue official who had no proprietary rights in the land from which he collected taxes.

ZIMMĪ (dhimmī). A non-Muslim living in a Muslim state. According to a strict interpretation of the Islamic law, only Jews and Christians were eligible for the status of zimmī. Each adult male zimmī had to pay jizya (q.v.). In practice, when Muslims conquered a country they tolerated others than the "Peoples of the Scripture." This was particularly true in India, where the Hindus were treated as zimmīs.

Suggested Readings

THE following list includes works that are especially valuable for giving more detailed treatment of certain topics than has been possible in this book. Most of them have bibliographies. Not all works referred to in the text have been included; reference should be made to the footnotes for primary sources.

General Historical Studies

Haig, Sir Wolseley et al., editors. *The Cambridge History of India*. Vols. III-V. Cambridge, 1928-37; Delhi, 1957-58.

Hardy, Peter. *Historians of Medieval India: Studies in Indo-Muslim Historical Writing*. London, 1960.

Lane-Poole, Stanley. *Medieval India under Mohammedan Rule, A.D. 712-1764*. New York, 1903; Calcutta, 1951.

Majumdar, R. C., editor. *The History and Culture of the Indian People*. Vols. V-IX. Bombay, 1957-. Vols. VII and VIII have not yet been published. Full bibliographies.

Prasad, Ishwari. *A Short History of Muslim Rule in India*. Allahabad, 1959.

Qureshi, I. H. *The Muslim Community in the Indo-Pakistan Sub-Continent*. 'sGravenage, 1962.

Tarachand. *Influence of Islam in India and Pakistan*. Calcutta, 1959.

Titus, Murray Thurston. *Islam in India and Pakistan*. Calcutta, 1959.

The Delhi Sultanate

Ahmad, M. A. *Political History and Institutions of the Early Turkish Empire of Delhi* (1206-1250). Lahore, 1949.

Day, U. N. *Administrative System of Delhi Sultanate* (1206-1413 A.D.). Allahabad, 1959.

Habibullah, A. B. M. *The Foundations of Muslim Rule in India*. Lahore, 1945.

Husain, A. M. *The Rise and Fall of Muhammad bin Tughluq*. London, 1938.

Lal, K. S. *History of the Khaljis, 1290-1320*. Allahabad, 1950.

Moreland, W. H. *The Agrarian System of Moslem India*. Cambridge, 1929.

Pandey, A. B. *The First Afghan Empire in India*. Calcutta, n.d.

Qureshi, I. H. *The Administration of the Sultanate of Delhi*. Lahore, 1944.

Srivastava, A. L. *The Sultanate of Delhi, 711-1526 A.D.* Agra, 1953.

Tripathi, Ram Prasad. *Some Aspects of Muslim Administration*. Allahabad, 1956.

The Mughal Empire

Chopra, P. N. *Some Aspects of Society and Culture During the Mughul Age, 1526-1707*. Agra, 1955.

Edwardes, S. M. and H. L. O. Garrett. *Mughal Rule in India*. London, 1930; Delhi, 1956.

Habib, Irfan. *The Agrarian System of Mughal India*. New York, 1963.

Ibn Hasan. *The Central Structure of the Mughal Empire and Its Practical Working up to the Year 1557*. London, 1936.

Moreland, W. H. *From Akbar to Aurangzeb: A Study in Indian Economic History*. London, 1923.

——*India at the Death of Akbar*. London, 1920.

Owen, S. J. *The Fall of the Mughal Empire*. London, 1912; Varanasi, 1960.

Prasad, Beni. *History of Jahangir*. London, 1922.

Prasad, Ishwari. *Life and Times of Humayun*. Bombay, 1955.

Qanungo, K. R. *Dara Shukoh*. Calcutta, 1952.

——*Sher Shah*. Calcutta, 1921.

Roychoudhury, M. L. *The State of Religion in Mughal India*. Calcutta, 1951.

Saran, Parmatma. *The Provincial Government of the Mughals*. Allahabad, 1941.

Sarkar, Sir Jadunath. *Fall of the Mughal Empire*. 4 vols. Calcutta, 1932-1950.

——*History of Aurangzib, Based on Original Sources*. 5 vols. Calcutta, 1912-52.

——*Mughal Administration*. 4th ed. Calcutta, 1952.

Sharma, Sri Ram. *A Bibliography of Mughal India (1526-1707 A.D.)*. Bombay, 1938.

——*Mughal Government and Administration*. Bombay, 1951.

——*The Religious Policy of the Mughal Emperors*. New York, 1962.

Smith, Vincent A. *Akbar the Great Mogul, 1542-1605*. London, 1917; Delhi, 1958.

Regional Kingdoms

Akbar, Muhammad. *The Punjab under the Mughals*. Lahore, 1948.

Caroe, Olaf K. *The Pathans 550 B.C.—A.D. 1957*. London, 1958.

Cunningham, J. D. *A History of the Sikhs*. H. L. O. Garrett, editor, with additional notes by R. R. Sethi. Delhi, 1955.

Datta, K. K. *Alivardi and His Times*. Calcutta, 1939.

Edwardes, Michael. *The Orchid House; Splendours and Miseries of the Kingdom of Oudh, 1827-1857*. London, 1960.

Khan, M. N. *Kashmir under the Sultans*. Calcutta, 1960.

Majumdar, R. C. and Jadunath Sarkar, editors. *History of Bengal*. 2 vols. Dacca; 1943-48.

Raychaudhuri, T. K. *Bengal under Akbar and Jahangir*. Calcutta, 1953.

Sardesai, G. S. *New History of the Marathas*. 3 vols. Bombay, 1946-48.

Srivastava, A. L. *The First Two Nawabs of Awadh*. 2d ed. Agra, 1954.

Venkata Ramanayya, N. *The Early Muslim Expansion in South India*. Madras, 1942.

The European Powers and the Mughals

Danvers, Frederick C. *The Portuguese in India*. 2 vols. London, 1894.

Hunter, Sir William W. *A History of the British in India*. 2 vols. London, New York, 1899-1900.

Khan, S. A. *Anglo-Portuguese Negotiations Relating to Bombay, 1660-1667*. London, 1922.

Rawlinson, Hugh G. *British Beginnings in Western India, 1579-1657*. Oxford, 1920.

Spear, Thomas G. *Twilight of the Mughuls*. Cambridge, 1951.

Literature and the Arts

Bailey, T. G. *A History of Urdu Literature*. Calcutta, 1932.

Brown, Percy. *Indian Architecture: The Islamic Period*. Bombay, 1956.

——*Indian Painting under the Mughals*. Oxford, 1924.

Fox-Strangways, A. H. *The Music of Hindostan*. Oxford, 1914.

Ghani, M. A. *Pre-Mughal Persian in Hindostan*. Allahabad, 1941.

Keay, Frank E. *A History of Hindi Literature*. 3d ed. Calcutta, 1960.

Saksena, Ram Babu. *A History of Urdu Literature*. Allahabad, 1940.

Welch, Stuart C. *The Art of Mughal India*. New York, 1964.

Index

Abbasids, 12-17 *passim*, 19, 44, 48, 59, 67, 115
Abdali, *see* Ahmad Shah
Abdul Hai, Maulvi, 281
Abdullah Khan, 145-46
Abdul Qadir, 182
Abdul Rahim Khan-i-Khanan, 144, 146, 166-67, 242, 243
Abdur Rahman, 175
Abdus Samad Khan, 256
Abu Ali, 16
Abu Bakr, 4
Abul Ata Sindhi, 18
Abul Fath Daud, 24
Abul Fazl, 158, 167, 178, 242; murder of, 146, 175, 180, 198; political opinions of, 150-51, 210, 215; and brother Faizi, 152-53, 242; and religion, 161-64; and the arts, 248, 251
Abul Fazl Gazruni, 153n
Abul Najm Zarir Shaybani, 30
Abu Maashar Sindhi, 18
Abu Nasr Farsi, 34, 35
Adhan Khan, 144
Adil Shahis, 83
Administration: 60, 195-96, 257-58, 269, 270-72, 296; Arab, 11-14, 20; of Ghazni, 23, 36; of Delhi Sultanate, general, 45-50, 79, 86-106, 109; Iltutmish's, 55, 55-60, Ala-ud-din's, 64-67; Mughal, general, 135-36, 209-22, 226-28, 237; Sher Shah's, 138-40; Akbar's, 144, 146-51, 164; Jahangir's, 176-78; Shah Jahan's, 185-86; Aurangzeb's, 189, 190, 198-200, 205-8; British, 277-78, 289-90, 292-93
Afghanistan, 22 ff., 60, 141, 295; Persian language in, 36, 241; and Babur, 84, 137; popularity of Bedil in, 204, 241-42
Afghans, 193, 259, 270, 273; in Delhi, 18, 287; contributions to Muslim success, 41, 45, 58-59; in power,
76-78, 258-59, 267; in Bengal, 83, 145; and Hamayun, 137-38, 248; and Sikhs, 194, 205, 281-83; and Safdar Jang, 266
Afzal Khan, 196
Agra, 77, 140, 141, 145, 197, 225, 254; and Babur, 78, 137; culture and education in, 136, 238, 241; and Humayun, 138, 142, 143; and Akbar, 146, 156, 246; and Aurangzeb, 183-84, 190; and Shah Jahan, 184, 247
Agriculture, 18-19, 74-75, 110, 227-28
Ahadis, 212-13, 218, 248
Ahmadabad, 79, 84, 123, 153n, 225, 227, 238, 247
Ahmad Chap, 62, 88
Ahmad ibn Majid, 85
Ahmadnagar, 83, 123, 129, 146, 181, 196
Ahmad Niyaltigin, 28-29, 33
Ahmad Shah (Abdali), 261, 265-67, 279
Aibak, Qutb-ud-din, 39, 40, 42-43, 45, 52, 55, 57, 86, 89, 92, 94, 105, 106, 120
Ain-i-Akbari (Abu Fazl), 150, 161-62, 216, 218, 221, 274
Ajmer, 24-25, 37-39 *passim,* 49, 105; buildings in, 42, 156, 247
Akbar, 135-36, 142, 146; cultural life and the arts, 67, 242, 246, 248-49, 251, 273, 279, 295; territorial expansion and control, 82, 84, 176, 180-82; coinage and revenue, 97, 214-16; government and justice, 103, 185, 206, 210-13, 220-21, 226; religion and toleration, 141, 156-65, 166-74, 194, 207, 235-36; military organization, 218-19, 274; trade and industry, 223-24; education, 238, 240-41
Akbar II, 278
Akbar, Prince, 197

Akbarabadi Mosque, 288
Akbar-Nama (Abu Fazl), 162, 242, 249
Akhla-i-Jalali (Dawwani), 153n
Akhund Darweza, 172
Alamgir II, 266, 267
Alam Shah, 76
Ala-ud-din Husain, 30-31
Ala-ud-din Husain Shah, 83
Ala-ud-din Khalji, 69-70; conquest and expansion, 45, 62-63, 72-73; religion, 64, 96; government and justice, 65-66, 89, 90, 100-1, 104, 106, 139, 207; military organization, 66, 98; revenue, 67, 94, 96, 110; culture and arts, 68, 112, 121
Ala-ud-din Masud, 53-54
Ala-ul-Mulk, 64-65
Al-Biruni, Abu Raihan, 26-28, 31-32, 131
Ali, 4, 5-6
Aligarh College, 280, 289
Aligarh movement, 265
Ali Hujwiri, 35-36
Ali Mardan Khan, 181
Alivardi Khan, 262, 268
Allahabad, 62, 183-85, 205, 220, 225
Allami Afzal Khan, 211
Almagest (Ptolemy-Al-Biruni), 26-27
Alptigin, 23
Aluniya, 52
Amalguzar, 215
Ambala, 75, 255
Amin, 139
Amir Fathullah Shirazi, 151, 153
Amir-i-dad, 91, 99-100
Amir-i-hajib, 91
Amir-i-Majlis, 90
Amir Khan, 193
Amir Khan Nawab, 281
Amir Khurd, 87
Amir Khusrau, 67-69, 98, 116-17, 119, 296
Amran, 12-14, 15
Anandpal, 24, 25
Anandpur, 194, 195
Arabia, 3-4, 127, 263; contact with, 36, 224, 238, 283-86
Arabian Nights' Entertainments, 16
Arabic characters and numerals, 15, 49
Arabic coinage and currency, 49, 97

Arabic language and literature, 19, 23, 35, 46, 84, 103, 115, 128-29, 138, 173, 264, 280, 291-92, 240, 252
Arabic traditions, 93, 154, 295
Arabs, 3-6, 22, 33, 110-11; conquests of, 6-11, 22; rule of, in Sind, 11-14, 19-21, 36, 109, 111, 164; cultural and intellectual influence, 14-17, 119
Architecture, 125; during Delhi Sultanate, 67, 75, 84, 113, 120-22, 149; during Mughal empire, 186-87, 202, 213-14, 217, 245-48, 287-89
Ariz, 66, 98-99, 104
Arjan, Guru, 175, 194, 233
Army, 33, 140, 226-27; during Delhi Sultanate, 41-42, 56-59, 65-67, 86, 94, 97-99; during Mughal empire, 139, 206, 211-14, 217-19, 257, 259, 274
Art, 79-80, 84, 120-21, 280, 195; Indian, 21, 149; during Delhi Sultanate, 119-22; during Mughal empire, 142, 184, 187, 202-4, 238-53
Artillery, 98, 137, 218, 274
Arya Samaj, 126
Arz-i-mumalik, 209
Arzu, 244, 245
Asad Khan, 210 211
Asaf Khan, 168, 176, 177, 179, 186, 205, 210-11
Ashoka, 75, 143
Asiatic Society, 291
Asirgarh, 146
Assam, 80, 82, 181, 190-91, 194, 283, 285
Astrology, 15, 16, 27, 230
Astronomy, 15, 26, 114, 118, 240, 263
Attock, 29, 192, 193
Aufi, Muhammad, 49, 116, 118
Aurangabad, 197, 260
Aurangzeb, 95, 99, 103, 151, 170-72, 181-85 *passim,* 189-208 *passim,* 254, 257, 266; religious policy, 189, 198-200, 251-52, 255; conquests, 190-98, 244; Afgans, 192-93; Sikhs, 193-95; Marathas, 195-97; East India Company, 200-1; character, 200-2; land revenue, 215-15; navy, 219; judiciary, 220-21; Hinduism, 227, 232-36; culture and arts, 238-43, 247, 251-52, 275; army, 274
Azad, Abul Kalam, 159-60

Azad Khan, 255, 256
Azam, 243
Azam Shah, Prince, 171, 206
Azim-ush-Shan, 255, 256

Babur, 78, 84, 94, 136-37, 138, 142, 145, 206, 265, 267, 274; arts, 242, 245-46, 248, 288
Badaun, 39, 43, 53, 76, 279
Badauni, 73, 151, 153, 154, 156, 157, 161-62, 220, 225, 242
Badrud-din-Sunqar, 53
Badshahi Mosque, 247, 255
Baghdad, 12, 14-18 *passim*, 20, 23, 26, 44, 46, 48, 56, 59, 88, 90, 112, 113, 120, 186
Bahadur Shah (Prince Muazzam), 195, 196-97, 242, 243, 254-55, 275, 278, 287
Bahadur Shah of Gujarat, 137
Bahadur Yar Jang, Nawab, 141
Baha-ud-din Gurshashp, 72
Bahmani, 73, 83, 114
Bahram, 30, 31
Bairam Khan, 143-44
Baji Rao I, 258
Bakhshi, 213
Bakhtawar Khan, 202
Bakhtiyar Khalji, 39
Balban, 45, 46, 50, 52, 54, 55-60, 61, 63, 67, 80, 88-94 *passim*, 97, 98, 102-7 *passim*, 112, 113, 116, 149, 150, 207
Baluchistan, 146
Banda, 195, 254-55, 256
Barani, Ziya-ud-din, 46, 50, 57, 63-66 *passim*, 72, 87-89 *passim*, 98, 101, 102, 106, 109-10, 112, 114, 118
Barid Shahis, 83
Barlas Turks, 75
Barmakid family, 14-15
Bartu, 43
Bayazid of Bistam, 16
Bedil, 204, 241-42
Behzad, 248
Benares, 29, 30, 32, 43, 119, 225, 229, 279
Bengal, 21, 37, 39-40, 55, 58-59, 72-73, 78, 82-83, 88, 138, 180-81, 261-62, 219; Mughal rule in, 145, 176, 191, 200, 205, 206; British in, 200-1, 268-70; industry, 111, 224; education,

113-14; architecture, 121; religion, 124, 126, 129-30, 165, 172-74, 245, 283-86
Bengali literature, 83, 118, 173-74, 192, 232, 245, 291-92
Berar, 83, 181
Bernier, François, 131, 187, 224, 226, 228, 238-40 *passim*, 274
Betel, 108, 231
Bhagwan Das Raja, 144, 165
Bhagwan Singh, 178
Bhaktamala, 128
Bhakti movement, 79, 125, 126, 128-30 *passim*, 195
Bhaku, 192
Bhatinda, 38, 39, 52
Bhikschachara, 32
Bhojpur, 58-59
Biana, 77
Bidar, 83, 183
Bihar, 32, 39, 55, 80, 112, 137, 138, 243
Bijapur, 80, 83, 119, 123, 153, 181, 183, 195-97 *passim*, 204, 205, 219, 244
Bilas Khan, 251
Birbal, Raja, 146, 153, 165, 243
Bir Singh Budhela, 146, 180
Bishvas Rao, 267
Bistam of Bayazid, 16
Blochmann, H., 161-62
Bombay, 20-21, 201, 214, 219, 225-26, 228
Brahmagupta, 15
Brahmajit Gaur, 140
Brahmanabad, 7, 11, 19
Brahmans, 21, 74, 108, 128, 158, 165, 232
Brahmaputra River, 80, 82, 191-92
Brahmo Samaj, 126
British in India, 85, 135, 139, 172, 205-6, 215-17 *passim*, 220, 222, 225-28 *passim*, 231-35 *passim*, 277-94; *see also* East India Company
Bu Ali Hasan, 29
Buddhism, 8-9, 11, 21, 124
Budhu Miyan, 284
Bughra Khan, 58-60, 80, 88, 116
Buhlul Lodi, 76, 77, 93
Bukhara, 22-23, 34, 36, 116, 155, 166, 182, 186, 241
Bundelkhand, 37, 180, 258

Burdwan, 175, 205
Bureaucracy, 105, 178, 275
Burhanpur, 197, 238
Burhan-ud-din, Maulana, 102-3
Burhan-ul-Mulk, 259
Buxar, 269-70, 272

Cairo, 14, 113, 120
Calcutta, 105-6, 214, 225-26, 268, 291
Calicut, 85
Caliph, 88, 282, 284
Cambay, 20, 226, 238
Canals, 95
Canning, Earl, 289
Caste, 130, 131, 226, 234
Cavalry, 52, 98, 110, 218
Central Asia, 32-33, 36, 40, 45, 56, 79, 103, 109, 112, 114, 119-22 *passim,* 136, 145, 146, 170, 182, 223
Central India, 63, 258, 267
Ceylon, 6, 20
Chach, 8-9
Chaghatai Turks, 136
Chaitanya, 126, 129-30, 165, 173, 233
Chand Bibi, 146
Chandu Lal, 175
Chaudharis, 105, 109
Chauhan kingdom, 49
Chausar, 16
Chess, 16, 108
Chihilgan, 57
China, 8, 74, 82
Chingiz Khan, 43, 136
Chin Qilich Khan, 257; *see also* Nizam-ul-Mulk
Chishti sufis, 119, 156
Chitor, 63, 140, 144
Chittagong, 118, 180, 191, 201, 224, 285
Christianity, 4, 126, 287
Christians, 144, 160
Chuti Khan, 118
Clive, Robert, 269
Coinage, 5, 49, 64, 72, 96-97, 176, 201, 254, 255, 277
Colleges, *see* Education
Commerce, 18-19, 109, 111, 179-80, 209-10, 219, 226-27, 290-94 *passim*
Constantinople, 186, 245-46
Conversion, 123-25 *passim,* 130-31, 148, 232-33, 234-35, 283, 295
Cooch Behar, 176, 190-91

Cordova, 112-13, **120**
Coromandal, 21
Cotton goods, 223-24
Counterfeiting, 72
Courts, 99, 220-22 *passim*
Cows, slaughter of, 17, 172, 235
Criminal law, 220, 277-78
Curzon, George Nathaniel, Marquess Curzon of Kedleston, 288
Customs duties, 140, 199, 200, 214, 223

Dacca, 40, 80, 140, 176, 190-91 *passim,* 219, 231, 283, 284
Dadu, 126, 127-28
Dahar, 6-11 *passim*
Dalhousie, James Ramsay, Marquess of, 290
Damascus, 5, 18, 110, 120, 164
Dance, 101, 102-3, 263
Danishmand Khan, 240
Dara Shukoh, 182-86 *passim,* 187-88, 189, 192, 193, 198, 243, 250, 295, 296
Dard, 244-45
Dars-i-Nizamiya, 205, 239
Dar-ul-harb, 284-85, 286
Dar-ul-Islam, 284-85, 286
Daswant, 249
Data Janz Bakhsh, 35-36
Daulatabad, 70, 72, 73, 114, 121, 181
Daulat Khan Lodi, 78
Dawwani, 153, 154
Debul, 6, 7, 10, 17, 19
Deccan, 98, 110, 141, 166-67, 257; regional kingdoms in, 73, 80, 83, 85, 261-62; Islamic culture in, 114-15, 119, 204, 243-45 *passim;* Mughal authority in, 146, 176, 177, 180-83 *passim,* 189, 195, 206, 208, 215, 219; Marathas in, 195-97, 205, 257, 273, 260
Delhi, 18, 20, 24-25, 37, 42, 72, 84, 88; culture in, 113, 119, 120, 136, 238-40 *passim,* 245, 248, 252, 279-82 *passim;* architecture in, 121, 184, 186, 246-48 *passim,* 263; Babur in, 137; Humayun in, 141-42; Marathas and, 257-58, 272; Nadir Shah in, 259-60; Shah Waliullah in, 263, 265; British in, 273, 277-79; in Indian Revolt, 287-89

Delhi College, 280-81
Deoband seminary, 239, 265, 280-81, 289
Dera Ismail Khan, 38
Devagiri, 62, 63-64, 70, 72, 73
Devi Singh, 233
Devkot, 113-14
Dilar Khan, 196-97
Din-i-Ilahi, 160-64 *passim*
Divorce, 230
Diwan, 104, 209, 210-11, 213; diwan-i-arz, 98-99; diwan-i-mazalim, 99, 220; diwan-i-khalsa, 211; diwan-i-tan, 211
Doab, 43, 55, 58, 104
Duperron, Anquetil, 188
Durbar, 277-78
Dutch in India, 85, 177, 200, 221, 224, 227

East Africa, 85, 110
East Bengal, 284-85
East India Company, 102, 179, 222, 254, 272, 276; and Aurangzeb, 200-1; in Bengal, 268-70; control of India, 277-79 *passim;* and British government, 289-90; language policy of, 292
East Pakistan, 82, 124, 191-92, 208, 283
Economy: Ala-ud-din Khalji's regulation of, 65-66; under Delhi Sultanate, 72, 94-96, 107, 110-12; Sher Shah's reforms in, 139-40; of Jahangir's reign, 178-79; under Aurangzeb, 189-90, 205, 207; development of in Mughal empire, 223-30
Education: in Delhi Sultanate, 113-15; and Akbar, 149, 154-55; and Aurangzeb, 198-99, 204-5; in Mughal empire, 238-41, 273-74; Shah Wali-ullah's role in, 263-64; at Delhi College, 280-81; English, in India, 291
Egypt, 5, 6, 14, 18, 224
Election, of ruler, 90-91
Elephants, 98, 110
Elliot, Sir Henry, 293-94
Eunuchs, 189
Europe and India, relations between, 6, 110, 135, 179, 191, 218, 223-24, 225, 228, 235, 236, 247, 274

Faizi, 151-53, 158, 167, 178, **242**
Fakhr-i-Mudabbir, 42, 86-88 *passim,* 91-92, 97-99 *passim,* 113, 116, 118
Fakirullah (Saif Khan), 252
Famine, 70, 72, 73
Faraizis, 284-85
Farangi Mahal, 205
Faridpur, 283, 284
Farrukh Beg, 249, 250
Farrukhsiyar, 256-57, 262
Fatawa-i-Alamgiri, 103, 205, 221
Fatawa-i-Jahandari (Barani), 87-88
Fathpur Sikri, 145, 149, 153, 156, **167,** 225, 246, 248-49
Fathullah Shirazi, 153-54, 216
Fazil Khan, 186, 240
Fidai Khan Kuka, 247
Fighani of Shiraz, 241
Fiqh, 114, 239
Fiqh-i-Firuz Shahi, 95
Firishta, 25, 114, 242
Firuz (Bahmani ruler), 114-15
Firuz Jang, 207
Firuz Kuh, 30, 31
Firuz Tughluq, 74-75, 82, 89, 93, 95, 103, 107, 113-14, 121, 207, 228
Food, 66, 108, 110, 140, 189-90, 295
Fortifications, 63, 137, 138, 140, 246, 288
Fort William College, 291
"Forty, the," 57
France, 5, 238

Games, 228, 231
Ganges River, 39, 40, 59, 73, 77, **84,** 104, 137, 138, 279
Gardens, 246
Garib, 128
Gaur, 79, 83, 138
Geography, study of, 238-39, **240**
Gezit, 96
Ghalib, 204, 242. 279, 289, 296
Ghanimah, 95
Ghausgarh, 270, 272
Ghazi Malik, 69; *see also* Ghiyas-ud-din Tughluq
Ghazi-ud-din, 239, 266, 267
Ghaznavids, 18, 48, 92, 94, 109, 241
Ghazni, 19, 26, 61, 63, 90, 113, 241, 259; and Muhammad Ghuri, 37-40 *passim;* government at, 45-46; and Iltutmish, 48-49; tradition of, 112

Ghias-ud-din Mansur, 154
Ghiyas-ud-din Shah, 82
Ghiyas-ud-din Tughluq, 31, 63, 69, 70, 72, 82, 92-94 *passim,* 104, 107, 117
Ghulam Husain Khan, quoted, 265
Ghulam Qadir, 270, 272
Ghur, 30-31, 37, 54
Goa, 85, 160
Golden Temple, 194
Golkunda, 80, 83, 119, 181, 183, 195-97 *passim,* 204, 205, 207, 244
Gosains, Vaishnava, of Mathura, 170
Governors, provincial, 103-5 *passim,* 139, 163, 213, 214, 220, 221, 236
Govind Rai, 38
Govind Singh, Guru, 194-95, 254, 255
Grain, 66, 70, 95, 110
Grammar, 238-39, 240
Greek ideas, 5, 26-27, 115, 153
Gujarat, 12, 21, 38, 63, 73, 84, 145, 179, 189, 219, 238, 258, 260, 274; textile industry in, 111, 225; kingdom of, 37, 83-84; music in, 79; architecture in, 121; conversions in, 233
Gujarati, 244, 292
Gulbadan, Begum, 240
Gulbarga, 79
Gunpowder, 274
Gurshashp, 106
Gwalior, 24-25, 43, 50, 55, 120, 137, 140, 143, 168, 184, 251, 252, 255, 270

Hadith, 114, 155, 238, 239
Hafiz, 82
Haji Muhammad Mohsin, 284
Haji Shariat Ullah, 283-84, 286
Hajjaj, 6-7, 8, 9-10, 11-12, 20-21
Hakim Abul Gilani, 154
Hakim Hashim Gilani, 114
Halhed, Nathaniel, 292
Hammans, 108
Hanafi school, 158, 264, 265
Hanbali, 265
Hargovind, Guru, 194, 233
Harsa, 32
Harun-al-Rashid, 12, 15
Hasain Sharqi, 119
Hasan, 115, 117
Hasan Abdal, 192

Hasan Abul, 29
Hasan Ali, 256-57
Hasan Nizami, 42, 118
Hastings, Lord, 278
Hauz-i-Shamsi, 49, 120
Hazabr-ud-din Hasan Adib, 39
Hazara, 282
Hazarajet, 31
Hazin, 242, 244
Hazrat Ali, 255
Hazrat Nasir-ud-din Chiragh-i-Delhi, 65
Hazrat Nizam-ud-din Auliya, 93, 107, 112, 113
Heber, Reginald, 293
Hejaz, 238
Herat, 30, 34, 79, 248, 258
Hibbari family, 14
Hidaya, 102, 103
Hijaz, 17, 82, 263
Hijra, 4
Himalayas, 112, 266-67
Himu, 143
Hindi, 35, 117, 139, 142, 243, 245, 291, 292
Hindus: and Arabs, 11-12, 17-18; and commerce, 19, 110-11, 226-27; and Ghaznavids, 24-26, 27-33 *passim;* in Muslim administration, 105, 140, 150-51, 175, 178, 195-06, 198-200, 211, 220-22 *passim;* under the Sultanate, 43, 48, 50, 55, 65, 69, 72-73, 75, 77, 78, 84-85, 87, 98, 102, 107-12 *passim,* 115; and Islamic culture, 79-80, 118-22 *passim,* 229-30, 246, 248-53 *passim,* 295-96; as zimmis, 96; revival of, 136-37, 171-72, 185-86, 283; and Islam, interaction of, 123-132, 187-88, 193-94, 231-37, 283-86 *passim;* and Akbar, 144, 148-49, 164-65, 170; and Aurangzeb, 227, 232-36; Hindu-Muslim separatism, seeds of, 291-94
Hindustani, 83, 125, 291, 292
Hisham, 12
History writing of, 26, 74, 87-88, 101, 107, 112-19 *passim,* 135, 238-39, 242-43, 292-93
Horses, horsemanship, 41, 66, 108, 110, 218, 228
Hospitals, in Mughal empire, 228-29

Hugli, 80, 82, 180-81, 200, 205
Hulagu Khan, 43, 59
Humayun, 94, 137-38, 140-42 *passim,* 241, 246, 248, 267
Husain, Iman, 5
Husain Ali, 256-57
Husain Shah, 118
Husain Shahi dynasty, 83
Husain Sharqi, 77, 84
Hyderabad, 141, 244, 250, 258, 261-62, 278, 290

Ibadat Khana (House of Worship), 145, 156-57, 160, 164-65
Ibn Battuta, 65, 74, 106, 107, 131-32
Ibn Hasan, 210
Ibn Haukul, 17
Ibn-Taimiya, 169-70
Ibn-ul-Athir, 32, 43
Ibrahim, Sultan of Ghazni, 30, 34, 35
Ibrahim Khan, 205
Ikhtiyar-ud-din Muhammad, 39-40
Ilbari Turks, 56, 60, 61
Iltutmish, 40, 43-54 *passim,* 56, 86-90, 92, 97, 113, 115, 120, 149
Ilyas Shahi dynasty, 82
Imad Shahis, 83
Imam-ud-din Maulvi, 285
Inayat Ali Maulvi, 285
Indian Councils Act (1861), 290
Indian Ocean, 6, 85, 219, 274
Indian Revolt (1857-58), 286-91
Indo-Muslim culture, 295-96
Indus River, 17, 19, 23-25 *passim,* 43, 140, 193, 260, 266-67
Industry: in Delhi Sultanate, 110-11; in Mughal empire, 223-25
"Infallibility Decree of 1579," 158-60, 164
Inheritance rights, 214
Interest, 109-10
Iqbal, 169, 296
Iqtas, 79, 103-4
Iran, 5, 22; influence on culture, 154, 176, 178, 179; *see also* Persian influence
Irani faction, 186, 257, 266
Iraq, 8, 18, 20, 34, 45, 83, 114
Irrigation, 74-75, 95
Isami, 49, 65, 118
Isfahan, 36, 79, 241
Islam Khan, 176

Islam Shah, 140-41
Ismail, 4
Ismailis, 6, 14, 24, 40, 52, 74
Ismail Khan Rumi, 186
Istanbul, 103, 224
Itimad-ud-Daula, 210-11
Izz-ud-din Kishlu Khan, 53-54

Jagat, Guru, 165
Jaget Seth, 227
Jagirs, 149, 175, 212
Jahan Ara Begum, 184, 241
Jahandar Shah, 252, 255-56, 266, 275
Jahangir (Prince Salim), 99, 145, 146, 156, 175-80, 181, 185, 210, 211, 222, 223, 225, 228-29, 236, 241, 274; and Islam, 166, 168-70 *passim,* 232-33, *passim;* and Sikhs, 194, and architecture, 246-47; and painting, 249-50; and poets, 279
Jahan Saz, 30-31
Jahiz, 17
Jains, 73, 160, 185, 227
Jaipal, 23, 24
Jaipur, 249, 263
Jaisi, 243
Jai Singh, Raja, 196-97
Jai Singh, of Jaipur, 263
Jalal-ud-din Firuz Khalji, 44, 61-62, 88, 99, 100, 116
Jala-ud-din Qazi, 53
Jala-ud-din Rumi Maulana, 114
Jalila, 77
Jamali, 77-78
Jamal-ud-din Mahmud, 153
Jama Masjid, 247, 288
Jami, 117
Janjira, sidi of, 219
Jaswant Singh, 183
Jats, 9, 12, 26, 58, 70, 267-68, 287
Jaunpur, 75, 77, 79, 82-84 *passim,* 93, 119, 137, 138, 140-41, 143, 160, 279
Javed Khan, 266
Jesuits, 160, 161, 166, 220, 235
Jihad, 82, 265, 281-82, 283, 285
Jizya, 5, 74, 84, 95-96, 144, 148, 172, 198, 233, 257
Junaidi, 48-51 *passim,* 92
Jurisprudence, 114, 239
Justice, in the sultanate, 91, 99-103; in provinces, 105-6; British, in India, 292

Kaaba, 3
Kabir, 126-32 *passim,* 243, 295
Kabul, 19, 22, 30, 63, 78, 136, 141, 142, 145, 148, 161, 182, 192, 193, 247, 248, 259, 260, 267
Kaiqubad, 60, 116
Kaksa, 10
Kalinjar, 24-25, 43
Kalyani, 183
Kam Bakhsh, Prince, 206
Kampili, 72, 73
Kamran, 138
Kanauj, 24-25, 30, 37, 39, 40, 119, 137, 138
Kangra, 25, 29, 75, 169, 176, 233
Kankalah, 17
Karachi, 6, 225-26
Karamat Ali Maulvi, 285-86
Karnal, 38, 259
Kashmir, 8, 12, 32, 84, 146, 164, 177, 181, 232, 236, 250, 252; culture of, 79, 118-19, 225, 245-47 *passim,* 251
Kathiawar, 73, 78
Kavi rai, 149, 243
Khafi Khan, 207-8, 242
Khajuha, 184
Khalid-al-Barmaki, 15
Khalil Ullah Khan, 183-84
Khaljis, 38, 41, 61-69, 82, 107, 148
Khandesh, 83-84, 146, 181
Khan-i-Azam, 166-67, 178
Khan-i-Davran, 259
Khan-i-Jahan, 107
Khan-i-saman, 213-14
Khan Jahan, 93
Khan Jahan Lodi, 180
Kharaj, 94, 96
Khattak tribe, 193
Khawaja Shah Mansur, 160
Khiyal, 119, 251, 252, 262-63
Khizr Khan, 76, 116
Khokhars, 25, 40, 58
Khurasan, 19, 22, 23, 34, 45, 68, 110, 258
Khurram, Prince, 176, 177, 179-80
Khushal Khan Khattak, 193
Khusrau, son of Jahangir, 175, 178 185, 194
Khusrau, Malik, 31
Khusrau Amir, 98, 107, 112, 115-18 *passim*
Khusrau Khan, 69, 117

Khusrau Quli, 249
Khwaja Abdul Samad, 248, 249
Khwaja Ahmed Hasan Maimandi, 33
Khwaja Baqi Billah, 166-68 *passim,* 172
Khwajah Abdus Samad, 142
Khwaja Jahan Sarvar-ul-Mulk, 93
Khwaja Muhammad Masum, 170-71
Khwaja Muhazzab-ud-din, 92
Khwaja Mansur, 151, 210
Khwaja Muin-ud-din, 156
Khwaja Qutb-ud-din, 124
Khwarizm, 22, 26, 43, 44
Khyber pass, 38, 161
Kingship, theories of, 89-90, 93, 150-51
Kirman, 22, 33
Koh-i-Nur, 63-64
Konkan coast, 20-21
Kotwal, 163, 214, 221, 226
Kufri, 167
Kurds, 33
Kurukshetra, 171

Ladi, Rani, 7
Lahore: Ghaznavids and, 18, 20, 25, 26, 28-31 *passim,* 33-36 *passim,* 92, 241; Ghuris and, 37-38, 40; Mongols and, 44, 58-59; Sultanate and, 50; Muslim conquest of, and Hindus, 108; tradition of, and Delhi, 112; Mughals and, 136, 137, 141, 145-46 *passim,* 186, 225, 238, 246-47, 289; Qulich Khan of, 166-67; conquest by Nadir Shah, 259; conquest by Marathas, 266
Lakshmansena, Raja, 40
Lalitaditya, 32
Lal Kunwar, 256
Lalluji Lal, 291
Land revenue: in Delhi Sultanate, 65-67 *passim,* 94, 109, 182; in Mughal empire, 139-40, 149, 178, 214-17, 227-28
Languages: in regional kingdoms, 79-80, 83, 118-19, 125, 204, 261, and literature in Mughal empire, 243-45; rise of new Indian, under British, 291-92
Law: Islamic, 48, 74, 89-90, 99-103 *passim,* 111; in Mughal empire, 157-60 *passim,* 185, 189, 198-200, 205,

207-8, 220-22 *passim,* 234-35, 281; schools of, 265; and British, 277-78, 292; Turkish influence on, 295
Libraries, 112-13, 241
Literature: in Delhi Sultanate, 68-69, 83, 112-13, 115-18, 120; in Mughal empire, 151-55 *passim,* 241-45, 279-81 *passim*
Lodi dynasty, 77-78, 84, 93, 121-22
Logic, 114, 154, 232, 238-40 *passim*
Lucknow, 78, 123, 248, 252, 279-80

Ma'bar, 72-73
Ma'dan-ul-Shrifa (Miyan Bhuva), 78
Madras, 20-21, 214, 225-26
Madrasa 49, 113-15, 239, 263
Madura, 64, 73
Maghs, 176, 184, 219
Mahabat Khan, 186
Mahabharata, 118, 173
Mahadaji Sindhia, 270-73 *passim*
Mahadwi movement, 140-41
Maham Anaga, 143-44
Maham Anga, 240
Mahipal, 29
Mahmud, of Ghazni, 14, 23-28 *passim,* 30-33 *passim,* 37, 87, 131, 148
Mahmud Tughluq, 75, 76
Majumdar, R.C., 9, 191, 294
Makhdum-ul-Mulk, 141, 156-58 *passim*
Makran, 7, 146
Malabar, 21, 124, 132
Maladhar Vasu, 118
Malik Hisam-ud-din Aghul Bak, 39
Maliki, 265
Malik Kafur, 61, 63-64, 69
Malik Shadi, 92-93
Malik Shah, Sultan, 30
Malik-ul-wazara, 92-93
Malwa, 37, 62, 63, 79, 83-84, 138, 144, 197, 233, 251, 263
Mamluk Ali Maulana, 280-81
Manka, 15-16
Manrique, Father, 235-36, 241
Mansabs, Mansabdars, 98, 178, 190, 191, 211-13, 217-18
Man Singh, 144, 148-49, 151, 165, 178
Man Singh, Raja of Gwalior, 120, 252
Mansur, 14
Mansura, 14, 17, 18-19
Manucci, Nicolo, 229, 231, 236
Marathas, 64, 83; language, 83, 119

232; religion, 128-29; and Aurangzeb, 195-97, 205, 206, 218; and Mughal empire, 258, 260, 266-67, 275, 279, 287; and British, 270-73 *passim,* 277
Marriage customs, 260
Marshall, Sir John, 121
Masud I of Ghazni, 26, 28-29, 33
Masud II of Ghazni, 30
Masud III, 30, 34
Masudi, 17, 18-19
Masud Razi, 34
Masud Sa'ad Salman, 34-35
Mathematics, 15, 26, 27, 119, 239
Mathura, 158, 165, 170, 198, 233
Maudud, 29-30
Mawara-un-Nahr, 22
Mazhar, 244-45
Mecca, 3, 4, 140, 144, 201, 263, 274, 282, 283
Medicine: Indian, 15-16; in Delhi Sultanate, 78, 115; in Mughal empire, 154, 228-30
Medina, 4, 5, 263
Mediterranean Sea, 110
"Mental sciences," 155, 238
Merchants, Hindu, 226-28
Mewar, 84, 137, 176, 258
Mewatis, 58
Mian Bhuwa, 115
Mian Mir, 187
Minhaj-us-Siraj, 43, 49, 51, 53, 90, 101-2, 105, 118
Mir, 244-45
Mir bakhshi, 99, 209-10, 211
Mir Fathulla Shirazi, 210
Mir Jafar, 268, 269, 272
Mir Jumla, 190-91, 219
Mir Madan, 269
Mir Qasim, 269, 272
Mir Saman, 209
Mir Sayyid Ali, 142, 248
Mirza Haider, 233
Mirza Hakim, 145, 160
Mir Zahid, 205
Mirza Jan, 154
Mirza Jani Beg, 146
Mirza Mehdi Ali Khan Nawab, 229
Mirza Nuhammad, 268; *see also* Siraj-ud-daula, 268
Mirza Salih, 233
Miskin, 128

Missionaries, 21, 61, 124, 125, 283 ff., 295
Money-lenders, Hindu, 109-10
Mongols: invasions, 36, 43-45, 55, 56, 59, 63, 68, 70, 79, 106, 108, 116, 122, 124; effect on culture, 41-42, 112, 114, 120, 153; and religion, 64
Monserrate, Father, 161, 220, 225, 235
Moreland, W.H., 94, 125
Mosques, 64, 69, 120, 245-47 *passim*, 287-88
Muawiyah, 5
Muazzam, *see* Bahadur Shah
Mubarak Shah, 69
Mughis-ud-din, qazi, 88, 100-1
Muhammad, 3-4
Muhammad, Prince, 116
Muhammad Amin Khan, governor of Kabul, 192
Muhammad Amin Khan, wazir, 257
Muhammad Aquil, 207
Muhammad bin Bakhtiyar Khalji, 40, 41, 80, 113-14
Muhammad bin Mansur, 116
Muhammad Farrukhsiyar, 256-57, 262
Muhammad Ghuri, 14, 26, 31, 32, 37-43 *passim*, 45, 46, 76, 86, 96-97, 101
Muhammad ibn Qasim, 7-12, 14, 18, 20, 39, 48, 105, 106, 108, 164, 199, 265
Muhammad Qasim Maulana, 280
Muhammad Iwaz, 52-53
Muhammad Khan, 59, 60
Muhammad Quli Qutab Shah, Sultan, 244
Muhammad Shah, 252, 257-62 *passim*
Muhammad Tughluq, 70, 72-74, 82, 106, 107, 115, administration of, 93; coinage of, 97; and provincial administration, 104-5; and architecture, 121
Muhammad Yazdi Mullah, 160
Muhandis, 188
Muhazzab-ud-din, 52-53
Muhibullah Bihari, 205
Muiz-ud-din Muhammad, 31
Muiz-ul-Mulk, 160
Muizziya, 113
Muizz-ud-din-Bahram, 52-53
Mujaddid Alif Sani, 167; *see also* Shaikh Ahmad
Mujaddidiya revival, 170

Mulla Abul Hakim, 185
Mullah Shah, 187
Multan, 8, 10, 14, 40, 55, 74, 108, 116, 186; Arab relations, 17-20; occupation by Muhammad Ghuri, 37-38; kingdom of, 83-84
Mumtaz Mahal, 176, 240-41
Munir, 186
Muqaddam, 105, 109, 214
Muqtis, 104
Murad, 182, 183-84
Muridi, 161-62
Murshidabad, 205, 227, 269, 293
Murshid Quli Khan, 208, 262, 268
Musa, 12, 15
Music: in Delhi Sultanate, 16-17, 67-68, 78, 108, 113, 117, 119-20, 125; in regional centers, 79-80, 84, 279; in Mughal empire, 142, 149, 157, 184, 190, 198, 202, 251-53, 262-63
Mustaufi, 91
Mutahar, 114
Mutamid Khan, 229
Mu'tazalis, 264
Mysore, 123-24
Mysticism, 16, 114, 123, 130, 286, 295

Naakali, 285
Nadir Quli, 258; *see also* Nadir Shah
Nadir Shah, 218, 222, 244, 249, 258-60, 262, 279, 287
Nadiya, 39-40, 41, 80
Naib, 92, 210
Najaf Khan, 270
Najd Desert, 265
Najib-ud-daula, 267-68, 270
Najm-ud-din Abu Bakr, 54
Namadeva, 128-29
Nanak, 126, 127, 129-32 *passim*, 193
Naqshbandi movement, 166, 167, 170
Nasiriya Madrasa, 113, 120
Nasir-ud-din Mahmud, 54, 55-56, 101
Nasir-ud-din Qabacha, 40, 43
Navy, in Mughal empire, 219, 274
Nawasa Shah, 24
Nawayat communities, 20-21
Nayak Mahmud, 120
Naziri, 241, 242
Nazr (gift), 278
Niniat Khan Ali, 170-71
Nirun, 8, 17
Nishapur, 29, 42

Nizam Shahis, 83, 181, 196
Nizam-ud-din Auliya, 117
Nizam-ud-din Bakshi, 78, 151
Nizam-ud-din Mulla, 205, 239
Nizam-ul-Mulk, Chin Qilich Khan, 208, 257-62 *passim,* 266, 280
Northwest frontier, 182, 192-93, 201
Nur Jahan, 175-79 *passim,* 185, 186, 202, 210, 246-47, 275
Nur-ud-din Mubarik Ghaznavi, 88
Nusrati, 244
Nusrat Shah, 83

Octroi, 189-90
Ordnance, 209-10
Ottoman empire, 103, 170, 245-46
Oudh, 39, 43, 65, 112, 116; and Mughal painting, 250; musicians, 252; regional kingdom, 259, 261, 269-70, 273, 278, 279, 287
Ovington, John, 228, 236-37

Painting: in Delhi Sultanate, 119; in Mughal empire, 142, 149, 184, 202, 246, 248-50, 263
Pakistan, 66, 217, 265, 286
Pala dynasty, 124
Pan, 108
Panchayats, 214, 220, 221, 226, 227, 234, 235
Panchtantra, 16
Pandua, 79, 83
Panipat: first battle of (1526), 78, 84, 98, 137; second battle of (1556), 143; third battle of (1761), 267
Paper industry, 110, 111
Pargana, 105, 139, 215, 216
Parsis, 160, 163
Pathans, 131, 172, 193-95 *passim,* 231, 282
Patna, 137, 225, 256, 282, 285, 288
Patwari, 217
Patyali, 58-59
Peacock Throne, 260
Pearl Mosque, 247
Pelsaert, Francisco, 236
Persia, *see* Iran
Persian influence: in Lahore, 36; on political theory and practice, 46, 89-90, 93, 211; on literature and language during Delhi Sultanate, 68, 78, 83, 84, 103, 114, 118, 122, 128-

29; on textiles, 110-11, 225; on music, 119; on architecture, 120; on literature and language during Mughal empire, 142, 148, 154-55, 161, 173, 185, 186, 195, 204, 240-45 *passim;* 291, 292; on architecture, 246, 247; on painting, 248-50 *passim;* general, 295
Peshawar, 22-25 passim, 29, 38, 108, 192, 193, 259, 282
Peshwa, 267
Pirates, 191, 192, 219
Pir Baba, 172
Pir Bodhan, 119
Pir Shams Tabriz, 124
Plassey, 269, 272, 292-93
Poetry: in Ghaznavid period, 34-36; in Delhi Sultanate, 68-69, 83, 107, 112-13, 115-17, 125, 128-29; in Mughal empire, 149, 151-53, 195, 202, 204, 240-45 *passim,* 279-81 *passim; see also* Hindi; Persian; Urdu
Political theory: of Delhi Sultanate, 86-88; of Mughal empire, 234-37 *passim*
Poll tax, 96
Polo, 108, 231
Polo, Marco, 32
Portuguese, 85, 180-81, 191, 200, 218, 219, 235, 274
Postal service, 5, 66-67
Price controls, 65-66, 110, 226
Printing, 241, 273-74
Prithvi Raj, 38-39, 105
Provinces, administration of: under the Sultanate, 103-6; during the Mughal empire, 213-14
Public works, 75, 99, 214
Punjab, 28, 55, 77, 183, 233, 246, 261, 262, 289; Arabs in, 8, 22; Ghaznavids in, 24, 29-30, 34; Muhammad Ghuri in, 38, 40; during Delhi Sultanate, 43, 63, 74, 78, 104; under Mughal empire, 136, 137, 143, 145-46, 175, 184; Sikhs in, 194-95, 254
Purdah, 230
Pushtu literature, 193, 245

Qadri order, 128
Qandahar, 19, 138, 146, 177, 181-82, 186, 258-59

Qanungo, K.R., 66-67
Qara Khitai Turks, 40
Qasim Khan of Bengal, 181
Qazi-i-mumalik, 100
Qazis, 99-101, 113, 207, 214, 2ᴸ0, 221, 239
Quran, 3-5 *passim,* 17, 69, 96, 114, 153, 154, 158-59, 167, 239, 264
Qureshi, I.H., 94, 105
Qutaiba ibn Muslim, 22
Qutb Minar, 49, 120
Qutb Shahis, of Golkonda, 83
Qutb-ud-din Husaiʀ, 54
Qutb-ud-din Khan Koka, 160, 175
Qutb-ud-din Mubarik Shah, 116-17
Qutb-ud-din Muhammad, 30
Quwwat-ul-Islam Mosque, 49, 120

Raghunath Rai, Raja, 211
Rai Chandra Bhan Brahman, 185
Raihan, Imad-ud-din, 56
Rai Raghunath, 185
Rai Rayan, 63
Raiyatwari, 215, 216
Rajaram, 197
Rajasthan, 63; *see also* Rajputana
Rajatarangini, 118-19
Rajmahal, 176, 205
Rajputana, 25, 84, 138, 144-45, 254, 258
Rajputs, 24, 25, 33, 38, 59, 112; and Mughals, 138, 140, 144, 148, 149, 158, 176, 185, 236, 259, 272
Ramadan, 3, 4, 172
Ramananda, 126
Ramayana, 118, 173
Ramchandra, Raja
Ram Mohan Roy, 278
Ram Singh, Raja, 140
Rana Sanga, 84, 137
Ranjit Singh, 247
Ranthambhor, 43, 55, 63, 115, 144-45
Raushan Ashtar, 257; *see also* Muhammad Shah
Raushaniya sect, 145-46, 172, 182, 193, 235
Raushan-ud-daulah, 239
Rawalpindi, 29, 192
Rawat-i-arz, 92, 116
Raychaudhuri, T.K., 230
Raziyya, 46, 50-52, 55, 89, 92
Red Fort, 247, 277

Red Sea, 110, 219
Refugees, from Mongols, 41-42, 45, 114, 120-21 124
Religion: and Delhi Sultanate, 88-90, 113-15 *passim,* 123-32; and Akbar, 144, 145, 148-49, 151, 153n, 156-65; orthodox reaction to Akbar, 166-74; and Dara Shukoh, 187-88; and Aurangzeb, 189-90, 198-200, 204, 207-8; and education, in Mughal empire, 238-39; in late Mughal empire, 263-65, 280-82; British policy on, 292-93
Revenue, land: Sher Shah's reforms in, 139-40; in Mughal empire, 178, 182, 227-28
Revenue systems: of Delhi Sultanate, 94-96; and provincial administration, of the sultanate, 104; and Mughal empire, 154, 191, 198, 205, 209, 213, 214-17, 257-58, 261-62
Revivalism: Islamic, 170, 185, 204, 283-86, 295, 296; Hindu, 232
Revolt, Indian (1857-58), 286-90
Reza, 49-50, 116
Roads, 140, 213-14, 223
Roe, Sir Thomas, 179, 224, 249-50, 274
Rohilkhand, 55, 261
Rohilla Afghans, 270
Rohri, 8, 14, 43
Rudaki, 23
Ruhani, 115
Rukh-ud-din Firuz, 50-51
Rumi, 204
Runi, Abul Farz, 34

Saadullah Khan, 184, 186, 187, 211
Sacha Badshah, 194
Sachau, E.C., 27, 28, 31-32
Sadarang, 262-63
Sadri-i-Jahan, 92, 100, 113, 167, 209-10, 214
Sadr-ud-din Arif, 102, 154
Sadr-ul-sadur, 143, 156
Safavids, 250, 258
Safdar Jang, 248, 266
Sahib-i-barid, 91
Saif Khan (Fakirullah), 252
Saif-ud-daula Mahmud, 34-35
Saif-ud-din, 30
Salim, Prince, *see* Jahangir

Salima Sultana, 240-41
Saljuq Turks, 29, 30, 31, 34
Sama, 101, 102-3
Samana, 116, 172
Samanids, 22-23
Samarqand, 22, 34, 75, 79, 136, 154, 186, 250
Samugarh, 183, 256
Sangreza, 115, 116
Sanskrit, translations of, 15-17, 20, 26-27, 33, 75, 83, 84, 115, 117-19 *passim,* 188, 232, 245, 291, 292
"Saracens," 32-33
Sar-i-khail, 98
Sarkar, Sir Jadunath, 191, 194, 218
Sarkar, 139-40, 214, 215
Sarmad, 188
Sarpanch, 214
Satgaon, 80, 226
Sati, 163, 189, 236-37, 291
Sauda, 244-45
Sayyid, caste, 131
Sayyid brothers, Husain Ali and Hasan Ali, 256-57
Sayyid Ahmed Brelvi. 281-83, 285
Sayyid Ahmed Khan, Sir, 265, 290
Sayyid Ali Shah Tirmiz, 172
Sayyid Maula, 100
Sayyid Muhammad Jaunpuri, 140-41
Sayyid Nur-ud-din Mubarik, 101
Sayyids, 76, 77, 173-74
"School of Manners," 242
Science: Indian, 15-16; study of, in Delhi Sultanate, 112-15 *passim;* study of, in Mughal empire, 238-39
Sena dynasty, 124
Sepoy Muting, 286-91
Sewand Rai, 33
Shafii, 265
Shah Abdul Aziz, 265, 280, 281, 285, 289
Shah Alam, 267, 269-73 *passim,* 278
Shahbaz Khan Kamboth, 160
Shahdara, 177, 246-47
Shah Ismail, 281
Shah Ismail Ghazi, 82
Shah Ismail Shahid, 265
Shah Jahan, 180-88, 191, 196; administration of, 199, 210-14 *passim,* 218; and culture, 202, 247-48, 250, 251, 275; and position of Hindus, 231-32, 234-36

Shah Jalal, 82
Shahji, 129, 196
Shahji of Admadnagar, **83**
Shah Mansur, 216
Shah Muhammad, **265-68**
Shah Muhibullah, 185
Shahryar, 177
Shah Sharif, 129
Shah Turkan, 51
Shahu, 197
Shah Waliullah, 169, 170, 204, 263-65, 280, 283, 286, 289, 296
Shaida, 186
Shaikh, caste, 131
Shaikh Abdul Haq Muhaddis, 89, 238
Shaikh Abdullah, 141
Shaikh Abdul Nabi, 156-58 *passim*
Shaikh Ahmad Sirhindi, 167-74 *passim,* 204, 234
Shaikh Alai, 141
Shaikh Ala-ud-din (Islam Khan), 176
Shaikh Budhan, 128
Shaikh Farid, 99, 166, 172, 178, 211
Shaikh Ibrahim, 103
Shaikh Mohammad Ghaus, 251
Shaikh Mubarik, 153*n,* 158
Shaikh Saif-ud-din, 171
Shaikh Salim Chishti, 145, 156
Shaikh Taqi, 126
Shaikh-ul-Islam (Makhdum-ul-Mulk), 157
Shambhuji, 197
Shams-ud-din Firuz, 80, 82
Shams-ul-Mulk, 113
Sharaf-ud-daulah, 239
Shariat, 89, 100, 111, 207
Sharifji, 129
Sharqui kings, 82
Shayista Khan, 183-84, 191, 196, **200-1,** 208, 219
Sher Afghan, 175, 177
Sher Kan Sunqar, 59
Sher Shah (Sher Khan Suri, Sher Khan Sur, Sher Shah Adil, Sher Khan), 83, 94, 137-41 *passim,* 148, 223
Shia sect, 6, 143, 160, 164, 168, 172, 255, 264-66 *passim,* 296
Shiq, 105
Shiqqdar, 139
Shiraz, 7, 10, 36, 186, **241**
Shirzad. 30. 34

Shivaji, 83, 129, 196, 219
Shuja Shah, 183-84, 200
Shuja-ud-daula, 269-70, 272
Shurta courts, 99
Sialkot, 38, 167, 238, 260
Sikandar Lodi, 77-78, 93, 95, 154
Sikhs, 127, 129, 172, 175, 233; and
     Aurangzeb, 193-95, 200; and con-
     quest of Punjab, 246, 247, 254-56
     passim, 260, 262, 267-68, 271-72,
     276; and Sayyid Ahmed, 265, 281-
     83 *passim*
Silk industry, 224, 225
Sinan, 245-46
Sind: and Arabs, 6-22 *passim,* 26, 36,
     48, 105, 108, 109, 111, 119, 130,
     164, 199; and Delhi Sultanate, 43,
     55, 73, 84; and Mughal empire, 138,
     146, 184, 262; and Sindhi language,
     245, 292
Sindhia, 277, 278-79
Sipah salar, 98, 213
Siraj-ud-daula, 268, 269
Sirhind, 76, 77, 167-69 *passim,* 255,
     261, 266
Sisakar, 10
Slave Kings, 40-41, 45, 60, 61, 101,
     109
Smith, Vincent, 160-61
Sobha Singh, 205
Somnath, 14, 25-26, 234
Sonargaon, 79, 80, 82, 140
Southeast Asia, 21, 110, 224
Spear, Percival, 277-78, 279
Spice trade, 6, 21, 108
Sports, 108, 228
Srikara Nadi, 118
Suba, 79, 215
Subahdar, 213
Subuktigin, 23, 24
Succession, in Mughal empire, 275-76
Sufism: in Delhi Sultanate, 16, 35-36,
     46, 61, 68, 101, 119, 124, 125, 126;
     in Mughal empire, 163-64, 179, 185,
     187-88, 243, 244, 263, 264, 284,
     286; in Bengal, 173, 283
Sugar industry, 110. 111
Sukhpal, 24
Sukkur, 43
Sulahkul, 148-49
Sulaiman, 8
Sultan, power of, 89-90, 99, 100, 151

Sunni sect, 6, 14, 90, 164, 172, 264,
     266, 281
Suraj Mal, 268
Surat, 200, 201, 219, 225, 226, 228,
     235
Sur dynasty, 142, 143, 156
Sushruta, 15
Syed Ahmed Khan, Sir, 280
Syed Jalal, 124
Sylhet, 80, 82

Tabriz, 79, 142, 251
Tafsir, 114, 155, 239
Tahmasp, 142
Taimur Shah, 266, 267
Tajiks, 41, 48, 51, 55, 241
Tajikstan, 204, 241-42
Taj Mahal, 186-87, 188, 202, 247
Talib, 241
Tansen, 251
Taqavi, 228
Tara Bai, 197
Tarain, 25, 38-39, 40, 41
Tatar Khan, 103
Tavernier, Jean, 236
Tawbar Muslims, 284
Taxation: in Delhi Sultanate, 5, 65-66,
     67, 74, 94-96, 110; in Mughal em-
     pire, 144, 189-90, 198, 200, 207,
     214-17, 234
Tegh Bahadur, 194
Tehsils, 215
Telingana, 93, 107, 181
Temples, destruction of, 25, 31-32,
     198-99, 232-35 *passim*
Textile industry, 110-11, 223-25 *passim*
Thanesar, 25, 29, 30
Thatta, 73, 146, 247
Tilak, 29, 33
Timur, 75, 76, 84, 94, 98, 136, 153
Timurid rulers, 223
Tinnevelly, 20-21
Tipu, Sultan, 123-24
Tirhut, 39, 70, 82
Todar Mal, 140, 148-49, 151, 153-54,
     178, 210, 216
Trade: Indian-Arab, 6, 18-19, 20-21;
     in Ghaznavid period, 32; in Delhi
     Sultanate, 109, 110, 140; in Mughal
     empire, 179-80, 223-24, 226-27, 231,
     232, 269-70; and East India Com-
     pany, 200-1

Translations, of Sanskrit, 75, 83, 84, 118-19, 188; into English, 86-87, 102, 153*n*, 161-62; into Persian, 117, 242, 264
Transoxiana, 22, 34, 44, 63
Tripathi, R.R., 94
Tughlaq Nama, 117
Tughluq dynasty, 69, 76, 89, 99-100, 103, 107; administrative policy of, 92-93; and architecture, 121
Tughril, 80
Tukaram, 128, 129
Tulasidas, 243
Turanis, 149, 178, 257, 266
Turkistan, 32-33, 225, 241
Turkmans, Ghuzz, 31
Turks in India, in Ghazni, 18, 22-36; and Delhi Sultanate, 40, 41, 46-48, 51-55 *passim,* 60, 61, 70, 76, 82, 86, 90, 107-9 *passim,* 131; and cuture, 117, 119, 142, 242, 295; and Mughal empire, 136, 148, 170
Tuti Namah, 117

Uch, 37-38, 43, 124
Ujjain, 24-25, 63, 183, 233, 263
Ulama, role of, 89, 102, 103, 157-60 *passim,* 164, 199, 239, 255, 279, 280
Umar, 4-5, 11
Umayyads, 5, 6, 12, 14, 18, 89-90
Urdu, 80, 204, 243-45, 252, 262, 263, 264, 289, 291
Urfi, 241, 242
Usman, 5
Ustad Isa, 186-87, 188
Uttar Pradesh, 32
Uzbegs, 136, 145-46, 149, 182

Vairagis, 233
Vaishnavites, 129-30, 165, 170, 283
Vajraditya, 32
Vakil, 210

Vindhyas, 62, 73
Vishnu, 129

Wahhabism, 170, 264, 265, 282-86 *passim,* 296
Waihind, 17, 22, 23, 24, 25
Wakil-i-dar, 91
Wakil-i-sultanat, 93
Wali, 204, 244
Walid, 6-7, 8
Walis, 104
Waqf, 65
Warangal, 63-64, 70, 73
Wasi, 255
Wazir, role of, 91-93, 98, 104, 209-11 *passim,* 257-58
Wazir Khan, 255
West Pakistan, 17, 20, 26, 33-36, 38, 124

Yahya, 118
Yahya the Barmakid, 12, 15
Yaqub ibn Lais, 22
Yezdegerd, 22
Yildiz, 43
Yusufzais, 145-46, 182, 193, 282

Zabita Khan, 270
Zafar Khan, 250
Zafar Khan Ghazi, 82
Zahuri, 242
Zain-ul-Abidin, 79, 84, 118, 164
Zakariya Khan, 262
Zakat, 95-96
Zamindars, 176, 284, 287
Zeb-un-Nissa, 240-41
Zia Muhammad, 115
Zimmis, 11, 17, 48, 96, 111
Zinat-ul-Masjid, 288
Ziya Nakhshabi, 117
Zulfiqar Khan, 206, 255-56 *passim*